This collection of essays by one of the preeminent Kant scholars of our time transforms our understanding of both Kant's aesthetics and his ethics.

Kant is still widely regarded as the father of the aesthetics of formalism and the doctrine of art for art's sake. Guyer shows, however, that Kant treats the disinterestedness of taste that is the core of his aesthetic theory as an experience of freedom and thus creates an essential connection between aesthetics and the interests of morality. At the same time Guyer reveals how Kant's moral theory includes a distinctive place for the cultivation of both general moral sentiments and particular attachments even on the basis of the most rigorous principle of duty.

The scope of the volume is broad. Kant's thought is placed in a rich historical context including such figures as Shaftesbury, Hutcheson, Hume, Burke, and Kames, as well as Baumgarten, Mendelssohn, Schiller, and Hegel. Topics treated include the sublime, natural versus artistic beauty, genius and art history, and duty and inclination.

These essays (half published here for the first time) extend and enrich the account of Kant's aesthetics in the author's earlier book *Kant and the Claims of Taste* (1979). They will be of particular interest to all Kant scholars, professional philosophers concerned with aesthetics and ethics, intellectual historians, and students of German literature.

# Kant and the experience of freedom

# Kant and the experience of freedom
## Essays on aesthetics and morality

PAUL GUYER

FLORENCE R.C. MURRAY PROFESSOR IN THE HUMANITIES
UNIVERSITY OF PENNSYLVANIA

CAMBRIDGE
UNIVERSITY PRESS

Published by the Press Syndicate of the University of Cambridge
The Pitt Building, Trumpington Street, Cambridge CB2 1RP
40 West 20th Street, New York, NY 10011-4211, USA
10 Stamford Road, Oakleigh, Victoria 3166, Australia

First published in 1993

Printed in Canada

*Library of Congress Cataloging-in-Publication Data*
Guyer, Paul, 1948–
Kant and the experience of freedom : essays on aesthetics and
morality / Paul Guyer.
p.   cm.
Includes bibliographical references and index.
ISBN 0-521-41431-8 (hard)
1. Kant, Immanuel, 1724–1804 – Aesthetics.   2. Kant, Immanuel,
1724–1804 – Ethics.   3. Aesthetics, Modern – 18th century.   4. Ethics,
Modern – 18th century.   5. Kant, Immanuel, 1724–1804 – Contributions
in doctrine of free will and determinism.   6. Free will and
determinism.   I. Title.
B2799.A4G86   1993
193 – dc20                                                          92–12656
                                                                              CIP

A catalog record for this book is available from the British Library

ISBN 0-521-41431-8 hardback

*For my daughter*
*Nora Francesca Foa Guyer*

# Contents

# Preface

This collection includes all but one of the essays on Kant's aesthetics that I have written since the publication of my earlier study, *Kant and the Claims of Taste*, in 1979 (Cambridge, Mass.: Harvard University Press), as well as several essays that directly explore the place of feeling, the paradigmatic form of aesthetic experience, in Kant's moral philosophy. (The one essay omitted from this collection, "Pleasure and Society in Kant's Theory of Taste," in *Essays in Kant's Aesthetics*, edited by Ted Cohen and myself [Chicago: University of Chicago Press, 1982], had actually been written in 1975, and while providing a useful introduction to *Kant and the Claims of Taste*, it does not extend its approach to the issues considered in these essays.)

These essays were written for different occasions and attack a set of variously interrelated issues from several angles. When I first published *Kant and the Claims of Taste*, I naturally assumed that I had said everything I could possibly have to say on the subject of the book and turned back to the *Critique of Pure Reason*, which had been my first love in Kant. But there were some glaring omissions in *Kant and the Claims of Taste*, and I did take the opportunity provided by several of the invitations that came to me in the wake of that book to rectify several of those in the oldest of the essays reprinted here, Chapter 6, on the differences between the beautiful and the sublime (originally published in 1982), and Chapter 8, on Kant's theory of genius and its implications for the conception of art history (originally published in 1983).

At that time, I had no plan for any systematic reconstruction of my interpretation of Kant's aesthetics, and my primary focus in the following years was indeed the work that culminated in my book on the *Critique of Pure Reason, Kant and the Claims of Knowledge* (published in 1987). As that work approached and reached completion, however, I found myself increasingly returning to Kant's aesthetics. I did not find myself revising the interpretative framework of *Kant and the Claims of Taste* but placing it in a larger context or, more precisely, in two contexts: the historical context of Kant's relation to eighteenth-century aesthetics, and the philosophical context of its relation to Kant's moral philosophy – which relation, I became increasingly convinced, provided the fundamental motivation for Kant's excursion into aesthetic theory. This connection between Kant's aesthetics and morality began to be the center of my concern in the various essays that are here presented as Chapters 1, 5, 7, and 9, which were written between 1985 and 1989. Constructing an historical account of the evolution of Kant's conception of the relation between aesthetics and morality then became the center of my interest in the three essays that I wrote in 1990 with the idea of something like the present volume already in mind, the present Chapters 2, 3, and 4. Finally, Chapter 10 was written at the end of 1991 specifically to complete this volume by explicitly addressing the issue of feeling and its connection to moral principle from the side of Kant's moral philosophy rather than from the side of his aesthetic theory.

I have retained the essay form rather than recasting this material as a systematic treatise, partly because I believe it would misrepresent Kant's thought on these issues to make it appear entirely systematic and partly in the hope that a collection of essays will reach a wider audience than another systematic treatise on Kant's aesthetics. Keeping the material in its original essay form does entail some overlap among the essays, and for that I apologize to those who sit down to read the work from beginning to end. The variety of approaches taken in these essays also means that they could have been arranged in a variety of ways. The order that I have chosen (including the grouping of the essays into two parts, historical and topical) does not reflect the order of the composition of the essays but is meant to supply some continuity in the treatment of various themes. However, it is not meant to be rigid. Chapter 1 introduces themes further discussed in both parts, and Chapter 7 makes extensive historical contrasts, and thus could easily have been included among the more historical papers of Part I had I not wanted it to continue the discussion of the sublime in Chapter 6. Only the first three chapters would best be read in the order in which they are printed.

My purpose in collecting these essays in the present form is not to supersede *Kant and the Claims of Taste* by revising or retracting any of its interpretation of Kant's basic framework for the analysis and justification of pure judgments of taste in the simplest form of judgments on natural beauty, but rather to illustrate how Kant enriched and expanded that framework through his discussions of such issues as the sublime, the fine arts, genius, and beauty's symbolization of morality. What I hope to show is that Kant at least suggested how to reconcile the assumption of the uniqueness of aesthetic experience and artistic creation, an assumption which was certainly becoming a fixture of modern thought by Kant's time, with the assumption that there must be a vital role for the aesthetic in the larger morality of mankind, an assumption which may be much older than the other yet has rarely been surrendered, even in the throes of modernism. Kant tried to show how aesthetic experience can have independent value even while only morality itself has unconditional value, leading to a subtlety and complexity in his thought that Kant himself was not always prepared for and that has continued to be rare in subsequent aesthetic theories. The following essays attempt to bring out some of this subtlety and complexity.

This book is the product of various periods of work spread out over the last decade, and I have accumulated many debts, both personal and institutional, in its production.

Above all, I would like to express my gratitude to Alexander Nehamas, who was my colleague at the University of Pennsylvania from 1986 to 1989, and my friend for many years before and since. He was my sounding board for many of these essays, especially for my reconception of Kant's place in the history of aesthetics, expressed in Chapters 2 through 5. He listened to me with unflagging interest and commented with insight and care on much of this work as it was written. An intellectual companion whose own interests and sensibilities are so different from one's own yet whose sympathy and support are so complete is rare and treasured. Words fail me.

Among the other friends who have listened to and talked with me about this work, I would also like to express special thanks to Noël Carroll, Donald Crawford, Juliet Floyd, Timothy Gould, Peter Kivy, Jerry Schneewind, Jay Wallace, and Tom Wartenberg.

In conjunction with specific essays, I would like to make the following acknowledgments. Chapters 2 and 3 were written and much of the work for Chapter 4 accomplished during the academic year 1989–90, when I was supported by research leave from the University of Pennsylvania and a research fellowship for senior university teachers from the National Endowment for the Humanities. I thank those institutions for their financial support.

Chapter 1 was originally presented at the meeting of the Eastern Division of the American Society for Aesthetics in 1989, and I thank the program committee for that meeting, chaired by Michael Krausz, for the invitation to speak on that occasion. Donald Crawford subsequently published the paper in the *Journal of Aesthetics and Art Criticism*, and I am grateful for his interest as well as his permission to reprint it here.

Chapters 2 and 3 were presented as lectures at a National Endowment for the Humanities Summer Institute on Art and the Emergence of Aesthetics in the Eighteenth Century at the Johns Hopkins University in 1990. I am grateful to Frances Ferguson and Ronald Paulson for their invitation to participate in that institute, to the Endowment again for its financial support, and to Jerry and Elizabeth Schneewind for their special hospitality on that occasion. A version of Chapter 3 was also given at a University of Rochester conference on Kant and Kantian Aesthetics in May 1990, and I thank Ralf Meerbote for the invitation to participate in that conference and Noël Carroll for his comments. I also thank Professor Meerbote for his understanding of my decision to reserve publication of this material for the present volume rather than allowing it to be included in the proceedings of his conference.

Chapter 4 was first presented at a bicentennial conference on the *Critique of Judgment* held at the New School for Social Research in New York in December 1990, and I am grateful to Wayne Waxman for the invitation to participate in that conference. I am also grateful to Professor Waxman for his understanding of my decision to reserve publication of this paper for the present volume.

Chapter 5 was initially presented at a conference on Hegel and the third *Critique*, organized by the Internationale Hegel-Vereinigung at Fiecht, Austria, in May 1989 and subsequently published in the volume *Hegel und die "Kritik der Urteilskraft,"* edited by Hans-Friedrich Fulda and Rolf-Peter Horstmann. I am grateful to both of them not only for this invitation but for their extraordinary hospitality on my trips to Germany. I also presented this paper at Northwestern University in October 1990, and I thank Meredith and Michael Williams for their interest as well as hospitality on that occasion. Kirk Pillow of Northwestern asked me some extremely useful questions then, subsequently reflected in what is now Chapter 4.

Chapter 7 was originally written for a *Festschrift* for Dieter Henrich, *Theorie der Subjektivität*, edited by Konrad Cramer, Hans-Friedrich Fulda, Rolf-Peter Horstmann, and Ulrich Pothast and published in 1987, and I am again grateful to Professors Fulda and Horstmann for the invitation.

Chapter 8 was written for a special edition of the *Monist* on "Purity and Integrity in Art and Morals" (1983), edited by Mary Mothersill, and I thank her not only for this invitation but for her interest in and enthusiasm for my work over many years. I also thank the *Monist* for permission to reprint the paper here.

Chapter 9 was originally presented at a conference on philosophy and the environment organized by the University of Lodz, Poland, in 1988, apparently the first philosophical conference on the environment ever held in any of the then Eastern Bloc countries. I am grateful to the members of the Department of Philosophy of the University of Lodz, especially Andrej Kaniowski and Ryzsard Panasiuk, for this invitation, and also to my friend Tom Wartenberg for his role in it. I thank the American Council of Learned Societies for their financial support of my attendance at this conference.

Chapter 10 has been specially written for this volume. I am grateful to one of the anonymous referees for Cambridge University Press for the stimulus to add this essay to the volume I originally submitted. My thanks to Terence Moore of the Press not only for his patience in waiting for this addition but for his unfailingly enthusiastic support for my work in general.

Finally, for their generous help in correcting the proofs, I would like to thank Lanier Anderson, Curtis Bowman, Rukesh Korde, Josefine Nauckhoff, Toomas Puhvel, Frederick Rauscher, Cynthia Schossberger, Lisa Shabel, Alison Simmons, and Jennifer Uleman.

# Note on citations

Quotations from Kant's works are located by volume and page number in the German *Akademie* edition of the works, *Kant's gesammelte Schriften*, 27 volumes, edited by the Königlichen Preußischen (later Deutschen) Akademie der Wissenschaften (Berlin: Reimer [later de Gruyter], 1900–). Where Kant used roman or arabic section numbers (the former generally in introductions to his books), these are also cited. The only exception to this rule is quotations from the *Critique of Pure Reason*, which are located by the pagination of the first edition of 1781 (cited as *A*) and the second edition of 1787 (cited as *B*). Unless otherwise indicated, translations from Kant as well as from other German authors are my own.

I have used the following abbreviations:

| | |
|---|---|
| *CJ* | *Critique of Judgment* |
| *FI* | "First Introduction" to the *Critique of Judgment* |
| *R* | *Reflexionen* (Marginalia and notes) |

For other works, I have used short titles. These include:

| | |
|---|---|
| *Groundwork* | *Groundwork of the Metaphysics of Morals* |
| *Logic* | *Logic: A Handbook for Lectures* (edited by G. B. Jäsche) |
| *Practical Reason* | *Critique of Practical Reason* |
| *Religion* | *Religion within the Limits of Reason Alone* |
| *Right* | *Doctrine of Right*, Part I of the *Metaphysics of Morals* |
| *Virtue* | *Doctrine of Virtue*, Part II of the *Metaphysics of Morals* |

Works which are referred to less often are cited by the full title.

# Introduction

For decades the *Critique of Judgment* received little attention outside of the narrow circle of Kant scholarship. What little notice it did receive in broader circles was usually confined to an obligatory bow to it as the philosophical source of the critical doctrines of aesthetic formalism and of the autonomy of art: the ideas, that is, that in all works of art our interest is properly confined to features of perceptual form and that appreciation and judgment of art must take place within parameters set by art itself, independently of any other or broader cognitive or practical concerns. In the last decade or two, however, Kant's third *Critique* has suddenly been transformed from a *tabula rasa* into a palimpsest of philosophical and critical theories. Instead of being the archetypical work of modernism, the *Critique of Judgment* has suddenly become the archetypical work of postmodernism, revealing the contradictions inherent in every idea of knowledge, rationality, culture, and art which it has suddenly become so fashionable to discover. No longer the paradigm of an irenic classicism or a more contemporary but equally imperturbable formalism, the last of Kant's trio of great *Critiques* has suddenly become the symbol of deconstructionism itself, a book that shows how every attempt to make firm distinctions between accident and essence, whether in theory or practice (and including the distinction between theory and practice), undercuts itself.[1]

In the present work I want to suggest that Kant's conception of the full range of natural and appropriate responses to aesthetic objects, whether works of art or beauties of nature, does indeed go beyond the narrow formalism which is, to be sure, suggested in certain sections of the opening of the "Analytic of the Beautiful," itself the first half of the *Critique of Judgment* (especially §§2–4 and §§13–16). I also want to show that Kant's attitude toward art, in particular, is much more complicated and, indeed, conflicted than is suggested by the traditional supposition that he was the founding father of the idea of "art for art's sake." But I want to present these complexities not by importing contemporary preconceptions and preoccupations into his work but in Kant's own terms. Kant cannot be reduced to a merely representative man of his own times, for he often saw far beyond what any of his immediate predecessors and contemporaries had thought. But neither can he be transformed, without distortion, into a figure of our own times. Kant himself set the terms in which he wanted to go beyond the simplicities of aesthetic formalism and artistic autonomy, and our first task must be to discover what these terms are.

I will argue throughout these essays that Kant did not simply deconstruct, or show the underlying incoherence of notions of aesthetic formalism and artistic autonomy, as so many have recently supposed, but rather that he showed how the uniqueness of aesthetic response and artistic creation could be reconciled with the vital role of the aesthetic in the larger morality of mankind. Kant believed in the intrinsic and independent value of aesthetic experience but also in the uniquely unconditional value of morality, or the primacy of practical reason (that is, the use of reason to determine what we ought to do rather than what is the case). One of my chief purposes in the following essays is to show how Kant tried to make these two beliefs not merely compatible but interdependent.

In my earlier work I was rash enough to suggest that Kant's discussions of such topics as the sublime and genius, which appear to be tied only loosely to the basic architectonic structure of the argument of the *Critique of Judgment*, were mere concessions to the literary fashion of his day, thus not essential to his fundamental argument about the conditions under which it is epistemologically justifiable to claim the universal validity of one's pleasurable response to a work of nature or art, the claim that is inherent in a judgment of taste. Few commentators on my work have spared me the embarrassment of quoting my dismissal of the significance of the sublime, for instance, although my own lack of interest in that topic, in a work conceived during the early and mid-1970s, certainly reflected the predilections of the analytical aesthetics of the period. Were it not for the risk of appearing equally rash (if not equally callow) in taking another similarly one-sided view, I might now be tempted to assert the opposite. If I succumbed to that temptation, I would claim that it is Kant's exclusive focus on the problem of the intersubjective validity of judgments of taste, in the "Analytic of the Beautiful," which is his mere concession to a literary fashion of his time, since he here adopts the genre of the essay on agreement in taste that had been popularized earlier in Britain by Hutcheson and Hume. I might also claim that the real heart of Kant's aesthetic theory and the underlying motivation for its creation is the connection to his moral theory which appears in his discussion of the sublime, of aesthetic ideas as the content of works of artistic genius, and of beauty as the symbol of morality.

But I trust that the stance taken in the following essays is more subtle than that. What I hope to reveal is that there is an intimate and indispensable connection between the analysis of aesthetic judgments and explanation of aesthetic response, which is the core of Kant's theory of pure judgments of taste, and the linkage of aesthetics to morality, which is clearly Kant's ulterior motive. The pleasurable yet disinterested sense of freedom from cognitive or practical constraint – that is, the sense of the unity of aesthetic experience without its subordination to any scientific or moral concepts and purposes – which is at the heart of Kant's explanation of our pleasure in beauty is precisely that which allows aesthetic experience to take on deeper moral significance as an experience of freedom. The meaning of the aesthetic cannot be fully plumbed as long as this realm of human experience is entirely isolated from the moral dimension, yet it is primarily through the experience of freedom which is captured by Kant's conceptions of the disinterestedness and purposelessness of aesthetic response that aesthetic experience is capable of taking on the deep moral import that Kant assigns to it. The coils of Kant's conception of the moral value of the aesthetic, in other words, are tightly wound around the armature furnished by his epistemological analysis and psychological explanation beginning with his discussion of pure judgments of taste.[2] And by tracing out this complex connection (especially in light of the variety of historical connections examined in Part I and Chapter 7), I hope that I can show that Kant's sense of the connections between beauty, art, and morality is more subtle than much of what was suggested not only before, but also since, he wrote.

Immanuel Kant, who was born in 1724, published his first scientific work, *Thoughts on the True Estimation of Living Forces*, in 1747, and his first philosophical work, the *New Exposition of the First Principles of Metaphysical Cognition*, in 1755; but although his lectures on logic and epistemology touched upon what we would now identify as issues of aesthetics from early in his career (our earliest extensive texts of these lectures date from 1770), Kant did not publish his views on aesthetics until the last of his three great critiques, the *Critique of Judgment*, which was first published in 1790, when Kant was already sixty-six years old. (An earlier work that sounds as if it would concern aesthetics, the *Observations on the Feeling of the Beautiful and the Sublime* of 1764, really concerns what we would now call moral psychology rather than aesthetics.) And although it is natural for us now to read Kant's three great critiques – the *Critique of Pure Reason*, first published in 1781 and extensively revised in 1787; the *Critique of Practical Reason* of 1788; and the *Critique of Judgment* – as if they were conceived as the continuous exposition of a single, coherent system, in fact each of the later two works was unplanned at the time of its predecessor and represents some considerable revision of it. Indeed, in the first edition of the *Critique of Pure Reason*, Kant had completely dismissed the possibility of aesthetics as an *a priori* theory of taste (A 21), a position which he only barely moderated in the second edition of the work (B 35–6), Kant's work on which was completed by March 1787. Nor was there any suggestion of the possibility of a third *Critique* in the *Critique of Practical Reason*, the manuscript for which was finished by the end of June 1787. The first hint that Kant had conceived of the possibility of a third *Critique* came only in December of 1787, in a letter from Kant to his then disciple Karl Leonhard Reinhold.[3] Yet the work was ready for the publisher by the beginning of March 1790, hardly two years later – two years in which Kant was by no means exclusively occupied with the *Critique of Judgment*, but was also working on the defense of some of the most basic doctrines of the *Critique of Pure Reason* in the most extensive polemic in which he ever engaged, his reply to the neo-Leibnizo–Wolffian critic J. A. Eberhard in his essay "On a Discovery according to which every new Critique of Pure Reason should be rendered dispensable by an older one."[4]

The *Critique of Judgment* was thus conceived and written in considerable haste, and this is evident in the text. The work treats not only aesthetics but also teleology, that is, the role of conceptions of purposiveness in our comprehension of nature, and the connection between the two is fraught with tension; moreover, the discussion of both of these topics is forced into the organizational scheme or "architectonic" originally developed in the *Critique of Pure Reason* for other subjects, and that can be confusing or even misleading.[5] Further, the treatment of aesthetics, although hardly long (153 pages, in the standard German edition), is particularly convoluted and repetitive. It may therefore be of some use to preface any discussion of the substance of the work with an outline of its structure.

The *Critique of Judgment* begins with a preface, followed by a general introduction, the latter of which exists in two different versions: the introduction that was published with the text and that was apparently one of the final sections to have been written, and an earlier version, which Kant had rejected, supposedly on grounds of length alone, but which differs in a number of interesting ways. This text, which Kant by no means disclaimed and even made available to some of his associates[6] but which was not published in its entirety until 1914, is now referred to as the "First Introduction" to the *Critique of Judgment.* Following the introduction(s), the *Critique* then is divided into two principal parts, the "Critique of Aesthetic Judgment" and the "Critique of Teleological Judgment," the former of which is the primary focus of most of the essays in the present volume. The "Critique of Aesthetic Judgment" has a complex internal structure. The "First Division" is comprised of two "books," the "Analytic of the Beautiful" (consisting of §§1–22 and the following "General Remark") and the "Analytic of the Sublime" (consisting of §§23–9 and the following "General Remark"). The first division also includes the "Deduction of Pure Aesthetic Judgments." Although this latter title should properly subsume only sections 30 through 40 or perhaps 42, in which Kant attempts to prove a claim about the intersubjective validity of judgments of beauty that he had made in the "Analytic of the Beautiful," the title is carried over to the quite independent discussion of the fine arts in sections 43 through 54. Finally, the "Critique of Aesthetic Judgment" concludes with the "Second Division," entitled the "Dialectic of Aesthetic Judgment" (§§55–9), which has as an appendix an essay on the "Methodology of Taste" (§60). (The "Critique of Teleological Judgment" also has a complex internal structure, but familiarity with that will not be necessary for our purposes).[7]

We can now turn to the main issue of these essays, the connections between Kant's aesthetics and his moral philosophy. In my earlier book, *Kant and the Claims of Taste,* these connections played a minor role in my account of Kant's aesthetic theory. That was because I confined my consideration of them there to the specific question of whether these links were necessary or sufficient for the completion of Kant's transcendental deduction of the intersubjective validity of judgments of taste, that is, his attempt to prove that agreement about judgments of beauty and sublimity is not only possible but even necessary, at least under ideal circumstances, a thesis that had been advocated by R. K. Elliott and Donald W. Crawford.[8] I argued that the various links to morality canvassed by Kant did not succeed in this specific objective, and, in spite of the vigorous criticism that my earlier work has received on this score, I am still inclined to believe that this judgment was essentially correct. But this is not to deny that Kant's links between aesthetics and morality are of profound interest and importance when considered apart from this narrow question. They must only be considered from the right point of view to appreciate their importance. This is why I wish to describe what is offered in the present collection of essays not as a retraction but as an enrichment of my previous treatment. Given this goal, however, it may be of use if I briefly characterize my earlier position and some of the criticism it has engendered.

According to the picture of Kant's aesthetic theory that I presented in *Kant and the Claims of Taste* and refined in some subsequent work (such as the essay on the distinction between the beautiful and the sublime included here as Chapter 6),[9] the core of Kant's theory is an epistemological interpretation of the claims made by judgments of taste and a psychological explanation of the responses, such as our feelings of pleasure in the beautiful and the sublime, that are expressed by such judgments.[10] (By a "judgment of taste," Kant means the proposition or the assertion of the proposition that a particular object is, for example, beautiful. Such a judgment is made or at least justified on the basis of reflection on the origin of the pleasure one feels in the object, when such reflection suggests that this feeling of pleasure is not merely a physiological response to the stimulus provided by sensation of the object but is the product of the harmonious reaction of the higher cognitive faculties of imagination and understanding to the perception of the object. Kant confuses the reader by suggesting that the process which leads to this feeling of pleasure, as well as that which leads from the feeling of pleasure to the assertion of the judgment of taste, are both acts of "reflective judgment."

There are good reasons for thinking of both of these as expressing a reflective use of judgment, but it should be clear that the enjoyment of an object, on the one hand, and the judgment that other persons should also enjoy it, on the other, are, at least in principle, psychologically and epistemologically distinct acts of mind.) In other words, my interpretation was an account of the significance of judgments of taste and the character of aesthetic response, constructed from the materials offered by Kant's theory of human cognition – the theory offered in the *Critique of Pure Reason* but also transformed, at certain key points, in the *Critique of Judgment* itself. The aesthetic theory, as I presented it, starts off with a logical analysis of the claims that are asserted in a judgment of taste, proceeds to offer an explanation which is essentially a psychological model of the underlying mechanisms of the aesthetic responses that are expressed by such judgments, and then attempts to conclude with a transcendental deduction (that is, a justification from the conditions of the possibility of experience in general) that would demonstrate that responses explained in the manner described at the second stage of the theory do in fact satisfy the logical demands raised at the initial stage of the analysis.[11]

On this approach, Kant commences with an analysis of the very idea of a judgment of taste as an *aesthetic judgment*,[12] which yields two fundamental claims. On the one hand, as *aesthetic* – that is, as essentially connected with feeling or sensibility – a judgment of taste cannot be made on the basis of the subsumption of its object under any determinate concept;[13] it must, rather, both be about that aspect of perception which can never become part of the objective cognition of an object, namely the pleasure (or, in the case of a negative judgment, the displeasure) it produces in an observer, and even be made primarily on the basis of such a feeling (see *CJ*, §1, 5:203–4, and *FI*, §VIII, 20:229). On the other hand, as a *judgment*, an aesthetic judgment claims acceptability not only by the person who asserts it on the basis of her own encounter with its object but by all others who might encounter it, at least under appropriate or ideal condi-

tions. Some utterances, such as mere judgments of agree-
ableness (what Kant calls "aesthetic judgments of sense"),
defeat the expectation of such intersubjective acceptability
by permitting the attachment of the restrictive phrase "to
me," which expressly limits their validity to the speaker, but
judgments of taste do not. One can appropriately say, "Olives taste good to me (but not to my daughter)," but one
cannot say, "The Chrysler Building is beautiful to me (but
not to my wife)." By calling something "beautiful," we mean
precisely that everyone ought to be pleased with it (*CJ*, §7,
5:212). In this regard, in fact, judgments of taste do not
differ from other empirical judgments.[14] In sum, then, a
judgment of taste is one in which one person, on the basis
of her own pleasurable response to an object, asserts that all
others who encounter that object under appropriate circumstances can also be expected to take pleasure in it. In Kant's
terms, in a judgment of taste the subjective response of
pleasure is connected with the object with the "quantity" of
"universal subjective validity" and the "modality" of "exemplary necessity" – that is, it holds not just for one person
but for everyone, and not accidentally but necessarily (*CJ*,
§8, 5:215, and §18, 5:236–7).[15]

This analysis obviously raises the question of *how* one can
reasonably assert that such a subjective response as one's
own pleasure in a particular object, whether that object is a
work of nature or of human art, must necessarily occur in all
others who encounter it, at least under the right conditions.
Kant sharpens this problem, and also tries to solve it, by
means of the theory of pleasure that underlies the *Critique of
Judgment*. Kant supposes that all pleasure is connected with
the satisfaction of an aim or objective, and that universally
valid pleasures must therefore be connected with the satisfaction of some universally valid objectives. This suggests that
the pleasure of aesthetic response must be connected with
the perception of its object as satisfying some determinate
cognitive objective or some determinate practical objective,
which would in any case presuppose a determinate cognitive
judgment of the object, although this would seem to be con-

trary to the underlying analysis of aesthetic judgment. Kant goes on to add, however, that pleasure is most noticeable when the satisfaction of the objective involved appears to be contingent rather than necessary and is therefore not obviously imposed by the basic laws of thought or practice themselves (*CJ*, § VI, 5:187–8). This sets the stage for his central explanation of our pleasure in beauty, which claims that this pleasure arises when the manifold of intuition produced by an object – that is, the variety of experiences the perception of it engenders in us – sets our faculties of imagination and understanding into a harmonious or free play that feels as if it satisfies our subjective goal in cognition, that of finding unity in all of our manifolds of intuition, without producing that unity by what is ordinarily the objective condition or guarantee of the possibility of cognition, namely the subsumption of the variety of our experiences under determinate concepts of the understanding (see especially *FI*, §VIII, 20:224–5). The harmony of imagination and understanding induced by a beautiful object is pleasurable precisely because it seems like the satisfaction of our fundamental cognitive aim for unity but also seems contingent because it is not produced by the application of any determinate concept to the manifold[16] which would guarantee the unification of the manifold.[17]

This preliminary explanation of aesthetic response is enriched as the exposition of the "Critique of Aesthetic Judgment" unfolds. In the case of judgments on the sublime rather than on the beautiful, Kant postulates a subjective satisfaction of underlying goals of reason rather than understanding, that is, our capacity not just to apply concepts to our experience but to seek and find coherence and completeness in our systems of theoretical and practical concepts themselves. In the case of works of art rather than nature, ideas as well as merely perceptual forms may contribute to our subjective sense of unity and satisfaction, and our sense of harmony may not have as its object mere perceptual form as contrasted to concepts but rather the interrelation of concepts and form. These amplifications of Kant's underlying theory will be among the issues to be pursued in the essays that follow. What we must briefly consider here, however, is the justification, or "deduction," of the claim to agreement in judgments of taste that Kant attempts to build upon the analysis of aesthetic judgments and explanation of aesthetic response that has just been outlined.

Restricting himself to the case of judgments of beauty,[18] Kant argues that although one cannot make an *a priori* judgment that an object is beautiful without an actual experience of pleasure on encountering it, nevertheless, once it has pleased one, one can make the *a priori* judgment that under appropriate circumstances others will also take pleasure in it, a judgment which is *a priori* in the sense that it does not depend upon any empirical investigation into the actual responses of others but only upon reflection on one's own response to the object (*CJ*, §36, 5:288). The justification for such a claim is, first, that the judgment of beauty involves the cognitive faculties of understanding and imagination, not merely a physiological response such as an agreeable sensation in response to some merely physical stimulus, and second, that the experience of beauty arises from an optimal condition of those faculties which may be expected to occur under the same circumstances, that is, in response to the same objects, in all who possess these basic cognitive abilities, that is, all cognitively healthy human beings (*CJ*, §38, 5:290, and especially §21, 5:238–9).

Unfortunately, although the first of these claims may seem plausible enough, the second is problematic. Even if everyone can reasonably be expected to be able to gain cognition of any particular object through the application of a determinate concept to it, it is by no means obvious that an object which is able to induce the harmonious play of imagination and understanding in one person *without* any concept need be able to bring about this state in everyone else who encounters the same object, even under similar circumstances. Precisely because it must seem contingent that a particular object should give a sense of the unity of the manifold it presents without being subsumed under a determinate concept, one might argue, it cannot be necessary that any object which has this effect on one person must have it on others.[19] Thus, Kant's explanation of our pleasure in beauty in terms of a distinctive employment of the underlying faculties of cognition – and, by extension, his subsequent explanation of other forms of aesthetic response in similarly cognitive terms – may be sufficient to make it reasonable to expect that all cognitive subjects should be capable of aesthetic response under some circumstances or other, and even reasonable for one person to engage in practices such as the critical exhibition and discussion of aesthetic objects that are aimed at getting others to experience an aesthetic response to those particular objects. But his argument does not seem sufficient to prove that particular objects must always produce the same aesthetic response in all subjects who encounter them under suitable circumstances. To this extent Kant's deduction of judgments of taste appears to fall short of its goal.

Since my original publication of this critical assessment of Kant's deduction of aesthetic judgments in *Kant and the Claims of Taste*, critics have objected that it is the restriction of my reconstruction of Kant's theory to its epistemological aspects which is at fault, and that the deduction seems incomplete, as I describe it, only because I omitted its indispensable moral dimension. Two writers who have pressed such a criticism are Salim Kemal[20] and Kenneth F. Rogerson.[21] Before briefly commenting on their views, however, I must point out that I had already scrutinized an earlier attempt to use Kant's connection of aesthetics and morality for the specific purpose of completing his transcendental deduction of judgments of taste, that offered by Donald Crawford in *Kant's Aesthetic Theory*, for it is by no means clear to me that the more recent writers have addressed the difficulties which I had previously noted in Crawford's analysis of the links which Kant suggests between aesthetics and morality.

Crawford had used Kant's claim that the beautiful symbolizes the morally good (because, as I point out in several of the following essays, there are analogies between our *experience* of beauty and the nature of moral judgment) to complete the deduction by arguing that the judgment of taste's demand for agreement could be grounded in a legitimate demand for "sensitivity to that which symbolizes the basis of morality."[22] In response to this proposal, I argued three main points. First, we must distinguish between grounds for defending the rational expectation that others *will* agree with our own aesthetic responses and grounds for demanding, "as a sort of duty," as Kant puts it (*CJ*, §40, 5:296), that they *ought* to agree with us.[23] Second, although a connection between beauty and morality might have been intended by Kant to supply a ground for the normative demand for agreement in matters of taste, the way in which we do not just expect but in some sense demand that others also have taste, any moral ground for the desirability of agreement in taste would not itself supply additional reasons for expecting such agreement, but would rather seem to presuppose that we already have adequate grounds for such an expectation, on the general principle that "ought" implies "can," that is, that morality can only demand of us what is indeed in our power.[24] Finally, I argued that even Kant's grounds for constructing the *demand* for agreement in taste seem inadequate: Kantian morality appears to hold that it is morally praiseworthy for us to do the actions required by duty only to the extent that we are motivated by the rational belief that those actions are our duty and not – indeed, notoriously not – motivated by any particular inclination toward those actions or the persons who are their objects. For this reason, I held, it was not apparent why a certain kind of sensitivity, whether a sensitivity directly to beautiful objects or to beauty as a symbol of morality, even if it would in some way be conducive to the development of a frame of mind compatible with morality, could be demanded of anyone as a requirement of morality.[25] Kantian morality may allow us to hope that we and others act out of feeling as well as reason, it seems, but certainly not to demand that anyone do so, and thus it is far from clear how a demand that anyone have or develop the capacity or susceptibility for any form of feeling could be defended within its framework.

I would now agree that the last of these objections depends on an excessively narrow reading of Kantian morality, equating Kant's conception of virtuous motivation with the whole object of our duties, and much in the following essays, culminating in the systematic discussion of duty and inclination in Kant's moral philosophy that is offered in Chapter 10, is intended to better illuminate Kant's complex and delicate thought about the proper role of feelings in our entire experience and practice of morality. On Kant's view, pure reason must certainly always remain the essence of both the fundamental principle of morality and virtue or morally praiseworthy motivation, but for embodied creatures like ourselves, reason will both need to make itself sensibly manifest to us and will also require that we bring our inclinations and emotions into harmony with it. To the extent that aesthetic experience can be conducive to either of these two aims, morality will clearly take a legitimate interest in it that will reasonably enough express itself in the form of a demand that moral agents also develop taste, "as a sort of duty." But it is far from clear that my recent critics have done much to address the particular objections that I originally raised to Crawford's attempt to appeal to Kant's connection between beauty and morality for the completion of the transcendental deduction of aesthetic judgments. In particular, neither Kemal nor Rogerson seems to have grasped the full force of the distinction between moral grounds for demanding agreement in taste and the possibility of using moral grounds for additional support for the expectation of agreement, which Crawford himself probably did. Nor is it clear that they have made much progress in showing how the moral significance of aesthetic experience, even once it is explained, could justify the demand not merely that others have some aesthetic experience in general but that they agree with us in their aesthetic response to particular objects as claimed by judgments of taste, although to justify this assumption is the specific burden of proof for the deduction of judgments of taste.

Kemal's argument is difficult to follow. He certainly recognizes the difference between proving the general desirability of the possession of taste and the rationality of expecting agreement in responses to particular objects, for he initially charges that Kant's deduction establishes only the possibility of agreement about taste in general, not agreement about particular judgments, and suggests that morality can be brought in to make a transition from ideal agreement, or the general possibility of agreement, to actual agreement.[26] But this seems to conflate the distinction between the general possibility of agreement and actual agreement about particulars with that between epistemological grounds for expecting agreement and moral grounds for demanding it, and simply to assume that moral grounds for demanding agreement in taste also bring along grounds for agreement about particular objects. However, it remains difficult to see how even a successful moral argument for the necessity of aesthetic sensitivity as somehow morally beneficial would require all persons to develop or exercise this morally beneficial sensitivity on the same particular objects of taste. Subsequently, Kemal seems to sense these problems and to argue that it is not morality at all but rather fine art which can secure the agreement about particulars which Kant's "merely epistemological" deduction falls short of providing. Here the idea seems to be that, as cultural artifacts, works of fine art are supported by or even part of the mechanism by which consensus is created in particular cultures, so that it is through works of fine art, above all, that agreement in response to individual objects is created in and by particular cultures.[27] But here not only does the original project of turning to morality for the completion of the deduction disappear (for, although Kant assumes that works of artistic genius paradigmatically have moral content [*CJ*, §49], this plays little role in Kemal's account); what is worse, Kemal also confuses actual agreement about responses to particular objects in a given culture with the ideal agreement about particular objects that transcends particular historical circumstances, in which Kant is interested. Particular cultures may indeed constitute, or be constituted by, agreement in evaluative and normative attitudes toward particular objects, but Kant is not interested in cultural agreement about particular objects per se; on the contrary, he is deeply suspicious of any agreement about artistic merit that he thinks may merely be a product of cultural conditions (see especially *CJ*, §41) and searches for the ideal conditions for agreement in judgments of taste, as opposed to any empirical conditions that may produce social agreement regardless of genuine aesthetic merit. By turning toward historical agreement about artistic traditions in particular cultures for the completion of Kant's deduction of aesthetic judgment, Kemal not only loses sight of the original connection between aesthetics and morality but completely undermines Kant's own conception of the kind of genuinely universal intersubjective validity sought by a true judgment of taste.[28]

Rogerson's argument takes a different tack. He tries to exploit Kant's moral (rather than merely epistemological) conception of aesthetic response and judgment to solve at least three different alleged problems in standard accounts of Kant's theory. First, he argues that Kant cannot explain how aesthetic judgment can be considered as a species of "reflective judgment," which always seeks to subsume a given particular under an idea that is not immediately given, in contrast to "determinant judgment," which always applies given concepts to objects (see *CJ*, §IV, 5:179–80), unless every aesthetic object does exemplify some sort of idea, even if not an ordinary empirical concept.[29] Second, Rogerson believes that although Kant's epistemological account of aesthetic response may explain how aesthetic response can be universally communicable, it does not explain why aesthetic response is pleasurable.[30] Finally, he argues that a merely epistemological interpretation cannot explain the normative aspect of judgments of taste, the way in which they demand agreement.[31] The fact that (as Kant once but only once claims) all beautiful objects, both natural and artistic, exemplify aesthetic ideas (*CJ*, §51, 5:320), Rogerson holds, can solve all these problems. That beautiful objects manifest a nondeterminate aesthetic idea suffices to make them fit candidates for reflective judgment; their moral significance makes them pleasurable; and their moral significance likewise makes it appropriate to demand that others attend to them and take pleasure in them. Again, however, Rogerson does not clearly separate the rationality of expecting agreement about judgments of taste from the justification for demanding it, and thus does not explain why the moral desirability of aesthetic response requires agreement in particular aesthetic judgments. Moreover, as Rogerson himself concludes (thus reiterating my own original criticism), it is by no means clear that Kant's ethical theory entitles him to demand sensitivity to what is a mere symbol or analogue of the fundamental principle of morality: "Put differently, it is one thing to demand that persons take an interest in determining their actions by the appropriate law of pure practical Reason, and quite another to demand that they take an interest in objects which express aesthetic Ideas."[32] This is the point in my original rejection of the use of the link between aesthetics and morality to complete the deduction of aesthetic judgments that I now believe requires the most extensive reevaluation, but Rogerson does not provide it.

In fact, only one author has directly confronted the issue of how a connection between aesthetics and morality could advance the specific objective of the deduction of judgments of taste by trying to show that such a connection could justify the demand that different persons not just have some aesthetic sensibility in general but agree in finding particular objects beautiful. This author is Anthony Savile, in his book *Aesthetic Reconstructions: The Seminal Writings of Lessing, Kant, and Schiller* (1987). Savile begins by accepting my own interpretation of the two stages of Kant's analysis of aesthetic judgment and explanation of aesthetic response, as well as my assessment of the shortcomings of Kant's official deduction of aesthetic judgments on the basis of the essentially epistemological explanation of aesthetic response. He then argues that the exemplification of moral ideas – that is, aesthetic ideas, which Kant seems to assume always have moral content – by individual works of *art* can justify the demand for agreement about particular objects, because of the individuality of the moral ideas expressed in each and the importance of gaining knowledge of all such moral ideas.[33] Further, Savile holds that the way in which the experience of *natural* beauty can suggest our moral relation to the world is so important that it needs to be reinforced by every possible particular experience of natural beauty, which no one can afford to miss.[34] However, Savile recognizes that if the connection to morality is given such a central role in the deduction of aesthetic judgments on both natural and artistic beauty, a fundamental issue must be confronted: What becomes of Kant's claim that aesthetic response and judgment must be disinterested and free of all constraint by determinate practical as well as theoretical concepts?[35]

Answering this question will be a continuing focus of the following essays, but especially Chapter 3. There I argue that the heart of Kant's connection between aesthetics and morality is the view that it is only by preserving its freedom from direct constraint by concepts, even didactic concepts of morality itself, that the experience of beauty can serve the purpose of giving us a palpable experience of freedom, which is its deepest service to the needs of morality. (The details of this idea are adumbrated in various essays that follow.) Before we can properly appreciate Kant's underlying idea, however, we must realize that much of the critical discussion that has just been recounted has obscured the real nature of Kant's thought by approaching the connection between aesthetics and morality with completely the wrong question in mind. Beginning with Crawford's thesis and my own criticism of it, and certainly continuing with the work of Kemal and Rogerson, if not Savile, it has been assumed that Kant meant the appeal to morality to solve an outstanding problem within his theory of taste, namely the problem of justifying the demand for agreement in particular judgments of taste. From this point of view, every attempt to interpret Kant's intentions has proved wanting, because, whatever our basis for taking a morally significant interest in taste, it never seems sufficient for demanding that everyone agree in particular judgments of taste. But our fundamental error has been in supposing that Kant ever intended the moral significance or content of aesthetic experience and objects to solve a problem within his aesthetic theory – a problem which in any case he did not recognize, for he thought his deduction of aesthetic judgments was successful. In fact, Kant did not look to moral theory to solve a problem in aesthetic theory; instead, he looked to aesthetics to solve what he had come to recognize as crucial problems *for morality:* how the rational ideal of autonomy that underlies morality – that is, the ideal of self-governance by the free choice always to act in accordance with the universal law of pure reason – cannot merely be understood by disembodied reasons but can be made palpable to fully embodied rational agents like ourselves, and how this ideal of pure reason can nevertheless lead to a set of duties that do not just ignore the sensuous aspect of our being but include it. It is not for the sake of agreement in taste that Kant connects it to moral ideas, but for the sake of moral ideas that Kant finds them to be central to taste, indeed ultimately characterizes taste as "at bottom a faculty for the estimation of the sensible rendering [*Versinnlichung*] of moral ideas" (*CJ*, §60, 5:356). Taste does not reach out to morality to increase its own security; rather, morality – that is to say the concern for morality which is primary in us all – spreads its wings over the realm of taste in its own behalf. Yet taste can serve moral autonomy only if morality can also recognize aesthetic autonomy: This is what I shall argue that Kant, like virtually no one before or since, recognized.

In arguing that Kant looked to the sphere of taste to solve unresolved problems in his moral theory, however, I do not wish my view to be confused with the ideological demystification of Kantian morality and aesthetics recently advocated by Terry Eagleton (*The Ideology of the Aesthetic*, 1989). Eagleton claims that Kant appeals to the noncoercive consensus of feeling which is central to his conception of aesthetics in order to mask the emptiness of his moral law – the fact that in its insistence on universalizability it treats all persons as abstract identities and interchangeable commodities. Kant's morality is supposed to leave no room for any genuinely felt consensus with real individuals, a deficiency which he hopes to make good by proffering such bonds of sympathy in the realm of taste instead. Like the "phallic signifier," Eagleton claims (in high fashion, if not itself in good taste), for Kant "reason is a mechanism which, like the commodity, effects formally equal exchanges between isolated individual subjects, erasing the difference of their needs and desires in its homogenizing injunctions" and taking regard of others "only at the abstract level of the understanding, not with any spontaneous sense of their complex particular needs."[36] The realm of taste can make up for the deficiency of morality by fostering such a sense or at least creating the ideological illusion that one exists. But even if taste offers a real possibility for a genuine consensus among noncommoditized individuals, Eagleton criticizes Kant for restricting the creation of community, or *Gemeinschaft*, to the merely cultural realm and not making community or solidarity a genuine ideal of politics itself. On Eagleton's account, "Culture thus sketches the ghostly outline of a non-dominative social order, [but] does so by mystifying and legitimating actual dominative social relations." As he continues,

> Kant's highly formalistic ethics prove incapable of generating any distinctive political theory of their own beyond a conventional liberalism; and though such ethics proffer the dream of a community where subjects are ends in themselves, they are finally too abstract to bring this ideal home to felt experience. It is this which the aesthetic is uniquely able to provide; but in doing so it reproduces something of the very social logic it is out to resist. Kant's selfless aesthetic judge, absolved from all sensual motivation, is among other things a spiritualized version of the abstract, serialized subject of the market place, who cancels the concrete differences between himself and others as thoroughly as does the leveling, homogenizing commodity.[37]

But these charges, although the authority of Hegel transparently lies behind them, rest on a tissue of misrepresentation and simplification.

First, Kant's fundamental principle of morality is formal but by no means empty. It is now well established that Kant's conception of the fundamental principle of morality does not ignore all differences of need among individuals and reduce them to faceless, interchangeable commodities, but treats all individuals alike only in the sense that the rationally acceptable needs of each must be equally considered in all actions affecting them.[38] The requirement of treating others as ends in themselves is not that one treat them all the same at the level of particular types of action (for instance, how much income each is allotted), and it is certainly not the requirement that one just treat them all the same way one treats oneself, however one likes to treat oneself. It is rather the requirement that one pursue only courses of action to which all those potentially affected by them, with all their differences yet in their common status as rational agents, could rationally consent. Kant does not simply require the mechanical universalization of one's own actions, but their universal rational acceptability.[39] We cannot, of course, know the needs and hopes of others *a priori* and may have to try to figure out the acceptability of our actions to others whose specific needs and desires are unknown to us, and sometimes even to themselves, by considering the consequences of our actions in a possible world in which the universalization of our own proposed maxim is a law of nature. But in this case, universalization is not an end in itself but an instrument for determining whether our actions could also be ends for the other real and distinct persons who may be affected by them. Kant's ethics may be formal and may seek to find rational rather than merely emotional motivations for concerning ourselves with the impact of our actions on others, but it does not reduce the others to abstract entities or pallid reflections of our precious selves. It seeks to construct nothing less than a rational framework in which the real differences among distinct persons may be successfully accommodated. Thus, even if Kant turns to aesthetics to make the moral motivation of reason more sensibly palpable to ourselves, he does not turn to aesthetics because his moral principle fails to tell us how to deal with real human subjects. His moral principle gives us all the formal guidance reason can give us in dealing with the real needs and desires of others; aesthetics may come in to make more palpable the freedom that we realize by being moral, but is not necessary to compensate for any commodification of human individuals in Kant's moral principle.

Second, Eagleton's objection to Kant's restriction of a consensus of feeling to aesthetics rather than politics misses one of Kant's profoundest insights, the necessity of confining law and politics to securing outward freedom of action and not using it as an instrument for any party's conception of how to improve the inward life of the spirit. Here, too, Eagleton's failure to appreciate Kant's wisdom goes back to Hegel, and the ensuing misunderstanding has caused no end of real misery in the century now at last drawing to a close. In Kant's view, the essence of politics is external or juridical legislation, and juridical legislation is coercion. Legal incentives to action are coercive, whether they take the subtle form of the use of taxation for the direction of social policy or the blunter form of incarceration or execution for violating the criminal law or political opposition. Thus Kant infers that politics can legitimately concern itself only with the prevention of violations of the freedom of external action of persons, not with all aspects of their welfare, including their spiritual well-being – justice is the authorization to use coercion when but only when it is necessary to hinder an unjust hindrance to the rightful freedom of others.[40] A true community of feeling among members of a polity may be a noble end, perhaps even an ultimate duty of virtue itself and thus a goal of morality, but in Kant's view it is not one which can justifiably (or for that matter successfully) be brought about by the use of the potentially coercive means which is all that law has available to it. For that reason, the establishment of any consensus of feeling, as contrasted with outward respect for freedom of external action, must be left to the individual's internal legislation of morality and to aesthetics rather than to politics, and if morality itself is to be confined only to the rational principle rather than emotional tone of individual motivation, then a consensus of feeling must be left to aesthetics alone – although as we shall see (especially in Chapters 9 and 10), that is to draw the line between aesthetics and at least Kant's ultimate conception of the moral duties of virtue much too sharply. Suffice it here to say that as long as the essence of politics must remain juridical legislation, politics and aesthetics, external freedom of action and consensus of internal feelings, must remain on opposites sides of the fence.

This is traditional liberalism, to be sure, but it is difficult indeed to see how anyone can continue to advocate the use of political means to create cultural cohesion in a century in which the deadly effects of nationalism and even more vicious attempts to make consensus of feeling the proper object of coercive political actions are still the subject of our daily headlines. As the blood of the French Revolution began to flow in earnest, Kant recognized that politics alone could create community only through violence, creating consensus simply by eliminating those who would be diverse. Kant never thought that the limits on individual action that are necessary to preserve maximally compossible freedom of action for all are anything more than a minimal or necessary condition of human civility and by no means thought of external justice as the highest good for human beings. He certainly considered that the realization of the highest good for human beings requires the culture of morality and taste. He just wanted us to be clear that any attempt to bring about the highest good possible for us through coercion rather than the noncoercive means of morality and taste would end up destroying us. About that, history has certainly proved him right.

This conclusion is more overtly political than anything that will follow, and a proper defense of Kantian liberalism is a matter for another occasion. Here I only wish to suggest that a formalistic ethics may not be an inhumane ethics but indeed the most humane ethics, and although the formalistic account of moral motivation that Kant seems to have suggested in his classical ethical writings of the 1780s may have needed to be supplemented by the moral aesthetics he developed in the 1790s, we will never be well served by blurring the lines between aesthetics, ethics, and politics. What I hope to illuminate from a variety of perspectives in the following essays is only some of the ways in which Kant thought aesthetics could come to the aid of morality without undermining the essential uniqueness of either.

# Kant's aesthetics in historical context

# Chapter 1

# Feeling and freedom: Kant on aesthetics and morality

## I. THE GULF BETWEEN NATURE AND FREEDOM

In the final section of the introduction to the *Critique of Judgment*, Kant speaks of the "great gulf" (*grosse Kluft*) that separates the "realm of the concept of nature" from that of "the concept of freedom." "The concept of freedom," he states, "determines nothing in regard to the theoretical cognition of nature; the concept of nature likewise [determines] nothing in regard to the practical laws of freedom." It does not seem possible to throw a bridge across this gulf, he continues, but in fact "the faculty of judgment yields the mediating concept between the concept of nature and the concept of freedom, which makes possible the transition from the purely theoretical to the purely practical, from the lawfulness of the former to the final purpose of the latter, in the concept of a *purposiveness* of nature." Such a mediating concept apparently must show that even though "the determining grounds of causality according to the concept of freedom (and the practical laws which it contains) are not founded in nature," "nevertheless their *effect*, in accord with these formal laws, should take place in the world" (*CJ*, §IX, 5:195–6).

Originally presented as an address at the meeting of the Eastern Division of the American Society for Aesthetics in 1989, this essay was published under the title "Feeling and Freedom: Kant on Aesthetics and Morality," *Journal of Aesthetics and Art Criticism* 48 (1990): 137–46. Reprinted here, with minor alterations, by permission.

Many writers have offered accounts of how the teleological concept of the purposiveness of nature, or more broadly the formal purposiveness of objects of both aesthetic and teleological judgment (that is, the perception of individual objects, of particular systems of natural objects, and of nature as a whole as if they were products of design, even in the absence of a theoretical assertion that they are), is supposed to bridge the gulf between the causality of nature according to theoretical laws and the causality of freedom according to practical laws. But few pause to ask the question, What gulf? What problem about the relationship between the legislations of nature and freedom remains to be solved, in the *Critique of Judgment,* that was not already solved by the *Critique of Pure Reason* and the *Critique of Practical Reason?* Had not the proof of the actuality of freedom in the second *Critique,* building upon the proof of its logical and epistemological possibility in the third antinomy of the first *Critique,* already solved the problem of the relation between the causality of nature and the causality of freedom? Kant's conception of morality, as well as the model of the relations between theoretical and practical reason that he had evolved by the time he completed the *Critique of Practical Reason* (which we might have conveniently called his "metaphysics of morals," if he had not preempted that title for his detailed description of our actual duties of justice and virtue in his last great work)[1] comprised several key claims. Above all was Kant's conception of virtue and moral worth as a quality attaching to agents on account of their attempts to perform actions intended to comply with the moral law solely on the ground that such actions are required by the moral law, that is, from the motive of duty alone: "It is not enough to do what is right, but it must also be performed solely on the ground that it is right" (*CJ,* §53, 5:327). Next, there was a claim about our knowledge of the moral law, the claim that pure practical reason alone can discover the moral law, without assistance from any other faculty of cognition. Third, there was a claim about our knowledge of the actuality of freedom. Although acknowledgment of the difference between phenomena and noumena (appearances and things in themselves) and recognition that the deduction of the universal applicability of the law of natural causation holds only for objects of empirical knowledge or appearances had been argued, in the solution to the third antinomy in the first *Critique*, to suffice for the proof of the *possibility* of a causality according to laws of freedom as well as laws of nature, only in the second *Critique* was it argued that purely rational cognition of the practical laws of freedom implies the *actual existence* of free will. Finally, and most puzzling for the *Critique of Judgment*'s assertion that there is a problematic gulf between the realms of natural and practical laws, the second *Critique* offered a metaphysical model of the relation between freedom in the noumenal realm and determinism according to natural laws in the phenomenal realm according to which freedom in the noumenal realm was not only total in itself but also total in its control of relevant events in the phenomenal realm. The universal validity of causal law *within* the phenomenal realm did not imply that the phenomenal realm as a whole was not totally subject to the free agency of the self as it is in itself but rather only that, if need be, the entire history of the phenomenal realm could be taken to reflect the free choice of a rational agent in the noumenal realm. (And since the lawfulness of the phenomenal realm itself was also supposed to be a product of the self as it is in itself, although in its theoretical rather than practical capacity, this should not even have seemed to be any very difficult task.) The free agency of the noumenal self could not be seen as intervening at particular moments in the history of the phenomenal world, but we could nevertheless rest assured in the conviction that the phenomenal realm of nature as a whole is always subject to the freedom of the will, no matter how recalcitrant to the demands of practical reason any sequence of events in the natural formation of a character might otherwise seem. So virtue lies in motivation by the moral law alone; reason alone suffices for knowledge of the moral law; knowledge of the moral law suffices for knowledge of the transcendental freedom of our will; and the freedom of our will implies total control over the phenomenal realm, in spite of (rather, along with) the total subjection of the latter to causal laws of nature. What gulf between the realms of nature and freedom remains to be bridged?

I propose to answer this question by arguing that the *Critique of Judgment* contains major developments in Kant's conception of the role and importance of feelings in the practice of morality, and of sensibility in our comprehension of morality. By 1790, Kant had come to feel that there was a gulf to be bridged between nature and freedom, because he had made certain essential modifications of his moral epistemology and moral psychology – or at least clarifications of his views to avoid misinterpretations of which many readers, both then and since, have been guilty. At no point in the *Critique of Judgment* does Kant imply any retraction of his criterion of virtue, or his conception that reason alone can discover the moral law and, given any set of circumstances, determine what is right, or his conception of the proof and power of freedom of the will. But he does suggest (contrary to what many at least had inferred from his presentation of his conception of virtue in the *Groundwork of the Metaphysics of Morals* of 1785) that the moral perfection of human beings does not lie in this sort of virtue alone, regardless of the presence or absence of the kind and sympathetic sentiments that other writers of his time had made into the whole of morality. On the contrary, he makes it clear that moral perfection requires the development of feelings compatible with and conducive to those intentions that are dictated by pure practical reason alone. Then he argues that the cultivation of susceptibility to aesthetic responses, to works of both nature and art (but preeminently to the former), can assist in this regard. In this way, Kant suggests that although virtuous *motivation* can be constituted by the thought of duty alone, such a restrictive state of mind is not what virtuous motivation itself aims to produce. He also suggests that the assumption that the free practical will can determine one to dutiful action without also being accompanied by what Kant now calls "moral feeling," "a disposition for the feeling for practical ideas" (*CJ*, §29, 5:265), is unrealistic.

Second, Kant also suggests that any idea that a comprehension of morality can proceed totally independently of sensible representation is implausible. Instead, he suggests that specific moral conceptions, the structure of moral action, and even the primacy of practical reason itself all stand in need of representation in a form that the senses, and creatures so dependent on the senses as we human beings are, can grasp – and again, that the aesthetic is especially suited to assist in this regard. The aesthetic, we should note, is not alone in this regard; teleological judgment also assists, through Kant's argument that nature as a whole can be seen as a purposive system only with respect to the necessary end of human freedom. But both the aesthetic ideal of human beauty in particular and the teleological conception of nature in general as a purposive whole culminating in humanity are sensible images of morality and derive their overwhelming importance precisely from Kant's recognition that we need such images: that although the content of the moral law must be deduced by ratiocination alone, we are not creatures who can really be expected to grasp the nature of morality itself by pure, unaided reason.

These developments in Kant's moral psychology and epistemology are characteristic of his thought in the 1790s; indeed, the *Critique of Judgment* should probably be seen as the first fruit of the profound ripening in Kant's conception of morality that took place in that final decade of his creativity. The idea that the motivation of duty should not simply act independently of, or even in opposition to, our feelings but that, instead, we both should and can work to make our feelings harmonious with our free will is central in both the *Religion within the Limits of Reason Alone* (1793) and the *Doctrine of Virtue* (Part II of the *Metaphysics of Morals*, 1797). Earlier, in the *Groundwork of the Metaphysics of Morals* (1785), Kant had illustrated the virtue of being motivated by the conception of duty alone by showing how the dutiful maxims of individuals "who endure their life, though without loving it," or in whom all "sympathy with the fate of others has been extinguished" by a "deadly insensibility" brought on by a cloud of misfortunes, can nevertheless have a complete "moral content" (4:398). In the *Religion*, however, perhaps stirred by what he took to be Friedrich Schiller's unfair criticism of such examples, which may have been intended only as a heuristic device, Kant makes it clear that an irremediable conflict between duty and desire is not really possible. Instead, the appearance of such a conflict would represent a lingering denial of the law of duty itself:

> Now if one asks: what is the *aesthetic* quality, as it were the *temperament* of virtue, brave and thus *joyous*, or anxiety-ridden and beaten down? then an answer is hardly necessary. The latter slavish determination of mind can never obtain without a hidden *hatred* of the law, and the joyous heart in *following* its duty (not complacency in the *acknowledgment* of it) is a sign of the genuineness of virtuous disposition . . . [T]he firm resolve to do better in the future . . . must bring about a joyous determination of the mind, without which one is never certain of having *come to love* the good, i.e., of having taken it up in one's maxim. (*Religion*, 6:23–4n.)

Kant holds that a hateful disposition cannot accompany virtuous motivation, at least over the long haul, and for that reason can cast doubt on the claim that a person having such feelings is motivated by duty. In the *Doctrine of Virtue*, Kant argues that the very character of duties to oneself is to place one's sensuous being (*Sinnenwesen*) under obligation to one's rational being (*Vernunftwesen*) (§3, 6:418). Duties to oneself are divided into "perfect duties," which are the duties not to damage or destroy one's moral personality and the physical being on which it depends, and "imperfect duties," which are those to perfect one's moral personality and physical being. The principle of imperfect duties to oneself, he says, can be summed up in the slogan "*Make yourself more perfect* than mere nature created you" (§4, 6:419).[2] This implies that the nature of one's feelings is not simply to be taken as a given, to be ignored by the free will and overridden when necessary, but that feelings, as part of one's natural being, should and can be modified to help perfect the harmony between one's natural and rational being.[3]

The *Critique of Judgment* fits into a moral framework in which it is necessary, as well as possible, to bring feeling into harmony with the rational demands of duty. But it was only seven years after the third *Critique* was published that the *Doctrine of Virtue* was to make explicit that the full panoply of our duties includes the cultivation of our feelings of sympathy toward natural objects other than human beings, for the sake of the cultivation of humane feelings within ourselves – "the disposition of sensibility . . . to love something without regard to use (e.g., beautiful crystallizations, the indescribable beauty of the realm of plants)," Kant says, "much advances morality, or at least prepares [us] for it," even though "it is not itself already moral" (*Virtue*, §17, 6:433) – as well as the cultivation of our more direct feelings of sympathy for fellow human beings (§§34–5, 6:456–7). One can therefore propose that the *Critique of Judgment* should be seen as Kant's first sustained discussion of the way in which our feelings toward ourselves and our fellow humans can be brought into harmony with the claims of the pure practical reason that makes us free agents in the strictest sense. The gulf that needs to be bridged is not that between noumenal and phenomenal causality but between feeling and freedom – that is, between the arbitrary realm of sensation and the law-governed autonomy of reason. In principle, the noumenal causality of the free will, the free agency of the self as it is in itself, always has the power to remake the phenomenal world of appearance and its natural laws of causation, but in practice it must do this by working with, not against, the feelings of the natural and embodied human agent. Aesthetic as well as teleological judgment assist in this enterprise by offering both sensible representations of key aspects of morality and opportunities for the cultivation of the moral feelings.

## II. THE LINKS BETWEEN AESTHETICS AND MORALITY

In this chapter I will not attempt to discuss at length the particular links between aesthetics and morality that Kant

suggests in light of this general scheme but will simply catalog them. My catalog will be divided into three parts. First,
Kant suggests direct connections between aesthetic judgment and the cultivation of moral feelings. Second, Kant
suggests ways in which both aesthetic objects (especially
works of fine art) and aesthetic experience itself offer sensible
representations of moral ideas, and even of the structure of
morality. Third, both aesthetic and teleological judgment
serve to represent nothing less than the primacy of practical
reason, that is, the unconditional superiority of the rational
use of reason over all other forms of value. These links can be
only briefly described here; several are explored more fully in
later chapters.

## Moral psychology

We will first consider the role of aesthetics in Kant's moral
psychology. The experience of beauty serves the purposes of
morality most directly by improving our propensity for moral
feeling. The relatively easily obtained experience of pleasure
in a disinterested state of mind, characteristic of the experience of beauty, accustoms us to disinterested enjoyment in
general and thus prepares us for the more difficult task of
joyfully superseding personal interests in the way that morality can often require. The achievement of a pleasurable state
of mind is not a direct aim of practical reason. But disinterested delight is a natural concomitant of the moral determination of the will and, as Kant suggests in the *Religion,* a sign of
true commitment to morality. The experience of beauty fosters this frame of mind.

Kant's remarks on this theme, in the part of the *Critique of
Judgment* entitled the "Critique of Aesthetic Judgment," are
quite brief. First, in his contrast between "free" and "dependent" judgments of beauty, he says that dependent judgments of beauty, which presuppose some classification and/or
interpretation of an object, offer a better prospect of "rules not

for taste, but for the unification of taste with reason, i.e., of the beautiful with the good." Beauty thus "becomes usable as an instrument of intention in respect of [the good], in order to bring that disposition of mind which preserves itself and is of subjective universal validity to the support of that manner of thought which can only be preserved through arduous resolution, but is objectively universally valid" (*CJ*, §16, 5:230–1). Second, in the "General Remark" which follows his analyses of beauty and sublimity, Kant argues that even though only the "*absolutely good*," which is grounded in an "*absolutely necessitating* law," "contains not a mere *claim* but also a *command* for approbation from everyone" (*CJ*, §29 General Remark, 5:266–7), experience of the beautiful nevertheless "cultivates, in that it also teaches [us] to attend to purposiveness in the feeling of pleasure"; the beautiful is "purposive in relation to the moral feeling" because it "prepares us to love something, even nature, apart from interest" (*CJ*, §29 General Remark, 5:267).[4] Finally, Kant concludes the "Critique of Aesthetic Judgment" by suggesting that morality requires not just the abstract universalizability of aims in a kingdom of ends but also communication among the individual inhabitants of an actual community. This leads to a final encomium on taste, described "as a sense [that is] common to all mankind" and that thus constitutes a part "of the art of the mutual communication of ideas between the most cultured part [of a commonwealth] and the ruder part, the tuning of the amplitude and refinement of the former to the natural simplicity and originality of the latter, and in this way first discovering the medium between the higher culture and common nature" (*CJ*, §60, 5:356).[5] Kant argues here that "the development of moral ideas and the culture of the moral feeling" is the "true propaedeutic for the founding of taste," thus reversing the order of priority suggested in Sections 16 and 29. But the very fact that either the disposition to moral feeling or the disposition to aesthetic response can be regarded as the propaedeutic to the other shows how intimately connected the two dispositions are and how the perfection of each goes hand in hand with that of the other.

## Moral epistemology

Kant's discussion of the role of the aesthetic in moral epistemology – that is, the ways in which aesthetic objects and experience afford sensible representation of moral ideas – is more extended and more complex than these passing comments on moral psychology and includes aesthetic representation both of crucial moral concepts and of the primacy of practical reason. First, in his accounts of the sublime, aesthetic ideas, and beauty as the symbol of morality, Kant suggests that aesthetic phenomena can offer sensible representations of practical reason, of specific moral conceptions, and finally, of the general relation between moral reason and moral feeling. Second, Kant suggests that the aesthetic ideal of human beauty and the teleological purposiveness of nature as a whole can represent the uniqueness of morality as a necessary end, thus furnishing sensible representations of the primacy of practical reason itself.

We will first consider the aesthetic representation of morality, beginning with the "sublime." The key to Kant's account of the sublime is the claim that "the feeling of the sublime in nature is respect for our own vocation, . . . which as it were makes intuitable the superiority of the vocation of reason over the greatest capacity[6] of sensibility" (*CJ*, §27, 5:257). Kant distinguishes two different types of the feeling of the sublime. The first, the experience of the "mathematical sublime," induces a feeling that represents the unlimited cognitive power of reason, "a feeling, namely, that we have pure, self-sufficient reason, or a faculty for the estimation of magnitude, the preeminence of which cannot be made intuitable through anything except" the efforts of sensibility and understanding to grasp such magnitudes (*CJ*, §27, 5:258). The second, the experience of the "dynamical sublime," is characterized as a feeling that specifically represents the dominion of practical reason over ordinary, natural inclinations. This form of the sublime is called "dynamical" because it represents our ability not to grasp nature but even to act against it if duty so requires. Here, fearful and threatening prospects in nature, towering seas and mountains, "elevate the strength of the soul above its usual mean and discover within us a faculty of resistance of quite another kind from that which may be assailed and endangered by external nature." This gives us the courage to measure ourselves against the physical power of nature and, in so doing, reveals the imperviousness of our purely moral character to threats from nature. The experience of the dynamical sublime, then, is a feeling that reveals our "physical incapacity" to withstand the power of nature over us as its creatures "but at the same time discovers our faculty for judging ourselves as independent of it." "Nature is here called sublime merely because it raises the imagination to the presentation of those cases in which it can make palpable [*fühlbar*] the proper sublimity of its own vocation over nature" (*CJ*, §28, 5:261–2).[7]

So Kant's original view of the unlimited freedom of the noumenal agent remains intact. What is added is the idea that a feeling engendered by aesthetic response can represent this metaphysical claim to us through our imagination, and that it is apparently quite important that the basis of morality receive this sensible representation:

> Just as we reproach someone who is indifferent in the estimation of a natural object which we find beautiful with lack of *taste*: so we say of one who remains unmoved by something which we judge to be sublime that he has no *feeling*. But we require both of every human . . . only with this difference, that we require the former of everyone since in it the faculty of judgment merely relates the imagination to the understanding as the faculty of concepts, but we require the second, since in it the imagination is related to reason as the faculty of ideas, only under a subjective presupposition (which however we believe ourselves to be able to impute to everyone and justified in so doing), namely that of the moral feeling in men. (*CJ*, §29, 5:265–6)

Kant does not spell out why we are justified in requiring moral feeling, as well as virtuous motivation, of everyone.

He does not argue that moral feeling may be required because it is the only sure criterion of virtuous motivation, although he suggests this in the *Religion*. But in recognition of the realities of our natural circumstances, he clearly does require a feeling, as well as rational cognition, of the basis of morality.

We now turn to the fine arts, which also play a vital role in Kant's expanded moral epistemology. Pure or simple aesthetic judgments on the beauty of crustacea and foliage, of course, are disinterested, but judgments on the more complex fine arts are never pure, because they always involve recognition of the human intentionality that lies behind works of art (*CJ*, §43, 5:303; §45, 5:306).[8] Perhaps just because works of fine art are products of human intentionality, we cannot keep our judgments of them entirely independent of assessment of their moral significance. In any case, Kant asserts that "where the fine arts are not brought into either close or distant connections with moral ideas, which alone bring with them a self-sufficient delight," then over time they must "dull the soul, gradually render the object disgusting, and make the soul moody and dissatisfied with itself through the consciousness that its disposition is contrary to the purposes of reason" (*CJ*, §53, 5:326). Kant is apparently presupposing not just that any products of human intentionality must be compatible with the fulfillment of duty, but also that at some level, and in the long run, all human activities must make some contribution to the advancement of morality and will inevitably be judged from that point of view. The arts, he argues, can satisfy this general requirement by rendering moral conceptions intuitable to the senses as aesthetic ideas.

Kant argues that the mere form of a work of art can satisfy the demands of taste, but that works of art are also expected to have "spirit" (*Geist*), something to serve as an "animating principle of the mind" (*CJ*, §49, 5:313). Aesthetic ideas fill this role. An aesthetic idea is a "representation of the imagination which gives much to think about, without any determinate thought, i.e., *concept*, being adequate to it, which therefore no language can fully reach and make comprehensible." Such ideas clearly prevent an aesthetic object from quickly being exhausted and becoming boring. But not just any ideas can fill this role. Rather, Kant supposes, only moral conceptions offer the permanent interest required of aesthetic ideas. These "representations of the imagination" are called "ideas" precisely because "they strive after something lying beyond the boundaries of experience and attempt to approximate a representation of concepts of reason (intellectual ideas). . . . The poet," he says, "dares to render sensible ideas of reason of invisible beings, the realm of the blessed, hell, eternity, the creation, etc." (*CJ*, §49, 5:313–14): in other words, not ideas of morality in general but specific moral conceptions. Aesthetic ideas render moral conceptions accessible to sensibility.

Kant sometimes writes as if this was in the interest of art rather than morality itself, as if art needs morality to retain its interest. But at the end of the "Critique of Aesthetic Judgment," Kant implies that the significance of taste lies in its unique capacity to provide sensible representation of moral ideas. This suggests that morality has its own interest in securing sensible representation of its central conceptions: "Taste is at bottom a faculty of judgment for rendering moral ideas sensible . . . from which the greater sensitivity for the feeling for the latter (which is called moral [feeling]) derives that pleasure which taste declares as valid for everyone and not just for the private feeling of each" (*CJ*, §60, 5:356). The importance of taste, in other words, derives not just from the disinterested delight that it affords but from its capacity to make moral ideas evident to the senses, and obviously this would not make taste important unless it was important that moral ideas be made evident to the senses.

Next, I turn to Kant's discussion of the beautiful as the symbol of the morally good. In Section 59 of the *Critique of Judgment*, Kant argues that "taste as it were makes possible the transition from the charm of sense to habitual moral interest without too violent a leap" because beauty is a symbol of morality. In this context, a beautiful object stands for the experience of beauty, which in turn "represents this imagination, even in its freedom, as purposively determinable for the understanding and even teaches us to take a free delight in objects of the senses without the charm of sense" (CJ, §59, 5:354). The free delight in beauty represents the dependence of moral feeling on an antecedent determination of the free will, and in light of this parallel beauty gives some sensible representation to the relation between reason and feeling in morality itself.

Kant begins Section 59 with the blunt statement that "intuitions are always required in order to demonstrate the reality of our concepts" (5:351); stated without restriction, this would seem to apply to moral concepts along with all others. But Kant adds that although examples can be given for empirical concepts and schemata for pure concepts, it is impossible to produce intuitions which directly confirm the reality of concepts of reason, that is, ideas. However, he next argues that "hypotyposis," or presentation of concepts to the senses (Versinnlichung), can also be accomplished "symbolically." In this case, although the concept is one which "only reason can think and to which no sensible intuition is adequate," there is nevertheless still some form of sensible intuition that counts as a representation of the concept. In the case of such a symbolic representation, what agrees with the concept is not the actual content of the intuition but "merely the form of reflection" on it (5:351). Kant illustrates this claim with an analogy between a "despotic state" and a "handmill": Although an observation of the latter is not itself an observation of the former, there are similarities between the ways these two things behave, and thus in the structure of our thought about them, even if not in the direct empirical content of our observation of them. In light of this, one can serve as a symbol of the other. Kant then applies this analysis of symbolism to the claim that "the beautiful is the symbol of the morally good." His argument is that the experience of aesthetic judgment furnishes us with some experience of both our own capacity for autonomy and the possibility of harmony between this capacity and nature outside it, which must be grounded in a supersensible basis for both. Because of partial parallels between the structure of aesthetic judgment (in this case pure aesthetic judgment on the beautiful in general, not specifically judgment on art with morally significant representational content) and moral judgment, aesthetic experience can serve as a symbol of moral judgment. The experience of both autonomy and the supersensible basis of agreement between our autonomy and nature that we enjoy in the aesthetic case can count as some sensible representation (*Versinnlichung*) of those as moral ideas as well.[9]

The parallels between aesthetic and moral judgment center on the relation between pleasure and the cognitive activity that produces it. The beautiful pleases immediately, disinterestedly, as the result of freedom of the imagination, and with universal validity. Virtuous motivation pleases immediately although independently of any antecedent interest, on the basis of a free employment of intellectual faculties, and with universal validity. There are also differences: Moral feeling depends on the freedom of the will rather than imagination, and is grounded upon concepts rather than independent of them (*CJ*, §59, 5:354). Still, in aesthetic judgment immediacy, disinterestedness, freedom, and universality are as it were palpable, and they make the analogous immediacy, disinterestedness, freedom, and universality of moral judgment palpable as well. The parallels between aesthetic and moral judgment also allow the symbolization of the subjective autonomy and objective harmony with it that ground the possibility of morality as well.[10]

## The ideal of beauty

Finally, I turn to Kant's accounts of the "ideal of beauty," in the "Critique of Aesthetic Judgment" (*CJ*, §17), and of "the ultimate end of nature as a teleological system" in the "Critique of Teleological Judgment" (*CJ*, §§83–4). Kant does not explicitly label either of these as a representation of the primacy of practical reason, but I suggest that we can make sense of Kant's motivation in these sections by supposing that he was searching for nothing less than vehicles for the representation of the primacy of practical reason itself. Such a search would be dictated not by the internal logic of aesthetic or teleological judgment itself but rather by Kant's increasing sensitivity to the need for access to the ideas of pure practical reason through natural human feelings.

First, let us consider Kant's conception of the "ideal" of taste. In the "Critique of Aesthetic Judgment," Kant argues that it is natural for us to seek not just exemplary objects of taste – that is, different objects that all of us can reasonably be expected to find beautiful – but a single, "highest model" of taste, an "archetype" or "*ideal*" (*CJ*, §17, 5:232). Such a single ideal of taste cannot be provided by any purely free beauty, or even by any ordinary case of dependent beauty; the ends or uses of a "beautiful residence" or a "beautiful garden," for instance, "are not sufficiently determined and fixed, consequently [their] purposiveness is almost as free as that of *vague* [i.e., dependent] beauty" (*CJ*, §17, 5:233). Nor can the ideal of beauty be arrived at by inducing any sort of norm or average from observed instances, even though the imagination is capable of discovering such norms without any rules. Any such norm would be inextricably linked to the empirical circumstances of the individual observer, and persons in different circumstances would arrive at different norms (*CJ*, §17, 5:234). Instead, Kant argues, only a representation of the human form as expressive of the *a priori* idea of morality itself suffices to fix an ideal of a single beautiful object valid for all: "Only that which has the end of its existence in itself, *man*, who determines his ends himself through reason, . . . this *man* is therefore an *ideal of beauty*, just as humanity in his person, as intelligence, alone among all objects in the world is capable of an ideal of *perfection*" (*CJ*, §17, 5:233). Human autonomy is the only candidate for a unique ideal of beauty.

In fact, Kant does not say why different human populations should be expected to arrive at a single image of the appropriate expression of the ethical ideal of humanity any more than at a single norm of merely physical stature or beauty, why, that is, the physical expression of the moral ideal of humanity should not vary from culture to culture, even if the moral ideal itself is the same. But this problem is not really very interesting. What is much more interesting is why Kant assumes we must search for any single ideal of beauty, whether in ourselves or other objects, in the first place, and thus why we need to find any *a priori* concept to fix a single ideal of beauty. Simply to assume that because every object which is beautiful must be capable of pleasing everybody there must therefore be some single object which maximally pleases everybody would be a bizarre mistake in quantification, in no way implied by Kant's antecedent analysis of aesthetic judgment. So what lies behind his argument?

The answer can only be that it is reason, not aesthetic judgment, which seeks to fix an ideal of beauty, for the very purpose of representing itself to sense. Thus Kant says that the archetype of taste transforms "the purposes of humanity, insofar as they cannot be sensibly represented, into a principle for the estimation of its form, through which the former can be revealed as through their effect in appearance" (*CJ*, §17, 5:233). It does this precisely because the ideal of beauty "rests to be sure on reason's indeterminate idea of a maximum" (5:232). In other words, it is reason which demands outward representation of its effects in a form of beauty, and indeed something maximally beautiful, in order to represent its own character as something maximal or unconditioned. "The ideal consists in the expression of the *ethical*, without which the object would not please . . . universally and positively" (*CJ*, §17, 5:235).

It may seem that nothing has been said about the *primacy* of practical reason or its superiority to any other form of feeling or cognition. Nor is it clear that Kant has explained why we must seek an object which is not just maximally but *uniquely* beautiful. But these two problems seem to be linked: A single ideal of beauty must be sought precisely because practical reason is unique, the sole unconditioned and unconditional end of mankind. An aesthetic ideal is not sought just as one more representation of reason, which we already have aplenty in the beautiful and sublime in general, but as a representation of its uniqueness. That lies only in the superiority of practical reason to all else. Remember, Kant has said that humanity alone admits of an ideal of beauty, because humanity, as intelligence, alone admits of perfection. It can only be practical reason which Kant has in mind here.

We can now turn to the moral significance of teleology. Kant's analysis of teleological judgment, in the "Critique of Teleological Judgment," culminates in an argument that a coherent view of nature as purposive is possible only in relation to a necessary "ultimate end" of creation, and that the only candidate for such an end is the unconditional end of human freedom itself. He thus suggests that a teleological view of nature must itself represent the primacy of practical reason, because such a view is possible only in acknowledgment of the unconditional necessity of the end of morality, indeed *as* an acknowledgment of that end.

This conclusion is not evident in the first two-thirds of Kant's treatment of teleological judgment, where his argument is essentially epistemological. Here Kant argues that due to the limits of our understanding (namely, its restriction to temporally unidirectional mechanical laws of causation), we cannot understand the self-maintaining and reproductive character of organisms except by conceiving of them as if they were "intrinsically purposive," or the product of intelligent design. Such a conception of them, however, is merely reflective or regulative (that is, it functions for the internal organization of our own thought but cannot be asserted as a theoretical truth about reality itself); thus, we are not licensed to assert that natural organisms are in fact the product of intelligent design, although we cannot understand them otherwise.[11] This argument then takes an unexpected turn when Kant goes on to suggest that an intelligent designer can be conceived to produce designed objects only in order to fulfill some ulterior objective or final end. In other words, intrinsic purposiveness cannot be coherently conceived on its own, but only in connection with extrinsic purposiveness. In Kant's words, "Since we must support the inner possibility [of an organized thing] on a causality of final causes and an idea, which is the basis of this, we cannot think of the existence of this product except as an end" (*CJ*, §82, 5:426). Obviously, the assumption is simply that it would be irrational for a designer to produce designs without some good reason to do so – a deeply Leibnizian thought.

Kant's argument then makes the following further move. The extrinsic purposiveness of natural systems must have something to do with the purposes of human beings, because they are "the only being[s] on earth who can form a concept of ends and by means of [their] reason make a system of ends out of an aggregate of purposively formed things" (*CJ*, §82, 5:426–7). But nature cannot be seen as purposive relative to the human end of maximizing happiness, both because it is obviously false that nature has made man "a special favorite" and, equally important, because happiness is too indeterminate and open-ended for nature ever to realize, even if it would. Instead, the final end of nature can only be human culture, the "aptitude and skill for all kinds of ends, for the sake of which nature (both external and internal) can be used" (*CJ*, §83, 5:430). But even here, a distinction must be drawn. The final end of nature cannot be culture as mere skill for the furtherance of any ends whatsoever but the "culture of discipline," or "the liberation of the will from the despotism of desires" (*CJ*, §83, 5:432). In other words, freedom of the will as governed by practical reason is the only possible ultimate end for the extrinsic purposiveness of nature:

> Now we have only a single sort of being in the world, whose causality is teleological, i.e., directed at ends, and yet so constituted that the law according to which they have to determine ends is represented as unconditional and independent of natural conditions but rather as necessary in itself. The being of this kind is man, but considered as noumenon: the only being of nature in whose constitution we can cognize a supersensible faculty (*freedom*) and even the law of the causality together with the object which it can set before it as its highest purpose (the highest good in the world). (*CJ*, §84, 5:435)

A teleological view of nature, Kant concludes, requires more than just seeing organisms as if they were designed. We must see organisms as if they were designed for a purpose that is not only compatible with our empirical observation of nature but also necessary; and only the end of human freedom – the objective, as well as the foundation, of morality itself – satisfies that description.

Kant does not sort out all the claims he might base on this connection. He simply says that "if now the things of the world, as dependent beings as regards their existence, require a highest cause acting according to ends, then man is the final end of creation" (*CJ*, §84, 5:435). At least three different theses are possible here. These are, first, that teleological judgment is simply a possibility for reflective judgment but one that must be grounded in the possibility of seeing human freedom as the ultimate end of nature; second, that teleological judgment of organisms is required by the exigencies of the human epistemological situation but turns out to require a moral conception of man as well; and, finally, that a representation of nature as amenable to human morality requires a teleological conception of it as subordinated to this sole unconditional end. But on any one of these accounts, Kant argues that nature can be seen as a "chain of mutually subordinated purposes" only in connection with humanity as "the subject of morality," and thus teleological judgment of nature becomes a representation of the unconditional value of morality or the primacy of practical reason.

In the end, perhaps, Kant wished to bridge the gulf between nature and freedom by having it both ways. The limits of theoretical cognition require a teleological and ultimately moral view of nature, and morality itself requires a teleological view of nature. If so, then he has certainly gone beyond the heroic view of the *Critique of Practical Reason*, on which the free will simply ignores the facts of nature. He has instead suggested that we must be able to represent the unconditional dominion of freedom within, as well as from outside of, nature.

Kant's subordination of a teleological view of nature to a

moral view of mankind itself does not threaten any incoherence with regard to the requirement of disinterestedness, for he never suggests that there is anything disinterested in either our theoretical or teleological conception of nature. His various suggestions that aesthetic responses to both nature and art subserve ultimate purposes of morality, however, obviously threaten his apparently fundamental claim that judgments of taste are independent of all conceptions of goodness, or are free of any interest (*CJ*, §4, 5:208, and §5, 5:210). How can he maintain that both our response to natural and artistic beauty and our creation of the latter satisfy this fundamental constraint that the aesthetic be free of determination by all theoretical and practical concepts and yet allow objects of taste to be put into the service of morality, even (as in such cases as the ideal of beauty) to be in some sense determined by the logic of morality rather than the logic of aesthetic judgment itself?[12] At a technical level, the answer to this question will lie in distinguishing between the narrow role of a concept in *determining* our response to an object and a broader role of its being in some sense *manifested* or *exemplified* by an object, its being illustrated by an object without itself dictating that we must take pleasure in the object. At a deeper level, the answer to this question lies in Kant's insistence that it is precisely in virtue of its freedom from all constraint, even that by concepts of morality itself, that aesthetic response can furnish us with the experience of freedom that allows it to symbolize morality. Even where morality itself is not what is symbolized but some more specific moral idea is exemplified (we might additionally suppose), the fundamental freedom of aesthetic response itself remains a *sine qua non*. The following essays, especially the other, more historical chapters in Part I, explore this indispensable presupposition of Kant's attempt to show that the aesthetic can serve morality without losing its own identity.

*Chapter 2*

# The dialectic of disinterestedness:
# I. Eighteenth-century aesthetics

According to standard histories of eighteenth-century aesthetics,[1] Anthony Ashley Cooper, third earl of Shaftesbury, and, under his influence, Francis Hutcheson, professor of moral philosophy at Glasgow, characterized our response to objects displaying beauty and other aesthetic properties such as grandeur or sublimity as "disinterested," or independent of our normal theoretical and practical interests. This characterization of what we now call "aesthetic experience" is supposed to have been accepted by the many writers on aesthetics who followed them, until Kant formalized the theory by elevating disinterestedness into the first criterial "moment" and the premise of all his further analysis of the judgment of taste.[2] Following Kant, writers such as Schopenhauer made disinterestedness the fundamental hallmark of the aesthetic, a position which it retained in Romantic and Idealist conceptions of the "autonomy" of art and in their progeny, the conceptions of "distance" or "detachment" in analytical aesthetics as an "aesthetic attitude" necessary to allow the genuine "aesthetic properties" of "aesthetic objects" to be observed and properly enjoyed.[3]

This little story drastically simplifies a much more complicated history. Shaftesbury did indeed introduce two themes that were to remain constant through the remainder of the

This essay was originally presented as a lecture at a National Endowment for the Humanities Summer Institute on Art and the Emergence of Aesthetics in the Eighteenth Century at Johns Hopkins University in 1990 and is first published in the present volume.

eighteenth century and influence aesthetic theory well into our own. These are, first, the idea that our response to a beautiful object is a natural and immediate response that is more like a sensory reaction than a protracted reflection or ratiocination; and, second, the view that this response transpires independently of any reflection on the *personal* or *private* interest or advantage of the agent enjoying it. But these hardly meant that he took the response to beauty to be independent of all theoretical and practical interests or values in general. On the contrary, Shaftesbury was a Neoplatonist, influenced more by the Cambridge Platonists than by his own teacher John Locke, and as such he held the beautiful, the true, and the morally good to be manifestations of the same underlying form and order in the universe. Shaftesbury used the sense of beauty to prove the existence of a moral sense, which it could readily do because it was not just analogous but identical to it. Despite all the homage that Hutcheson paid to Shaftesbury, when Hutcheson characterized the sense of beauty as a unique "internal sense" which is independent of all reflection on use or advantage whatsoever and is *analogous* to the sense of virtue, he was tacitly rejecting the Neoplatonism of his influential predecessor. But almost no author between Hutcheson and Kant was willing to follow Hutcheson in this radical separation between the aesthetic and the practical. Shaftesbury's anti-Hobbesian separation of aesthetic response from private interests was accepted virtually without need for further discussion, and the view of Shaftesbury and Hutcheson that aesthetic response was natural and immediate like a sensory reaction was widely accepted, not only in empiricist Britain but even in rationalist Germany. But the main task of aesthetic theory between Hutcheson and Kant was to show, often with fairly explicit reference to Hutcheson, that in spite of these features of immediacy and impartiality, aesthetic response is not detached from other sources of human interest and value but rather that it is important precisely because it is so intimately connected with the most fundamental sources of theoretical and practical value, knowledge and virtue. The theoretical

problem was precisely to preserve the uniqueness of the phenomenon of taste while simultaneously securing its foundations in the most general sources of human value.

This was still the ultimate task faced by Kant's aesthetic
theory, a task made all the harder by the fact that only with
Kant did disinterestedness, in the sense of independence not
just from considerations of private advantage but from practical value in general, return to the forefront of aesthetic
theory. But when it did return, it did not come back in the
simple form that Hutcheson had envisioned. For Kant, after
all, practical reason enjoyed primacy over all else, but what
he recognized was that aesthetic response could serve the
interests of practical reason or morality in the long run, as the
critics of Hutcheson demanded, only if it were to remain free
of any direct constraints of theoretical as well as practical
reason in the short run, as Hutcheson had suggested. In
other words, in aesthetics as elsewhere Kant was trying to
resolve an antinomy created by his predecessors. Far from
merely accepting an already dominant theory of disinterestedness, he wanted to resolve a historical controversy representing a real theoretical antinomy by demonstrating that
aesthetic experience can only be understood as a delicate
balance between the disinterestedness which constitutes its
own freedom and the broader sense of freedom which underlies our most fundamental forms of attachment in the world,
the freedom of reason on which the bonds of morality are
based.

## I. SHAFTESBURY AND HUTCHESON

Modern aesthetic theory in both Britain and Germany commences with the nearly simultaneous work of Shaftesbury,
published in his *Characteristics of Men, Manners, Opinions,
Times* in 1711, and Joseph Addison, in his famous essays on
"The Pleasures of the Imagination," published in the *Spectator* in 1712. But for the debate about the disinterestedness of
aesthetic response, rather than, say, its characteristic vari-

eties such as the beautiful and the sublime, it is Shaftesbury and his reception by Hutcheson that must be the starting point of our discussion.

Shaftesbury presented his view that our response to beauty is natural and immediate in formulations that were to reverberate for decades to come, although his formulations also make it instantly clear that he was interested in the aesthetic as evidence for his moral theory rather than as the subject of a theory of taste and its objects in its own right. The characters in his dialogue *The Moralists* speak thus:

> For you will allow, without doubt, that in respect of bodies, whatever is commonly said of the unexpressible, the unintelligible, the I-know-not-what of beauty, there can lie no mystery here, but what plainly belongs either to figure, colour, motion or sound. Omitting therefore the three latter, and their dependent charms, let us view the charm in what is simplest of all, mere figure. Nor need we go so high as sculpture, architecture, or the designs of those from whom this study of beauty have raised such delightful arts. 'Tis enough if we consider the simplest of figures, as either a round ball, a cube, or dye. Why is even an infant pleased with the first view of these proportions? Why is the sphere or globe, the cylinder and obelisk preferred; and the irregular figures, in respect of these, rejected and despised?
>
> I am ready, replied he, to own there is in certain figures a natural beauty, which the eye finds as soon as the object is presented to it.
>
> Is there then, said he, a natural beauty of figures? and is there not as natural a one of actions? No sooner the eye opens upon figures, the ear to sounds, than straight the beautiful results and grace and harmony are acknowledged. No sooner are actions viewed, no sooner the human affections and passions discerned (and they are most of them as soon discerned as felt) than straight an inward eye distinguishes, and sees the fair and shapely, the amiable and admirable, apart from the deformed, the foul, the odious, or the despicable. How is it possible therefore not to own "that as these distinctions have their foundation in Nature, the discernment itself is natural, and from Nature alone"?[4]

Shaftesbury's dialogue suggests several claims. First, even an infant is pleased with the beauty of regular figures, on which we can assume that the more complex beauties of architecture and sculpture are grounded. Thus the response to beauty is "natural" in the sense of being founded in inborn capacities or receptivities that require only exposure to their proper objects but no instruction or acquired knowledge in order to come into operation. Second, the mode of operation of these faculties is immediate, like that of the ordinary external senses with which they are so closely linked. "No sooner" do we observe a beautiful object under appropriate conditions than we are pleased with it, just as no sooner do we open our eyes under appropriate circumstances than we indeed see what is there to be seen. Or, as Shaftesbury also suggests, there is no gap between discerning the object and feeling the aesthetic response of pleasure in it. There is no need for any intervening process of reflection, and if the response to the beauty of an object is not indeed actually part of merely seeing it – as we shall discover that it cannot be, on Shaftesbury's Neoplatonic theory – then it is at least very much analogous to so doing. Finally, however, Shaftesbury is interested in the character of our response to the "natural beauty of figures" as evidence of a similarly natural and immediate (although also in the end not merely sensory) response to, a virtual sense for, the "amiable and admirable" in human actions, affections, and passions.

The natural response to beauty, whether of figures or actions, transpires independently of any calculations of personal advantage or private interest – as indeed it must, if even the infant is capable of it. Any individual's sense of the beauty of an object is independent of a prospect for individual use or consumption of the object or any personal advantage to be obtained from it:

> Suppose (my Philocles) that, viewing such a tract of country as this delicious vale we see beneath us, you should, for the enjoyment of the prospect, require the property or possession of the land.

The covetous fancy, replied I, would be as absurd altogether as that other ambitious one.

O Philocles! said he, may I bring this yet a little nearer, and will you follow me once more? Suppose that, being charmed as you seem to be with the beauty of those trees under whose shade we rest, you should long for nothing so much as to taste some delicious fruit of theirs; and having obtained of Nature some certain relish by which these acorns or berries of the wood become as palatable as the figs or peaches of the garden, you should afterwards, as oft as you revisited these groves, seek hence the enjoyment of them by satiating yourself in these new delights.

The fancy of this kind, replied I, would be sordidly luxurious, and as absurd, in my opinion, as either of the former.[5]

Tacit in this interchange are two distinct claims: first, that it is contemptible to suppose that our appreciation of the beauty of something which is in fact usable or consumable is based on the prospect of our own personal consumption of it, and, second, that it is absurd to suppose that beauty is always connected to even the possibility of human use or consumption of an object. Again, Shaftesbury does not pause to make these distinct claims explicit. Nor does he need to; dispelling the unremitting egoism of the likes of Hobbes and Mandeville does not require an argument but only a lucid statement of fact. And few writers in the decades to follow even felt the need to reiterate Shaftesbury's completely persuasive separation of aesthetic response and *personal* interest.

Yet for Shaftesbury the sense-like immediacy of our pleasure in the beautiful and the separation between this pleasure and the prospect of personal consumption meant neither that our response to beauty is entirely disconnected from our higher faculties of mind nor that there is no connection between the beautiful and other sources of value whatsoever. On the contrary, Shaftesbury was a convinced Platonist, who believed, first, that the beauty perceived in the physical world is only a superficial manifestation of an underlying order both created by and perceived by mind, and, second, that the order which is perceived by the senses as physical beauty is the same as that which gives rise to "utility and convenience" from a global (although not a personal) point of view.

Many passages evince Shaftesbury's underlying Platonism; the one I quote next is particularly interesting, because it transforms a traditionally Aristotelian connection of beauty to form rather than matter into an argument for the ultimately mental foundation of beauty – a step that will also make it easy to suggest an identity, rather than mere analogy, between beauty and virtue:

> "That the beautiful, the fair, the comely, were never in the matter, but in the art and design; never in body itself, but in the form or forming power." Does not the beautiful form confess this, and speak the beauty of the design whenever it strikes you? What is it but the design which strikes? What is it you admire but mind, or the effect of mind? The mind alone which forms. All which is void of mind is horrid, and matter formless is deformity itself.[6]

A few pages later, Shaftesbury supplements this claim with an argument that since we share senses with the brutes, but the brutes are attracted to objects only by savoriness, hunger, and thirst, not beauty, it cannot be our senses alone which perceive beauty: "Neither can man by the same sense or brutish part conceive or enjoy beauty: but all the beauty and good he enjoys is in a nobler way, and by the help of what is noblest, his mind or reason."[7] Although the sense of beauty is natural and immediate, then, it is not, strictly speaking, the product of our senses, whether external or otherwise, which can operate independently of reason. Rather it depends upon the latter.

Finally, a passage in the *Characteristic*'s concluding "Miscellaneous Reflections" makes clear Shaftesbury's view that although the sense of beauty cannot be connected to a prospect of personal possession or private interest, still there is an underlying identity between the beautiful and the practically valuable: The beautiful is the sense-like appearance not of that which is of personal use to oneself, or even to one's own species, but of that which is fit in the grand scheme of things:

> 'Tis impossible we can advance the least in any relish or taste of outward symmetry and order, without acknowledging that the proportionate and regular state is the truly prosperous and natural in every subject. The same features which make deformity create incommodiousness and disease. And the same shapes and proportions which make beauty afford advantage by adapting to activity and use. Even in the imitative or designing arts . . . the truth or beauty of every figure or statue is measured from the perfection of Nature in the just adapting of every limb and proportion to the activity, strength, dexterity, life and vigour of the particular species or animal designed.
>
> Thus beauty and truth are plainly joined with the notion of utility and convenience.[8]

So aesthetic response is disinterested rather than private, but far from being detached from the most fundamental sources of practical value. On the contrary, "What is beautiful is harmonious and proportionable, what is harmonious and proportionable is true; and what is at once both beautiful and true is, of consequence, agreeable and good."[9] We can, to be sure, have a natural and immediate perception of beauty, but that is only because we can also have such a perception of truth and goodness; and although we have such an immediate sense of beauty, that does not mean that our perception of beauty is due to the senses alone, but rather that the senses must be completely infused with mind and reason. Shaftesbury introduces the idea of disinterestedness, then, but certainly not the idea that either aesthetic response or its object is detached from underlying theoretical and practical sources of value.

In light of Shaftesbury's ultimate identity between beauty, truth, and goodness, Francis Hutcheson's suggestion, in *An Inquiry Concerning Beauty, Order, Harmony, Design* (the first of the two treatises comprising his inaugural *Inquiry into the Original of our Ideas of Beauty and Virtue* of 1725), that there is no need for him to "recommend the Lord Shaftesbury's writings to the world"[10] is perhaps best taken as a gentle irony. Of course he agrees with "my Lord Shaftesbury" that we cannot "deduce every approbation or aversion," including our pleasures in the beautiful and the grand, "from rational views of private interest."[11] But he refuses to combine this with Shaftesbury's underlying identity between the beautiful and the good and the concomitant ascription of the recognition of beauty to the same faculty of mind which recognizes truth and goodness. Instead, in what he cannot have but meant as criticism of Shaftesbury, he goes on to argue for a radical separation between the sense of beauty and rational insight into practical value in general. He asserts an analogy, rather than an identity, between the sense of beauty and the sense of virtue and uses this analogy as evidence for the existence of the latter, but it remains an analogy. Hutcheson does not share Shaftesbury's rejection of Locke; instead, he clothes his Lockean rejection of Shaftesbury's Neoplatonism in Shaftesbury's own language.

Hutcheson's general objective in his *Inquiry into the Original of our Ideas of Beauty and Virtue* is to undermine the Hobbesian conception that calculations of self-interest or personal advantage underlie all of our practical attitudes and behavior. He attempts to reach this goal by arguing that such calculations always presuppose an antecedent and independent assignment of pleasure and pain to the experience of objects: "Advantage, or interest, cannot be distinctly conceived till we know what those pleasures are which advantageous objects are apt to excite, and what senses or powers of perception we have with respect to such objects."[12] His "principal design" is to make this argument in the case of moral judgments, where he wants to show that "human nature was not left quite indifferent in the affair of virtue, to form to itself observations concerning the advantage or disadvantage of actions"; rather, the "Author of nature . . . has given us strong affections to be the springs of each virtuous action."[13]

The demonstration that we have a natural tendency to be pleased with the appearance of such properties as *"uniformity, order, arrangement, imitation"*[14] in sensible objects, offered in the first treatise of the *Inquiry*, that *Concerning Beauty, Order, Harmony, Design*, is meant to prepare the way for the claim that we have a natural tendency to be pleased with certain patterns of human intention and behavior, perhaps by appealing to intuitions which had not been rendered as controversial by the sophistries of Hobbes and Mandeville as had those concerning moral motivation itself. But there is no suggestion that the sense of beauty and the sense of virtue are products of identical operations within the subject or are focused on what is ultimately the same property in their objects.[15]

Hutcheson's general argument that rational calculations of interest must presuppose some antecedent sense of pleasure in objects does not itself suffice to prove that any particular kind of pleasure is itself primitive and irreducible; it would be compatible with this premise that all pleasures were ultimately grounded in (for example) consumption of objects leading to the satisfaction of biological needs or in the perception of patterns of human intention and behavior manifesting benevolence to others (which is Hutcheson's characterization of the object of the moral sense). In such cases, the pleasure in beauty, although not the product of rational calculation of interest, would still be a manifestation of another and more practical underlying source of value. Hutcheson therefore needs a direct argument that we have a sense of beauty which is not only independent of rational calculations of advantage but also of other natural senses of pleasure. This is what his first *Inquiry* sets out to provide.

Hutcheson defines "sensations" as "ideas which are raised in the mind upon the presence of external objects" where the mind "is passive and has not power directly to prevent the perception or idea, or to vary it at its reception";[16] the capacity to receive a specific variety of such sensations is a "sense." He also maintains the factual premise that some sensations are pleasant: "Many of our sensitive perceptions are pleasant, and many painful, immediately, and that without any knowledge of the cause of this pleasure or pain, or how the objects excite it, or are the occasions of it, or without seeing to what farther advantage or detriment the use of such objects might tend."[17] From the general premise that the mind is passive in sensation, incapable of directly varying the content of sensation, it follows that no reflection on the use or other practical value of an object can affect the quality of our sensation of it, including the pleasurableness or painfulness of that sensation: "Nor would the most accurate knowledge of these things vary either the pleasure or pain of the perception, however it might give a rational pleasure distinct from the sensible, or might raise a distinct joy from a prospect of further advantage in the object."[18] Hutcheson then proceeds to argue that these theses hold not only in the case of simple ideas of objects, such as ideas of their color, texture, temperature, or taste, but also that "there are far greater pleasures in those complex ideas of objects, which obtain the names of *beautiful, regular, harmonious*." So he asserts,

> Thus everyone acknowledges he is more delighted with a fine face, a just picture, than with the view of any one colour, were it as strong and lively as possible; and more pleased with a prospect of the sun arising among settled clouds, and colouring their edges with a starry hemisphere, a fine landscape, a regular building, than with a clear blue sky, a smooth sea, or a large open plain.[19]

Precisely because of the independence of this tendency to be pleased by certain regular and harmonious complex ideas from any other source of pleasure, including that of the pleasures that may be naturally attached to particular simple ideas included in the complex ones (such as particular colors), no sort of argument other than an appeal to experience can be offered for the existence of this tendency; it cannot be derived as a logical consequence from anything else. Because this sense of beauty cannot be directly derived from the tendency to take pleasure in any of the simple ideas offered by the ordinary five external senses of sight, hearing, touch, taste, and smell, and also because he intends subsequently to argue that this sense of beauty can be stimulated by non-sensible objects such as mathematical theorems, Hutcheson calls the sense of beauty an *"internal sense."*[20] This is a far more rigorous doctrine than Shaftesbury's: Hutcheson does not just argue that the sense of beauty is natural and immediate, but he also excludes from its operation precisely the kind of manifestation of the faculty of reason which is ultimately central to Shaftesbury's Neoplatonism, in spite of his emphasis on the sense-like immediacy of aesthetic response.

Having appealed to the similarity between the immediate pleasurability of certain simple ideas of the external senses and the natural pleasurability of certain complex ideas to establish that our recognition of beauty should be categorized as a sense, Hutcheson then draws inferences from his original characterization of sensation. "The ideas of beauty and harmony, like other sensible ideas, are *necessarily* pleasant to us, as well as immediately so." Thus, "the pleasure does not arise from any *knowledge* of principles, proportions, causes, or the usefulness of the object, but strikes us at first with the idea of beauty," and since such knowledge is inoperative in the origination of our pleasure in a beautiful object, "neither can any resolution of our own, nor any prospect of advantage or disadvantage, vary the beauty or deformity of an object. For as in the external sensations, no view of interest will make an object grateful."[21]

Thus, Hutcheson does not derive the separation between pleasure in beauty, on the one hand, and any recognition of use or advantage, on the other, from any special definition or characterization of aesthetic response or attitude, as in modern theories, but rather from a general characterization of the nature of sensation and the subsumption of the special case of beauty under this more general characterization. The necessary and immediate connection between the perception of certain objects and the occurrence of certain sensations in us and the passivity of the mind, that is to say the inertness of reason or reflection in the process of sensation, are features of

all sensory perception. The disinterestedness of aesthetic response, in other words, is a consequence of the mechanism of
sensation. It should also be noted that the character of
Hutcheson's argument makes it plain that he does not mean
to exclude just *private* interest from the sense of beauty, although he did mention that in his preface; the general exclusion of intervention by reason in the mechanism of sensation
excludes consideration of one's own interests, the interest of
the human species in general, or the interests of any species
whatever from any essential role in our pleasure in the beautiful. Hutcheson accepts Shaftesbury's characterization of response to the beautiful as a natural sense, but by exploiting a
Lockean conception of sensation reaches a conclusion diametrically opposed to Shaftesbury's. For the Neoplatonist, the
natural sense of beauty perceived an outward manifestation
of the inward order and goodness of the universe; but for
Hutcheson, precisely because we perceive beauty by means of
sensation, its perception must be independent of any rational
insight into the theoretical or practical structure of reality.

Hutcheson's inference from the sensory nature of aesthetic
response to its essential detachment from all rational insight
into practical value is our primary concern here, but one other
point must be mentioned. Hutcheson divides the genus of
beauty into the two species of "Original or Absolute Beauty"
and "Relative or Comparative Beauty," a division that influenced most writers in the ensuing decades, arguably as late as
Kant.[22] Absolute beauty is that "which we perceive in objects
without comparison to anything external"; relative beauty is
"that which we perceive in objects commonly considered as
*imitations* or *resemblances* of something else,"[23] thus that form
of beauty most characteristic of works of fine art. In the case of
absolute beauty, the characteristic *cause* of our sensation of
pleasure is asserted to be the perception – although of course
not rational calculation or conception of – "*uniformity amidst
variety.*"[24] This is an empirical claim, which Hutcheson de-
fends by the inductive argument that the intensity of pleasure
in beautiful objects increases correlatively to increases of variety with constant uniformity or to increases of uniformity with

constant variety.[25] Now, the recognition of uniformity amidst variety is also a key to theoretical cognition of a complicated universe for "beings of limited powers" such as ourselves.[26] This does not mean, however, that when we take pleasure in the perception of uniformity amidst variety we are taking pleasure in the *recognition* of the fulfillment of a valuable cognitive objective, and thus in the satisfaction of a theoretical (if not practical) interest. On Hutcheson's account, "There does not appear to be any necessary connection, antecedent to the constitution of the Author of nature, between regular forms, actions, theorems, and that sudden sensible pleasure excited in us upon observation of them." The connection between uniformity amidst variety as a source of knowledge and as a source of pleasure is a contingent connection; there is "a great moral necessity," but no logical necessity, that "the Deity [be] so kind as to connect sensible pleasure with certain actions or contemplations beside the rational advantage perceivable in time."[27] In other words, it is natural to suppose that a benevolent creator has connected an immediate sense of pleasure to the perception of a property which is also of great theoretical value to us, but that does not mean that we take pleasure only in a recognition of the cognitive value of this property or need to recognize this value in order to feel the pleasure. For Hutcheson, the connection between aesthetic response and cognition is entirely external, not internal as it is later to be not only for Kant but also for British writers such as Gerard and Kames. The cognitive significance of uniformity amidst variety does not undermine Hutcheson's insistence that the sense of beauty operates independently of any intellectual recognition of any other theoretical or practical source of value.

## II. BERKELEY, HUME, AND BURKE

Hutcheson, of course, rejects the idea that pleasure in the beautiful has anything to do with "private interest," but what he explicitly argues for is the much broader claim that it has nothing to do with the recognition of *any* form of use or advantage. This detachment of the aesthetic from all other sources of value is presented as a direct consequence of the sensory nature of pleasure in beauty. British writers for the next three decades or more almost uniformly accepted and expanded upon Hutcheson's characterization of aesthetic response as essentially sensory but rejected his inference that this entails the detachment of the aesthetic from all other sources of value. On the contrary, it seems hard to describe the project of such writers as Hume, Burke, Gerard, and Kames as anything other than that of showing how deeply the sense of beauty – and the senses of the sublime, the novel, and so on – are embedded in the most fundamental sources of human value. Indeed, although on first reading the extensive literature on taste of eighteenth-century Britain one might think of it as the product of a legion of opportunistic writers looking to cash in on the dilettantism of a growing class of moneyed and leisured gentlemen, beneath the polished prose one can sense an urgent, perhaps post-Reformation, Enlightenment argument that only if the aesthetic is deeply rooted in the most fundamental sources of theoretical and practical value can it command the respect which it once derived so easily from its service to religion. [28]

The first criticism of Hutcheson's view was offered by George Berkeley, in *Alciphron or the Minute Philosopher*, his criticism of Mandeville, Shaftesbury, and other "freethinkers," published in 1732. Unlike subsequent critics, Berkeley balked at Hutcheson's characterization of the aesthetic as essentially sensory. He recognized that Hutcheson's argument was that because the perception of beauty is an immediate sense it cannot involve reason, and because it does not involve reason it therefore cannot depend upon a recognition of use, advantage, or interest; with impeccable logic, he controverted Hutcheson by arguing that the perception of beauty plainly does involve the recognition of fitness and usefulness, and therefore must involve reason and cannot be purely sensory.

*Alciphron* is written as a dialogue, with many targets and

characters; I can only touch upon one interchange. After arguing that the proportions of beautiful objects in different species, both animate and inanimate (such as oxen and horses,
tables and chairs) differ from each other, Berkeley's spokes-
man secures assent to the following series of questions:

> And, to make the proportions just, must not those mutual
> relations of size and shape in the parts be such as shall make
> the whole complete and perfect in its kind? . . .
>
> Is not a thing said to be perfect in its kind when it answers
> the end for which it was made? . . .
>
> The parts, therefore, in true proportions must be so re-
> lated, and adjusted to one another, as that they may best
> conspire to the use and operation of the whole? . . .
>
> But the comparing parts with one another, the considering
> them as belonging to one whole, and the referring this whole
> to its use or end, should seem the work of reason: should it
> not? . . .
>
> Proportions, therefore, are not, strictly speaking, perceived
> by the sense of sight, but only by reason through the means
> of sight. . . .
>
> Consequently beauty . . . is an object, not of the eye, but of
> the mind.[29]

Although Berkeley favors the plain appeal to experience at
least as much as Hutcheson, here he puts it into service of a
more traditional aesthetic theory, indeed one closer to that of
Shaftesbury's own Neoplatonism, though much of *Alciphron*
is an attack upon Shaftesbury's moral theory, the Platonism
of which perhaps Berkeley does not entirely acknowledge.
What is beautiful in a horse would not be pleasing in an ox,
and vice versa, he is arguing, and thus our pleasure in
beauty cannot be a mechanical sensory response to any perceptual invariants; instead, it must depend upon an appropriate conceptualization of the proper plan and end of any object and must therefore involve the faculty of reason as well
as (if not instead of) the senses.

In a pregnant aside, Berkeley acknowledges that our recognition of beauty cannot always be linked to the literal useful-

ness of an object. In a discussion of the components of Greek architecture, which (at least tacitly) recognizes that its masonry style incorporated features of its wooden predecessor, Berkeley mentions that our satisfaction depends upon "use or the appearance of use." In this regard a true child of his times, he then comments on "the grand distinction between Grecian and Gothic architecture, the latter being fantastical, and for the most part founded neither in nature nor in reason, in necessity nor use, the appearance of which accounts for all the beauty, grace, and ornament of the other."[30] The introduction of the term "appearance" of use, as well as actual use, will shortly be seen to give great scope for the involvement in aesthetic experience of the imagination, as well as (if not, indeed, instead of) reason.

Hutcheson replied to Berkeley in a note appended to the fourth edition of his *Inquiry* (1738). The note is brief and certainly takes no notice of the subtlety just mentioned. Here Hutcheson is just concerned to argue that fitness to a use could not be the *sufficient* condition for beauty, since a chair with legs in four different styles would work as well as one with stylistically uniform legs, or a coffin-shaped door, wider at shoulder height than at the bottom, would work as well as a rectangular one, yet clearly neither of the former objects would be as beautiful as the latter; and he also argued that it could not even be a *necessary* condition of beauty, since we can discern beauty "in Plants, in Flowers, in Animals whose Use is to us unknown."[31] This last comment was still to reverberate a half century later in Kant's *Critique of Judgment.* In the meantime, however, critics tried to undercut this dispute between Hutcheson and Berkeley by rejecting the premise accepted by both: that there is an essential connection between the recognition of usefulness or advantage on the one hand and the employment of reason rather than sense on the other. Instead, the next generation of writers was largely concerned to show that Hutcheson's sensory model of aesthetic response was in fact compatible with an intimate connection between beauty and more general sources of value.

Perhaps the first to argue this way was David Hume. This assertion may seem surprising, since the theory of his essay "Of the Standard of Taste" seems deeply Hutchesonian, apparently asserting a natural and immediate (but also irreducible or unanalyzable) connection between certain external forms and our sense of pleasure: "Some particular forms or qualities, from the original structure of the internal fabric, are calculated to please, and others to displease."[32] But this essay, a later production not published until 1757, does not represent the full scope of the aesthetic theory hinted at in the *Treatise of Human Nature,* published in 1739–40 when Hutcheson was clearly still much on Hume's mind. In that work, the purely formalistic sort of beauty suggested in the later essay represents only one species of a much richer genus, and the broader characterization of beauty in the *Treatise* is clearly designed to reject Hutcheson's simplistic detachment of the sense of beauty from the wider range of our values. This broader theory can also be conceived of as picking up the hint offered by Berkeley's distinction between "use or the appearance of use."[33]

As in the works of Shaftesbury and many others of the period, in Hume's *Treatise* aesthetic matters are only touched upon in passing, in illustration of claims in moral theory. Nevertheless, the work suggests an extensive theory of beauty. Ontologically, Hume treats all cases of beauty as consisting in a relationship between the form of a particular object and the pleasure that it induces in an observer: "Beauty is nothing but a form, which produces pleasure, as deformity is a structure of parts, which conveys pain."[34] However, the process intervening between the form of the object and the feeling of pleasure which it causes is not identical in all cases. Instead, Hume divides the genus of beauty into more specific classes. He explicitly suggests a twofold classification, distinguishing between one kind of beauty, in which the form of the object acts directly on our senses by the *"primary constitution* of our nature"[35] without the involvement of any other ideas or capacities, and another kind, involving further ideas and processes, especially the idea of utility and the processes of sympathy and imagination. "Thus the beauty of all visible objects causes a pleasure pretty much the same, tho' it be sometimes deriv'd from the mere *species* and appearance of the objects; sometimes from sympathy, and an idea of their utility."[36] In fact, we shall see that what he ultimately employs is a tripartite division. There is first the purely sensory beauty of *species*, or appearance – the Hutchesonian case; second, there is beauty connected to utility (as it turns out, in several different ways); and finally there is the case where the pleasure of beauty is connected with the recognition that an internal purpose of art, rather than an external purpose of utility, is or appears to be satisfied. In a sense, then, Hume does not so much reject Hutcheson's theory of beauty as supplement it, but he also makes it clear that Hutcheson's cases of immediate, purely sensory beauty are very much in the minority and that most cases of beauty involve ideas of utility and the operation of the imagination, as well as the senses: "A great part of the beauty, which we admire either in animals or other objects, is deriv'd from the idea of convenience and utility";[37] "Ideas of its utility and its contrary, though they do not entirely determine what is handsome or deformed, are evidently the source of a considerable part of approbation or dislike."[38]

About the first kind of beauty, the product of the direct action of perceptible forms on our sense of pleasure, Hume, remaining true to his Newtonian stance of restraint from explanatory hypotheses,[39] finds little to say: "Some of these qualities produce satisfaction in [us] by particular *original* principles of human nature, which cannot be accounted for."[40] He places confidence neither in Hutcheson's induction that the sense of beauty is always caused by the perception of uniformity amidst variety nor in his theological explanation of that generalization. Instead, he just leaves open the possibility that there may be a variety of perceptible properties which, because of inexplicable features of our psychological and physiological constitution, are always pleasurable to behold.

Perhaps Hume also feels little need to explain the origination of mere beauties of "*species* or appearance" because they represent such a small part of our larger experience of beauty; in any case, his reticence on this first form of beauty certainly contrasts with his elaborate explanations of the second main class of beauty, that linked with the idea of utility. As we have seen, Hume contrasts beauty of mere appearance to beauty deriving from ideas of utility and convenience; as he also puts it, in a fairly obvious slap at Hutcheson, the latter "is a beauty of interest, not of form."[41] However, since " 'Tis certain our own interest is not in the least concern'd" in virtually all such cases – here is the unquestioned acceptance of Shaftesbury's rejection of *private* interest – some other mechanism for connecting utility and our own feeling of pleasure must be found. In fact, Hume suggests that the link is established by three different forms of imagination, which we might label *sympathy*, *generalization*, and the *association of ideas*.

Hume gives great prominence to the case of *sympathy*, as befits his larger objectives in moral philosophy. "Most kinds of beauty are deriv'd from this origin; and tho' our first object be some senseless inanimate piece of matter, 'tis seldom we rest there, and carry not our views to its influence on sensible and rational creatures." In the case of a well-designed, useful, and convenient house, for instance, even if we do not ourselves stand to benefit by its virtues, we share in the pleasure of the owner who will: "It must delight us merely by communication, and by our sympathizing with the proprietor of the lodging. We enter into his interest by the force of the imagination, and feel the same satisfaction, that the objects naturally occasion in him."[42] We do not need a personal bond of friendship to another in order vicariously to enjoy his benefits from his own beautiful possessions; sympathy is a more general effect of the imagination:

> To this principle, therefore, is owing the beauty, which we find in everything that is useful. How considerable a part this is of beauty will easily appear upon reflection. Whenever an object has a tendency to produce pleasure in the possessor, or in other words, is the proper *cause* of pleasure, it is sure to please the spectator, by a delicate sympathy with the pos-

sessor. Most of the works of art are esteem'd beautiful, in proportion to their fitness for the use of man, and even many of the productions of nature derive their beauty from that source. Handsome and beautiful, on most occasions, is not an absolute but a relative quality, and pleases us by nothing but its tendency to produce an end that is agreeable.[43]

This principle of sympathy is the most direct way in which a felt pleasure in an object can be communicated from one person to another, but it presupposes that at least one person is in a position to derive a nonaesthetic benefit from the actual use of an object. Thus it does not create a principle of pleasure distinct from enjoyment of the actual use of an object but rather communicates that pleasure beyond the actual particular user of the object. However, Hume also introduces two other mechanisms of the imagination, which create a sense of beauty in cases where there is and can be no actual use of an object at all.

The first of these other processes of the imagination is what we might call its tendency to *generalization*. This is the propensity of the imagination to fill in gaps in our experience, the most notorious cases of which are the imagination's tendency to carry inductions beyond our limited evidence, thus producing causal laws, and its tendency to fill in the gaps between similar impressions, thus creating the very fiction of enduring physical objects themselves.[44] Similarly, the imagination fills in gaps in our perception of utility:

Where any object, in all its parts, is fitted to attain any agreeable end, it naturally gives us pleasure, and is esteem'd beautiful, even tho' some external circumstances be wanting to render it altogether effectual. . . . A house, that is contriv'd with great judgment for all the commodities of life, pleases us upon that account; tho' perhaps we are sensible, that no-one will ever dwell in it. . . . A man, whose limbs and shape promise strength and activity, is esteem'd handsome, tho' condemned to perpetual imprisonment. . . . Where a character is, in every respect, fitted to be beneficial to society, the imagination passes easily from the cause to the effect, without considering that there are still some circumstances wanting to render the cause a complete one.[45]

By its tendency to generalization, the imagination allows us to take pleasure in the *appearance* of utility, even in cases in which there is no one who actually enjoys its benefits.

In the kind of cases just considered, the objects themselves are actually suited to use, and what the imagination is adding is the idea of the pleasure of a missing person to enjoy that use. In another kind of case, however, where the object is not even potentially useful, the imagination deploys its tendency to the *association of ideas* to suggest the satisfaction of an end nevertheless. Hume's example of this tendency is noteworthy, because it is the only one of all those we have considered where he draws on the fine arts, rather than applied or decorative art, and also because in this case he deals with the negative case of pain rather than the positive case of pleasure:

> There is no rule in painting more reasonable than that of ballancing the figures, and placing them with the greatest exactness on their proper centers of gravity. A figure, which is not justly ballanc'd, is disagreeable; and that because it conveys the ideas of its fall, or harm, and of pain: Which ideas are painful, when by sympathy they acquire any degree of force and vivacity.[46]

If the appearance of an ill-balanced figure suggests ideas of pain and harm to us, then presumably the appearance of a well-balanced figure suggests ideas of security and well-being. By the same process of association, images of stately homes, well-muscled or graceful humans, and swiftly sailing ships must suggest to us the same sort of ideas that observation of their originals would induce. The association of ideas can fill in any gaps in our enjoyment of appearances left by sympathy and generalization.

Finally, Hume also suggests, in the essay "Of the Standard of Taste," that works of art have internal purposes and that we enjoy the successful accomplishment of those purposes, as well as the imaginative satisfaction of purposes external to works of art:

> Every work of art has also a certain end or purpose for which it is calculated; and it is to be deemed more or less perfect, as it is more or less fitted to attain this end. The object of eloquence is to persuade, of history to instruct, of poetry to please, by means of the passions and imagination. These ends we must carry constantly in our view when we peruse any performance; and we must be able to judge how far the means employed are adapted to their respective purposes.[47]

In some cases, such as those of eloquence or history, the purposes of persuasion or instruction may seem external to purely artistic intentions, and the pleasures they produce may not seem very different from the pleasure of utility; but in other cases, such as poetry, it seems more likely that the objective of the artist is to create pleasure by a satisfactory exercise of the imagination itself. Here Hume seems to suggest a source of pleasure involving the imagination but neither mere appearance nor the idea of utility, although he says little to elaborate this suggestion and hardly develops any theory of the internal purposes of works of art.

As we saw at the outset, however, Hume believes that most cases of beauty are cases of the imaginative enjoyment of utility. In this, his view seems to be closely related to Berkeley's. There is also a deep difference, however. Berkeley inferred from the recognition of usefulness to the indispensable involvement of reason in the experience of beauty, but there is no hint of such an inference in Hume. There hardly could be, given his restrictive conception of reason as a faculty which merely calculates from premises given to it and which certainly has no capacity to originate any impression, including impressions of pleasure or pain, on its own.[48] In fact, at the most general level Hume's philosophy can be seen as a profound extension of Hutcheson's sensory model as well as a rejection of the rationalism of the later Berkeley. Where

Hutcheson was content to argue that the sense of beauty and the moral sense must be antecedent to calculations of reason, Hume argues that the entire framework of our beliefs – theoretical and practical as well as aesthetic – must be the product of natural and immediate tendencies to experience certain sentiments in certain situations rather than the product of rational inferences among rationally justified beliefs. But in order to paint this larger picture, he has to replace Hutcheson's original notion of sensation with the broader one of imagination.[49] By so doing he makes it possible for us to have natural and immediate responses to ideas such as those of utility and convenience without invoking the faculty of reason. The imagination can involve such ideas, even if, as Berkeley (and indeed Shaftesbury) had argued, the unaided external senses could not. In the most general terms, then, Hume accepts Hutcheson's idea of aesthetic response as natural and immediate rather than inferential, thus rejecting Berkeley's lingering rationalism, without accepting Hutcheson's inference that this entails the exclusion of all ideas of use and advantage from our sense of beauty. On Hume's account, there is thus no need to drive a wedge between the underlying sources of aesthetic value and the broader sources of value, action, and passion in our lives: All of these depend upon imagination rather than mere reason.

In the "Introduction on Taste," which Edmund Burke added to the second edition of *A Philosophical Enquiry into the Origin of our Ideas of the Sublime and the Beautiful* two years after its first publication in 1757 (the same year as Hume's "Of the Standard of Taste"), Burke plainly rejected Hutcheson's postulation of a sense of beauty independent of our other sources of value:

> I cannot help taking notice of an opinion which many persons entertain, as if the Taste were a separate faculty of the mind, and distinct from the judgment and imagination; a species of instinct by which we are struck naturally, and at the first glance, without any previous reasoning with the excellencies,

or the defects of a composition. . . . To multiply principles for every different appearance, is useless, and unphilosophical too in a high degree.[50]

However, Burke does not simply follow Hume's *Treatise* in arguing that we can have an immediate sense of utility by virtue of an expanded conception of the imagination. Rather than following Hume by attempting to break Hutcheson's and Berkeley's shared assumption of a connection between utility and reason, Burke accepts the premise but follows Hutcheson rather than Berkeley by denying that there is any connection between the perception of beauty and the recognition of utility. "In framing this theory," he mercilessly writes, "I am apprehensive that experience was not sufficiently consulted." For example, "On that principle, the wedge-like snout of a swine, with its tough cartilage at the end, the little sunk eyes, and the whole make of the head, so well adapted to its offices of digging, and rooting, would be extremely beautiful."[51] But Burke does follow Hume in rejecting Hutcheson's idea that there is a separate sense of beauty that works independently of the rest of our passions and affections. Instead, he follows Hume's hint that fundamental principles of our constitution, our psychology, and even our physiology lead us to have a natural reaction of pleasure or delight to certain objects, though he is less restrained than Hume in inventing explanations of these principles.

My purposes here do not require a detailed examination of Burke's elaborate contrast between the beautiful and the sublime, especially its extension into the realm of physiology. My objective of demonstrating the rejection of Hutchesonian disinterestedness will be served by a general account of Burke's theory of the psychological foundations of our pleasure in the beautiful and delight in the sublime.[52] According to Burke (who here adopts the fundamental psychology of the natural law tradition as formulated by Samuel Pufendorf),[53] our affective life is governed by two primary passions: "Most of the ideas which are capable of making a powerful impression on the mind, whether simply of Pain or

Pleasure, or of the modifications of those, may be reduced very nearly to these two heads, *self-preservation* and *society*."[54] These passions are entirely general sources of affection, hardly confined to any detached sphere of aesthetic experience. But aesthetic experience depends on them.

In particular, the experience of the sublime is an experience of delight in our self-preservation, engendered by the appearance of great danger when that is present without the real pain of actual danger. "The passions which belong to self-preservation, turn on pain and danger; they are simply painful when their causes immediately affect us; they are delightful when we have an idea of pain and danger, without being actually in such circumstances; . . . Whatever excites this delight, I call *sublime*."[55] The experience of beauty, by contrast, is grounded in our passion for society. This passion, in turn, takes two forms: "The society of the *sexes*, which answers the purposes of propagation; and next, that more *general society*, which we have with men and with other animals, and which we may in some sort be said to have even with the inanimate world."[56] Beauty, then, lies either in features of perceptible objects that we associate with what we find sexually stimulating, "those qualities in bodies by which they cause love, or some passion similar to it,"[57] such as the "smoothness; the softness; the easy and insensible swell" of "that part of a beautiful woman where she is perhaps the most beautiful, about the neck and breasts"[58] – Burke intimates that there are features of the male appearance which are equally pleasing to the female, but his own point of view is most decidedly masculine – or in features that stimulate passions connected with society in the more general sense, such as "*sympathy, imitation, and ambition*."[59] Burke does not suggest what sorts of physical properties should be correlated with these latter passions, but he does argue at length that abstract categories such as "proportion" and "fitness" do not stand in any direct correlation with the particular physical qualities that make us find objects lovely.[60]

Burke pushes on to provide physiological foundations for these psychological claims, arguing that the perception of characteristically sublime objects tenses and invigorates our organs, while that of smooth and small beauties relaxes them (although this hardly fits well with his sexual explanation of the sense of beauty). We need not follow him in these excursions. We need only to observe that although he shares Hutcheson's separation between the sense of beauty and any recognition of utility or advantage, he by no means separates aesthetic experience from the rest of our emotional life. On the contrary, he explains the power and attraction of the sublime and the beautiful precisely by showing how they bring into play our most fundamental passions. Of course, Burke does not link aesthetic response to the gratification of purely private interest and argues that these psychological principles "are the same in all." "Love, grief, fear, anger, joy, all these passions have in their turn affected every mind; and they do not affect it in an arbitrary or causal manner, but upon certain, natural, and uniform principles."[61] But it is perfectly clear that for Burke its separation from anything private hardly implies the detachment of the aesthetic from the general principles of all our action and passion.

### III. GERARD AND KAMES

The responses to Hutcheson offered by Berkeley, Hume, and Burke might be taken to canvas the major theoretical alternatives for rejection of the idea of aesthetic detachment: Berkeley revives the rationalist idea that our pleasure in beauty depends upon a fundamentally rational insight into utility; Hume retains the primacy of utility but broadens Hutcheson's idea of sense into a concept of imagination which allows for a natural and immediate response to the perception of utility or its appearance, without the intervention of reason; and Burke rejects the connection to utility altogether but roots aesthetic response deep in our psychological sources of valuation, which he identifies with passions for self-preservation and society. Hutcheson, Hume, and Burke were also undoubtedly the British writers on taste who were most significant for

Kant, and so for historical as well as theoretical reasons we could easily terminate our discussion of the pre-Kantian debate on disinterestedness here. However, two figures who illustrate additional aspects of the rejection of Hutcheson's conception of aesthetic detachment are worthy of at least brief notice. These are the Scottish professor Alexander Gerard and the Scottish jurist Henry Home, Lord Kames (cousin to David Hume). Kames's *Elements of Criticism* (first published in 1761) was well known to Kant, and it is likely that the work of Gerard was as well.

Gerard's *Essay on Taste,* published in 1759, just two years after Hume's "Standard of Taste" and Burke's *Enquiry,* adopts Hutcheson's language of senses, and indeed seems to go well beyond Hutcheson's affirmation of a detached conception of the sense of beauty by identifying separate senses, or "simple principles," of novelty, sublimity, beauty, imitation, harmony, and oddity and ridicule as well as virtue.[62] But he accompanies his acceptance of the Hutchesonian assimilation of the aesthetic to sensation with an argument that "internal senses are not ultimate principles" but can be explained in terms of more fundamental principles of the mind; and his detailed analyses of the several aesthetic senses or tastes show that he regards them as thoroughly interpenetrated by our most basic cognitive and practical principles, rather than isolated from them. Let us look first at his theoretical rejection of Hutcheson and then at his practice.

In a section of his essay asking "How far Taste depends on Imagination," which clearly demonstrates the influence of Hume's enfranchisement of the latter, Gerard includes a long footnote arguing that the classification of a response as a sense does not imply that it is an *"ultimate* and *original"* principle incapable of further analysis and explanation.[63] Plainly following Hutcheson as well as Locke, he argues that taste is properly classified as a sense because it (1) "supplies us with such *simple* perceptions, as cannot be conveyed by any other channel to those who are destitute of that sense," (2) "receives its perception *immediately,* as soon as its object is exhibited," and (3) "is a power which exerts itself *independent of volition.*" Because the experiences of beauty, sublimity, harmony, and the like satisfy these criteria, "the powers of taste are therefore to be reckoned senses."[64] But, he continues,

> whether they are ultimate powers, is a subsequent question. Those who are unacquainted with philosophy reckon all our powers ultimate qualities of the mind. But nature delights in sympathy, and produces numerous effects, by a few causes of extensive influence; and it is the business of philosophy to investigate these causes, and to explain the phenomena from them. On enquiry it appears that the internal senses are not ultimate principles, because all their phaeonomena can be accounted for, by simpler qualities of the mind.

Gerard then illustrates this general claim with an account of the sense of beauty as rooted in theoretical and psychological principles connected with the value of cognition in general, arguing that such a foundation of an aesthetic response in more general tendencies of human nature is not incompatible with its classification as a "sense," because "the sentiment of beauty arises, without our reflecting on this mixture. This sentiment is compound in its *principles*, but perfectly simple in its *feeling.*"[65] In modern terms, we might say, Gerard is arguing that Hutcheson was mistaken to infer from the phenomenological immediacy of the sense of beauty its theoretical detachment from more general sources of value.

It is worth lingering for a moment over Gerard's discussion of the sense of beauty. Following the tradition begun by Hume, his account is in fact highly pluralistic. He distinguishes the beauty of figure, which is in turn resolvable into beauties of uniformity, variety, and proportion,[66] from the beauty of "utility, or the *fitness* of things for answering their ends,"[67] and then further separates both of these classes of beauty, as responses to what are in fact complex properties of objects, from the beauty of simple properties, exemplified by color.[68] In contrast to Hutcheson, he describes the formal beauties of figure as seamlessly blending with the beauty of utility,

76

but as yielding precedence to the latter where a choice must be made: "Though the most perfect art falls infinitely short of nature, in combining the useful with the regular; yet none of its productions is reckoned a master-piece, in which these excellencies do not meet; and to obtain utility, forms of inferior beauty [of figure] are, for particular purposes [of utility], constantly preferred, even where beauty is far from being neglected."[69] Even more interesting, however, is the way in which Gerard explains the formal beauties of figure. Whereas Hutcheson had taken our pleasure in uniformity amidst variety to be inexplicable, and thus only contingently although benevolently correlated with our cognitive purposes, for Gerard the fact that such beauties of figure as uniformity, variety, and proportion satisfy the basic requirements of cognition itself is directly responsible for our pleasure in them: "Facility in the conception of an object, if it is moderate, gives us pleasure."[70] Such facility is treated in both theoretical and psychological terms: We directly enjoy "perspicuity of thought" and also benefit from the adjustment of the tenor of mental activity to the proper pitch between excitement and languor. Moreover, the pleasure of taste is not detached from a reflexive attitude toward our own nature: "Nothing gives us greater pleasure, than what leads us to form a lofty conception of our own faculties."[71] Yet, for all their deep connection to general principles of cognition, the pleasure which uniformity, variety, and proportion give us is "an immediate sensation, prior to our analyzing them, or discovering by reason that they have these qualities."[72] As in the case of Hume, Gerard can accept Hutcheson's sensory model of taste without its theoretical consequence of the detachment of the aesthetic from other human interests, thanks to a broader conception of sensation than Hutcheson employed.

Gerard also insists upon an intimate connection between the sense(s) of taste and moral approbation, but one that falls short of identity.[73] Perhaps the intimate connection between taste and practical value, in this final stage of the development of classical British aesthetics, would be better illustrated by reference to Kames, however, since his views on this issue were clearly influential in the evolution of Kant's own views.

Kames certainly stands in the Hutchesonian tradition of treating aesthetic response as a kind of sense, and he follows Gerard's precedent in proliferating internal senses, distinguishing senses of beauty, grandeur and sublimity, motion and force, novelty, risibility, resemblance and dissimilitude, uniformity and variety, congruity and propriety, and dignity and grace.[74] This list alone would make it clear that on Kames's view there can be no hard-and-fast distinction between the sources of aesthetic value and the more general sources of value in human life. Two general features of his discussion make this equally clear.

First, unlike his cousin Hume, Kames traces the source of our pleasure in all the varieties of taste to an underlying principle of human nature which clearly grounds our theoretical and practical values as well. "We are framed by nature," he writes, "to relish order and connection. When an object is introduced by a proper connection, we are conscious of a certain pleasure arising from the circumstance." Kames uses this principle to explain a variety of responses to nature, for instance, not only our pleasure in beauty but also that in grandeur; he then extends the principle to explain our pleasure in art as well: "Every work of art that is conformable to the natural course of our ideas, is so far agreeable; and every work of art that reverses that course, is so far disagreeable. Hence it is required in every such work, that, like an organic system, its parts be orderly arranged and mutually connected."[75] There is no suggestion that the order which is the object of aesthetic response is merely analogous to that which underlies knowledge and virtue; instead, Kames really seems to reaffirm Shaftesbury's Platonic identity of the ultimate objects of beauty, truth, and goodness in the more modest and scientific language of midcentury empiricism.

This is not to say that the idea of disinterestedness has totally disappeared from view in Kames. He preserves a place for it, but an empirically grounded place which does not require the theoretical detachment of the aesthetic from other sources of value. Aesthetic responses fall under the general rubric of love and hate, agreeable and disagreeable reactions to objects. All of these responses satisfy the Hutchesonian criterion of immediacy: "Such is our nature, that upon perceiving certain external objects, we are instantaneously conscious of pleasure or pain: a gently-flowing river, a smooth extended plain, a spreading oak, a towering hill, are objects of sight that raise pleasant emotions."[76] However, the basic class of pleasurable and painful responses can be divided into two classes, emotions and passions, distinguished by the fact that the latter inevitably produce *desire* for their objects while the former do not:

> We proceed to an observation of considerable importance in the science of human nature, which is, That desire follows some emotions, and not others. The emotions raised by a beautiful garden, a magnificent building, or a number of fine faces in a crowded assembly, is seldom accompanied with desire. Other emotions are accompanied with desire; emotions, for example, raised by human actions and qualities. . . . The pleasant emotion produced in a spectator by a capital picture in the possession of a prince, is seldom accompanied with desire; but if such a picture is exposed to sale, desire of having or possessing is the natural consequence of a strong emotion.[77]

Freedom from at least any personal interest in possession or consumption of an object, Kames suggests, is at least a typical characteristic of aesthetic response, but it is a contingent and far from invariable feature. There is no principled distinction between the etiology of emotions and passions, and instances of even the same emotion can be free of desire on some occasions but not on others. Disinterestedness is apparently reduced to a statistically frequent concomitant of aesthetic response, rather than an essential characteristic or inevitable consequence of it.

Finally, we should observe that Kames sanguinely assumes a direct and beneficial influence of aesthetic experience on the virtue of those who enjoy it. He starts off his work by justifying the study and development of taste in social and moral terms. "The science of rational criticism tends to improve the heart no less than the understanding," he confidently asserts, and goes on: "Delicacy of taste tends no less to invigorate the social affections, than to moderate those that are selfish" and "necessarily heightens our feeling of pain and pleasure; and of course our sympathy, which is the capital branch of every social passion." (Hume had argued that taste *depends* upon sympathy, but Kames goes beyond him in arguing that it *improves* sympathy.) And finally, "One other advantage of rational criticism is reserved to the last place, being of all the most important; which is, that it is a great support to morality. . . . No occupation attaches a man more to his duty, than that of cultivating a taste in the fine arts."[78] And Kames concludes his discussion of beauty with the same sentiments, arguing that "the perception of beauty greatly promotes industry" but this effect is slight "compared with the connections that are formed among individuals in society by means of this singular mechanism . . . . External beauty . . . concurs in an eminent degree with mental qualifications to produce social intercourse, mutual good-will, and consequently mutual aid and support, which are the life of society."[79]

Hutcheson had argued that there is an analogy between the sense of beauty and the moral sense. This argument had the theoretical or philosophical advantage that the former could provide evidence for the existence of the latter while retaining its detachment from any direct moral value itself. Far from accepting this idea of the disinterestedness of aesthetic response, Kames concedes even the freedom of aesthetic pleasure from private interest only a contingent status and bluntly asserts that aesthetic response has direct practical value in establishing social bonds and should be cultivated for that reason. It seems safe to say that this attitude was far more typical of the generation of British aestheticians following Hutcheson than Hutcheson's own isolation of the aesthetic from our more fundamental values. It was also readily accepted by the young Kant, among many other German writers. Only in his philosophical maturity did Kant recognize that the connection between aesthetic and moral value had to be much more subtle than this. Before we turn to Kant's mature resolution of the dialectic of disinterestedness, however, a brief look at some of his German predecessors is required. They were perhaps not as important for Kant as the British writers we have just considered, but they were certainly not completely absent from his thought.

## IV. FROM LEIBNIZ AND WOLFF TO BAUMGARTEN, MENDELSSOHN, AND MORITZ

The tradition of aesthetics in eighteenth-century Germany begins with Leibniz and Wolff, neither of whom developed anything that could be called an explicit aesthetic theory but both of whom contributed premises that were developed into such a theory by immediate disciples of Wolff such as Johann Christoph Gottsched and by members of the next generation such as Alexander Gottlieb Baumgarten and Moses Mendelssohn. Leibniz contributed a definition of sensory perception as the "clear but confused" or "indistinct" perception of the same objects or states of affairs that the intellect could, at least in principle, apprehend through clear and distinct cognition,[80] a definition which he often illustrated precisely by analogizing sensory perception in general to judgments of taste in particular and which he subsequently used for an explicit definition of taste as well: "Taste, as distinguished from understanding, consists of confused perceptions for which one cannot give an adequate reason."[81] Leibniz also contributed the general framework of his perfectionist ontology, on which the actual world is considered the best of all possible worlds, on which each of its individual components can also be conceived of as a perfection at least relative to the limits of its compossibility with other components, and in which perfection in turn is defined as the maximal combination of uniformity and variety.[82] But Leibniz did not combine these two elements of his thought into an explicit account of aesthetic judgment.

In his *Vernünfftige Gedancken von Gott, der Welt, und der Seele des Menschen* of 1720, commonly known now as the "German Metaphysics," as well as in later Latin works, Christian Wolff did combine these two elements into a general theory of value judgments, but not a special theory of aesthetic judgments. Like Leibniz, Wolff often illustrated his general theory of judgment with judgments of taste, but precisely in so doing demonstrated that he did not regard these as a special class detached from other judgments of value. Wolff accepted Leibniz's definition of sensory perception as "clear but confused" cognition, or "at most clear, but not distinct."[83] Wolff then defined pleasure as a perceptual or "intuitive cognition of perfection."[84] This is a general definition applying to all feelings and judgments of pleasure, and the perfection which is the object of such sense perception is also defined in entirely general terms as simply harmony in the manifold of things, or the harmony in the manifold of any particular thing in relation to its essential end or purpose.[85] Wolff illustrates his general definition of perfection by the case of representational painting, where the purpose of the artwork is similarity and therefore its perfection consists in the harmony of the manifold of the painting with that purpose;[86] but there is no suggestion that in giving this example he is isolating an essential characteristic which detaches art or the aesthetic from any other locus of pleasure and value. On the contrary, Wolff offers a unified account of pleasure according to which all feelings of pleasure are responses to objective perfections, or states of the world which are objectively good in themselves and for us as well, which therefore naturally produce desire, and in which there is no place for a special category of the aesthetic detached from goodness and desire:

> Since the good makes us and our condition more perfect, and the intuition of perfection excites pleasure, so must the intu-

itive cognition of the good excite pleasure . . . . On this account we call what brings pleasure naturally good.[87]

Out of the indistinct representation of the good arises the
*sensual desire*, which is accordingly nothing other than an inclination of the soul toward the subject of which we have an
indistinct concept of the good.[88]

All feelings of pleasure are sensory perceptions of goodness
which naturally produce an inclination in favor of their object. There is no hint in Wolff of a conception of aesthetic
response as generally disinterested, that is, as in any way
isolated from these general relations between goodness, pleasure, and desire, although undoubtedly he would have
agreed with Shaftesbury in detaching the response to beauty
from merely private interest.

Wolff's conception of pleasure as the sensory cognition of
objective perfection completely dominated aesthetic theory
in Germany for the next fifty or more years. Some writers
looked for criteria to demarcate the aesthetic from other perceptions of goodness or to add special character to it, but
none detached it from this general theory of value or sub-
scribed to Hutcheson's conception of disinterestedness, even
though his views were well known in Germany. Gottsched
applied Wolff's principles in an *Essay on a Critical Art of Poetry
for the Germans*, published only a decade after the latter's
"German Metaphysics." This work was intended as a practical poetics rather than as a theoretical treatise, but it explicitly
asserted three Wolffian dogmas. First, Gottsched appropriated the Leibnizo–Wolffian conception of judgments of taste:
"The metaphorical as well as common taste have to do only
with clear, but not entirely distinct, concepts of things."[89]
Second, Gottsched held that each form of fine art has its
proper perfection, and that in spite of the sensory nature of
aesthetic response it is possible to master the creation and
judgment of an art form by rules rationally derived from its
inherent perfection. One finds the criterion for judgments of

taste "in the rules of perfection, which apply to each particular kind of beautiful thing, such as buildings, paintings, music, etc., and which are distinctly comprehended and demonstrated by proper masters of them."[90] But, finally and most crucially, the perfections of works of art are grounded in metaphysical perfections of the objective world: "The rules which are introduced in the liberal arts do not come from the mere idiosyncrasy of humans: rather they have their ground in the unalterable nature of things themselves; in the agreement of the manifold; in order and harmony."[91] On this account, art must be mimetic, because it derives its perfection from the perfection of the objective world which it imitates: "The beauty of a work of art does not depend upon an empty darkness, but has its firm and necessary ground in the nature of things. . . . Natural things are beautiful; and therefore if art wishes to bring forth something beautiful, it must imitate the example of nature."[92] There seems little room here for an account of the value of beauty separate from an entirely general account of the perfection of the actual world.

Alexander Gottlieb Baumgarten, who introduced the term "aesthetics," in its modern sense, in his early dissertation on poetry in 1735 and in his unfinished but monumental *Aesthetics* of 1750–8, also presented his thought in the literary form of a practical poetics, but engaged in more theoretical discussion than Gottsched.[93] In his theoretical moments, he attempted to distance himself from the Wolffian treatment of taste by creating room for a more autonomous conception of aesthetic value. He did this in part by definition; whereas Wolff had defined all pleasure, including that in the beautiful, as the sensory or intuitive cognition of perfection, Baumgarten twisted the formula so as to define "the aim of aesthetics" as "the perfection of sensitive cognition as such."[94] This definition, like Baumgarten's earlier definition of a poem as a "perfect sensitive form of speech" (*oratio sensitiva perfectiva*), that is, the perfection of a form of speech "whose parts tend towards the cognition of sensitive representations,"[95] was meant to indicate that although sensory cognition had to be theoretically understood as clear but confused representation, it was not just a degenerate form of thought but had perfections of its own distinct from those of logical or scientific thought, which could be exploited as a unique source of pleasure in the fine arts. Baumgarten also made his point by a tripartite analysis of artistic beauty as consisting of "the beauty of things and thoughts," that is, the beauty of the object imitated; "the beauty of order," a general metaphysical category; but also "the beauty of signification," that is, the special property of the "harmony of signs [or means of expression] among themselves" independent of the merits of the represented object.[96] This last category was certainly meant to indicate that works of art contained sources of merit and pleasure independent of other values inherent in the objective world signified by the content of works of art.

Baumgarten extended this doctrine by ascribing to works of art a series of merits which he conceived in analogy to the merits of purely theoretical thought (thus he sometimes called the faculty of taste the *analogon rationis*); these were aesthetic richness, magnitude, truth, clarity, and cognitive liveliness (*vita cognitionis*).[97] These were supposed to be formal properties of successful artworks. Here, however, Baumgarten ultimately showed his distance from the doctrine of aesthetic disinterestedness, for these categories ultimately turned out to be essentially connected with the representation of objectively valid *moral* virtues: "Magnitude," especially, was a requirement for the "moral greatness of an object" represented in a poem or the "dignity of the subject matter."[98] Ultimately, Baumgarten found the source of our attachment to great poetry to lie above all in *"magnanimitas et gravitas aesthetica."*[99] On his account, then, although art has additional sources of value in the formal merits of a special form of cognition, its fundamental source of value for us is deeply connected to the ontological and moral perfection of the world it represents. There is no room for a general conception of disinterestedness in this account.

Baumgarten's definitional divergence from Wolff was not observed even by his own colleague and disciple Georg Friedrich Meier, whose *Anfangsgründe aller schönen Künste und Wissenschaften* (1748–9) appeared in print a year before Baumgarten's own work but which, its own author said, was largely based on Baumgarten's lectures; Meier reproduced Wolff's original definition of the pleasure in beauty as "the sensitive cognition of perfection" (§23) rather than his more immediate master's inversion of this formula. And Moses Mendelssohn, the most influential German philosophical writer on aesthetics between Baumgarten and Kant, took up Baumgarten's tripartite analysis of artistic beauty, with its emphasis on the pleasurable potential of the sign as well as object, but used Wolff's definition of pleasure and Baumgarten's definition of beauty interchangeably.

Mendelssohn, whose most important writings on aesthetics were published between 1755 and 1771, was well acquainted with the British as well as the German tradition in aesthetics. But his allegiance was clear. Like Burke, he explicitly rejected Hutcheson's separation of the sense of beauty from our other faculties and wrote that

> one should not create with the English[100] philosopher a new sense for beauty, which the Almighty has set in our soul with wise intentions, as it were by decree. This is the closest thing to suddenly cutting off all lines of rational investigation, and as it were transforming the complete whole, nature, into a patchwork.[101]

Instead, Mendelssohn found our pleasurable response to beauty to be deeply entrenched in our most fundamental sources of value. The language he used to express this view, however, was not Burkean but Wolffian, and he found the source of beauty in a sensory response to the perfections of objective existence and of our own condition considered as part of objective reality.

Mendelssohn usually gave a Wolffian definition of beauty: "*Beauty depends*, according to the opinion of all philosophers, *on the indistinct representation of a perfection*";[102] "now if the cognition of this perfection is sensitive [*sinnlich*], then it is called beauty."[103] Without acknowledgment of any difference, he sometimes substituted the Baumgartian definition:

> We have now found the general means, through which one can please our soul, namely the *sensitively perfect representation*. And since the final purpose of the beautiful arts is to please, we can presuppose the following principle as indubitable: The essence of the beautiful arts and sciences consists in an *artistic sensitive-perfect* representation, or in a *sensitive perfection represented through art.*[104]

Mendelssohn does not suggest that Baumgarten's definition represents any theoretical advance over Wolff's. In fact, however, his use of both definitions is appropriate, because his own view combines a Wolffian view that the fundamental value of the aesthetic lies in its representation of objective perfection with the Baumgartian view that the potential perfection of artistic media of representation is itself an additional source of pleasure in perfection.

Let us consider the Wolffian elements in Mendelssohn's thought before turning to his appropriation of Baumgarten. Following Wolff, Mendelssohn argues that our feelings of beauty are a response to the perfections of reality, at least insofar as they can be represented by means of the senses. He then supplements Wolff's view by arguing that our sense of pleasure in the aesthetic includes a response to the perfection of our own bodily condition in the perception of beauty. Mendelssohn reasserts the Wolffian view thus:

> Everything which is capable of being represented to the senses as a perfection can also yield an object of beauty. Here belong all perfections of external forms, i.e., of lines, planes, and bodies and their movements and alterations, the harmony of manifold tones and colors, the order in the parts of a whole, their similarity, multiplicity, and agreement, their transference and transformation into other forms, all capacities of our soul, all skills of our bodies; and even the perfections of our external conditions, by which one understands

honor, comfort, and wealth, cannot be excluded if they are suited to be represented in a manner striking to the senses.[105]

Here there is a tacit distinction between aesthetic and purely intellectual or conceptual modes of representation, but no separation between the *objects* of aesthetic response and other forms of valuation, and thus no suggestion that aesthetic response is disinterested in any general sense of being detached from other sources of value, even the value of external goods. This impression is strengthened when Mendelssohn includes the representation of our own perfections under the rubric of beauty, and assigns these all to the perfection of our thinking and willing (*Denken* and *Wollen*) – "If the essence of a spirit consists in thinking and willing, then he must himself become more perfect the more perfect are his concepts and the objects which he represents, and his happiness grows with the amount and magnitude of the perfection which he has brought forth through his free will"[106] – for this allows no source of perfection in human beings other than the general perfection of theoretical and practical reason. On this basis, Mendelssohn can say that a single conception of perfection is "the goal of all our desires and wishes, the measure of our actions and omissions; . . . the highest principle in ethics, in politics, and in the arts and sciences of enjoyment."[107]

We should note that the last comments concern the underlying sources of perfection for a *spirit;* Mendelssohn does go beyond Wolff in adding that our pleasure in beauty also includes a sensitive representation of the increase in the perfection of our *bodies* or physiological condition that is offered by the experience of beautiful objects:

> The effect of a perfect object on our nerves brings our body into a condition which serves its preservation, . . . and the soul receives an obscure concept of the improved condition of the body. The soul must therefore have a double enjoyment in the contemplation of a perfect object. One from the concept of its perfection . . . and secondly out of the obscure concept of the perfect condition of its body.[108]

However, the potential for bodily as well as spiritual pleasure in aesthetic response only serves to integrate the aesthetic further into our general sources of value rather than to isolate it.

In fact, Mendelssohn's view is that all experiences of pleasure constitute a single continuum of negative to positive feeling, ranging from aversion to desire, with differences in degree but no fundamental differences in kind. He writes that

> our sensations are always accompanied by a determinate degree of delight or displeasure. One can no more conceive a spirit without the faculty for love and aversion than one without the power of representation. All different degrees and alterations of this delight and displeasure, all of our inclinations and passions, must be explained from this fundamental faculty [*Grundvermögen*] of love and aversion.[109]

Again there is no suggestion that there is any essential distinction between our pleasurable response to beauty and to any other form of perfection. Of course there are differences of degree among our sensations of delight, and there is at least a phenomenological distinction between the sense of desire that accompanies some pleasurable sensations and an outright stimulus to action – but these are no more than differences of degree: "As I have presented *enjoyment*, it is distinguished from *willing* only by degree."[110] Aesthetic response is not fundamentally separated from desire and the motivation to practical action.

Mendelssohn's position on the underlying uniformity of all forms of valuation is directly inherited from Wolff. Following Baumgarten, he does add the sign or medium of aesthetic representation itself as an additional source of perfection and thus pleasure. Not surprisingly, he does this in the language of Wolffian (or even Cartesian) metaphysics. He points out that not only are the objects of representations real properties or entities, but also that the representations themselves are "positive characteristics" or "affirmative determinations" of the soul,[111] and that they may thus have their own perfections and be objects of pleasures in themselves. This metaphysical foundation creates the possibility for an explanation of our enjoyment of the representation of objects which are not themselves perfections and enjoyable, such as in the case of tragedy: Even "the knowledge of an evil action and disapproval of it are affirmative characteristics of the soul, are expressions of the powers of the spirit in knowledge and desire, are elements of perfection, which must necessarily arouse pleasure and delight in this connection."[112] Mendelssohn speaks of the "object" and its "projection" (*Gegenstand* and *Vorwurf*) as separate sources of perfection and pleasure.[113] He also uses this metaphysical doctrine as the basis for a tripartite analysis of the "composite sensation which is aroused through the work of art," similar to though not quite identical with Baumgarten's, in which there figures a pleasurable response to (1) the perfection of the object itself, (2) the perfection of the object's imitation of the object, and (3) the skill of the artist as well, "since all works of art are visible impressions of the capacities of the artist, who, so to speak, gives us his whole soul for intuitive cognition."[114] Here Mendelssohn follows Baumgarten in recognizing the additional sources of value available in the artistic representation of the external world. But even with this emphasis on the special sources of artistic value, he is far from suggesting that aesthetic response is in any way detached from the general source of value in the perfection of the world; on the contrary, the "perfection of a rational being" is itself one of the highest and most important constituents of the perfection of the world as a whole.

Mendelssohn wrote with full knowledge of Hutcheson's proposal of a disinterested sense of beauty, but rejected it in behalf of an expanded version of the theory of a unitary basis of objective perfection that had prevailed in Germany since early in the century. Indeed, the rejection of the idea of aesthetic disinterestedness must have prevailed in Germany until very shortly before the time of Kant's own *Critique of Judg-*

*ment,* as can be inferred from the fact that as late as 1785 Karl Philipp Moritz still thought it worthwhile to attack the reduction of beauty to usefulness. In an influential article of 1785, which Kant could hardly have missed,[115] Moritz argued, first, that usefulness is always a source of value external rather than internal to an object (many other objects can serve the same use equally well); and, second, that if beauty is just usefulness then everything useful must be beautiful, which is obviously not the case. Instead, he held, the beautiful object is contemplated as something *"perfected in itself,* which constitutes a whole in itself, and thus grants me pleasure *on its own account."* It does not serve some purpose which I have independent of it, and which is thus external to it, and thus does not exist "on account of the perfection of something else, but rather exists on account of its own internal perfection."[116] The doctrine that beauty is equivalent to usefulness which Moritz is attacking is crude and had long before been refined by Hume and Gerard, or even Berkeley, to avoid such obvious objections, nor did the Wolffian doctrine of pleasure as perception of perfection have any such simplistic consquence, but Moritz must have been responding to an attitude still prevalent in popular (if not professional) thought. The doctrine of the internal perfection which Moritz proposes in its stead may represent a departure from the view of Baumgarten and Mendelssohn that the perfection of the sign is a source of perfection and pleasure additional to that of the represented world, instead finding the locus of aesthetic value within the aesthetic object alone, and may thus represent a first step toward much idealistic and contemporary aesthetic theory. But it is not only vague, but also retains at least the language of the Leibnizo–Wolffian world view, which allows little room for aesthetic disinterestedness or a doctrine of the autonomy of art. Nevertheless, the very fact that Moritz should have felt compelled to launch such a protest as late as 1785 shows how far from being a widely accepted dogma the doctrine of disinterestedness introduced by Hutcheson was, in Germany as well as Britain.[117]

It should now be clear that the conception of a general detachment of aesthetic response from our underlying framework of theoretical and practical values, although it may have been suggested early in the eighteenth century, was far from widely accepted. Instead, the project of most eighteenth-century writers, whether in Britain or Germany, seems to have been that of justifying an interest in artistic and natural beauty, apart from the subservient role in religion which had served this purpose for a millennium or more, precisely by showing how deeply rooted in our most basic theoretical and practical projects is our pleasure in the aesthetic. Of course, everyone accepted Shaftesbury's view that our sense of beauty cannot be based in the satisfaction of personal or private interests, but this was not generally taken to mean that it had therefore to be detached from our most widely shared interests. When Kant began his analysis of the four moments of the judgment of taste with the requirement of disinterestedness, therefore, he was by no means just incorporating into his own philosophical system a doctrine that already enjoyed wide acceptance apart from it. Instead, although he started off with the noncontroversial detachment of our sense of beauty from personal use or consumption (*CJ*, §2), he then pointedly revived the far more controversial Hutchesonian position that aesthetic response is independent of our gratification in the agreeable and pleasure in the good altogether (*CJ*, §§3–5). Unlike Karl Philipp Moritz, however, he did not make this move in behalf of a purely internalist or autonomous conception of the perfection of works of art.[118] Instead, he recognized the position of the critics of Hutcheson that the enjoyment of the aesthetic can only be sustained if there is a deep connection between our sense of beauty and our deepest, especially practical, values. But he did not accept the direct links between the aesthetic and the practical that writers such as Hume or Burke or Kames or all the Wolffians had accepted; rather, he argued that it is only by means of its detachment from any direct service of the interests of reason that aesthetic experience can more indirectly serve these interests by providing us with a sensible image of our freedom itself and of the primacy of practical reason; the disinterestedness of our delight in the beautiful is itself that which serves the interest of reason. It will be the aim of Chapter 3 to trace out the details of this resolution to the controversy (rather than consensus) about disinterestedness which we have now found to be central to the history of aesthetics in the eighteenth century.

*Chapter 3*

# The dialectic of disinterestedness: II. Kant and Schiller on interest in disinterestedness

As we have seen, the traditional account of the role of disinterestedness in the emergence of philosophical aesthetics in the eighteenth century needs revision. It is usually supposed that early in the century, Francis Hutcheson, the first professor to make a significant contribution to modern British philosophy, sanitized some ideas of the less rigorous Lord Shaftesbury, and described the workings of an alleged sense of beauty as an immediate response of pleasure to the perceived proportionality of an object that was prior to any conceptualization of the object, and therefore independent of any conception of an interest the object could serve, thereby offering the first theoretical characterization of the aesthetic as an independent form of experience. Toward the end of the century, then, Kant is supposed to have taken over this characterization of disinterestedness as the cornerstone of his attempt to show that judgments of taste could be founded on the subjective feeling of pleasure yet make a synthetic *a priori* claim to the agreement of all human beings that is parallel to the synthetic *a priori* claims of theoretical and practical reason, (that is, those claims that are the informative yet universal and necessary, and therefore nonempirical, principles

This essay was originally presented as a lecture at a National Endowment for the Humanities Summer Institute on Art and the Emergence of Aesthetics in the Eighteenth Century at the Johns Hopkins University in 1990. A shorter version was presented at the University of Rochester conference on Kant and Kantian Aesthetics in May 1990. It is published here for the first time.

which Kant had held lie at the foundation of both natural science and morality.) The intellectual challenge for Kant, on this account, was to show how a form of experience divorced from the constraints of scientific theory on the one hand and moral action on the other could nevertheless raise the same claim to universal validity as those obviously more rule-governed domains of human thought and action.

As I have argued, however, such a story simplifies the original relation between Shaftesbury and Hutcheson as well as omitting the generation between Hutcheson and Kant entirely, and in so doing misunderstands what is in fact Kant's by no means direct reception of Hutcheson's original idea of disinterestedness. British writers such as David Hume, Edmund Burke, and Henry Home, Lord Kames, although they were all influenced by Hutcheson's interpretation of aesthetic response in terms of Lockean sensation rather than reflection, largely if not entirely rejected Hutcheson's supposition that our attachment to objects of taste, whether beautiful or sublime, could be explained without appeal to more general sources of value. Hume, for instance, was willing to recognize the appeal of some forms of objects as an original, which is to say inexplicable, feature of our mental constitution, but many more cases of beauty were to be explained as grounded in the sympathetic enjoyment of actual utility or the appearance of utility. Burke explained the enjoyment of the beautiful and the sublime in terms of general instincts toward society and toward self-preservation. Such theories must be seen as rejections rather than reconstructions of Hutcheson's conception of disinterestedness as the criterion for aesthetic response in general or for particular aesthetic judgments. And midcentury German writers, such as the Wolffians Alexander Gottlieb Baumgarten and Moses Mendelssohn, while concerned to differentiate the aesthetic from both the cognitive and the practical, nevertheless also rejected the idea that the aesthetic is simply an autonomous form of experience and instead interpreted it as a special form for the representation of ontological and moral perfection which could, although not with the same kind of feeling, be represented in other forms of thought as well.

Kant knew these writers, both British and German, very well; indeed, during the vital formative years of the early 1760s they constituted a large part of his reading. He therefore could not possibly have conceived of himself as simply incorporating the Hutchesonian conception of disinterestedness into his own philosophical system. Instead, I suggest, in aesthetics as elsewhere in his philosophical enterprise he must have seen himself as reconciling opposed but only apparently incompatible points of view. For what he actually argued is that paradigmatic judgments of taste are disinterested in their origin but can serve the supreme interest of morality precisely in virtue of their disinterestedness. At the most immediate level of response, aesthetic judgment must be free of external constraints, including the constraints of morality, but in virtue of this freedom the experience of aesthetic judgment can represent and in some degree prepare us for the exercise of freedom in morality itself. In the long run, Kant also suggested, disinterested aesthetic judgment can retain its interest for us only if in this way it freely serves the interest of morality itself. For Kant, the autonomy of the aesthetic is in the service of the primacy of practical reason, but the aesthetic serves practical reason in virtue of nothing less than its freedom from constraint by practical as well as theoretical reason.

Evidence for this interpretation can be found in the way in which Friedrich Schiller appropriated Kant's aesthetics. In his *Letters on the Aesthetic Education of Mankind*, Schiller took the occasion of the crisis of the Terror in the French Revolution to attempt nothing less than the refutation of Plato's charge that poetry would undermine the stability of the republic; he attempted to accomplish this fundamental philosophical task by arguing that only aesthetic education could show how to reconcile feeling and freedom, sense and reason, in the way necessary to allow a transition from dictatorship to democracy without a passage through terror. But aesthetic education could do this, he argued, only if its exemplary objects were free of didacticism, thus did not dictate a moral theory or political system to us but instead allowed and encouraged us to freely develop capacities equally necessary for the enjoyment of beauty and the enjoyment of freedom in its moral and political application. In this argument, I suggest, Schiller sought to refute Plato by applying what he rightly took to be the deepest lesson of Kant's aesthetics.

## I. KANT: THE INTEREST OF DISINTERESTEDNESS

At the beginning and the end of the "Critique of Aesthetic Judgment," the first half of his *Critique of Judgment* of 1790, Kant makes apparently incompatible statements about the moral interest of the aesthetic. At the conclusion of the "First Moment" of the "Analytic of the Beautiful" (itself the first section of the "Critique of Aesthetic Judgment"), summing up what is presented as the initial step of his argument, he states that "*Taste* is the faculty for estimating an object or manner of representation through a delight or displeasure *without any interest*" (CJ, §5, 5:211). In the final paragraph of the work, however, he writes that

> taste is at bottom a faculty for estimating the sensible rendering [*Versinnlichung*] of moral ideas (by means of a certain analogy of the reflection about both) . . . so it becomes clear that the true propaedeutic for the foundation of taste is the development of moral ideas and the culture of moral feeling, since only when these are brought into connection with sensibility can genuine taste assume a determinate, inalterable form. (CJ, §60, 5:356)

These statements seem diametrically opposed: The first suggests that the exercise of the faculty of taste and the pleasure it can yield (when it does not disappoint) must proceed independently of any interest, *a fortiori* independently of a moral interest, yet the second statement says that the development of taste is dependent on the cultivation of moral reasoning and the disposition to morality, which would seem to make sense only if the exercise of taste was crucially dependent on rather than entirely independent from morality.

One might think to escape this apparent contradiction by appeal to Kant's distinction between the beautiful and the sublime. The claim that taste is entirely independent of any interest, after all, occurs in the section of the *Critique* entitled "Analytic of the Beautiful," whereas in the separate section entitled the "Analytic of the Sublime" Kant claims that the experience of sublimity makes palpable or sensible the existence within us of a capacity for moral reasoning and moral determination of the will which is unconditional both in what it demands of us and what it can accomplish. Kant characterizes the experience of sublimity as one in which "the irresistibility of [nature's] power over us, considered as natural beings [*Naturwesen*], certainly yields knowledge of our physical incapacity, but at the same time reveals a faculty for judging [ourselves] as independent of her and a superiority over nature on which is grounded a self-preservation of an entirely different kind from that which is attacked by nature outside of us" (*CJ*, §28, 5:261), that is, the immunity of our moral character from injury from any merely physical source. Given the way in which the experience of the sublime reveals the dominion of our moral over our physical being, it seems natural for Kant to treat the sublime as a sensible rendering of the capacity for morality itself and then to continue, as he does, "that the intellectual, in itself purposive (the morally) good, estimated aesthetically, must not be represented so much as beautiful but rather as sublime, so that it arouses more the feeling of respect (which scorns charm) rather than love and intimate inclination" (*CJ*, §29 General Remark, 5:271). Then one might conclude that the statements of Sections 5 and 60 do not contradict each other, because they concern different forms of aesthetic experience: The experience of beauty is independent of any interest, including the moral, but the experience of the sublime depends upon the prior cultivation of moral sensitivity.

Such a solution to our paradox, however, is precluded by

the fact that Kant is clearly talking about the beautiful rather than the sublime in Section 60. For in the preceding section Kant has claimed precisely that "the beautiful is the symbol of the morally good; and only in this respect (a relation, which is natural to everyone, and which every one also imputes to others as a duty) does it please with a claim to the agreement of everyone else, whereby the mind at the same time is conscious of a certain ennoblement and elevation above mere receptivity to pleasure through impressions of sense" (*CJ*, §59, 5:353); and there is no evidence that he has changed the subject between Section 59 and Section 60. The sublime in fact has dropped from view at this particular point in Kant's argument, and the specific features of aesthetic experience on the basis of which it is argued that there is an analogy between the aesthetic and the moral which satisfies the requirements for symbolic representation are features of the experience of beauty rather than sublimity. So Kant's distinction between the beautiful and the sublime does not resolve the apparent contradiction between his statements in Sections 5 and 60, but instead creates a second paradox: If Kant holds in Section 29 that it is the sublime rather than the beautiful which *represents* the morally good, why does he hold in Section 59 that it is the beautiful rather than sublime which is the *symbol* of morality?

In fact, the answers to the two questions we now have before us are closely connected. The judgment of beauty must be independent of all interest because it is grounded in a harmony of imagination and understanding which is free of determination by any rules whatever, including the rules of morality; but precisely because the experience of beauty can count as an experience of such freedom, Kant argues in Section 59, it is also suited to serve as a symbol of morality, insofar as the essence of morality is freedom itself, although in this case the freedom to determine ourselves by the law of reason as contrasted to the necessity of being determined by the laws of nature. The experience of the sublime, however, is an experience which is pleasurable for us at all *only* because it reveals our morality to us; in this sense, the experience is dependent upon our morality rather than an independent experience which can serve as a symbol of it. Kant also suggests that the experience of the sublime is even an experience to which morality *compels* us. In the case of the sublime, "the effort and the feeling of the unattainability of the idea through the imagination . . . compel us to *think* of nature itself in its totality as the representation of something supersensible" (*CJ*, §29 General Remark, 5:268); and because this interpretation of our experience comes across as if necessitated, Kant concludes that "the delight in the sublime in nature is therefore also only *negative* . . . namely a feeling of the robbery of the freedom of the imagination through itself, insofar as it is purposively determined by another law than that of its empirical use" (*CJ*, §29 General Remark, 5:269). The experience of the sublime, although it reveals to us the existence of our capacity for morality and its utter dominion over the threats and blandishments of the physical world, is not directly an experience of freedom itself. In Section 59, Kant therefore does not think of it as suited for *symbolizing* the basis of morality, because there he is focusing, above all, on the freedom inherent in morality. The experience of beauty, however, precisely because it is not dictated by morality, is thereby suited to symbolize morality, which is to say to make our freedom palpable to us. In other contexts, however, Kant has no hesitation in thinking of the experience of the sublime as a fit symbol of morality, particularly when he is thinking not so much of the freedom of the moral agent's rational will but rather of the way in which that freedom itself requires a law that can appear as a constraint upon the sensuous inclinations and desires of the embodied rational agent (*CJ*, §29 General Remark, 5:271). When Kant is thinking of freedom per se, beauty is its most apt symbol, but when he is thinking of how rational freedom depends upon a law which can constrain sensuous nature, then the sublime may seem the better choice.[1]

Before we can examine further the links that Kant establishes between aesthetics and morality, however, we must consider the notion of disinterestedness by which he initially separates them and through the medium of which they are to be reconnected. The exposition in the "Critique of Aesthetic Judgment" is superficially clear (at least in comparison with Kant's other major works), but it is difficult to discern the underlying pattern of argument. Nowhere is the appearance of a straightforward and univocal argument more deceiving than in Kant's opening discussion of disinterestedness, for here Kant in fact exploits two distinct definitions of disinterestedness and suggests two different accounts of its position in his argumentation. Officially, disinterestedness is defined in terms of *existence:* Kant says that "interest [is] the delight which we connect with the representation of the existence of an object" (*CJ,* §2, 5:204), and disinterestedness is correspondingly defined as being "entirely indifferent in this regard." A disinterested delight, in other words, is one in which "the mere representation of the object in me is accompanied with delight, no matter how indifferent I may be to the existence of the object of this representation" (*CJ,* §2, 5:205). However, at least in his contrast between the beautiful and the good, Kant suggests that the disinterestedness of our pleasure in the beautiful ought to be defined in terms of the absence, from our response to it, of a *concept* of its value: "To find something good," he says," I must always know what sort of thing the object is to be, i.e., have a concept of it," whereas that is not necessary in the case of the delight in the beautiful (*CJ,* §4, 5:207). It is not immediately clear what the first of these two criteria means, for since (according to Kant) existence is not an informative predicate, it is not clear what it would mean to value the existence of something as opposed to any of its represented features. Nor is it clear that these two criteria are coextensive, since it would seem possible both to value the mere representation of something for conceptual reasons and also to respond favorably to the existence of something without the mediation of a concept. Perhaps, however, we can see what Kant really intends only by putting the two criteria together. An interest would be present in the case in which we value the existence of a thing only under a certain conception of its possible use or significance;

in Kant's words, interested pleasures in the good and agreeable "are determined not merely through the representation of the object, but through the represented connection of the subject with the existence of it" (*CJ*, §5, 5:209), where the means for the representation of the connection to existence must be a concept of what makes that existence good or agreeable. Conversely, our delight is disinterested when it is independent of any such conception and is thus produced purely by immediately represented qualities of the object, as opposed to such ramifications of its existence as can only be comprehended through a determinate concept of it. "The judgment of taste, on the contrary, is merely *contemplative*, i.e., a judgment which, indifferent in regard to the existence of an object, only compares its constitution with the feeling of pleasure and displeasure. But this contemplation itself is not directed to concepts" (*CJ*, §5, 5:209). Note that on this definition, however, what we contemplate are the *represented qualities* of an actual object; the gross distinction between representation and existence drops out, to be replaced by a subtler distinction between an immediate response to an object as represented and a response mediated through determinate conceptions of the value of a thing as represented.

Even if we attempt to reconcile Kant's two suggested definitions of disinterestedness in this way, however, it remains unclear just how Kant intends to argue for the thesis that response to the beautiful must indeed be disinterested. On the one hand, it can appear that this thesis is meant to serve as the opening premise of a philosophical argument which is supported itself only by an appeal to pretheoretical common sense. When Kant asserts that "if the question is whether something is beautiful, one does not want to know whether the existence of the object is of importance for us or anyone else . . . but rather how we estimate it in mere contemplation (intuition or reflection)," he appeals to our intuitive understanding that, for instance, Jacobin objections to the cost of producing the object are irrelevant to the question of its beauty (*CJ*, §2, 5:204–5). This suggests that he thinks that the requirement of indifference to existence and pleasure in the mere representation of a thing follows from common sense. On the other hand, the preceding section (*CJ*, §1) suggests that Kant begins his argument with a philosophical definition of aesthetic judgment as one "the determining ground of which *cannot be other than subjective*," which therefore cannot be any concept, for concepts are objective, *a fortiori* cannot be any determinate concept of the use or value of the existence of an object (*CJ*, §1, 5:203–4). On this account, the determining ground of aesthetic judgment must instead be the pleasure taken in the mere representation of the thing, for the reason that both of these – pleasure and representation – and only these, are subjective in the requisite sense.

Now, other things being equal, it might seem advisable to begin a philosophical argument from common sense rather than from a technical definition, that is, from beliefs shared in our linguistic community independently of any specific theory. It would therefore seem most charitable for us to think of Kant as having intended to start his argument from such a position. But there are problems with such an account of Kant's strategy in arguing for disinterestedness. First, what he appears to present as common sense was *not* common sense in his community: Hume and Burke and Kames and Wolff and Baumgarten, all highly influential authors, uniformly agreed that aesthetic pleasure is intimately connected with the general conditions for the value of the existence of objects, not entirely dissociated from it. Second, even conceding the force of the appeal to pretheoretical intuition, its implications would not be sufficiently general. Even if we grant that the Indian sachem would be wrong to call the palaces of Paris ugly because he prefers the restaurants or Rousseau wrong to do so because he objects to the social costs of their production (*CJ*, §2, 5:204–5), it would not follow that the proper grounds of aesthetic evaluation have nothing to do with *any* conceptualization of the existence of such objects and can lie only in an immediate response to the mere representation of them. Common sense is "common" only because it does not have such precise philosophical implications.

For these sorts of reasons, then, it seems best to regard Kant's requirement of disinterestedness as a consequence rather than first premise of his theoretical analysis and explanation of aesthetic pleasure. Such a theoretical foundation would be supported the way any serious philosophical theory is, namely through the illumination it offers of our total package of scientific as well as quotidian beliefs rather than through correspondence with any single Archimedian point in common sense outside of it, although of course its potential for reconstructing particularly prominent features of common sense will be a major test of it. And if the requirement of disinterestedness follows from a more fundamental philosophical theory of aesthetic experience, then the sense and force of this requirement, and thus the conditions under which it can be reconciled with the interests of morality, will also be determined by that theory.

So what is Kant's basic philosophical theory of our pleasure in the beautiful? His key assumption is that every experience of pleasure is linked to the experience of the attainment of some objective (*CJ*, §VI, 5:187), but where pleasure is to be especially noticeable it cannot appear to be guaranteed by any concept, and likewise where the grounds of judgment are to remain subjective this experience of fulfillment cannot be grounded in the subsumption of a represented object under any determinate concept of its significance, whether theoretical or practical. Instead, mere reflection upon the form of an object independent of its subsumption under a concept must nevertheless be experienced as revealing a sort of unity or harmony which, as it were, satisfies our craving for cognition without offering us any conceptually determinate claims to knowledge.[2] Kant tries to put this point by saying that the representation of a beautiful object induces harmony between our faculties of imagination and understanding rather than itself directly harmonizing with any determinate concept:

> For since the ground of the pleasure is set merely in the form of the object for reflection in general, thus in no sensation of the object and also without relation to a concept which con-

tains any intention: so it is only the lawfulness in the empirical use of the imagination in general (unity of imagination and understanding) in the subject, with which the representation of the object in reflection, the conditions of which are *a priori* universally valid, is in agreement; and since this agreement of the object with the faculties of the subject is contingent, the representation effects a finality in regard to the cognitive faculty of the subject.[3] (*CJ*, §VII, 5:190)

Kant supposes that this reflection must proceed in the same way for everybody, at least under ideal circumstances. This controversial point need not concern us here.[4] What is crucial for our purposes is simply his basic idea that a beautiful object must appear to satisfy our cognitive craving for unity if it is to please us, but that it equally well must appear to satisfy this objective without subsumption under any determinate concept if it is to please us. A beautiful object pleases us because in our perception of it the pattern of features presented to intuition and sustained in imagination appears to accord freely with the understanding's requirement of unity rather than to be dictated by any concept applied to the object presenting that pattern. In summing up the "Analytic of the Beautiful," Kant stresses the freedom of the imagination in the experience of beauty: "The result of the prior analyses," he says, "amount to this concept of taste: that it is the faculty for estimation of an object in relation to the *free lawfulness* of the imagination" (*CJ*, §22 General Remark, 5:240). However, he continues, to suppose that the imagination was both literally *"free* and yet *lawful of itself"* would be a contradiction, for only understanding actually produces a law:

> Hence only a lawfulness without a law and a subjective harmony of the imagination with the understanding without an objective one, where the representation would be related to a determinate concept of an object, is compatible with the free lawfulness of the understanding (which can also be called purposiveness without a purpose) and with the peculiarity of a judgment of taste. (*CJ*, §22 General Remark, 5:241)

The disinterestedness of a judgment of beauty must, then, be interpreted on the basis of this theoretical model. When it is, it becomes clear that the claim of disinterestedness goes solely to the etiology of aesthetic response. A beautiful object is one that pleases without any antecedent conceptualization of it, *a fortiori* without an antecedent conception of any purpose it serves or function it fulfills, whether of one's own or of any one else, such as its artificer or owner, if it has one of these. In addition, the free accord of the imagination with the general but not specific conditions of understanding which gives rise to this pleasure cannot be expected to give rise to any determinate conception of a *class* of objects, instantiated by the particular beautiful object at hand, further members of which can rationally be expected to be equally satisfying solely on the basis of their satisfaction of any determinate conceptual criteria for membership in such a class. But there is no basis in Kant's theory for supposing that it must be impossible for the gratification afforded by an object's inducement of an unconstrained harmony between imagination and understanding itself to be put to serve larger purposes, or for attachment to the continued existence of any beautiful object to be generated by the very fact of the conceptually unconstrained pleasure in it. In particular, the suggestion that "judgments of taste do not in themselves ground any interest" (*CJ*, §3, 5:205n.) would be a *non sequitur*, or would be so unless an interest was defined as an attachment to the existence of all members of a *class* of objects the extension of which is determined through a *concept* that is determinant in the production of the pleasure we take in its initial and subsequent instantiations.

The scope and force of Kant's claim that the judgment of taste is independent of any interest is therefore determined, and limited, by Kant's theory that such a judgment expresses a harmony between imagination and understanding that occurs freely rather than through the constraint furnished by any determinate concept. We can now see how Kant can consistently reconcile this notion of disinterestedness with his concluding claim that taste for the beautiful is ultimately a faculty for rendering moral ideas sensible in a way in which even the experience of sublimity is not.

Kant's conception of the moral significance of aesthetic experience contains two elements which he does not always clearly distinguish. On the one hand, the freedom of the imagination in the *experience* of beauty affords us a sensible representation of fundamental aspects of the *nature* of practical reasoning, and on the other hand the natural *existence* of beautiful objects[5] affords us palpable evidence of the *efficacy* of practical reason. In initiating his final argument that the beautiful is the symbol of the morally good, Kant expounds these two claims together. The beautiful as the symbol of the morally good, he writes, is that product of taste by means of which

> even our higher faculties of cognition agree and without which their nature, compared with the claims made by taste, would arouse clear contradictions. In this faculty judgment does not, as is otherwise the case in empirical estimation, find itself subjected to the heteronomy of a law of experience: in regard to the object of such a pure delight it gives itself the law, as reason does in respect to the faculty of desire; and, on account of this inner possibility in the subject but also of the outer possibility of a nature agreeing with this, it finds itself in relation to something in the subject and outside of it, which is not nature and also not freedom but which is connected with the ground of the latter, namely the supersensible, in which the theoretical faculty is connected in a unity with the practical in a common and unknown way. (*CJ*, §59, 5:353)

This sentence suggests two claims. The independence of the faculty of judgment from external or heteronomous determination by a concept, in the case of a judgment of beauty, is analogous to the freedom of reason when it determines our desires by its own principles instead of heteronomously; and the existence of external objects which freely induce this harmony within our cognitive faculties – the "external possibility" of beauty in nature gratifying the "internal possibility" of the experience of beauty within our cognitive faculties – is analogous to the existence of a natural realm in which our practical reason can be efficacious. The harmony between imagination and understanding in the experience of beauty is analogous to the freedom of practical reason to *determine* our intentions, while the fact that external objects naturally exist which can yield this internal harmony is analogous to the fact that our autonomous practical reason can be efficacious in *realizing* our intentions in the realm of nature, a possibility which Kant here feels compelled to explain by reference to a common, supersensible ground of the realms of nature and freedom.[6]

Given Kant's connection between interest and existence, it is natural for him to connect the second rather than first of these parallels to the concept of a moral interest in the beautiful. Thus his discussion of the first parallel, in the next paragraph, does not use the term "interest": Kant asserts that the beautiful's role in symbolizing the morally good is what justifies our exaction of taste from others as a sort of duty (*CJ*, §59, 5:353; cf. §40, 5:296),[7] without explicitly saying that it produces an interest in it, and he reserves talk of interest for our attitude toward the *existence* of beautiful objects rather than the *experience* of beauty. This second parallel, and thus the explicit theme of a moral interest in the beautiful, is actually explored in an earlier section of the *Critique* (§42), but since the parallel between the internal experience of beauty and practical reasoning which Kant pursues in the remainder of Section 59 is logically prior, I will conclude the discussion of this later section before turning to the earlier one.

Kant's statement of the analogy between the experience of beauty and the exercise of practical reason is unusually clear:

1) The beautiful pleases *immediately* (but only in reflecting intuition, not like morality in concepts). 2) It pleases *without any interest* (the morally good is to be sure necessarily connected with an interest, although not with one which precedes the judgment on the delight, but rather with one which is first produced by that). 3) The *freedom* of the imagina-

tion . . . is represented as harmonious with the lawfulness of the understanding in the estimation of the beautiful (in moral judgment the freedom of the will is conceived of as the agreement of the latter with itself according to universal laws of reason). 4) The subjective principle of the estimation of the beautiful is represented as *universal,* i.e., as valid for everyone, but not as cognizable through any universal concept (the objective principle of morality is also expounded as universal for everyone, i.e., for all subjects and also for all actions of the same subject, [but] thereby also as cognizable through a universal concept). (*CJ,* §59, 5:353–4)

The key elements of the comparison are that both aesthetic and moral judgments produce a feeling of pleasure, although of course that is not all moral judgment produces; both are achieved without antecedent desires for their objects; both are free of any heteronomous determination; and both are universally valid. They are thus parallel in a number of ways. However, the parallel role of freedom and what depends on it, such as immediacy, is what is really unique to these two; universal validity, for instance, would also characterize conceptually constrained judgments of ordinary cognition. So the freedom of the imagination seems to be the heart of its special analogy to the morally good, insofar as self-determination is also the fundamental characteristic of practical reasoning.

Two questions leap to mind, however. Why does Kant describe this *parallel* between the experience of beauty and moral reasoning as the former *symbolizing* the latter rather than, for instance, vice versa? And why does the fact that the experience of beauty symbolizes the morally good give anyone ground for demanding or exacting this experience from others as a sort of duty? The answers to both of these questions are connected, although only dimly adumbrated by Kant earlier in Section 59. Kant starts the section with the general claim that "intuitions are always required to display the reality of our concepts" (5:351). He then goes on to state that it is impossible to so confirm the "objective reality of concepts of reason," because "no intuition entirely appropriate to them can be given." But he does not then simply drop the demand for sensuous presentation of intellectual concepts. Instead, he introduces the idea of *symbolic* rather than *schematic* representation: that is, representation by means of the sensuous presentation of properties merely analogous to those predicated by the intellectual concept rather than by means of those properties actually specified by the concept through its schema. Putting these statements together, one can arrive at the conclusion that the intellectual concepts of morality need some kind of representation in intuition for the sake of our cognition of the nature and requirements of morality itself, but that there is no direct schematization of these concepts in experience. So something which is analogous to them but which is directly experienced, namely the experience of beauty, can and indeed must be pressed into service for this purpose. This is why beauty symbolizes morality but not vice versa: The experience of beauty is paradigmatically sensuous, whereas practical reasoning is paradigmatically not. And how would this justify the claim that we should exact experience of beauty from others? Apparently Kant must assume (although he hardly explicitly argues this) that knowledge of the nature of morality is a condition of the possibility of compliance with the demands of morality itself, and that insofar as we are not merely entitled but are required to demand the latter of others, we must also demand sensitivity to the only available symbolization of morality from them.

Of course, for such an argument to go through the implicit condition of that last clause must be satisfied. That is, beauty must indeed be the only available symbol of morality, and it may seem as if Kant's analogy falls short of proving that. But although Kant has not explicitly argued that the experience of freedom so prominent in the experience of beauty is unique, he must surely have supposed that it was plainly, if not demonstrably, so. Or maybe it is even more likely that Kant just assumed that practical reason is such a dominant force in our lives that it simply seizes upon any opportunity for its own representation to our inexorably sense-dependent imagination. In particular, practical reason may be thought of as seeking ways to make our freedom palpable to us short of situations *in extremis:* Threatened with the gallows for doing what morality requires, we can become sure of our freedom to comply with morality nevertheless (*Practical Reason,* 5:30), but practical reason may also seize upon less rare and, we might even say, more comfortable opportunities to make itself palpable to us.[8]

This would also explain Kant's argument in his otherwise mystifying discussion of the "ideal of beauty" (*CJ,* §17). Here Kant argues that we need a "highest model" of some single maximally beautiful thing and that only the human figure, as the expression of the human capacity for morality, can play this role.[9] But if considered on the basis of the internal logic of aesthetic judgment alone, the premise of this argument is a numbing *non sequitur,* for from the fact that any object which is beautiful must ideally be pleasing to all (the requirement of subjective universal validity) it certainly does not follow that there must be some *one* object which is maximally pleasing to all, or even to each. So whence does the requirement of an ideal of beauty arise? It can arise only from practical reason itself, as indeed Kant indicates: "The archetype of taste . . . rests on reason's indeterminate idea of a maximum" (*CJ,* §17, 5:232), which "then proves that estimation according to such a standard can never be purely aesthetic, and that estimation according to an ideal of beauty is no mere judgment of taste" (*CJ,* §17, 5:236). Instead, reason seeks sensible representation in the sensible image of human beauty, although of course what counts as such beauty must itself be constituted on aesthetic grounds alone.[10]

Let us now turn to what Kant patently treats as a *moral* interest in the beautiful, that is, interest in the natural existence of beautiful objects as analogous to the external realization of our virtuous intentions. Kant discusses this under the rubric of the "intellectual interest in the beautiful" (*CJ,* §42). The basis of Kant's argument here is the general supposition that reason is "interested in its ideas (for which it effects an immediate interest in moral feeling) also having objective reality"; that is, practical reason does not merely demand to determine our *intentions* through freedom of the will but also looks toward the *realization* of those intentions in nature outside the will, above all, in our own behavior as a natural phenomenon. Thus, Kant continues, it is of interest to reason that

> nature at least show a trace or give a clue that it contains in itself some ground for assuming a lawlike harmony of its products with our delight independent of all interest . . . : therefore reason must take an interest in every manifestation in nature of a harmony similar to this; consequently the mind cannot reflect on the beauty of *nature* without finding itself interested. This interest however is related to the moral; and whoever takes this interest in the beauty of nature can do so only insofar as he has already well grounded his interest in the morally good. (*CJ*, §42, 5:300)

There are really two kinds of claims that could be made here. On the one hand, we could argue that we have a completely general interest in nature satisfying our objectives, whether disinterested or not, and that our interest in the existence of beautiful natural objects is just an instance of this. On this account, interest in natural beauty would be analogous to our interest in finding nature hospitable to virtue rather than, say, finding it a rich source of food, in that it would not presuppose an antecedent interest in any given class of objects, but it would not be otherwise unique. On the other hand, we could suppose that *only* morality creates a genuine interest in nature's being hospitable to our own objectives, and that any other instances of interest in natural existence, such as in the natural existence of the beautiful, must be grounded in that primordial moral interest. The conclusion of Kant's argument, which, unlike Section 59, says not just that interest in the natural existence of beauty is analogous to moral interest in the realizability of virtue but that it must be founded in it, clearly supposes the latter. But for that very reason, Kant's argument seems weak. Given the analogy between our interest in the realization of morality and our interest in the existence of beautiful objects, the moral interest might well be a *sufficient* condition of taking a similar interest in the existence of beauty. But given Kant's own definition of pleasure as a "condition of the mind . . . as a ground either to preserve itself (for the condition of mutually facilitating powers of the mind in a representation preserves itself), or to bring forth its object" (*FI*, §VIII, 20:230–1), the existence of a moral interest in nature does not seem to be a *necessary* condition for an interest in the existence of beauty; the nature of pleasure itself seems an adequate explanation for that.

But again we should probably conclude that such an objection would fail to do justice to Kant's overwhelming assumption of the dominance of practical reason in our lives. That is, although we may quibble about formal relationships, Kant in all likelihood simply took it to need no argument that we naturally have an interest in nature's being hospitable to our virtue and naturally search for evidence that this is so. Then, although we may have a self-explanatory interest in the natural existence of beautiful objects – of course we must always remember that these, unlike virtuous actions (and most other things), do not constitute a determinate class that is well defined by any determinate concept – we also seize upon such objects as additional evidence of nature's hospitality to our morality and intensify our pleasure in beauty for that reason.

Several puzzles about Kant's account of the intellectual interest in the beautiful remain. First, why does Kant insist that this interest is evidenced only in attachment to naturally beautiful objects such as wildflowers and birds and not in attachment to works of art? Second, why do we take this interest only in the beautiful and not in the sublime?

The first puzzle arises because of Kant's theory of genius. According to this theory, truly successful works of fine art always manifest a degree of unity of form and of harmony between form and content beyond anything which could be found in the determinate intentions and precepts of the artist, and which must therefore be ascribed to a "gift of nature" that "gives the rule to art," or to "talent" that "as an innate productive faculty of the artist itself belongs to nature" (*CJ*, §46, 5:307). But if the existence of beautiful works of art as well as beautiful flowers and birds must also be ascribed to nature (although, in this case, to nature working inside the skin of human beings, instead of outside it), then why is the very existence of fine art not as much evidence of nature's hospitality to our interests, aesthetic and moral, as the existence of natural beauties in the more ordinary sense?[11] In fact, there seems to be no good answer to this question, except that Kant is suspicious of the intentions we can all too easily form in connection with art. Some of his suspicions are obvious; he is clearly distrustful of the way in which we can all too easily use the arts for gratification of the ego, whether by literally adorning our persons or by surrounding ourselves with adornments of our more extended selves, for example refined and (often more importantly) expensive collectors' prizes. But Kant is worried about a subtler problem as well, namely the danger that the intentions of others which are embodied in works of art, that is, the goals and conceptions of those who produced these works, can rob each of us, as a member of their audience, of his own freedom which must be the foundation of any morally significant interest in the aesthetic. Sometimes Kant expresses this qualm by worrying about crude cases of actual deception. For example, if a joker exploits the mimetic potential of artistic techniques to trick us into thinking we are hearing a real nightingale or seeing real flowers when none are there, our response, even if pleasurable (as long as the deception goes undetected), is hardly free (*CJ*, §42, 5:299). But even when deception is excluded, Kant seems to think that an art object will still come across as the product of "an intentional art visibly directed to our delight" (*CJ*, §42, 5:301), and thus that it will still deny us the room for the exercise of our own freedom of the imagination which must be the basis for the moral significance of the aesthetic. To be sure, as he continues Kant recognizes that the beauty of art can only be explained as the product of a delicate balance between intention and nature: "Nature was beautiful if it also appeared like art; and art can only be called beautiful if we are conscious that it is art, and yet it appears like nature to us" (*CJ*, §45, 5:306); and in the theory of genius Kant clearly comes to recognize the compatibility of freedom and intentionality on the side of the *artist*.[12] But his suspicion that the autonomy of the *audience* of art is always dominated by the intentions of the artist seems to remain, or is at least not explicitly retracted.

Our second puzzle was why Kant supposes that we can take an intellectual interest only in the beautiful and not in the sublime. Kant does not spell out his explanation of this position, but the most obvious explanation would seem to be simply that in the case of the sublime, *nature* pleases us only indirectly. It is not its free harmony with our needs but rather ·its very *opposition*, at least to our natural interest in continued material existence, which reveals the existence within us of another plane of being that is utterly indifferent to the threat of physical injury, the moral freedom of rational agency. In the experience of the sublime, we have no evidence that nature itself will gratify our interests, including our moral interest, but rather evidence that we have a capacity for morality which is independent of nature's indifference to us. To put the point in other terms, we might say that the experience of the sublime can serve as a figure of our *virtue*, our capacity to will what is morally correct even in the face of opposition from our own inclinations, but that we take intellectual interest in evidence of the reality of the *highest good*, that is, happiness in proportion to our virtue as worthiness to be happy. Only the natural existence of beauty serves as evidence of the reality of the highest good.

In the end, Kant interprets aesthetic experience within a framework dominated by the primacy of practical reason, the view that all sources of value, even if they arise independently, must be compatible with the unconditional validity of the moral point of view. The moral point of view is inescapable for us, and no form of our intentional activity can remain isolated from its reach; perhaps that is why Kant seems just to take it for granted that works of genius will always have ideas of reason as their content (*CJ*, §49). The moral point of view is also that which is of most enduring interest to us; this, combined with the fact that the purely aesthetic response shares something of the nature of surprise, and thus by itself tends to fade with familiarity,[13] may explain why the fine arts must be "brought into a close or distant connection with moral ideas" in order to avoid the fate of dulling our spirits (*CJ*, §52, 5:326). Kant claims that only moral ideas "bring a self-sufficient delight" with them (*CJ*, §52, 5:326), which is too strong; on Kant's account, purely aesthetic pleasure is certainly self-originating, even if not completely self-sustaining. And in any case, a moral interest in the beautiful could not be sustained if the beautiful were not itself an experience of freedom from constraint, including undue constraint by the ideas of morality itself. That is precisely why ultimately only genius can successfully bring the moral and the aesthetic together. Only in works of genius can concepts inform without constraining the products of our intentional activity, and it is only such a delicate balance between rule and freedom which can symbolize and serve the interests of morality itself. Genius "is the exemplary originality of the natural endowment of a subject in the *free* use of his cognitive faculties" (*CJ*, §49, 5:318). As such, the *work* of geniuses (although not exactly their *works*) sets an example for later artists.[14] But it also offers an image of the freedom of morality itself and sets the terms under which we can take a moral interest in the aesthetic. We cannot remain interested in the aesthetic unless we can find moral significance in it, but we can find such significance only by experiencing the freedom of the aesthetic from heteronomous constraint.

## II. SCHILLER: AESTHETIC EDUCATION AND THE EXPERIENCE OF FREEDOM

Friedrich Schiller understood Kant's idea that the aesthetic can serve the purposes of morality only by remaining free of constraint, including constraint by morality itself. Sounding paradoxical, he wrote,

> Beauty produces no particular result whatsoever, neither for the understanding nor the will, it accomplishes no particular result, neither intellectual nor moral, it discovers no individual

truth, helps us to perform no individual duty and is, in a word, equally unfit to found the character and enlighten the head. By means of aesthetic culture, therefore, the personal worth of a human, or his dignity, insofar as this can depend solely on himself, remains completely indeterminate; and nothing more is achieved by it than that it is henceforth made possible *by nature* for him to make of himself what he will – that the freedom to be what he ought is completely restored to him.

But precisely thereby something infinite is achieved. For as soon as we recall that it was precisely of this freedom that he was deprived by the one-sided compulsion of nature in sensation and the exclusionary legislation of reason in thinking, then we are bound to consider the capacity which is restored to him in the aesthetic mood as the highest of all gifts, the gift of humanity.[15] (Letter 21, pp. 146/147)

Schiller's suggestion is that it is precisely because aesthetic experience is free of servitude toward any particular cognitive or practical objective that it can facilitate the realization of that freedom which is the precondition of successful moral action. But his argument is on a bolder scale than Kant's. In the end, Kant gave a rather modest assessment of the concrete political potential of the aesthetic: It offers the possibility of "an art of mutual communication of ideas between the refined and crude parts" of society, a medium between "high culture and worthy nature" (*CJ*, §60, p. 256). For Schiller, however, the aesthetic offers nothing less than the possibility for a new theory of justice within the soul – that is, harmony among the parts of the soul that will ground harmony among the parts of society – which will refute Plato by showing that aesthetic education grounds rather than undermines political stability. But even with this larger objective, Schiller remains true to Kant's insight that it is nothing less than the freedom of the aesthetic from the constraints of moralistic didacticism which allows it to serve the ultimate interest of morality and human freedom.[16]

Schiller's first major effort at an aesthetic theory, a series of letters written in early 1793 to his friend Christian Gottfried

Körner outlining a never-completed essay on beauty to be entitled *Kallias* (after which the letters themselves have come to be known as the "*Kallias* letters"), represented a modest development of Kant's theory that the beautiful is the symbol of the morally good. Revealing the continuing influence of Baumgarten's conception of the aesthetic as the *analogon rationis*, Schiller began by revising the Kantian analysis of beauty so that its analogy with morality became essential or constructive for it. Kant had characterized the aesthetic by means of a tripartite division: Aesthetic reflective judgment was initially characterized as a paradoxical case of cognition or theoretical judgment, the distinguishing feature of which – namely its freedom from conceptual determination – then allowed it to serve as a symbol of practical reasoning. Schiller, perhaps attempting to explain Kant's own distinction between aesthetic and teleological judgment at a higher level of abstraction than Kant himself did, but also driving a sharper wedge between the aesthetic and the theoretical than Kant did or than he himself was later to accept, employed a fourfold distinction, in which he characterized the teleological as the analogue of theoretical cognition and the beautiful as the analogue of freedom or autonomy in appearance.[17] As he put it,

> Estimation of concepts according to the form of cognition is logical: estimation of appearances according to this same form is teleological. An estimation of free effects (moral actions) according to the form of pure willing is moral; an estimation of non-free effects according to the form of pure willing is aesthetic. *Agreement* of a concept with the form of cognition is *agreement with reason* [*Vernunftmäßigkeit*] . . . , analogy of an intuition with the form of cognition is *similarity to reason* [*Vernunftähnlichkeit*] . . . , agreement of an action with the form of pure willing is *morality*. Analogy of an appearance with the form of pure willing or freedom is *beauty* (in the broadest sense).[18]

The essence of the comparison between actual freedom and beauty as the appearance of freedom is self-determination, that is, autonomy, or at least the absence of determination from without, that is, heteronomy. Schiller takes Kant's most profound contribution to philosophy to be the conception of a free action as above all one determined from within the agent by practical reason rather than one determined by anything outside the agent; he then takes himself to be grounding aesthetics on Kant's most important legacy when he argues that the appearance of freedom is found in a natural object when its form appears to be determined entirely by its own nature rather than by any external agent:

> Certainly no greater word has been spoken by *any* mortal man than this Kantian one, which is the content of his entire philosophy: Determine yourself through yourself. . . . This great idea of self-determination beams back at us from certain appearances of nature, and we call these *beauty*.[19]

Schiller also makes the point in the language of "form" and "matter":

> Practical reason, applied to free actions, demands that the action take place solely on account of the manner of action (form) and that neither matter nor purpose (which is always matter) have had influence on it. Now if an object shows itself in the sensible world to be determined through itself, if it presents itself to the senses so that one notices no influence of matter or of a purpose in it, then it is estimated as an *analogon* of the pure determination of the will (though not as the product of a determination of the will). Now since a will which can determine itself according to mere form is called *free*, that form in the sensible world which appears to be determined merely through itself is called a *presentation of freedom*.[20]

At first glance, this account of beauty seems to avoid several of the complexities of Kant's theory. On Kant's account, a beautiful *object* was really only indirectly a symbol of the morally good, deriving that status from the analogy between morality and the *judgment* or *experience* of beauty; on Schiller's model, the direct analogy between the nature of freedom and the appearance of beauty seems to avoid that indirectness. Further, Kant's account of the pleasure of beauty depended upon a complicated theory of the harmony of faculties and its production of pleasure that cannot ultimately be understood except as a psychological theory; Schiller's account seems at first to avoid such dependence on speculative psychology. In the end, however, the real criterion for whether an object is an appearance of autonomy or not is whether or not we feel compelled to search for an external explanation of its form: "A form therefore appears free when we neither find its ground outside it *nor are induced to seek it outside it.*"[21] Whether we start on the side of the object, like Schiller, or on the side of the subject, like Kant, to describe the aesthetic is ultimately to highlight certain characteristics of our own experience.

Having argued that beauty is essentially the analogical appearance of freedom, Schiller does nothing further to explain the importance of beauty for us; he must simply assume that the value of a representation of freedom is self-evident. The one further step he does take, however, is to use his theory as the basis for an argument against didacticism or explicit moralizing within art itself: if the form of a work appears to be determined by a specific moral conception, then it will appear to be determined from without rather than within and will not itself be an appearance of autonomy. In his words,

> If we suppose that we realize a moral intention with an object, then the form of this object will be determined through an idea of practical reason, therefore not through itself, [and] it will therefore suffer heteronomy. Thus the moral purposiveness of a work of art, or also an action, contributes so little to its beauty that it must rather be well hidden and have the appearance of arising entirely freely and uncompelled from the nature of the thing if this, its beauty, is not to be lost.[22]

The *Kallias* letters thus offer no explicit explanation of the value of beauty, apparently taking the value of a representation of freedom to be self-evident, but they do make it clear that whatever this value is it will be undermined by art that is patently directed at the achievement of moral ends. Although Schiller has not yet made explicit his own account of the moral value of the aesthetic, he is clearly following Kant in his recognition that this value can be fulfilled only if the aesthetic is free of direct constraint by morality.

Schiller's letters *On the Aesthetic Education of Mankind*[23] drop the attempt to improve upon Kant's characterization of the beautiful *object*, but instead constitute Schiller's attempt to provide an extended explanation of the moral value of aesthetic *experience* and thereby to justify the centrality of aesthetic education in the political progress of mankind. As Plato's attack against poetry had begun with a theory of the human soul, so does Schiller's refutation. Plato had divided the soul into the capacity to reason, a disposition to such self-assertive or self-protective states as pride and anger, and the sensual appetites, and had argued that order could be created within an individual life, and thus among individuals living together in a state, only if reason firmly rules the lower emotions and appetites through its knowledge of the form of the good. Aesthetic education, trading in mere simulacra of real knowledge, could ultimately strengthen only emotion and appetite and had to be banned from (or at least strictly regulated in) the just *polis* for that reason. Schiller, however, rejected the idea that the path to individual moral development, and thus political progress, lies through the simple subordination of our whole being to an abstract form of reason. He argued instead that neither of our two fundamental tendencies, the drive to abstract thought or reason on the one hand and to sensible or particular experience on the other, could healthily rule by itself. Rather, both must be brought into cooperation, not by some third, superior faculty of mind but rather by nothing less than the experience of beauty itself. The cooperation between sense and reason that could be learned through that experience would then allow these two faculties to be successfully employed in moral and political cooperation as well.

For our purposes here we do not need to consider all of the metaphysical model of human nature which Schiller attempts to construct, under the influence of Fichte as well as Kant. We can begin with his distinction between the two fundamental forces or drives in human nature. The first of these is the "sense drive," which directs us toward the ever-changing succession of sensations of physical existence which is the content of time (Letter 12, pp. 78 / 79). The second is the "form drive," which points us toward eternal necessities free of the relentless tendency to change (pp. 80 / 81). It is clear from the outset that success in both theory and practice depends on harmony between these two drives: "If the first drive furnishes only *cases,* the second gives *laws* – laws for every judgment, where knowledge is concerned, laws for every will, where deeds are concerned" (pp. 80 / 81). Kant's dictum that "thoughts without content are empty, intuitions without concepts are blind"[24] is obviously close to hand; rational knowledge of laws must be combined with experiential knowledge of cases for us to know our world and how to act in it. But it is all too easy for us to identify ourselves exclusively with one or the other of these drives. Schiller offers some characterization of the theoretical consequences of such exclusive identification, but even more compelling images of the practical consequences. If we let our attraction to the particularities of experience reign unhindered, then "feeling can only say: this is true *for this subject* and *in this moment,* and another moment, another individual, can come along which revoke the assertions of the present sensation," and "Inclination can only say: this is good for *your individual self* and *your present inclination,* but your individual self and your present need will be torn along by change, and that which you presently fiercely desire will become the object of your aversion" (Letter 12, pp. 82 / 83). Submersion in the particularity of experience alone makes impossible a stable set of beliefs and a stable set of desires and intentions, whether in an individual or a community. But an exclusive focus on reason leads to an unrealistic level of abstraction at which we cannot actually live. The moral and political dangers of this are particularly clear to Schiller. He writes, for instance, "The state should not only honor the objective and generic character of individuals, but also their subjective and specific character, and in extending the invisible realm of morals it should not depopulate the realm of appearance" (Letter 4, pp. 18 / 19). In this brief remark, Schiller makes the transition from the abstract metaphysics of universal and particular to his moving critique of the terror to which the French Revolution had degenerated.

It is easy for Schiller to provide abstract descriptions of the ideal relationship between these two drives which will avoid these pitfalls and dispose us to stable beliefs and intentions. "We are led to the concept of a reciprocal action between both drives, where the efficacy of each is at the same time grounded in and limits the other, and in which each attains to its highest manifestation" (Letter 14, pp. 94 / 95); "Let there be a community between the form-drive and the matter-drive, . . . since only the unity of reality with form, contingency with necessity, passivity with freedom perfects the concept of humanity" (Letter 15, pp. 102 / 103). And it is easy for him to make the general claim that beauty is nothing less than the image of "living form" where particularity and generality, matter and form, are brought into harmony (Letter 15, pp. 100 / 101), so that exposure to beauty should in some way obviously facilitate the reconciliation of the two drives in our lives more generally. But when we try to descend from this level of generality, it is important to note that Schiller suggests several different claims which it is worth distinguishing.

The following passage is fundamental to Schiller's brief for aesthetic education:

> Since the world is something extended in time, alteration, the perfection of that faculty which puts man in connection with the world must be its greatest possible alterability and extensity. Since the person is that which endures in alteration, the perfection of that faculty which is to oppose change must be its greatest possible self-sufficiency and intensity. The more multifacetedly his receptivity develops, the more mobile it is . . . the more world can the man *apprehend* . . . the more

force and depth of personality, the more freedom reason wins, the more world can the man *comprehend. . . .* His culture will therefore consist: *first*, in creating for the receptive faculty the most multisided contacts with the world and, on the side of feeling, developing passivity to the highest; *second*, in securing for the determining faculty the greatest independence from the receptive and, on the side of reason, developing activity to the highest. Where both these qualities are united, there man will combine the highest independence and freedom with the greatest fullness of being and, instead of losing himself in the world, will rather draw the entire infinity of its appearances into himself and subject it to the unity of his reason. (Letter 13, pp. 86–8 / 87–9)

Appropriate exposure to beauty – which here, unlike in the *Kallias* letters, must be conceived of as the sensuous presentation of cognitive as well as theoretical harmony between matter and form – is supposed to lead us toward this perfection of our two drives and to prepare them for cooperation in other spheres as well. But in fact, at least two significantly different claims are made in this passage.

At one level, Schiller is making the rather traditional, although anti-Platonic, *psychological* claim that exposure to beauty can have a beneficial effect upon our *affective* or emotional condition and thereby improve our prospects for appropriate action in practical circumstances. At another level, however, he is suggesting that aesthetic education fosters an *epistemological* improvement in our condition, maximizing our attention to both particularity and principle and to the possibility of bringing them together, which is necessary for truly effective exercise of either individual morality or political justice.

The psychological theory is suggested by Schiller's use of the distinction between passivity and activity in the passage just quoted and is emphasized in several subsequent letters. The basic idea is that sensitivity or receptivity to the particularity of experience is passive, and reasoning active (again, the influence of Kant is obvious) and thus that excessive preoccupation with the particularities of experience results from an excessively passive character, whereas excessive abstraction at the cost of due attention to experience results from excessive activity. The experience of beauty is then called upon to balance these tendencies. We respond to a beautiful object with a balance of passion and action, or, as Schiller also suggests, with a balance of relaxation and energy, and apparently the beneficial effects of that spread beyond the moment of aesthetic experience itself. Thus Schiller states,

> A simultaneously releasing and tensing effect is to be expected from the beautiful: a *releasing* effect, in order to hold the sense-drive as well as the form-drive within their boundaries; a *tensing* effect, in order to preserve both in their strength. Ideally, however, these two kinds of effect should be a single one. It should release by tensing both natures uniformly, and tense by uniformly releasing both natures. (Letter 16, pp. 110 / 111)

In actuality, however, an individual (or individuals or communities at historical stages of development) will usually suffer from an excess of one tendency or the other, and actual beautiful objects for that individual or in that culture will therefore usually address one excess or the other. So Schiller distinguishes between relaxing and invigorating instances of beauty: "The ideal-beauty, although indivisible and simple, displays in different relations a melting as well as energetic quality; in experience *there is* a melting and an energetic beauty" (pp. 112 / 113). As he also puts it,

> Actual, thus limited humans are found either in a condition of tension or a condition of relaxation, according as either the one-sided activity of individual forces disturbs the harmony of their being or the unity of their nature is grounded on the uniform enervation of their sensible and spiritual forces. Both of these opposed limits, as will now be proved, are removed through beauty, which restores harmony in the tense man and energy in one who is relaxed. (Letter 17, pp. 116 / 117)

Although a pure Kantianism as well as Platonism might seem to imply that sensibility must always be directly ruled by reason, Schiller's view is that exclusive domination of either faculty by the other is a tyranny which robs humans of their full potential for rational experience and action. Thus "every *exclusive* domination by either of his two basic drives is a condition of compulsion and violence for [man], . . . and freedom lies only in the cooperation of both his natures" (pp. 118 / 119). Exposure to beauty, Schiller supposes, will limit such domination and prepare the way for such cooperation, thus facilitating the possibility of freedom of the will itself as a natural reality, not just a theoretical possibility (see, e.g., Letter 20, pp. 138 / 139).

The details differ, and the tone is more pretentious, but the force of such an argument does not really differ much from the traditional kind of psychological argument offered, for instance, by Hume's assertion that "a cultivated taste for the polite arts . . . rather improves our sensibility for all the tender and agreeable passions; at the same time that it renders the mind incapable of the rougher and more boisterous emotions."[25] As such, this sort of argument has probably rarely seemed significantly less plausible than Plato's fear of the deleterious consequences of going to the theater, but equally its force has probably always been recognized to have natural limits.

As I suggested, however, Schiller's original statement of the moral benefits of aesthetic education contains another element, the idea that through the experience of beauty we can maintain the force of our reason while *maximizing our contacts* with the world or our *apprehension* as well as *comprehension* of it. Here his claim seems to be epistemological as well as psychological: To act well, we need to know as much as we can, not only about moral principles but also about the circumstances of the world in which we act and the people to, for, with, or against whom we act. Experience of the aesthetic directly offers us some such information and more generally strengthens the resolve to get it, since in the case of the aesthetic it is clear that beauty depends on variety of matter as well as unity of form.

Schiller does not spell this point out as explicitly as the last, but he clearly has it in mind. Thus, Letter 18 opens with the statement that "through beauty sensuous man is led to form and thought; through beauty spiritual man is led back to matter and restored to the world of sense" (pp. 122 / 123) and concludes with the assertion that "the essence of beauty [is] not lawlessness but harmony of laws; . . . the determinacy which is rightly required of beauty does not consist in the *exclusion of certain realities,* but rather in *the absolute inclusion of all*" (pp. 124 / 125). Or, as he puts it in Letter 21, immediately preceding the paragraphs quoted at the beginning of this section, "Aesthetic freedom of determination . . . must be conceived as a *filled infinity*" (pp. 144 / 145). The idea seems to be that in order to maximize our success in both thought and action, we must not just balance our inclinations to sense and reason but also maximize our experience of the world as well as our comprehension of theoretical and practical principles, and that aesthetic education offers a crucial avenue to the latter as well as the former. Put thus, Schiller's thesis is indisputable, although of course the uniqueness as well as scope of aesthetic education in this regard must again be matters for empirical investigation. But even with its natural limits, Schiller's application of the ultimately Leibnizian idea of beauty as the harmony of variety and unity is a valuable corrective not to the excessive but to the exclusive emphasis on the role of principles in practical reasoning which Kant can seem to have suggested, even when his ethical writings are read in light of his aesthetics. Schiller's point is not that moral principles can be too strong but that they cannot be applied alone.[26]

This is not the whole of Schiller's idea about the benefits of aesthetic education for moral epistemology, however. A further thought is suggested quite late in the letters when Schiller comes to the characterization of beauty as *Schein,* unhappily translated as either "semblance" or "illusion." This thought is the idea that it is through aesthetic experience that we can first, or at least most readily, come to understand that our image of the world is not simply *given* to us but must be *created* by us. Such a recognition may seem to be of purely epistemological import, but it is not, for the first step in practical reasoning must be the recognition that we have the responsibility for determining not only how to act in a situation but what our situation really is. In practical pursuits an initial conceptualization of our situation is no more simply handed to us than it is in theoretical inquiries; we must take responsibility for it ourselves.

Schiller puts this point by describing "contemplation," which is of course the paradigmatic form of aesthetic experience, as "the first liberal relation of man to the universe which surrounds him" (Letter 25, pp. 182 / 183), where by "liberal" he means to convey precisely the way in which the world does not itself necessitate a unique response to it but requires that we actively form our image of it through our own thought. He explicitly uses the language of "form" in this context:

> From being a slave of nature, which he remains as long as he merely senses it, man becomes its lawgiver as soon as he begins to think it. That which hitherto dominated him merely as *power*, now stands before his view as *object*. That which is object for him has no power over him, for in order to experience it as object he must experience his own power. So far as he gives matter form, and as long as he gives it, he cannot be injured by its effects; for nothing can injure a spirit except what robs it of its freedom, and he indeed demonstrates his freedom by giving form to the formless. (Letter 25, pp. 184 / 185)

A part, at least, of learning to act freely is learning that our freedom (and therefore, of course, our responsibility) begins with the very interpretation of our circumstances, and we can at least begin to learn this in the experience of beauty: "Beauty is to be sure the work of free contemplation, and with it we enter into the world of ideas" (Letter 25, pp. 184 / 185).

That the aesthetic object is never simply a simulacrum of a predetermined reality, in other words, teaches us that our understanding itself is never a mere mirror of preformed reality and that the conditions for practical reason are likewise not determined without our own thought. At the same time, Schiller is clear that there is a difference between a freely but responsibly created image of our world and a simple flight into illusion, and he is alive to the danger that we can all too easily be tempted to cross the fine line between these by allowing aesthetic semblance to degenerate into mere fantasy and illusion. The "sovereign right" of the poet to create a world entirely of his own choice exists only in the purely aesthetic sphere,

> the unreal [*wesenlosen*] realm of the imagination, and only so long as he scrupulously refrains from predicating real existence of it in the case of the theoretical and as long as he renounces imparting existence to it in the case of the practical. You see, the poet oversteps his boundaries in the same way if he attributes existence to his ideal as if he aims to achieve some determinate purpose by its means. (Letter 26, 196 / 197)

The world invoked by art is not the real world, and it is as much of a mistake to determine the form of the work of art by a determinate moral conception as it is to think that a determinate moral objective can be satisfied within a mere world of semblance. But insofar as art remains "*upright* (expressly renounces all claim to reality), and . . . *autonomous* (doing without all support from reality)," not only does it yield aesthetic "semblance" but it also can teach us that autonomy in conceiving of our world which is presupposed by autonomy of action in it.

Schiller's final word on aesthetic education is unmistakably aimed at Plato: "Taste alone brings harmony into society, because it founds harmony in the individual" (Letter 27, pp. 214 / 215). He does not simply equate taste with morality, or aesthetic education with moral development, but argues that the development of taste is a precondition for the realization of moral autonomy: "Man in his *physical* condition merely suffers the dominion of nature; he frees himself of this power in the *aesthetic* state, and rules it in the *moral*"

(Letter 24, pp. 170 / 171). Of course, he does not prove his claim that the aesthetic is the only path to the moral. But he certainly deepens Kant's insight that aesthetic experience can add a great deal to our moral development, above all to the epistemological framework within which moral development must take place, not only while it remains disinterested but indeed only if it remains disinterestedly free of external constraints, including the direct constraint of morality itself.

# Chapter 4

## The perfections of art:
## Mendelssohn, Moritz, and Kant

According to the account that I have been attacking in the preceding two essays, the heart of eighteenth-century aesthetics – indeed, the thesis that defined the independence of this new discipline itself – was the belief that the human experience and judgment of beauty, sublimity, and other of what we now call aesthetic properties must be essentially independent of any other fundamental sources of value connected with the theoretical and practical principles of human life. Such a thesis is supposed to have been introduced under the name of "disinterestedness" by Lord Shaftesbury and Francis Hutcheson at the start of the century, and to have been made the cornerstone of the analysis and deduction of judgments of taste in Kant's *Critique of Judgment* at its end. Further, because Kant's notion of disinterestedness has been thought to apply straightforwardly to our judgments about artistic as well as natural beauty, Kant has also been thought to be the father of the subsequent conception of the autonomy of art, the idea of "art for art's sake": that is, the view that the production of art, and therefore the most appropriate and enlightened response to and criticism of works of art, must be motivated by purely aesthetic concerns intrinsic to art (or specific media of art) rather than by extrinsic moral and political concerns. I have argued in Chapter 2 that the

This essay was presented as an address at a bicentennial conference on Kant's *Critique of Judgment* held at the New School for Social Research in New York in December 1990 and is published here for the first time.

supposition of a uniform adherence to a broad notion of disinterestedness radically falsifies the deeply controversial status of this concept in eighteenth-century aesthetics. Although Hutcheson (but not Shaftesbury) did assert such a complete separation between the origins of aesthetic value on the one hand and of all other forms of value on the other, subsequent writers, both British and German, largely rejected this separation. In Chapter 3, I argued that the notion of disinterestedness was, then, not so much inherited as it was revived by Kant, but only in a dialectical context in which he argued that the freedom of aesthetic response from direct constraint by concepts, including concepts of purpose and thus of morality, is precisely what makes aesthetic experience an experience of freedom which can indirectly serve our most fundamental end, morality itself. In the present essay I want to carry this argument further into the details of Kant's treatment of the fine arts. I will argue that Kant by no means asserted the subsequent idea of art for art's sake, but instead advocated a complex conception, on which both the production of and response to art must have room for the freedom of the imagination characteristic of pure aesthetic response to simple natural beauties but also for the moral dimension which can never be left out of account in products of human intentionality.

I will develop this account by pursuing several historical contrasts, some but not all of which were touched upon in Chapter 2. I will begin by considering Moses Mendelssohn's theory of art, which can be regarded as the culmination of the rationalist tradition in aesthetics grounded upon Leibnizo–Wolffian foundations by Alexander Gottlieb Baumgarten. In a number of essays, first published in the late 1750s and then reissued in book form in 1771, Mendelssohn developed a complex conception of aesthetic value as our pleasurable response to the dimensions of perfection inherent in represented objects, the representations of those objects, and the artistry involved in the production of such representations. The complexities of Mendelssohn's account were rejected, however, by the novelist and essayist Karl Philipp Moritz, who in a 1785 essay in the *Berlinische Monatsschrift* (likely to have been seen by Kant, since he published an essay of his own in the same issue)[1] argued that a work of art can only be properly appreciated as perfect in itself independently of any extrinsic use or value, even of the most noble sort. This essay can be regarded as a true ancestor of the later conception of the autonomy of art. In fact, however, Moritz's account merely retained Mendelssohn's metaphysical language of perfection while failing to provide any substantive explanation of our pleasure in works of art in terms of any of our own capacities or interests as human beings; and indeed the emptiness of Moritz's account was quickly recognized, especially by critics under the general influence of Kant, although not yet of the *Critique of Judgment*, such as the Leipzig aesthetician Karl Heinrich Heydenreich.[2] Kant himself can then be seen as having followed a strategy diametrically opposed to that of Moritz. Kant rejected Mendelssohn's metaphysics, substituting his own account of the subjective finality of aesthetic experience for Mendelssohn's ontologically objective perfectionism, but building upon his distinguished predecessor's substantive insight into the complex dimensions of the value of art in developing his own account of fine art as requiring a delicate balance between the freedom of the imagination and the primacy of practical reason. Whatever its subsequent effect, Kant's intention was clearly to rescue the Enlightenment recognition of art's intrinsic connection with the most fundamental sources of human value from an inadequate metaphysical foundation rather than simply to cut art loose from the rest of our life.

## I. MENDELSSOHN

Mendelssohn built his analysis of art and his resolution of a number of the outstanding issues of eighteenth-century aesthetics upon twin foundations. On the one hand, he accepted Wolff's fundamental explication of sensory perception as "clear but indistinct" representation and then of pleasure as the response to the sensory perception of ontologically objective perfection. As Mendelssohn put it in the letters *On the Sensations*, which first brought him to public attention in 1755, "According to the opinion of all philosophers, *beauty rests on the indistinct representation of a perfection.*"[3] And in an essay on "The Chief Principles of the Beautiful Arts and Sciences," published in 1757, he wrote:

> Every concept of perfection, of consensus, and of the un-flawed, is preferred by our soul to that which is flawed, imperfect, and unharmonious. This is the first degree of delight and displeasure, one or the other of which accompanies all of our representations. . . . Now if the cognition of this perfection is sensible, then it is called beauty.[4]

On this principle, our sense of beauty arises from the perception, by means of our senses, of objective perfections that are at least in principle apprehensible by intellect as well and thus do not have any intrinsic connection to the nature of our senses. On the other hand – although like many others at the time (and since) he did not clearly distinguish this from Wolff's position – Mendelssohn also accepted Baumgarten's thesis that our sense of beauty is a pleasurable response to the perfection of the distinctive possibilities for representation which are afforded by the senses as such, independently of objective grounds of value in the object of representation that might be apprehended by the intellect instead of the senses. As Mendelssohn put the point, a page after the just-cited definition of beauty, in "The Chief Principles of the Beautiful Arts and Sciences,"

> We have now found the general means through which one can please our soul, namely the *sensorily [sinnlich] perfect representation*. And since the ultimate end of the beautiful arts is to please, we can therefore presuppose as indubitable the following principle: The essence of the beautiful arts and sciences consists in an *artistic sensorily perfect* representation, or in a *sensory perfection represented through art.*[5]

Perhaps Mendelssohn did not feel a need to draw an explicit distinction between the Wolffian and Baumgartian principles, for even if they are not identical, they are certainly compatible with each other. We can take pleasure in the representation of something through our senses which is perfect and therefore intrinsically valuable, and we can equally well take pleasure in the perfection of our sensory media of representation itself. Indeed, the basis for Mendelssohn's analysis of the complexity of our pleasure in art was precisely his recognition that we can take pleasure in both what art represents and how it represents it.

Mendelssohn's formulation of the Baumgartian thesis conceals a second ambiguity, that between pleasure in the internal perceptual experience of an external object on the one hand and on the other hand pleasure in an artistic representation of an object where that artistic representation, for instance a painting, is itself the external object of a perceptual experience. Mendelssohn clearly had the former alternative in mind when he argued for this fundamental duality in the sources of aesthetic response by employing an ontological framework going back to Leibniz and even Descartes, supposing that perfection always lies in a reality or "affirmative" rather than "negative" characteristic or property (*Merkmal*), and then arguing that not only represented objects have affirmative properties the perception of which can cause pleasure but also that our representations are themselves affirmative properties of the soul, consciousness of which is as such accompanied with pleasure. As he put it,

> We sense pleasure or displeasure concerning the arrangement and constitution of the object [*Sache*], depending on whether we perceive realities or their lack in it. But in relation to the thinking subject, the soul, the perception and cognition of properties . . . is something *object-like* [*Sachliches*] which is posited in itself, an affirmative determination pertaining to the soul; therefore every representation, at least in relation to the subject, has something pleasing about it as an affirmative predicate of the thinking being.[6]

Taken literally, this argument implies that all representations are pleasing, those produced by works of art no more so than any others. And, as "affirmative realities," all real objects should be pleasing as well. This is precisely the kind of shoal on which the rationalist ontology always runs aground because of its description of properties as "perfections." But all that Mendelssohn is really assuming is that there is potential for pleasure in the perception of an object as well as in the object perceived. A perfect representation of a perfect object can be doubly pleasing, but in any case there is room for pleasure in a representation of an object which is not pleasing in itself, or even one which is evil and thus in itself distressing. As Mendelssohn writes, "Even the cognition of an evil action and the disapproval of it are affirmative characteristics of the soul, are expressions of the powers of the spirit in cognition and desire, elements of perfection which must necessarily arouse pleasure and delight in this connection."[7]

Mendelssohn's use of his argument also suggests that he is more interested in the distinction between an object and the representation of it in an artistic medium (which is itself the object of a mental representation) than in the original distinction between an external object and the internal representation of it. Although it is not originally introduced with this sense, Mendelssohn's distinction between an object (*Gegenstand*) and its projection (*Vorwurf*) is ultimately interpreted in this sense. The "projection" of an object is originally interpreted as another designation for the internal representation of it, and the same dualism already expressed in terms of representation is expressed by means of the contrast between object and projection as well: "The good and evil properties, excellences and lacks, virtues and vices of things . . . must be evaluated in a twofold relation, in relation to the *object*, or the thing, which they pertain to outside of us, and in relation to the *projection*, or to the thinking being, which perceives them."[8] But Mendelssohn soon switches to interpreting the "projection" as the artistic representation of an external object rather than the direct sensory representation of it, and thus claims that in the response to any work of art there is room for pleasure (or another emotion) in response to that which is represented by the work as well as room for pleasure in response to the character of the artistic representation of that objective content. This is the basis for his view that works of art are capable of affording us a "mixed sensation" (*vermischte Empfindung*), which is the central concept of his aesthetics:

> This representation through art can also be sensorily perfect, even if its object would be neither good nor evil in nature. . . . Through artistic representation that which is disagreeable in the object is moderated, and that which is agreeable is as it were elevated. That which is agreeable in art increases the delight. . . . As often as works of art have a model in nature which they imitate, so can this model in and for itself just as well be disagreeable as agreeable, yet in both cases arouse delight in its imitation. Yet this difference is to be noted: the agreeable model in nature will in and for itself arouse pleasure in relation to the object and in relation to the projection [*Vorwurf*]. This will be elevated through the beauties of art. . . . But models which in nature are disagreeable arouse a far more mixed sensation in their imitation.[9]

The potential for pleasure which lies in one's internal representation of an object is focused on the artistic representation of it, or perhaps we should say, is exploited by means of artistic representation. So Mendelssohn's original distinction between the perfection of external objects and the perfection of the cognitive states of the soul itself is transformed into the basic distinction between the pleasure we attach to objects which are intrinsically pleasing and the additional dimension of pleasure which we can attach to perception through the artistic representation of objects. This then becomes the basis for Mendelssohn's solution to the problem of our pleasure in the representation of tragic events[10] and for his argument that the beauty of art does not lie merely in the imitation of natural beauty but contains additional dimensions of perfection of its own.[11]

In Mendelssohn's fullest classification of the potential dimensions of pleasure inherent in our response to art, how-ever, the original distinction between external object and mental representation is not entirely subsumed in that be-tween external object and artistic representation but appears in a modified form. We have to assemble suggestions from several works in order to see the whole scheme, but when we do, what we see is something like this. Most of this pic-ture is presented in the essay on the chief principles of the fine arts, but not all of it.

(1) Mendelssohn of course begins his argument by stress-ing the potential for perfection in an external object or event (whether historical or not) itself, and the corresponding plea-sure (or otherwise) in our response.[12] He then proceeds to analyze additional dimensions of a work of art, understood as an imitation of an object in nature:

> Let us consider the composite sensation which is aroused by the work of art somewhat more precisely, and from that de-rive the rules for the expression as well as the constitution of the object of art. If the work of art has a model in nature, then in the first place the expression must be true.

Mendelssohn interprets "truth" or similarity as the paradig-matic perfection of an imitation, so he next infers that (2) "every imitation in and for itself already carries the concept of a perfection with it, and if our senses can perceive the similar-ity of an imitation then it is capable of arousing a pleasant sensation."[13] Although Mendelssohn is only considering re-semblance in this context, which, he points out, is by no means an exclusively artistic phenomenon – we also take pleasure in the reflections of objects in still water for the same reason – we can take his reference to mimesis to be his para-digm for all of those aspects of representations, in both the artistic and internal senses, which we can enjoy in addition to or even in distinction from the object which is represented. This broad category would include all of those features of form as well as content – shape, color, tone, composition, and so on – which constitute perfections of artistic representations. In Mendelssohn's words,

> Everything, which is capable of being represented to the senses as a perfection, can also yield an object of beauty. Here belong all perfections of external forms, that is, of lines, surfaces, and bodies and their movements and alterations, the harmonies of manifold tones and colors, the order of the parts of a whole, their similarity, multiplicity, and harmony.[14]

But further, Mendelssohn argues, our pleasure in the representation of an object is not confined to its sensible features or the sensible fact of its resemblance to its model. (3) We also admire, and thus enjoy, the skill or artistry which has gone into the production of an artistic imitation:

> In the imitations of art there is also the perfection of the artist, which we perceive in them; for all works of art are visible impressions of the capacities of the artist, who, so to speak, gives us intuitive knowledge of his entire soul. This perfection of the spirit arouses an uncommonly greater pleasure than the mere similarity, because it is worthier and far more complex than that. It is all the more worthy as the perfection of a rational being is more sublime than the perfection of a lifeless thing.

Naturally, the pious Mendelssohn does not miss the opportunity to remind us that the creativity of the divine artificer of the universe as a whole is even more admirable than that of human artists. But the basic point remains that we can have a pleasurable response to the artistry manifest in the production of an artistic representation that adds to our pleasure in what it represents as well as in the sensible properties of this representation itself. Thus "we find more to admire in a rose by Huysum than in the image of this queen among flowers which is reflected in [a] river."[15]

We have thus far arrived at a threefold classification of the potential for pleasure in our response to art into (1) pleasure (or other emotion) engendered by the represented object, (2) by the representation of the object, and (3) by admiration for the artistry manifested in the latter. Elsewhere Mendelssohn adds one more dimension, which is reminiscent of other contemporary theories of aesthetic response such as that of Edmund Burke: (4) A beautiful representation, now understood once more in the sense of an internal or mental representation of an object rather than the representation of it in an artistic medium – although of course the latter will be one of the sources of the former – has a beneficial effect not only on our mind but on our body, and a sensation of pleasure in that effect is also a part of the composite pleasure aroused by a beautiful object. As Mendelssohn put it, in a sketch which was not published until the modern edition of his works,

> The effect of a perfect object on our nerves brings our body into a condition which serves for its preservation[,] and the soul attains an obscure concept of the improved condition of the body.
>
> The soul must therefore have a double enjoyment in the contemplation of a perfect object. First from the concept of its perfections . . . and secondly from the obscure concept of the perfect condition of its body.[16]

But he also made the point in one of his published essays:

> As far as the pleasant sensation is concerned, it is an effect of perfection, a gift of heaven, which is inseparable from knowledge and the choice of the good; but it can be analyzed and resolved into the original drive to perfection. Pleasant sensation is nothing other in the soul but the *clear but indistinct intuition of perfection,* and insofar as it is accompanied by a sensible pleasure, a comfortable condition of the body, or a harmonious tension of the nerves, the soul also enjoys a sensible but indistinct intuition of the perfection of its body.[17]

Through its effect on the body, the mental representation of the external object, which itself can be an artistic representation, reasserts its presence. Thus the full outline of Mendelssohn's conception of the dimensions of pleasure potentially present in the response to a work of art emerges: On his account, we can enjoy (1) the represented content or theme of the work; (2) the formal properties of the work of art by means of which it represents this object; (3) the skill or artistry which has gone into the production of this work; and (4) the internal representation of all of this as a state of the soul with pleasurable effects on the body as well.

Although still expressed in the terms of Leibnizo–Wolffian metaphysics (and, as we shall see, subject to criticism on that score), Mendelssohn's analysis of the composite sensation of pleasure engendered by works of art gave him a rich framework for the discussion of many particular problems of aesthetics and issues in criticism, such as the problem of tragedy, the different potentials of different artistic media (in which he laid down the philosophical basis for Lessing's *Laokoön*),[18] and more. All of this was rejected, however, in Karl Philipp Moritz's insistence that a work of art could be understood only as "perfected in itself" rather than as referring to perfections lying outside of itself.

## II. MORITZ AND HEYDENREICH

Although Moritz dedicated his "Attempt at a Unification of all the beautiful Arts and Sciences under the Concept of *That which is Perfected in Itself*" to Mendelssohn, the position that the essay espouses is clearly intended to repudiate the kind of explanation of our pleasure in art which Mendelssohn had offered.[19]

Moritz begins his discussion with the commonplace distinction between the beautiful and the merely useful. Something that is useful serves some purpose in a user other than itself, and it has no value apart from serving such a purpose located in such a user other than itself. In particular, Moritz assumes, individual persons tend to evaluate useful objects in reference to their own individual purposes; as we will see, Moritz employs the idea of sympathy (but not a Humean conception of sympathy as a mechanism by which the appreciation of utility is extended to objects the use of which one cannot enjoy oneself). Thus, he claims that in the case in which I approve of an object as useful,

> I make myself as it were into the central point, to which all the parts of the object are related, i.e., I consider them merely as means, for which I myself, insofar as my perfection can be advanced thereby, am the end. The merely useful object is therefore nothing whole or perfected [*Vollendetes*] in itself, but first becomes that when it attains its purpose in me or is perfected in me.[20]

The gist of his description of the beautiful is then simply a reversal of the conception of the useful. Since the useful pleases because it serves a purpose lying outside of itself and is for that reason incomplete in itself, yet the beautiful is not the useful, the beautiful must please because it is complete or perfect in itself, serving only a purpose lying within itself rather than beyond itself:

> In the consideration of the beautiful, however, I remove the purpose from myself and back into the object: I consider it as something which is *perfected* not in me *but in itself*, which therefore constitutes a whole in itself, and grants me enjoyment on its own account. . . .
>
> Since the useful does not have its purpose in itself, but rather *outside* of itself in something else, the perfection of which is thereby increased . . .
>
> In the case of the beautiful it is the opposite. This does not have its purpose outside itself, and does not exist on account of the perfection of something else, but on account of its own inner perfection.[21]

To this point, Moritz's alternative account of the beautiful is merely rhetorical; he has said nothing more about the beautiful than that it is not useful.[22] Nevertheless, Moritz extends his argument, inferring that since we take pleasure in a useful object because it satisfies a purpose external to it, thus not for its sake but for our own, our pleasure in a beautiful object must conversely be an, as it were, sympathetic response to its satisfaction of an inner purpose of its own, which he posits without explanation. Drawing a remarkable conclusion from this, he explains that we are upset when a play is given before an empty house because that represents a rejection of what is important to the work of art itself (not, please note, the actors, producers, or other human agents):

> Thus the displeasure at an empty theater, even if the presentation itself is excellent. If we felt pleasure in the beautiful more for our own sake than for its, what would we care if it were known by anyone other than ourself? We strive to provide admirers for the beautiful, wherever we may find it; indeed we even feel a kind of sympathy for a beautiful work of art that is trodden in the dust, which is contemplated with an indifferent glance by passers-by.[23]

The beautiful artwork is personified, treated as if it were an agent with purposes of its own, the frustration of which commands our sympathy. We cannot speak of value in a vacuum, without relation to the purposes of agents; so having denied that the value of a work of art can lie in our own purposes external to it, Moritz writes as if the work of art were itself an agent, with ends the satisfaction of which is the source of its own pleasure and, as it were, only by sympathy of ours.

Moritz recognizes that reference to some purpose may be necessary to support an ascription of value to a beautiful object, but provides only a verbal satisfaction of this condition by introducing the idea of an "internal purposiveness": If something is useful because it satisfies a purpose of some agent external to itself, then it must be beautiful because it satisfies a purpose internal to itself, he infers, but he does not explain what this purpose is. In words that sound like those Kant is to use five years later but that, as we shall see, contain none of the substance of Kant's account, Moritz writes,

> Now that which is useless or nonpurposive cannot possibly be enjoyed by a rational being. Therefore where an object

lacks an external use or purpose, this must be sought in the object itself, . . . or I must *find in the individual parts of it so much purposiveness that I forget to ask, what is the real point of the whole?* In other words: I must find enjoyment in a beautiful object only on its own account; to this end its lack of external purposiveness must be made good by its internal purposiveness; the object must be something perfected in itself.[24]

The existence of a purpose within the object which is satisfied by some order of its parts is simply postulated in order to satisfy rationality's requirement of a purpose; no attempt is made to explain what such a purpose is or how it can subsist without relation to purposes of our own. The Mendelssohnian language of perfection is retained, but it is not supported by reference to either the objective perfections of that which is represented by a work of art or subjective perfections in the perceiver of the work. It is grounded only in the unexplained concept of the internal purposiveness of the work of art itself.

Even Moritz was ultimately forced to recognize that the value of a beautiful work of art could not be explained in abstraction from all human purposes, and in a subsequent essay he tacitly conceded that its value could only lie in satisfying an underlying principle of human nature. He wrote, "The beautiful is to be contemplated and felt as well as brought forth merely on its own account. – We contemplate it, because it is there, and stands in the midst of the series of things; and because we are contemplating beings, in whom restless activity makes room for moments of still contemplation."[25] The value of beauty, in other words, cannot be explained without taking into account its relation to beings like ourselves, for whom contemplation of a certain sort is valuable. But this grudging concession to the relational ontology of more traditional theories of beauty was not elaborated, nor did it have the impact of Moritz's bolder assertion that art exists for its own sake and not for ours.

Although later generations were to echo Moritz's bold claim of beauty for beauty's own sake in the slogan "Art for art's sake," his own generation was quick to find fault. Before we turn to Kant, let us briefly consider the response of Karl Heinrich Heydenreich, who was influenced by Kant but whose own *System der Ästhetik* also appeared in 1790 and was thus not specifically influenced by the *Critique of Judgment*.[26] Heydenreich offers a general criticism of the rationalist tradition of aesthetics that had culminated in the work of Mendelssohn, but also offers specific criticism of Moritz's 1785 essay.

Heydenreich's specific criticism of the rationalist analysis of beauty as perfection perceived by the senses is preceded by a general argument that all cases of beauty cannot be reduced to any single essential characteristic, and that there are instead a variety of grounds of pleasure in objects which lead us to call them beautiful. He enumerates four: (1) Objects may please us because of their "immediate impression . . . on our senses, without the intervention of any judgment"; (2) objects may charm us because of the "contingent association of certain images and representations"; (3) there are beauties "the efficacy of which rests on an essential relation of certain forms and tones to certain conditions of a human as a being sensitive to weal and woe," by which Heydenreich means to suggest the power of objects (e.g., landscapes) to evoke moods; and finally (4) there are beauties which "arouse enjoyment through the relation of certain objects, images, representations, thoughts, and actions to the laws of the understanding, of the speculative or practical reason."[27] Given what he clearly takes to be the empirical evidence in behalf of the existence of these different principles of beauty, which are not reducible to any single explanation, Heydenreich is suspicious of any attempt to analyze our pleasure in beauty in terms of any single metaphysical concept.

Heydenreich's insistence on multiple sources for beauty might have made him hospitable to Mendelssohn's explication of the *vermischte Empfindung* produced by works of art, but he is too critical of the perfectionist framework of the Wolffian–Baumgartian aesthetics which Mendelssohn still employed to see beyond its problems. In order for this theory to be sustained, he argues, it would have to pass the test posed by three questions: "(1) Can perfection be sensorily cognized? (2) Does the perception of perfection take place in all cases of beauty? (3) Can one derive all the feelings which beauty arouses from the perception of perfection?"[28] Heydenreich then argues that the perfectionist theory does not pass this test. First, he argues that the concept of unity by means of which the concept of perfection is traditionally glossed is equivocal and can mean either the wholeness of an object, its subsumption under a concept, or its fulfillment of a purpose, and that in any of these cases the senses cannot perceive it alone but only in conjunction with the intellect.[29] Second, he holds that experience "tells us that many objects are universally held to be *beautiful* without our being conscious of having cognized any perfection in them,"[30] thus that there is no evidence for the universal validity of the perfectionist theory. Finally, he holds that even in those cases where there does seem to be a recognition of perfection, that cannot "exhaust all of the effects of beauty, whether of nature or art"; in the case of a poem, for instance, there will be many touches which arouse pleasures that are genuinely part of the aesthetic effect of the poem but which cannot be brought under any single conception of the perfection of the whole.[31]

Heydenreich recognizes that Moritz's account of the beautiful as perfect in itself is meant to avoid the snares of the perfectionism of the rationalists, but he also sees that Moritz's alternative is empty. In particular, he recognizes that it does not follow from the platitude that the beautiful is not useful that it is not essentially related to us and our constitution; it just shows that the beautiful does not please by answering those sorts of needs which are satisfied by those things which are typically called useful. So he rejects Moritz's attempt to characterize beauty as if it were ontologically a property of objects considered on their own and insists that beauty lies in a relation to us or creatures like us:

In the things themselves, without relation to representing and feeling beings, nothing is *beautiful*. In this word there already lies the original influence of an object on enjoyment, I therefore cannot think of any object as *beautiful* without also representing a being who feels it, and if I speak of a thing as beautiful in itself I am deceiving myself and introducing a whole series of circular explanations.[32]

He argues, for instance, that the beauty of a Mozart or Haydn sonata simply cannot be understood "without relation to the sensitivity of yourself or another, without regard to a being who is interested in the imitation of feelings, harmony, and rhythm in series of tones."[33] Moritz's conception of perfection within the object, or of purely internal purposiveness, fails to do justice to the most obvious ontological fact about beauty, which is precisely that it consists in the appeal of an object, for one reason or another, to creatures with faculties of sense, understanding, and feeling like our own.

Heydenreich uses this critique of Moritz to prepare the way for his own theory that the specific beauty of works of art lies in their "relation to a being whose sensitivity they can pleasantly touch" by means of their capacity for expressing emotions.[34] Kant does not adopt this particular conception of the appeal of art. He agrees with Heydenreich in explicitly rejecting the rationalist explanation of the pleasure of beauty as arising from the perception of perfection through a sensory grasp of concepts, which was still employed by Mendelssohn, but Kant clearly retains the latter's sense of the fundamental complexity of our response to art. For this reason his position also represents a clear rejection of the simplistic position of Moritz, whose conception of the *internal* purposiveness of the beautiful work of art is replaced by the similar-sounding but very different and firmly relational conception of the *subjective* purposiveness of beautiful objects, both natural and artistic, as a foundation on which a complex account of our response to art can be erected.[35]

## III. KANT

Like much else in the *Critique of Judgment*, Kant's insight into the complex structure of our response to art is not well served by his exposition. The opening stage of his analysis looks like a paradox resolved by a verbal trick. On the one hand, Kant's general analysis of aesthetic judgment emphasizes that all genuine judgments of taste "must determine the object in regard to delight and the predicate of beauty independently of concepts" (*CJ*, §9, 5:231). That is, they cannot be grounded upon the subsumption of their object under any determinate concept or even, as Kant sometimes insists, upon the use of any concept to recognize any significant content in the object (cf. e.g., *CJ*, §3, 5:207). On the other hand, Kant analyzes a work of art as the result of "production through freedom, i.e., through a capacity for choice [*Willkür*] which grounds its actions in reason" (*CJ*, §43, 5:303) or in an exercise of intentional agency that, unlike, for instance, the agency of bees, must be guided by concepts. He then insists that "one must be conscious that a product of fine art is art and not nature" (*CJ*, §45, 5:306), which would seem to mean that one must recognize the intentionality of the work of art by connecting it to the concepts which guided that intentionality. Kant's first move is to try to reconcile these apparently contradictory requirements for the perception of beauty in art simply by turning the paradox into its own solution:

> Nature was beautiful when it also appeared as if it were art; and now art can only be called beautiful if we are conscious that it is art and yet it appears to us as nature. . . . The purposiveness in the product of fine art, although it is certainly intentional, must therefore not appear to be intentional; i.e., fine art must be able *to be regarded* as nature although one is still conscious of it as art. (*CJ*, §45, 5:306–7)

This passage has certainly been influential in the subsequent history of aesthetics.[36] Yet its insistence that we must somehow juggle our awareness of the intentionality inherent in works of art, and therefore the concepts embodied by them, with the simultaneous suppression of this awareness is entirely unnecessary. Instead, Kant's subsequent, more detailed discussion of fine art shows that in the paradigmatic case of a work of genius (for instance, the infinitely suggestive embodiment of an inexhaustible idea of reason in a poem or visual symbol), we can be conscious of the conception which is embodied in a work of art and of the concepts which typically constitute its content without sacrificing the freedom of the imagination which is the source of our pleasure in the beauty, indeed, that the freedom of the imagination of both the artist and the audience of a work lies precisely in the way that the form of a work of art gives expression to a concept but goes beyond anything that could be derived by any rule furnished by that or any other concept. In arguing that our pleasure in a work of art is ultimately grounded in our favorable response to both its content and the freedom of the imagination which takes its form beyond that content while harmonizing with it, Kant does justice to Mendelssohn's recognition that we take pleasure in both what a work of art represents and how it represents it but without relapsing into Mendelssohn's metaphysics of perfection. Both the content and the form of a work of genius provide infinite satisfaction of cognitive and moral objectives of our own without sacrificing the freedom of the imagination which is essential to the aesthetic, as would happen if this form and content were subsumed under objective concepts of perfection as Kant understands the latter.

In order to fully appreciate Kant's complex but nonparadoxical reinterpretation of the tradition represented by Mendelssohn, we must briefly review some of the basic claims of Kant's analysis of aesthetic judgments.[37] Kant's argument can be regarded as beginning from an analysis of the concept of an aesthetic judgment itself. As a form of *judgment* like any other, an aesthetic judgment raises a claim to intersubjective agreement which is not defeated by adding the qualifying expression "to me" to it (*CJ*, §7, 212); but as a judgment which is *aesthetic*, it must in some sense both concern and be made on the basis of a feeling which is necessarily subjective and cannot be transformed into any ordinary predicate for the cognition of an object (see *FI*, §VIII, 20:228). Our feeling of pleasure (or pain) is the only such feeling, so an (affirmative) aesthetic judgment (for instance, a judgment of beauty) must be one which ascribes an intersubjectively valid response of pleasure to an object on the basis of nothing other than an experience of that pleasure itself, or one "the ground of determination of which lies in a sensation which is immediately connected with the feeling of pleasure and displeasure" (*FI*, §VIII, 20:224; see also *CJ*, §1, 5:203–4, and *Metaphysics of Morals*, 6:211–12).

This basic analysis of the aesthetic judgment implies that it cannot be grounded on the subsumption of an object under any determinate concept applying to that object, for then that concept rather than the feeling itself would be the ground of the judgment. We do not find a flower beautiful because we classify it as a good reproductive organ and have a reason for approving of something so classified. This leads directly to Kant's rejection of the view that an aesthetic judgment is based on the recognition of a perfection in its object, whether by means of the senses or otherwise, for such a recognition always requires the subsumption of the object under a concept of that perfection. This rejection is most elaborately stated in Section 15 of the *Critique of Judgment* but most straightforwardly argued in the "First Introduction" to the *Critique of Judgment*. Here Kant explicitly examines the "definition of pleasure as the sensory representation of the *perfection* of an object," distinguished from "other logical judgments" only, "as is alleged, by the confusion which attaches to the concept (which is what some presume to call sensibility)" (*FI*, §VIII, 20:226). He argues that the concept of perfection may be understood in two senses, either as a purely "ontological concept" of the "mere completeness of the manifold insofar as it collectively constitutes a unity" or as such a unity which is in addition subsumed under "the concept of something as a goal," whether a "practical goal," that is, something conceived of as an end by practical reason, or a merely "technical" goal, that is, something recommended by theoretical reason as a means to some antecedent end (*FI*, §VIII, 20:228). In the case of the merely ontological conception of something as a perfection, not only must an object be subsumed under a concept in order to be cognized as a perfection, in violation of the analysis of aesthetic judgment, but in any case such a "subordination . . . has not the least to do with the feeling of pleasure and pain." In contrast, the judgment of something as an "objective perfection" which is also an end or goal "presupposes or includes a pleasure in the existence of the object" but requires the subsumption of the object under the concept of that determinate end as a condition of taking pleasure in it (*FI*, §VIII, 20:228). So in neither case can a judgment of perfection be equivalent to an aesthetic judgment. Even where such a judgment has anything to do with pleasure at all, it must be grounded on a concept of the object, whether that is clearly represented or not, and that is excluded by the analysis of aesthetic judgment.[38]

Yet Kant is far from thinking that this rejection of perfectionism means that the pleasure of aesthetic response is not to be explained by the relation of beautiful objects to fundamental human objectives. Rather, he holds that every feeling of pleasure (or at least every such feeling which is not to be explained entirely in merely physiological terms) must be seen as connected with the satisfaction of some objective. And if the pleasure in an object of taste is to be universally valid, then the objective which it somehow satisfies must also be, although if the object is to be found pleasing apart from its subsumption under the concept of any determinate goal then this objective cannot be one of empirical or pure practical reason. Thus Kant reaches the fundamental premise in his explanation of our pleasure in beauty, that it must arise from a condition which serves as the satisfaction of the fundamental aim of cognition yet without the subsumption of an object under a concept:

> The attainment of every aim is connected with the feeling of pleasure; and if the condition of the former is an *a priori* repre-

sentation . . . then the feeling of pleasure will also be determined through an *a priori* ground and as valid for everyone:
and indeed only through the relation of the object to the
faculty of cognition, without the concept of purposiveness
taking the least regard for the faculty of desire and therefore
entirely distinguishing itself from all practical purposiveness
of nature. (*CJ*, §VI, 5:187)

Kant is thus led to characterize the most fundamental level of
the pleasurable experience of beauty as arising from a feeling
that an object satisfies our basic aim for cognition without the
subsumption of the object under any determinate concept of
the object which would guarantee such satisfaction. Indeed,
Kant suggests, the absence of such a concept can be seen not
only as a requirement of the analysis of aesthetic judgment
but also as a consequence of this explanation of beauty to
which the analysis leads, for although the feeling of pleasure
is dependent upon a sense of "agreement with our faculty of
cognition," it is also noticeable only where there is a sense
that this agreement is "contingent" (CJ, §VI, 5:188), and the
subsumption of the object under any determinate concept
would undermine precisely this sense of contingency.

  Kant tries to characterize the condition in which the perception of a beautiful object pleasurably satisfies the fundamental aim of cognition without the use of a determinate concept
in a variety of ways, which are variants of the general claim
that in this experience the faculty of judgment "perceives a
relation of the two cognitive faculties," imagination and understanding, "which is the subjective, merely sensitive condition of the objective use of judgment (namely the harmony of
these two faculties with each other) in general" (FI, §VIII,
20:223–4). The gist of his explanation appears to be that the
subjective aim of cognition is the unification of our manifolds
of intuition as such, where the imagination presents manifolds and the understanding seeks unity, and that the subjective satisfaction of this aim, or the "subjective condition" of
cognition in general, is a feeling that the unity of the manifold offered to the imagination by an object constitutes a

unity even though that unity or organization is not seen as dictated by the ordinary working of the understanding, namely the subsumption of the manifold under any concept of a sort of object it is supposed to constitute or represent. Thus, although an oil refinery may appear to be an ugly jumble of pipes the unity of which can only be recognized by an engineer who understands their function, the soaring beauty of the Chrysler Building offers us a sense of unity entirely independent of any understanding of the requirements of structural engineering or New York's 1917 zoning law. Kant characterizes this condition as one of *subjective purposiveness*, meaning precisely that a beautiful object satisfies the fundamental *subjective purpose* of cognition without being brought under a determinate concept, in particular of any determinate end or *objective purpose*. The pleasure in a beautiful object "can express nothing other than its suitability to the faculties of cognition which are in play in reflective judgment, so far as they are in play, therefore merely a subjective formal purposiveness of the object" (*CJ*, §VII, 5:189–90).

Thus Kant rejects Mendelssohn's explanation of aesthetic pleasure as a response to the sensory perception of objective perfections. But he also rejects Moritz's strategy of simply positing a – vacuous – purposiveness in the object considered in itself. Instead, Kant explains the sense of beauty as due to the fact that an object seems to satisfy one of our most fundamental objectives, the goal of cognition itself, although without the usual mechanism of subsumption under a concept. Such a relation can be characterized as subjective purposiveness because it is the satisfaction of a purpose in the subject and also a satisfaction through merely subjective rather than objective means. Aesthetic response is unique, but that does not imply that it is not to be explained in terms of even more fundamental human goals and values.[39]

On Kant's full account of aesthetic judgment, beautiful objects are not only subjectively purposive for cognition. They are also subjectively purposive for morality or practical reason, in the sense of serving the interest of morality without being subsumed under any determinate moral concept, let alone judged to have been designed to advance any determinate interest of morality. The key to this additional argument is Kant's further description of the response to beauty as one involving not just the harmony of imagination with the understanding but the *freedom* of the imagination. As he puts it, "everything comes down to the concept of taste as the faculty for the estimation of an object in relation to the *free lawfulness* of the imagination" (*CJ*, §22 General Remark, 5:240). He thus interprets the aesthetic sense of unity in the absence of a concept as an experience of *freedom from constraint by concepts*. Kant can then argue that aesthetic response can furnish us with something which morality requires but (as he had stressed in the *Critique of Practical Reason* two years earlier) cannot furnish itself, namely an experience of freedom – although aesthetic response furnishes us with this experience only insofar as it is free of any direct constraint from outside the imagination, including a direct constraint by moral concepts themselves. Of course, this experience of freedom is an experience of the freedom of the imagination, not the will (*CJ*, §59, 5:354), so beauty, through the character of our experience of it, can furnish only a "symbolic" rather than "schematic" (that is, literal) representation (*CJ*, §59, 5:351) of the morally good; but in this way the "beautiful is the symbol of the morally good," and indeed, Kant adds, "It is also only in this respect (a relation which is natural to everyone, and which may also be imputed to everyone as a duty) that it pleases with a claim to the agreement of everyone else" (*CJ*, §59, 5:353).

This is Kant's most general account of the dual purposiveness of the beautiful for both cognition and morality, and it captures, without the metaphysics of rationalism, the insight of Mendelssohn's most basic distinction. The free harmony of the imagination and understanding that is induced by reflection on a beautiful object takes over the role of the perfection of representations as themselves affirmative properties of the soul; and the symbolic representation of the freedom of the will, which is essential to morality through the experience of the freedom of the imagination in the feeling of beauty, puts this cognitive condition into the service of the most fundamental form of human value, Kant's substitute for the objective perfection of the rationalist universe, without violating its uniqueness. For reasons which are revealing but not compelling, Kant confines this account to natural beauty, but there is no fundamental reason why it cannot be extended to artistic beauty as well.[40] But Kant also has a more particular account of how works of fine art can be subjectively purposive for both cognition and morality that preserves even more of the substance of Mendelssohn's insight into art without its metaphysical trappings. I will turn to that now.

As we saw, Kant holds that making an aesthetic judgment on a work of art requires conceptualizing it as the product of intentional agency which is itself guided by concepts, yet at the same time suggests that this recognition of the intentionality that is expressed in the artwork must be suppressed in responding to the beauty of an artwork (*CJ*, §45). However, Kant's analysis of aesthetic response contains resources to avoid this paradoxical suggestion, and in Kant's most detailed discussion of fine art he fully exploits those resources, although without announcing that he is doing so. Here he comes closest to incorporating Mendelssohn's insight into the complex experience of art into his own nonmetaphysical account.

Immediately after attacking the rationalist theory of perfection in Section 15 of the *Critique*, Kant introduces a distinction between *free* beauty, which "presupposes no concept of what the object ought to be," and *merely dependent* or *conditioned* (*bedingte*) beauty, which does conceive of objects "as standing under the concept of a particular purpose" (*CJ*, §16, 5:229). Kant does deny that the latter kind of beauty (which he illustrates primarily with works of human artistry, such as a church or an arsenal, where the intended purpose of the object constrains aesthetically acceptable forms for it) is the object of *pure* judgments of taste, but, contrary to what one might expect, he does *not* deny that dependent beauty is a kind of beauty at all. He merely says that in this case the judgment of taste is "restricted" by a purpose (*CJ*, §16, 5:230).

This suggests that dependent beauty is "conditioned," in the sense that the concept of the object's intended purpose places some restraint on the freedom of the imagination in responding to it, but that this concept is not sufficient to determine the form of the object. The concept of the object leaves its form indefinite although within limits, and thus leaves room for freedom of the imagination in the production of and response to forms consistent with this purpose. The medieval requirement that a cathedral have a cruciform floor plan, for instance, excludes some forms of building for churches altogether, but hardly suffices to determine the form of a beautiful cathedral. Both beautiful and indifferent or ugly buildings can satisfy this requirement, so the difference between those which are beautiful and those which are not must lie in the way that the perceptual form of the former but not the latter induces a harmony of imagination and understanding within the limits of the underlying concept of a cathedral, or, one might also say, in the way the form of a beautiful cathedral goes above and beyond any idea of the form which could be dictated by the mere concept of a cathedral. Only in this way can we explain why dependent beauty is still a kind of beauty at all. But if this is so, then recognition of the concept under which an object with dependent beauty is to be subsumed may constrain the imagination but hardly deprives it of its freedom to produce or respond to beautiful forms. It just sets the imagination the more difficult task of finding its freedom within limits.

On this analysis of dependent beauty, there is no need to suppress the conceptualization of the object in order to enjoy its beauty. One recognizes the classification of the object and even the constraints it implies, yet still feels the freedom of the imagination – indeed, feels it precisely in the way in which it goes beyond these restraints while conforming to them. And although Kant does not explicitly refer to his concept of dependent beauty in his discussion of works of genius as the paradigmatic products of fine art, this is the model of aesthetic response that he there employs. Paradigmatic works of fine art are works of artists with genius. As rational agents, artists have conceptions of the ends to be fulfilled by their works, of themes to be expressed by them, and of forms to be given to their works in order to express these themes and fulfill these goals. Yet genius, as a gift of nature, manifests itself precisely in the way in which the harmony of form and the harmony between form and content in what artists produce go above and beyond anything that could be derived from any rule implied by any of these concepts. In the case of genius, Kant states, the imagination "is free to provide, beyond agreement with the concept, an unsought wealth of undeveloped material for the understanding, of which this did not take account in its concept, which it therefore applies not objectively for cognition, but subjectively for the quickening of the cognitive powers" (*CJ*, §49, 5:317). The audience for a work of artistic genius can therefore respond both to the concepts the work embodies and to the freedom of the imagination that it represents and induces in themselves, without having to suppress either.[41]

Kant suggests these points in his most extensive analysis of genius. We find, he says,

> that as a talent for art it must presuppose a determinate concept of its product as a purpose, thus understanding, but also an (even if indeterminate) representation of the material, i.e., intuition, for the presentation of this concept, thus a relation of the imagination to the understanding; [second], that it does not reveal itself in the execution of the given purpose in the presentation of a determinate *concept* as much as in the delivery or expression of *aesthetic ideas*, which contain rich material for that aim, thus the imagination represents itself in its freedom from all guidance by rules but nevertheless as purposive for the presentation of the given concept; finally, . . . that the unsought, unintentional subjective purposiveness in the free harmony of the imagination with the lawfulness of the understanding presupposes a proportion and disposition of this faculty which cannot be brought about by any following of a rule, whether of science or mechanical imitation, but only by the nature of the subject. (*CJ*, §49, 5:317–18)

The key elements of this account are that a work of art is typically an intentional representation of a theme in a form or medium suited to that theme, but that neither the richness of the theme itself nor the most suitable form for its expression can be derived from any determinate concepts or rules. To go back to our example of the cruciform cathedral – and, obviously, to distribute the work of genius over a series of artists rather than a single one – genius would manifest itself in the recognition that the form of the instrument of Christ's death could itself serve as a symbol of the inexhaustible content of a religion; in the recognition that the floor plan of a Roman basilica could be transformed into an infinitely variable representation of this symbol; and, finally, in the choice or discovery of one particular form from the infinite variety of forms of, for example, windows and columns that will make a building into a beautiful cathedral. Our response to a work of art so produced can thus be seen to be a complex pleasure arising from recognition of its kind and content on the one hand, but also from the freedom of the imagination in the way it goes beyond these, on the other.

The freedom of the imagination in response to a work of genius is not just a response to the subjective purposiveness of its relation between form and content, but also a response to the way in which the content itself has a richness exceeding any rules. This is part of what Kant is saying by calling the content of such a work an "aesthetic idea," for such an idea is characterized as "a representation of the imagination associated with a given concept, which is connected with such a manifold of partial representations in the free use of that faculty that no expression designating a determinate concept can be found, which therefore adds much that cannot be named to a concept, [and] the feeling of which quickens the cognitive faculty" (*CJ*, §49, 5:316). The kind of unified yet inexhaustible richness which produces the sense of harmony between imagination and understanding is found not just in the relation between form and content in a true work of fine art, but within the content as well, and here too we are given a complex set of relationships to which to respond with the pleasure of beauty.

Kant's introduction of the notion of the aesthetic idea adds another dimension to his analysis of our complex response to art. Kant assumes that the central concepts in aesthetic ideas will typically be "concepts of reason (intellectual ideas)," that is, ideas about morality and the moral properties of humans and higher beings, such as "the kingdom of the blessed, hell, . . . envy, and all vices, as also love, fame, and the like" (*CJ*, §49, 5:314). Works of art are thus purposive for morality not merely by offering a general experience of freedom of the imagination which can symbolize moral freedom of the will, but also by illustrating specific moral conceptions yet still without surrendering the freedom of the imagination.

Kant does not offer any specific argument for his claim that the content of fine art typically consists of ideas connected with morality, or indeed for his underlying assumption that works of art typically have not just a guiding concept but a *content* as well. One argument for this assumption must have seemed so obvious to him that it needed no statement: Art is the product of human agency, human agents have an inescapable concern with morality, and that will manifest itself in their art as well as every other form of their expression. A second thought is more explicit, however. Following his classification of the fine arts which itself follows his discussion of genius, Kant observes that "if the fine arts are not brought into near or distant connection with moral ideas, which are alone accompanied by a self-sufficient delight," the same fate awaits them as awaits mere sensations of charm, namely that over a period of time they will "make the spirit dull, the object gradually repulsive and the mind dissatisfied with itself because of its consciousness that its disposition is contrary to the purpose of reason" (*CJ*, §52, 5:326). Two thoughts are suggested. First, we will eventually turn against any pleasure that does not ultimately serve morality. Second, the pleasure of art, perhaps precisely because it rests on an element of cognitive contingency that is a bit like surprise, cannot sustain itself in the way only the pleasure of morality itself in

fact can; so if we want the pleasure in art to be truly enduring, it must be connected with the latter. For these reasons,
there must be some connection to morality in the content of
art, but art does not have to sacrifice the freedom of imagination to establish this connection, and we can without contradiction take both moral and more purely aesthetic pleasure in
a truly accomplished work of art.

It should now be clear that Kant rejects Mendelssohn's
metaphysics of perfectionism without lapsing into Moritz's
conception of the purely internal purposiveness of the work
of art, the untenable idea that a work of art has a value
because of a purpose in itself unconnected with our own
most fundamental purposes. Instead, Kant's theory of the
subjective purposiveness of the beautiful in general and fine
art in particular holds that beautiful works of art serve our
underlying purposes in both cognition and morality in a
way uniquely characterized by the freedom of the imagination. In responding to a work of genius, we can take pleasure in the freedom of imagination in its response to the
form of the work as well as to the moral significance of its
content, and the experience of this freedom can serve as a
more general symbol of morality itself. Finally, although
Kant does not make this point explicit, we can respond to
the existence of genius itself as a sign of cooperation between nature and our own aims (see *CJ*, §42); this can stand
as a parallel to Mendelssohn's recognition of our admiration
of the artistry that lies behind a work of art. In offering this
complex account of the subjective purposiveness – if not ontological perfections – of art, Kant is obviously placing the
Enlightenment's recognition of the connection between art
and the most fundamental values of human life on foundations that can withstand his own critique of metaphysics but
certainly not isolating art from the rest of our lives. Kant is
not an advocate of art for art's sake, but of art for our sake.

# Chapter 5

# Hegel on Kant's aesthetics: necessity and contingency in beauty and art

The differences between the aesthetic theories of Kant and Hegel are both less, and greater, than meet the eye. In Hegel's fullest account of his understanding of the place of art in absolute spirit, the posthumously published *Lectures on Fine Art*,[1] it first looks as if Hegel has overstated the similarity between Kant's analysis of pure aesthetic judgments of beauty and his own conception of the theoretical significance of works of art; the interpenetration of concept and object which is central to Hegel's account of art and which he also claims to find in Kant's analysis of pure aesthetic judgment is not really there, although something which sounds similar – namely, harmony between our *faculties* of concepts and intuitions – is. However, when we turn from Kant's initial analysis of pure aesthetic judgments to his more developed theory, especially (but not only) of art, it may look as if Hegel may even have understated the similarity between his own account and Kant's. Kant's fully developed conception of art and aesthetic experience is not the exercise in formalism that might have been expected from his initial analysis of aesthetic judgment, but insists upon a deep connection between the experience of beauty, and sometimes the perceptible form of a work of art,

This essay was originally presented as an address at a conference on Hegel and the third *Critique*, organized by the Internationale Hegel-Vereinigung at Fiecht, Austria, in May 1989. It was originally published in *Hegel und die "Kritik der Urteilskraft,"* ed. Hans-Friedrich Fulda and Rolf-Peter Horstmann, Veröffentlichungen der Internationalen Hegel-Vereinigung, no. 18 (Stuttgart: Klett-Cotta, 1990), pp. 81–99. Reprinted with permission.

and an idea of reason, in terms that sound very much like Hegel's own. There is one essential difference, however. For Kant, the idea which must interpenetrate the work of art is a moral idea, indeed perhaps the idea of morality itself, whereas for Hegel it is something much less particular, something more like the broader, metaphysical idea of spirit's entire relation to the world. So there is an element of necessity, indeed one might also say urgency, in Kant's account of art and beauty that Hegel seems to omit, namely the necessity that, without sacrificing its disinterestedness or becoming didactic, art be final for the purpose of morality. Yet, even when Kant's concept of the moral necessity of art and beauty is understood, there is a way in which Hegel's ultimate criticism that Kant's conception of the aesthetic contains an unreconciled element of subjectivity, an insuperable chasm between our internal condition and the world, remains in place – not as the diagnosis of some simple, isolated mistake in Kant, to be sure, but rather as evidence of a profound difference between these two philosophers' conceptions of mankind's place in, or perhaps better, its hold or grasp on the world. The comparison between Kant's and Hegel's conceptions of art is not an exercise in academic aesthetics but leads straight to the underlying difference in *Weltanschauung* which grounds so many of their more particular disagreements.

These assertions will be refined, as well as illustrated, in what follows. Before turning to details, however, it may be useful to have one text before us. Hegel summarizes his discussion of the four "moments" of Kant's analysis of pure aesthetic judgment as follows:

Now what we find in all these Kantian propositions is an inseparability of what in all other cases is presupposed in our consciousness as distinct. This cleavage finds itself canceled in the beautiful, where universal and particular, end and means, concept and object, perfectly interpenetrate one another. Thus Kant sees the beauty of *art* after all as a correspondence in which the particular accords with the concept. Particulars as such are *prima facie* accidental, alike to one another and to the

universal; and precisely this accidental element – sense, feeling, emotion, inclination – is now not simply, in the beauty of
art, *subsumed* under universal categories of the understanding,
and *dominated* by the concept of freedom in its abstract universality, but is so bound up with the universal that it is inwardly
and absolutely adequate to it. Therefore thought is incarnate in
the beauty of art . . . so that nature and freedom, sense and
concept, find their right and satisfaction all in one. But this
apparently perfect reconciliation is still supposed by Kant at
the last to be only subjective in respect of the judgment and the
production [of art], and not itself to be absolutely true and
actual. (*WA* 13:88–9; Knox 1:60)

This paragraph touches all three points I want to make. First,
Hegel creatively misinterprets Kant's analysis of aesthetic response and judgment. For Kant, a beautiful object suggests
the contingent satisfaction of both imagination and understanding but contains no actual interpenetration of concept
and object. Second, however, successful art especially, but
also aesthetic experience more generally, do indeed make
incarnate – or at least, as Kant would say, make sensible – an
idea of reason, although not (*pace* Hegel) the idea in the
abstract, but the idea of freedom and morality in particular.
But third, even so, there remains an element of contingency
or subjectivity in Kant's account of the link between aesthetics and morality that Hegel cannot endure. For Kant it is, to
be sure, necessary for us to strive to be free through reason
and morality, but it is in some sense contingent that the
world is receptive to our freedom as well as to the production
of art capable of representing this freedom. For Kant, neither
our harmony with the world around us nor our harmonious
representation of our relation to the world is as inevitable an
outcome of the evolution of the spirit as Hegel would have it.

## I. HEGEL'S TRANSFORMATION OF KANT

Let us begin with Hegel's exposition of the four moments of
Kant's analytic of the beautiful. Hegel's account is hardly

inaccurate, but it does introduce elements which are in fact absent from Kant's analysis of pure aesthetic judgment. These additions, however, are not simply Hegelian misinterpretations which are altogether alien to the spirit of Kant's aesthetics. On the contrary, they do anticipate aspects of Kant's expanded conception of the aesthetic which are not included in the initial conception of pure judgments of beauty that Hegel is ostensibly discussing.

Hegel's account of each of the four moments starts off sounding very much like Kant's own assertions. He starts off with the general statement that

> Kant interprets the *aesthetic* judgment as proceeding neither from the understanding as such, as the faculty of concepts, nor from the sensible intuition and its variegated manifold as such, but rather from the free play of understanding and imagination. In this harmony [*Einhelligkeit*] of the cognitive faculties the object is related to the subject and its feeling of pleasure and delight. (*WA* 13:85; Knox 1:58)

This is a textbook rendition of Kant's conception of pure aesthetic response, or the feeling which underlies and is expressed by a judgment that an object is beautiful. Each of Hegel's subsequent descriptions of the four moments of the pure judgment of taste also begins with a textbook formulation. Hegel begins his descriptions of the disinterestedness, universality, merely formal purposiveness, and exemplary necessity of the beautiful in terms which do not seem to differ significantly from Kant's own. First, he says, "this delight is to be without all interest, that is, *without relation* to our *faculty of desire*. . . . The aesthetic judgment lets the external presence [*Vorhandene*] subsist freely for itself and proceeds out of a pleasure to which the object accords on its own account" (*WA* 13:86; Knox 1:58). Second, he reports, Kant says that the beautiful "should be that which, without a concept, that is a category of the understanding, is represented as the object of a *universal* pleasure. . . . The beautiful . . . should awaken a universal delight immediately without such a relation" of correspondence to a universal concept (*WA*, 13:86–7; Knox 1:58). Third, he reports, "The beautiful should have the form of *purposiveness* insofar as the purposiveness is perceived in the object without any representation of a purpose" (*WA* 13:87; Knox 1:59). "Finally," he says, "the Kantian consideration of the beautiful affirms fourthly that it is acknowledged without a concept as the object of a *necessary* delight. . . . Such a necessity of delight the beautiful has entirely in itself without relation to concepts, that is, to categories of the understanding" (*WA* 13:87–8; Knox 1:59–60). None of these characterizations departs from Kant's own formulations (see *CJ*, §§5, 9, 11, 17, 18, and 22).

However, in at least three of these four cases Hegel also adds a gloss that subtly transforms Kant's own account. In these glosses, rather than conforming to Kant's stated view that our response to a beautiful object is independent of any connection to concepts and ends whatever, Hegel suggests that the beautiful object contains a concept or an end in itself, although in a connection of unusual intimacy with rather than separation from it. Thus, he does not just say that disinterested pleasure lets the external object subsist freely by itself, but adds that such a pleasure "allows the object to have its end in itself" (*WA* 13:86; Knox 1:58). Next, in glossing the universal validity of pleasure in the beautiful, he adds that "in the consideration of the beautiful we are not conscious of the concept and of the subsumption under it, and the separation of the individual object and universal concept, which is otherwise present in judgment, does not occur here" (*WA* 13:87; Knox 1:59). The same idea, that is, that the beautiful object presents a concept and its object in a special relation of intimacy rather than separation, is also present in his gloss on Kant's conception of merely formal purposiveness. Here Hegel says that "the beautiful . . . exists as purposiveness in itself, without means and end showing themselves separated as different sides" (*WA* 13:87; Knox 1:59). Finally, although the terms of the relation are less clear in the final moment, perhaps Hegel also intimates the idea that the beautiful is distinguished not by its independence of concepts but rather precisely by its unusual intimacy with a concept, in his gloss on Kant's conception of exemplary necessity: "Necessity," he says, "is an abstract category and indicates an internally essential relation of two sides" (*WA* 13:87–8; Knox 1:59). But even if not in this last case then certainly in the first three, Hegel seems to depart from Kant's view. Whereas for Kant our response to beauty involves our *faculty* for concepts but no particular empirical or categorial concepts whatever, Hegel's idea seems to be instead that a beautiful object is distinguished precisely by the way in which it presents a concept, perhaps a concept of the end of the object, as inseparable from the object. In ordinary experience, it would seem to be suggested, we are not conscious of concept and object as inseparable, and it at least seems to us as if we can be aware of an object without a, or a particular, concept of it, and conversely that we can contemplate a concept without simultaneous acquaintance with any, let alone a necessary, instantiation of it; but in our response to a beautiful object Hegel's view seems to be that we must be conscious of the inseparability of the object and some, indeed presumably some particular concept in (and perhaps of) it.

While Hegel's account of Kant's analysis of pure aesthetic judgment obviously prepares the way for his own theory of art as "mediating the freely reconciled totality" of the "idea" as its content and "sensible, imaginable configuration" (*sinnliche bildliche Gestaltung*) as its form (WA 13:100; Knox 1:70), it also certainly seems to mischaracterize Kant's analysis and explanation of our response to beauty, and in so doing to suggest an element of necessity in a response that Kant characterizes precisely in terms of its apparent contingency. This is evident both from Kant's typical choice of examples of objects of pure aesthetic judgment and from several aspects of his theory of the beautiful.

As far as his examples are concerned, it is clear that Kant is attempting to illustrate the nonconceptual nature of pure aesthetic judgment by choosing objects which, whether natural or artificial, are appreciated independently of both classifica-

tion and interpretation: We need neither to have a *concept of*
nor find a *concept in* an object of a pure judgment of taste in
order to find it beautiful. Thus, in his initial contrast between
judgments of the beautiful and judgments about the good,
Kant says that "flowers, free designs, lines intertwining without aim, under the name of foliage" (note that the list suggests both naturally and artificially produced patterns) "sig-
nify nothing, depend on no determinate concept, and yet
please" (*CJ*, §4, 5:207). Kant's assertion that such objects "sig-
nify nothing" seems to deny precisely that these beautiful
objects have any conceptualizable content at all, let alone a
content which seems inevitably inseparable from their form,
and the claim that they depend on no concept suggests that
our response to them is independent of any conception of
them or their appropriate classification, let alone any conception of them that is as it were inevitably suggested by their
appearance.

The same sorts of examples recur when Kant subsequently
contrasts "free beauty" to "beauty which is merely dependent." Here again Kant emphasizes products of both nature
and art which are appreciated independently of classification
as well as interpretation, whether in terms of function or
content. Thus, "flowers are free beauties of nature," and
even a botanist who knows the function of the flower "pays
no attention [to it] when he judges it by means of taste," and
the same goes for birds and crustacea. Moving from the natural to the artificial, "designs *à la grecque*, foliage for borders
and wallpapers," and "musical fantasias (without a theme),
and indeed all music without text" please "freely and in themselves" while "representing nothing, no object under a determinate concept" (*CJ*, §16, 5:229). None of these paradigmatically beautiful objects displays an exceptionally intimate
connection with a concept or an end, a connection even more
inseparable than that between concept and object in ordinary
quotidian or scientific experience. On the contrary, our experience of these objects as beautiful is supposed to be utterly
independent of any application of a concept to the object or
any awareness of the applicability of a concept to the object.

Kant's theoretical statements about pure aesthetic judgment, as well as his examples of it, are also incompatible with Hegel's glosses on his analysis. As Hegel's opening (but not concluding) statement suggested, Kant explains our pleasure in the beautiful in terms of an unusual harmony between our *faculties* for conceptualization and sensuous representation, that is, understanding and imagination, but not in terms of a special relationship between the usual *products* of these faculties, that is, concepts and sensible representations of objects. Many passages make this point; a few will have to stand for the rest. We can take one from what is apparently Kant's first attempt to explicate his mature theory of taste, the essay often called the "First Introduction" to the *Critique of Judgment:*

> But since in mere reflection on a perception it is not a matter of reflecting on a determinate concept but in general only of reflecting on the rule of perception to aid the understanding, as a faculty of concepts, it can be seen that in a merely reflective judgment imagination and understanding are considered in the relationship in which they must stand to one another in the judgment generally, in contrast to the relation in which they really stand in the case of a given perception. (*FI*, §VII, 20:220)

For the sake of variety, we can consider another passage from one of Kant's later expositions, the account of aesthetic judgment which immediately precedes his attempt to give a transcendental deduction of judgments of taste. Here Kant unmistakably emphasizes his view that aesthetic response involves our faculty for conceptualization but no particular concept whatever:

> But the judgment of taste is not determinable through concepts, so it is grounded only on the subjective formal conditions of a judgment in general. The subjective condition of all judgments is the faculty for judging itself, or the power of judgment. Employed in regard to a representation through which an object is given, this requires the agreement of two powers of representation: namely of the imagination (for its

intuition and the combination of the manifold thereof) and the understanding (for the concept of the representation of the unity of this combination). Now since no concept of the object lies at the base of the judgment in this case, it can only consist in the subsumption of the power of imagination itself (in the case of a representation through which an object is given) under the condition that the understanding in general advance from intuition to concepts. That is, just because the freedom of the imagination consists in the fact that it schematizes without a concept, the judgment of taste must rest on a mere sensation of the mutually enlivening imagination in its *freedom* and understanding with its *lawfulness*. (*CJ*, §35, 5:287; see also §VII, 5:190, and §9, 5:217, 219)

In each of these passages, Kant insists that our response to the beautiful involves some form of harmony between our capacity for sensible representation and our capacity for conceptual unification that does not involve the actual application of any particular concept to the object or the recognition of a concept in it. The uniqueness of aesthetic experience lies precisely in the fact that imagination can somehow satisfy the understanding's ordinary demand for unity without the ordinary means for fulfilling this demand, namely, a concept. In Hegel's own terms, Kant's explanation of aesthetic response is "subjective" precisely in the sense that it postulates a certain condition of our cognitive faculties without any room for the sort of concepts that would ordinarily be produced as well as applied by these faculties.

Perhaps Hegel is not the only one to blame for his misinterpretation of Kant. Some of Kant's own turns of phrase suggest that our response to beauty involves not just our faculty for concepts but also some sort of general, indeterminate concept. Thus, the paragraph following that last cited from the "First Introduction" carries the argument on thus:

If, then, the form of a given object is so produced in empirical intuition that the *apprehension* of its manifold in the imagination agrees with the presentation of a concept of the understanding (regardless of which concept), then in mere reflection under-

standing and imagination mutually harmonize for the furtherance of their business, and the object is perceived as purposive
for the power of judgment alone, thus its purposiveness itself
is considered merely subjective. (*FI*, §VII, 20:220–1)

And, immediately following his first use of the example of
flowers and foliage in Section 4, Kant goes on to state that "the
delight in the beautiful must depend upon reflection on an
object which leads to some concept ([it is] indeterminate
which) and is thereby differentiated from the agreeable,
which rests entirely on sensation" (*CJ*, §4, 5:207). In Section 9
(5:217), he says that in the case of the free play of the imagination and understanding no "determinate concept restricts
them to a particular rule of cognition"; this at least leaves room
for the thought that an indeterminate concept – whatever
that would be – might be involved. Given such statements, it
would not be unreasonable for Hegel to think that Kant must
believe that the beautiful always involves a concept; and then
it would also be reasonable for Hegel to suggest that Kant's
idea that the beautiful involves either an arbitrary or an indeterminate concept should be replaced with the theory that the
beautiful is always a sensuous embodiment of the very abstract but still specific metaphysical concept which Hegel will
call the "Idea."

However, it should be clear that these statements of Kant's
are only somewhat clumsy formulations of his basic idea that
the estimation of the beautiful involves the satisfaction of the
*condition* of conceptualization, that is, the apparent unification of manifolds, without the application of *any* – and therefore of course any particular – concept to the object. This is
especially obvious in the remark from Section 4, which is
most naturally read as saying that the delight in the beautiful
depends upon the occurrence of the kind of *reflection* which
ordinarily leads to application of concepts, but in special circumstances in which it stops short of that result. It makes
more sense to interpret Kant's ambiguous passages this way
than to fly in the face of his unequivocal assertions that the
beautiful involves no concept of the object.

That imagination and understanding can even enter into a satisfying relationship under such conditions would seem anomalous rather than inevitable, and indeed Kant's underlying explanation of why this peculiar relationship is in fact the source of an appreciable pleasure depends precisely on the fact that the occurrence of such a condition apart from the kind of concept which ordinarily guarantees its possibility must appear contingent rather than necessary to us. This point is made at the outset of the *Critique of Judgment*, in the only passage where Kant suggests anything like a general theory of pleasure to ground the particular hypothesis by means of which he explains our pleasure in the beautiful. The basis of Kant's theory is the supposition that "the attainment of every objective is connected with the feeling of pleasure," but that such pleasure is "very noticeable" only when the attainment of the objective in question does not seem to "proceed necessarily" from the normal operations of our cognitive faculties but is rather "a harmony for our cognitive faculties which we regard as merely accidental" (*CJ*, §VI, 5:187–8). When we recognize the unity of the manifold presented to us by an object of intuition under the guidance or even compulsion of a concept applied to the object, the unity seems to us inevitable, necessitated by the concept, and there is thus nothing noticeably pleasing about fulfilling our underlying objective of unifying our manifolds of intuition in this way. But when our manifold of intuition seems unified in spite of the absence of any concept dictating its unity, that seems like an accidental or contingent satisfaction of our underlying cognitive objective and is the ground of an appreciable pleasure for that very reason. Thus, while it is the apparent lawfulness of our imagination which pleases us, the apparent contingency of such lawfulness or unity is indispensable to Kant's explanation of aesthetic response. If the unity of the manifold presented to us by a beautiful object were distinguished by its apparent necessity rather than contingency, as Hegel suggests, then Kant's explanation of our pleasure in beauty would be undermined. Since the pleasure we take in beauty is not a central element in Hegel's own account, perhaps we should not be surprised that he did not attend to this point. But it is clear nevertheless that his emphasis on the apparent necessity of inseparability between concept and object pushes his exposition of Kant away from Kant's own analysis of beauty.[2]

I should note that in a passage subsequent to his exposition of Kant's aesthetics Hegel does draw attention to an element of contingency in the experience of the beautiful. Concluding his discussion of the "Concept of the Beautiful as Such," he writes:

> But finally, however much the separate sides, parts, members of the beautiful object also agree with each other in an ideal unity and let this unity appear, yet this harmony must only become visible in them so that they preserve the appearance of self-sufficient freedom against one another. . . . Both must be present in the beautiful object: the *necessity*, posited through the concept, in the belonging together of the various sides and the appearance of their *freedom*. . . . Such necessity to be sure must not be lacking in beautiful objects, but it may not come forth in the form of necessity itself, but must rather be hidden behind the appearance of unintentional contingency. (WA, 13:156–7; Knox 1:115)

But it must be clear that this passage does not really represent an assimilation of Kant's view. For Hegel, the key to beauty remains necessity, and he can even speak of the relations among the elements of a beautiful object as following from a concept; the contingency of their connection is just an appearance, or perhaps even an illusion (*Schein*). But for Kant the contingency of a beautiful object's satisfaction of our interest in cognitive unity is the heart of his explanation of the pleasure we take in it.

## II. KANT ON ART AND MORALITY

Comparing Hegel's exposition of Kant's analysis of the judgment of beauty to its original, therefore, it must seem as if Hegel misstates Kant's theory and thereby overstates the

similarity between his own conception of beauty as the sensuous embodiment of the idea and Kant's. But when we turn
from Kant's initial analysis of pure aesthetic judgment to its
subsequent elaboration, especially (but not only) in his account of fine art, Hegel's interpretation seems closer to the
mark. For once he gets past his initial examples of flowers
and foliage, Kant turns to paradigms of beauty which seem
both inseparably and inevitably tied to, indeed embodiments
of, key concepts or even ideas of reason. In fact, here there
are some ways in which Kant out-Hegels Hegel.

For purposes of illustration, I will consider three topics:
Kant's treatment of the "ideal of beauty"; his conception of
aesthetic ideas and their role in artworks as products of genius; and his theory of beauty as the symbol of morality.

Kant's conception of the ideal of beauty is obviously a
profound inspiration for Hegel's aesthetics. It is also a puzzling anomaly in Kant's analytic of the beautiful. After adum-
brating the fundamental concepts of disinterestedness, universal agreement, and formal purposiveness, Kant raises a
question about the grounds on which we would be entitled
to introduce the idea of something *uniquely* beautiful, or an
"archetype" or "ideal" as "the representation of a particular
as a being adequate to an idea," in this case apparently to the
idea of beauty (*CJ*, §17, 5:232). He then goes on to argue that
such an ideal cannot be reached by any empirical process of
averaging or abstracting yielding merely an "aesthetic *normal
idea*," nor can it be found in beautiful objects which are either
entirely or even nearly independent of concepts, such as
either flowers or even suites of furniture, the most pleasing
forms for which are only minimally constrained by concepts
of their appropriate use. Instead, he argues, such an ideal of
beauty can be found only for "that, which has the end of its
existence in itself, *man*, who through reason determines his
ends himself. . . . *Man* is therefore an ideal of *beauty*, just as
the humanity in his person, as intelligence, is alone among
all the objects in the world capable of the ideal of *perfection*"
(*CJ*, §17, 5:232–3). In particular, he asserts, the ideal of the
beautiful is to be sought only in the "*human form*" (*mensch-*

*lichen Gestalt*) as the "expression of the *ethical,* without which the object would not please universally and positively (not just negatively, [on account of its] academically correct presentation)." Such an ideal "as it were makes visible" or serves as a "visible expression of the ethical ideas which govern humans internally" (*CJ,* §17, 5:235).

This argument is puzzling, first because it is no more obvious that there must be a single form for the outward expression of the morality of human beings than that there must be a single form of furniture suitable for commodious dining, and even more because it is not obvious why a single, maximally beautiful object should be expected or sought at all. The possibility, let alone actuality, of such an ideal does not follow from the logic of aesthetic judgment – from the proposition that any beautiful object must be pleasing to everyone, it does not follow that there is some one object which is maximally pleasing to everyone. But perhaps the answer to the puzzle is as obvious as the puzzle itself: Kant is not assuming that the logic of aesthetic judgment dictates a search for an ideal which can succeed only if taste is supplemented by morality, but is rather assuming that morality, in its own need for sensible representation, imposes the search for an ideal upon taste. As Kant says, the archetype of taste "rests on reason's indeterminate idea of a maximum" (*CJ,* §17, 5:232), although in this case it is practical rather than theoretical reason which demands representation of the unique and unconditional demand that it places upon us. A uniquely beautiful object is sought, and found in the unique beauty of the human form, to make sensible the unique demand of morality. So for Kant, an ideally beautiful object is indeed a sensible expression of pure ideas of reason, but specifically of the pure idea of morality and its unconditional demand itself.[3]

In Section 51, in which he gives a classification of the kinds of fine art, Kant begins by asserting that "beauty (whether natural or artistic) may in general be called the *expression* of aesthetic ideas" (*CJ,* §51, 5:320). He does not do much to sustain the claim that beautiful objects in nature really express any ideas, and elsewhere he suggests more plausible accounts of why we find natural beauty morally significant than the thought that they communicate moral ideas to us. But there is no doubt that he is committed to the view that the most successful works of fine art, that is, works of genius, always consist in the especially successful expression of aesthetic ideas, which are defined as imaginative presentations of ideas of reason through an apt image suggesting the indefinable and inexhaustible import of such an idea. The work of genius consists in hitting upon both "ideas for the given concept," or the expressive theme, as well as the sensible form for the expression and communication of such ideas to an audience through the actual media of the fine arts (*CJ*, §46, 5:307–8, and §49, especially 5:317). But an aesthetic idea is not the sensible presentation of *any* sort of conceptualization; an aesthetic idea is the "presentation of a concept of reason (of intellectual ideas)" (*CJ*, §49, 5:314). More specifically, an aesthetic idea is the sensible presentation of an idea of practical reason. Kant's initial examples suggest that aesthetic ideas are moral ideas only in the broadest sense: "The poet dares to make sensible ideas of reason of invisible beings, the realm of the blessed, hell, eternity, creation . . . death, envy, and all vices" (*CJ*, §49, 5:314). But as he continues, he suggests that at least the most satisfying aesthetic ideas are sensible presentations of moral ideas in a stricter sense:

> For example a certain poet says, in the description of a beautiful morning, "The sun spilled forth, as rest from virtue springs." The consciousness of virtue, even when one puts oneself in the place of a virtuous man only in thought, spreads in the mind a multitude of sublime and restful feelings and a boundless outlook into a happy future, which no expression appropriate to a fully determinate concept fully attains. (*CJ*, §49, 5:316)

Kant clearly supposes that only ideas of morality in the proper sense have the depth and breadth to sustain the pleasure we expect from a work of genius.[4]

Again a question arises about the source of what Kant here expects from art. Once again, the logic of aesthetic judgment itself does not seem to explain Kant's thought. That a work of art should have to represent anything at all, let alone a concept of morality, could hardly be dictated by Kant's initial analysis of aesthetic judgment, which it rather seems to contradict. But again it seems clear that works of genius, like the ideal of beauty, are required by morality itself rather than mere taste. Kant seems to think it hardly necessary to expand upon such a point; he merely observes that art with no moral content soon becomes boring, mere diversion like background music, but that art which disposes the soul to ideas makes it "receptive of more . . . pleasure and entertainment" (*CJ*, §52, 4:326). Perhaps his thought is that precisely because the pleasure in a pure judgment of taste depends upon the appearance of contingency, in the very nature of things it cannot be long sustained; only the self-sustained pleasure of morality is truly enduring. But whatever his reasons, it is clear that Kant thinks that although the pure and free beauty of crustacea and foliage signifies nothing, enduring works of artistic genius make moral ideas or ideas of practical reason sensible. The aesthetic in general may be independent of concepts, but for Kant, as for Hegel, works of art are sensible embodiments of ideas – although again specifically ideas of morality and not metaphysical conceptions in general.

In his discussion of the beautiful as the symbol of the morally good, finally, Kant argues that analogies between the experience and process of aesthetic judgment and the experience and process of moral judgment allow the object of the former, beauty, to serve as a symbol of morality itself. Without antecedent concepts or interest, the beautiful nevertheless pleases immediately, through a freely attained harmony between imagination and understanding, and on the basis of a principle which although only subjective is also universally valid. The concept of the morally good pleases immediately and apart from any other antecedent interest; the freedom of the will consists in harmony between our capacity for choice with reason; and the objective principle of morality is also universally valid (*CJ*, §59, 5:353–4).[5] Morality requires a concept, and aesthetic judgment precludes it, but the other similarities, combined with the obvious palpability of the experience of beauty, allow it to serve as a sensible symbol of morality – not quite an intuition that can "display the reality of our concept" of morality (*CJ*, §59, 5:351), but close enough to it to make the nature of morality evident to creatures of sense like ourselves. It should also be noted that although it is the beautiful object which serves as the symbol of morality, it does so in virtue of the experience of beauty of which it is itself, as it were, the symbol; there is no requirement that the beautiful object itself have any explicitly moral content, *a fortiori* that it be the kind of object which can reasonably be thought to have content, that is, a work of art rather than nature. Here Kant is postulating moral significance for the aesthetic in general rather than for works of art in particular.

In this case Kant makes it explicit that it is morality rather than taste which seeks for such significance in the aesthetic object. His discussion begins with the general thesis that concepts need intuitions to confirm their objective reality (ideas of reason not excepted, even though no intuition completely adequate to them can be given) and then turns to the aesthetic experience for at least symbolic satisfaction of this general requirement (*CJ*, §59, 5:351). But here he also suggests that there is a demand stemming from the side of taste which can only be satisfied through a link to morality. It is in the nature of taste to make a "claim to the agreement of everyone," but it is only as a symbol of morality that regard for the beautiful can be "imputed to everyone else as a duty" – although luckily sensitivity to this relation between the beautiful and the morally good is apparently "natural to everyone" (*CJ*, §59, 5:353). So in the end Kant's view seems to be not just that morality imposes certain additional constraints upon taste but also that taste itself makes demands which can only be satisfied by a link to morality.

How Kant can allow morality to place all these demands on art and the aesthetic without entirely undermining his original conception of the freedom of the imagination and without lapsing into crude didacticism is an issue which I have pursued in previous chapters. Hegel also wishes to avoid a didactic conception of the vocation of art, so both philosophers have an equally delicate task before them. The point here is just that in spite of the insistence on the absence of all concepts from aesthetic experience in Kant's initial analysis, which seems to be misrepresented by Hegel as more conceptual than it really is, Kant's more extensive interpretation of art in particular and aesthetic experience in general seems to share considerable similarities with Hegel's conception of art as the sensuous embodiment of the Idea.

Indeed, one might even suggest that in the end Hegel does not overstate the Kantian conception of the necessity that the beautiful be inseparable from a concept but that he actually understates it. For Kant the idea of reason which is expressed or symbolized by artistic or natural beauty is always a moral idea or even the idea of morality itself; and although Kant does not explain why morality requires sensible representation of the sort which only beauty can afford, it is clear that in the expanded conception of morality toward which the *Critique of Judgment* takes the first steps he thinks that it does. For creatures like us, finding a sensible representation of morality is apparently a demand of morality itself.[6] So finding aesthetic ideas for the concepts of morality and an aesthetic symbol of morality are apparently to be invested with the same necessity, indeed urgency, as is satisfying the demands of morality generally.

Thus, while at one level Kant's analysis of taste turns on contingency, at another it seems to turn on the highest sort of necessity recognized by Kant, the necessity of practical reason. And here Kant seems to go beyond anything that Hegel is quite prepared to argue. For Hegel, the idea which art embodies is not the specific idea of morality but the much more general, metaphysical/epistemological idea of spirit's relation to its world. But this is never available to art (or any other form of absolute spirit except philosophy) in its most general form, but rather only in the form of the self-conception of humanity and its relation to both spirit and world that is available to a particular culture at a particular time and place. As Hegel puts it in the *Encyclopedia,*

> The sensuous externality in the beautiful, the *form of immedi-acy* as such, is at the same time *determination of content,* and God has with his spirituality at the same time the determination of a natural element or existence. . . . It is not the absolute spirit which enters this consciousness. On the subjective side the community has of course ethical life, aware, as it is, of the spirituality of its essence. . . . But branded with immediacy, the subject's liberty is only an ethos [*Sitte*].[7]

So while in one sense it is always the same idea – of the spirituality of the world – which is expressed by art, at another level it is always a more particular conception of humanity and its place in the world which is expressed by particular works of art. There may, of course, be a certain kind of historical necessity that such conceptions occur when they do and find expression as they do, but at the same time it is clear that on Hegel's account there must also be an element of historical contingency in art's embodiment of the idea.

For Kant, then, there seems to be a single idea of morality which both art and the aesthetic always strive to express; for Hegel, the idea embodied by art is not quite that unique. Furthermore, although for Hegel there is obviously some sort of metaphysical and epistemological necessity that spirit express itself through an embodiment in art, whatever exactly this necessity is it is not a moral necessity. For Hegel, it may be inevitable that art embody the idea; for Kant it seems obligatory that it do so. It is not clear that Hegel is willing to follow Kant in claiming practical necessity for the aesthetic.

### III. A CONTINUING DIFFERENCE

So there is at least one sense, the practical, in which Kant seems more willing to impute necessity to artistic and natural beauty than Hegel is. Yet, as we saw, Hegel criticizes Kant's aesthetics as excessively "subjective," as failing to attain a "higher grasp of the true unity of necessity and freedom, particular and universal, sensible and rational" (*WA*, 13:89; Knox, 1:60–1). Does this mean that Hegel just failed to see how Kant himself went beyond his initial analysis of the beautiful to a theory of the practical necessity in both art and the aesthetic?

It is unlikely that Hegel just failed to see the centrality of the link between aesthetics and morality in Kant's expanded as opposed to initial statement of his theory of taste. Rather, Hegel and Kant had radically different conceptions of what would count as an acceptable theory of the efficacy of practical reason, and Hegel's criticism of Kant's aesthetics is but an expression of his fundamental opposition to one of the most pervasive features of Kant's metaphysics – his conception of the possibility of a gulf between practical reason and free will on the one hand and nature on the other, and thus the possibility that the fulfillment of an intention the formation of which is absolutely necessary for the will of a rational agent may yet seem radically contingent as far as nature is concerned. In fact, Hegel makes it quite plain at the outset of his discussion of Kant's aesthetics that his real problem is with Kant's ethics:

> In general Kant made self-relating rationality, freedom, self-consciousness finding and knowing itself as infinite the foundation for intelligence as well as will. . . . But since Kant fell back again into the fixed opposition of subjective thought and objective objects, of abstract universality and sensible particularity of the will, he it was above all who emphasized the . . . opposition [in] morality. . . . Given this fixity of opposition cognized through thought of the understanding, nothing remained for him but to express unity only in the form of subjective ideas of reason, for which an adequate reality can never be demonstrated. (*WA*, 13:84; Knox, 1:56–7)

For Kant, freedom consists in our ability always to form the morally requisite intention, even if nature may well frustrate the desired outcome of such an intention. If need be, Kant suggests, we can always rewrite the entire history of our own character to make an otherwise inexplicable choice explicable – for any "action . . . together with everything past that determines it, belongs to a single phenomenon of one's character, which one creates oneself" (*Practical Reason*, 5:98) – but he does not suggest that we can always rewrite the history of nature itself so as to ensure that our intentions have the desired outcomes. Hegel, however, expects a theory of rationality to overcome this opposition as well:

> Freedom is the highest vocation of the spirit. First, on its purely formal side, it consists in the subject finding nothing alien, no boundary and limit, in that which is opposed to it, but only itself. Even according to this formal determination all need and every unhappiness has disappeared, the subject is reconciled with the world, is satisfied with it and has solved every opposition and contradiction. . . . What . . . man seeks is the region of a higher, more substantial truth, in which all oppositions and contradictions of the finite can find their final solution and the freedom of their complete satisfaction. (*WA*, 13:134, 137; Knox, 1:94, 99)

For Hegel, freedom is not something internal to the will but a harmonious relation between the will and the world, so Kant's conception of freedom of the will, for all the necessity it may claim, inevitably seems merely subjective to him; it fulfills the subjective but not the objective condition of freedom. Since the aesthetic embodiment of the idea of morality in Kant represents freedom as Kant conceives it, it too is open to the charge of subjectivity in precisely the same sense. It may be necessary that we attempt to symbolize or even embody moral ideas in the beautiful, but contingent that we can succeed in doing so. Indeed that is exactly why Kant thinks that genius, which is nothing less than a "natural endowment" or gift of nature (*CJ*, §46, 5:307), is needed to produce original fine art. Kant's account of genius itself can stand as a symbol of his conception of a certain kind of contingency in the success of any human action.

So Hegel's insistence on the subjectivity of Kantian aesthetics is not as it were a diagnosis of Kant's theoretical mistake but an expression of a radically different world view. To be sure, we should not let Hegel get away with too much stress on the opposition between freedom and nature in Kant. In fact, the *Critique of Judgment* may well represent the beginning of a period in Kant's moral thought in which, perhaps in contrast to the impression created by the *Groundwork of the Metaphysics of Morals* of 1785, Kant tries to create closer connections between feeling and freedom. In the *Metaphysics of Morals* of 1797 Kant suggests that the necessary ends of virtue include perfection of one's natural as well as intellectual character, which includes both preservation and cultivation of feelings (see *Virtue,* especially §§16 and 17);[8] in the *Religion within the Limits of Reason Alone,* Kant suggests that an enduring opposition between an agent's consciousness of duty and his inclinations is not, contrary to the caricature of his philosophy, necessary for virtue or even really permissible, but is rather a sign of an underlying maxim in opposition to duty: "What is the *aesthetic* quality, as it were the *temperament* of virtue, brave and thus *joyous,* or anxiety-ridden and beaten down? . . . The latter slavish determination of mind can never obtain without a hidden *hatred* of the law, and the joyous heart in *following* its duty . . . is a sign of the genuineness of virtuous disposition" (6:23–4n.). So Kant ultimately thinks that morality requires a reconciliation of the natural and the rational within human character. But even then he is never willing to admit that we can reasonably expect and therefore reasonably require a complete reconciliation between human intention and nature in the broader sense, as our outward arena of action, or between happiness and the worthiness to be happy. That must remain a mere postulate of pure reason.

In fact, several elements of Kant's aesthetic theory must remain incomprehensible on the Hegelian view, turning as they do precisely on the contingency of harmony between reason and nature. One of these is Kant's conception of the sublime, which, it should be noted, plays no role in Hegel's exposition. Stripped of its subtleties,[9] Kant's account of the sublime is just that this aesthetic experience, akin to the feeling of respect, reveals the imperviousness of our character as rational agents even to nature's worst threats of physical destruction; its point is just that our virtues can necessarily withstand the utter contingency of our natural existence (see especially *CJ*, §28, 5:261). Without a sense of the radical contingency of our natural existence relative to our moral being, Kant's conception of the special, as it were painful pleasure in the sublime would make no sense. The second is Kant's conception of our intellectual interest in the existence of natural beauty. Again, we cannot enter here into the intricacies of Kant's account,[10] but the basis of Kant's argument is the idea that we can add pleasure in the fact of the existence of naturally beautiful objects to our primary pleasure in their form precisely because the existence of such objects is at least a "trace" or "hint" that nature "contains in itself some sort of ground for assuming a lawful harmony of its products" with our disinterested delight (*CJ*, §42, 5:300). If it were not contingent that nature were so accommodating to us, it is hard to see why we should take special pleasure in this discovery. On the contrary, it is just because Kant's moral philosophy – like, in the end, his epistemology[11] – recognizes a certain contingency in the fulfillment of the conditions for successful human existence that the existence of natural beauty can be laden with the significance of an intellectual interest. For Kant, unlike Hegel, there is no guarantee that we must reach an accommodation with nature, although we cannot coherently conduct action, any more than inquiry, except by postulating that we can reach such an accommodation.

# Kant's aesthetics and morality:
## topical studies

# Chapter 6

## The beautiful and the sublime

### I. INTERPRETATIONS OF THE SUBLIME

In *Kant and the Claims of Taste*, I argued that Kant's analysis of the sublime does not materially add to his argument for the intersubjective validity of aesthetic judments, and narrowly speaking that may be true. But more broadly, I also wrote that Kant's analysis of the sublime "will not be of much interest to modern sensibilities, and thus . . . most of what we can or will learn from Kant must come from his discussion of judgments of beauty."[1] No statement in that book has come in for more criticism than this remark, and justifiably so. By way of mitigating circumstances, I can only plead that my dismissal of the sublime accurately reflected, not its centrality in Kant's own thought, but at least the prevailing attitude in the analytical aesthetics of the preceding two decades, which (for better or worse) provided the background for my initial work on Kant's aesthetics during the 1970s. But at least my decision not to discuss the sublime at that time saved me from saying any nonsense about it. I cannot say as much for everything else that has recently been written on the topic.

In the years since I published that unfortunate remark, or perhaps even beginning a few years before 1979, the sublime

This essay was originally published as "Kant's Distinction between the Beautiful and Sublime," *Review of Metaphysics* 35 (1982): 753–83. Reprinted with permission. The introductory section has been added for the present volume. One paragraph has also been added to Section VI, and lesser additions and changes have been made throughout.

has become a topic of great interest, certainly (but by no means exclusively) among literary theorists. But much of what is said about the sublime, or even specifically about the Kantian sublime, has little to do with Kant's own intentions in his treatment of this fashionable eighteenth-century idea. Instead, the sublime seems to have become a palimpsest for theoretical concerns of our own day, and much of what is written about it has little connection indeed with anything that Immanual Kant himself did think or could possibly have thought about it. I do not wish to tax the reader with an extensive review of contemporary interpretations of the sublime. But a brief catalog may be useful, in order to make clear the need for the more literal kind of interpretation of Kant's own views about the sublime that I attempt to offer in this and the following chapter, partly in atonement for my own earlier sin of omission, but more importantly, to try to clip the wings of some of the wilder flights of speculation currently on offer.

Contemporary treatments of the Kantian sublime might be brought under three headings. These are what can be called the *deconstructionist*, the *psychoanalytic*, and the *ideological* approaches.

What I call the "deconstructionist" approach to the sublime has appeared in many forms, but the central idea is that the sublime reveals the underlying and irremediable impossibility of determinate thought by showing how every attempt to grasp experience in any definitive fashion is bound to be undermined by the inescapable inadequacy and instability of the instrument used. As an influential essay by Paul de Man asks, "Are we not made to swallow the more than paradoxical but truly aporetic incompatibility between the failure of the imagination to grasp magnitude with what becomes, in the experience of the sublime, the success of this same imagination as an agent of reason, are we not made to swallow this because of a constant, and finally bewildering alternation of the two terms[?]"[2] This thought occurs in many forms, but perhaps a general distinction might be drawn between its linguistic and its perceptual forms. On the linguistic account, the sublime reveals how beyond any attempt to say what experience is like there lurks the abyss of the unsayable; the perceptual form shows how not only the attempt to describe the world but even that to have a determinate perception of it is dissolved in a larger sea of the ungraspable. The linguistic interpretation has been popularized by de Man and Jacques Derrida and the many writers influenced by them. One example from a writer of the Yale school can serve for many: "In the Kantian moment of the sublime the surface is broken, the discourse breaks down, and the faculties are checked or suspended: a discontinuity opens between what can be grasped and what is felt to be meaningful."[3] The key idea here seems to be that the sublime reveals how all discourse is limited yet we still have a sense of meaningfulness lying beyond the limits of whatever discourse we can find.

The perceptual interpretation is perhaps less often clearly stated, but here is one example:

The proportion of normal experience originates in the abnormal experience of the sublime; the regularity of proportion has its ground in the irregular violence of the sublime; and the life-enhancing form of beauty is traced back to the violent outrage which the imagination visited upon itself. . . . The disposition of activity and passivity in resistance is the same phenomenon as the violence of the mathematical sublime. When encountering objects in time we are subject to their might; but we bring them under our dominion when we arrest them in space and determine them according to our proportions.[4]

On this account, all ordinary perception, symbolized by the beautiful, is actually the violent imposition of determinate form upon indeterminate matter, and the violence of the very nature of perception itself appears in the experience of the sublime.

In what I am calling the "psychoanalytic" interpretation of the sublime, the sublime is not interpreted as a symbol of the essential inadequacy and violence of ordinary discourse or perception but rather as a symbol of the inevitable manifestation of the irrational forces suppressed by the superego of human rationality, where reason is not our own essence but is rather (unfortunately or not) alien to that which is most deeply characteristic about us. As Stanley Cavell puts it, "The idea of a majesty alienated from us is a transcription of the idea of the sublime as Kant characterizes it. Then the sublime . . . bears the structure of Freudian transference."⁵ The sublime is here interpreted as an experience of the tension between reason and irrationality, contesting without end for supremacy in human nature.

Finally, in the "ideological" interpretation of the sublime, the awesome scope and power of the sublime is taken to be a tool to teach the individual fear and submission, the stick complementing the carrot of consolation offered by the beautiful. As Terry Eagleton writes;

> Both of these operations, the beautiful and the sublime, are in fact essential dimensions of ideology. For one problem of all humanist ideology is how its centering and consoling of the subject is to be made compatible with a certain essential reverence and submissiveness on the subject's part. . . . The sublime in one of its aspects is exactly this chastening, humiliating power, which decentres the subject into an awesome awareness of its finitude, its own petty position in the universe, just as the experience of beauty shores it up.⁶

The experience of the sublime is used to teach the subject nothing less than the lesson of his own moral and political insignificance. Eagleton leaves untouched some nasty questions: Who is it who uses the sublime to teach this lesson, and to whom is it taught? The answer to the latter question would seem to need to be the bourgeoisie, for who else is the primary audience for both art and the aestheticization of nature, but isn't the answer to the first question likely to be the bourgeoisie as well? But these details are not the real problem with the ideological approach.

Instead, the ideological approach, like the others, fails to gauge the centrality of reason in Kant's own account of the sublime. As reflections of twentieth-century anxieties about the primacy of reason – above all, practical reason – they may be accurate enough, but they can have little to do with Kant, who used the idea of the sublime to symbolize the secure dominance of reason in human life. It is crucial to realize that although for Kant the experience of the sublime may reveal the limits of the senses, imagination, and understanding, and in this regard be accompanied with an element of displeasure, the sublime is ultimately a satisfying experience which makes clear the vocation of reason. For us now it may be doubtful whether reason or the irrational will triumph, and we may try to suppress or sublimate our fear of that doubt, but for Kant there was no such doubt. And although for Kant there may be limits to what can be grasped or perceived by the senses or imagination, these are by no means limits on comprehension as such; on the contrary, they reveal the extent of reason's power of comprehension.[7] And above all, it must be recognized that for Kant the faculty of reason as it manifests itself in the experience of the sublime cannot repress what is essential to human beings, whether that repression be psychological or ideological, but it celebrates what is essential to human nature both individual and social. For Kant reason is universal, and it is inconceivable to think that it could be used to repress any segment of the population or teach it submission to any other. On Kant's conception, reason teaches us humility about our individual merits but pride in our humanity in general, pride in a faculty of our own in whose image God himself is created (rather than vice versa). Reason so understood cannot be enlisted in the serive of any form of suppression of the human agent or alienation of the human from the image of reason.[8]

Much of what has recently been written about the sublime thus reflects little of Kant's own view about the nature of reason. If we are to make clear our own sense of the limits of reason, which is obviously what so many contemporary writers are really trying to do, it should be understood that in this case Kant's conception of the sublime is not our model but rather that which must be rejected, and in order to do that we at least ought to understand his own idea. That is what I try to do in this and the following chapter. In this chapter, most of my attention is directed to the formal interpretation of how Kant's explanation of the sublime fits into the logic and psychology of his theory of taste; in Chapter 7, I focus on broader issues about the place of the sublime among other aesthetic phenomena in Kant's view of morality.

## II. KANT'S ANALYTICAL FRAMEWORK

Shortly after opening the "Analytic of the Sublime" in his *Critique of Judgment*, Kant writes,

> As far as the division of the moments of the aesthetic estima-
> tion of objects in relation to the feeling of the sublime is con-
> cerned, the analytic can proceed according to the same princi-
> ple that figured in the analysis of the judgment of taste. For as
> a judgment of the aesthetically reflective faculty of judgment,
> the delight in the sublime, just like that in the beautiful, must
> be representable as universally valid as regards its *Quantity,*
> as without interest as regards its *Quality,* as subjective finality
> as concerns its *Relation,* and the latter must be representable
> as necessary as regards its *Modality.* (*CJ,* §24, 5:247)

This has been taken to mean that Kant intended to *define* the two distinct predicates "beautiful" and "sublime" by one and the same set of criteria; yet this seems both paradoxical in itself and incompatible with any further discrimination of distinct aesthetic predicates within the constraints of Kant's theory of aesthetic judgment.[9]

Any air of paradox, however, may quickly be dispelled. It derives from the supposition that in describing the four "mo-ments" of the judgment of taste on beauty and the parallel four moments in the case of the sublime, Kant intended to state formal and specific *definitions* of the two forms of judg-ment. But this is clearly false. First, the term *Erklärung,* which

Kant used to label his capsule summaries of the four "Moments" of the "Analytic of the Beautiful" (*CJ*, §5, 5:211; §9, 5:219; §17, 5:236; §22, 5:240) as well as several characterizations of the sublime elsewhere in the *Critique of Judgment* (e.g, *CJ*, §25, 5:248 and §29 General Remark, 5:267), although translated by J. C. Meredith as "definition,"[10] is one which Kant himself explicitly contrasted to the technical term "definition" as altogether looser in meaning. In the *Critique of Pure Reason*, Kant expressly lamented that "the German language has for the [Latin] expressions *exposition, explication, declaration* and *definition* nothing more than the one word *Erklärung*" (A 730 / B 758). Second, although Kant's theory of formal definition requires that such a definition be a "complexus notarum primitivum" including only "essentialia in sensu strictissimo" and no "attributes" which are "consequences" of such "*primitive* and *constitutive* characteristics" (*Logic*, 9:60–1), Kant clearly held that some among the four moments of the "Analytic of the Beautiful" are logical consequences of the others. Thus, he claimed that the *Erklärung* of the beautiful as universally valid "can be deduced" (*gefolgert*) from the prior account of its disinterestedness (*CJ*, §6, 5:211),[11] which he certainly would not have said if he had intended the four "Moments" of this analytic collectively to comprise a formal definition of the beautiful. But perhaps most important, it was long a theme of Kant's methodology that formal definitions are not possible in the case of philosophically interesting concepts. As he wrote in the first *Critique*, "No concepts . . . allow of definition except only those which contain an arbitrary synthesis that admits of *a priori* construction," as in mathematics [A 729 / B 757]. Moreover, this was a thesis which Kant had explicitly applied to aesthetic concepts as long as he had held it at all. In the very essay in which he first stated his view on the place of definitions in philosophy, the *Enquiry Concerning the Clarity of the Principles of Natural Theology and Ethics* of 1764, Kant illustrated it by writing that "many concepts can scarcely be analyzed at all, for example, the concept of *representation*, the concept of being *next to* or *after one another*; other concepts can only be partially analyzed, as for example the concept of *space, time,* of the various *feelings* of the human soul, of the feelings of the *sublime,* of the *beautiful,* of the disgusting, etc." (2:280). Although many aspects of Kant's aesthetic theory did change between the 1760s and the publication of the third *Critique* in 1790, there is no evidence that his view on the possibility, let alone necessity, of definitions in aesthetics was among them.[12]

It is thus most unlikely that Kant could have intended the moments of his analytics of the beautiful and the sublime to provide formal definitions of any aesthetic concepts at all, *a fortiori* a single definition of two distinct concepts. Nevertheless, problems about the theoretical status and force of Kant's distinction between the beautiful and the sublime remain, because neither of the two obvious strategies for accounting for the different meanings of judgments on the beautiful and the sublime while analyzing them according to a common principle looks as if it should be available to Kant. On the one hand, while we might notice that the common moments of quantity, quality, relation, and modality are in both cases meant to apply to feelings of "delight" and then suppose that the different meanings of judgments of beauty and sublimity and the predicates they contain must lie in qualitative or phenomenological differences between the feelings of pleasure to which they give expression, there are several difficulties with such a supposition. One is that Kant seems to deny that there *is* such a thing as a qualitative difference between numerically distinct feelings of pleasure, allowing instead only quantitative differences between them. Thus he writes in the *Critique of Practical Reason* that

> the representations of objects may be so dissimilar, they may be representations of the understanding or even of reason as opposed to representations of sense, yet the feeling of pleasure . . . (the agreeableness, the enjoyment that one expects from them . . . ) is not only of one and the same kind insofar as it can always be known only empirically, it is also one and the same insofar as it affects one and the same life force, which expresses itself in the power of desire, and in this

regard one pleasure can differ from another only in degree.
(*Practical Reason*, 5:23)

Further, even when offering his original "comparison of the three specifically different kinds of delight" in the "Analytic of the Beautiful," Kant seems always to speak of the "feeling of pleasure" itself in the singular and to distinguish such apparently different kinds of pleasure as those in "the agreeable, the beautiful, and the good" only in terms of "different relations of representations to the feeling of pleasure and displeasure, with respect to which we distinguish different objects or modes of representations from one another" (*CJ*, §5, 5:209–10). Such differences do not appear to be qualitative differences. But then, given these two considerations, why should we think that "beautiful" and "sublime" may be meaningfully differentiated by phenomenological differences between the feelings of pleasure they express?

On the other hand, however, if there are no phenomenological differences between the feelings of beauty and sublimity, or if such differences, although perhaps incidentally mentioned by Kant, are not meant to ground the distinction between the judgments on the beautiful and the sublime, and the meaning of such judgments is supposed to be determined instead by the purely logical and/or epistemological aspects of their form, another problem arises. This is just that if the four moments of quantity, quality, relation, and modality exhaust the significance of both forms of judgment, yet if universality, disinterestedness, subjective finality, and necessity are assumed to be determinate logical or epistemological requirements which are simply satisfied or not by any particular judgments, then there seems to be no basis for attaching distinct senses to the predicates "beautiful" and "sublime" and different meanings to judgments employing these predicates.

These considerations present difficulties for interpretations which see either the phenomenology of feelings of pleasure or the logical analysis of aesthetic discourse as the only essential or permissible elements of Kant's theory of aesthetic judgment.[13] But in fact what Kant's statement in Section 24 describes is neither a principle for pure phenomenology nor a guideline for a purely logical or linguistic analysis. Instead, it is a compact statement of a *theory* of aesthetic judgment according to which the significance of particular forms of aesthetic judgments as well as the differences between them may be understood by showing how a variety of related but phenomenologically distinct forms of feeling and the related but distinct psychological processes which explain their occurrence satisfy a single but abstract set of requirements of logical and epistemological status in a variety of specifically distinct ways. Once Kant's four moments are understood to describe a complex set of relations among feelings of aesthetic response, explanations of such responses, and the status of the judgments which give expression to these responses, it can be seen how they can both characterize a single form of judgment and yet allow for meaningful distinctions among specific aesthetic predicates. Indeed, once the abstract and generic nature of the requirements of Kant's aesthetic theory is understood, it might well become possible to define far more than the two specific aesthetic predicates he mentions within it, but I will attempt to show how Kant's theory works only in the two cases to which Kant himself applied it.

In other words, Kant's distinction between the beautiful and sublime can be understood only if we appreciate the complexity of his aesthetic theory, instead of reducing it to pure phenomenology or psychology or epistemology or linguistic analysis, each of which has a part in it, but none of which exhausts it. This can best be demonstrated by the comparisons of the feelings of beauty and sublimity, their explanations, and the ways in which they satisfy the four moments of his analysis that are provided in Sections III, IV, and V of this chapter. First, however, I will sketch the answers to our two problems about the phenomenological and logical force of Kant's distinction which these comparisons suggest.

Concerning Kant's phenomenology of pleasure, there are two points to be made. First, although there is indeed no evidence to suggest that Kant ever surrendered the *Critique of Practical Reason*'s view that feelings of pleasure differ only in degree and not in kind, the "Analytic of the Sublime" suggests that this restriction applies only to pure or simple feelings of pleasure, whereas the aesthetically relevant conception of "delight" is more complex. It subsumes not only simple feelings of pleasure but also mixed or complex feelings that are on balance pleasurable yet include elements or moments of displeasure and that are phenomenologically distinct from feelings of beauty for precisely this reason. Second, although Kant's distinction between the pleasure in the beautiful on the one hand and that in the agreeable and the good on the other is indeed a nonphenomenological distinction, this does *not* imply that phenomenological distinctions cannot be relevant to the distinction between different forms of *aesthetic* judgment and their predicates; the argument of Section 5 of the *Critique of Judgment* can be taken to mean that phenomenological differences are not the basis for the distinction between aesthetic judgment in general and such entirely distinct forms of judgment as the cognitive and the moral but it provides no reason to assume that such differences cannot contribute to meaningful distinctions *within* the general category of the aesthetic.

As far as the second problem is concerned, the following comparison will show that Kant's four "Moments" do not state determinate requirements which either are or are not fully satisfied by particular judgments – and especially not determinate requirements of logical form which are or are not satisfied simply by the structure of the propositions that are asserted by aesthetic judgments. Instead, these "Moments" characterize general constraints on the epistemological status of aesthetic judgments and on the epistemological structure of the psychological processes that give rise to aesthetic responses, which constraints may be satisfied in a variety of specifically distinct ways. Kant's general analysis of aesthetic judgments requires that all such judgments both concern and be made on the basis of a particular pleasurable feeling (*FI*, §VIII, 20:229), and that they impute that pleasure to others as the inevitable consequence of an appropriate encounter with the object of art or nature that occasions it in oneself without the connection of that pleasure to any determinate concept that may apply to that object (*FI*, §VIII, 20:225). These requirements mean that the epistemological status of aesthetic judgments must be that of intersubjectively universal and necessary validity, and that the state of mind which produces an aesthetic judgment must involve common qualities of intellect – in order to be universally valid – yet involve them in a way that is free and disinterested rather than determinate and objectively purposive, in order to avoid the inappropriate connection of pleasure to a concept. Yet these requirements can be satisfied in a variety of ways. Phenomenologically distinguishable although ultimately pleasurable feelings may be explained by psychological states involving different faculties of mind – imagination and understanding alone, or imagination, understanding, and reason in a variety of possible combinations – and these differences may produce further differences in the ways in which the epistemological requirements of universal and necessary validity are satisfied and in the precise manner in which the abstract conceptions of disinterestedness and subjective finality are instantiated. Thus, complexes of response and judgment with specifically different phenomenologies, psychologies, and even epistemologies may all satisfy Kant's general constraints on aesthetic judgment yet give rise to specifically distinct aesthetic predicates connoting precisely such differences.

Crucial to this account is the supposition that the disinterested and merely subjective final state of free play of the higher faculties of the mind that is the cause of all universally and necessarily valid aesthetic response may be instantiated by a psychological state which is a harmony between imagination and understanding *or* by one which may even involve disharmony between these two faculties but a harmony with the further faculty of reason instead. Yet it may immediately be objected to this contention that in the very place where Kant first defines what I have been loosely calling "aesthetic judgment" by distinguishing the more properly named "aesthetic judgments of reflection" from mere "aesthetic judgments of sense" (that is, simple expressions of agreeable feelings for which no claim of intersubjective validity is even considered) he makes the harmonious relation between the imagination and understanding essential to the very conception of an aesthetic judgment of reflection, and thus precludes the generic theory of aesthetic judgment which I am ascribing to him:

> A merely *reflective* judgment about a particular object can be *aesthetic*, however, if even before it contemplates comparing the object with others, the judgment, with no concept antecedent to the given intuition, unites the imagination . . . with the understanding . . . and perceives a relation between the two cognitive faculties which forms the subjective and merely sensitive condition of the objective employment of the faculty of judgment – namely, the harmony of those two faculties with one another. (*FI*, §VIII, 20: 223–4)

This passage comes from the first draft of his introduction to the *Critique of Judgment*, which Kant did not use, but the first general description of aesthetic judgment in the introduction which Kant did publish with his finished text likewise seems to specify that aesthetic judgment necessarily involves a harmony between the specific faculties of imagination and understanding (*CJ*, §VII, 5:190).

But these passages can only be understood as initial illustrations of a generic concept by a specific instance of it, for as Kant proceeds into the "Analytic of the Sublime," numerous passages make it clear that he does indeed mean to be contrasting specifically different varieties of a general form of "aesthetic universally valid estimation" (*CJ*, §29 General Remark, 5:267). The opening section of this "Analytic" makes this evident by employing the basic conception of the harmony of the faculties itself as a generic rather than specific conception: Kant writes that the beautiful and the sublime agree "in that both please for themselves" and depend upon neither a mere sensation nor a determinate concept, so that it must be the case that in both "the delight is connected with the mere presentation [of an object] . . . through which the faculty of presentation, or the imagination, is regarded as being in harmony, in the case of a given intuition, with the *faculty of concepts* of understanding *or* reason" (*CJ*, §23, 5:244; second emphasis added). Several sections later, Kant clearly treats not only the idea of a "subjective play" of the faculties of mind but also the idea of an aesthetic judgment itself as a generic notion when he says that in spite of the qualitative difference between the "restful contemplation" of the beautiful and the "motion" of the mind in its response to the sublime, the judgment on the sublime nevertheless "remains purely aesthetic because, without being grounded on any determinate concept of the object, it represents merely the subjective play of the faculties of mind (imagination and reason) as harmonious even through their contrast" (*CJ*, §27, 5:258). And finally, the "General Remark on the Exposition of Aesthetic Reflective Judgments," which contrasts the just-concluded analysis of the sublime with the preceding examination of the beautiful, makes it clear by more than its generic title alone (*CJ*, §29 General Remark, 5:266) that Kant has meant to describe specific distinctions within a genus of aesthetic judgment flowing from differences in the ways in which both pleasures themselves and their explanations may satisfy such requirements of the aesthetic as universal validity and subjective finality; for here Kant says that although the beautiful and the sublime may be *distinguished* by means of the two "short *Erklärungen*" that the beautiful is "that which pleases in mere estimation" and the sublime is "that which pleases immediately through its resistance to the interest of the senses," yet on *both* of these statements, precisely *as "Erklärungen* of aesthetic universally valid estimation, [the beautiful and sublime both] are related to the subjective grounds, namely on the one hand to sensibility as it is final in behalf of the contemplative understanding, on the other as it is contrary to this but final for the purposes of practical reason" (*CJ*, §29 General Remark, 5:267). Regardless of its opening statements, then, Kant's discussion of the beautiful and sublime certainly concludes with a generic account of aesthetic "estimation" within which more specific senses of particular aesthetic predicates may be distinguished by differences of phenomenology, psychology, and epistemology.

Rather than consider any more general claims for or against this thesis, however, I will now examine first the structure and then the content of the series of comparisons between the beautiful and the sublime by which Kant illustrates it.

## III. THE STRUCTURE OF THE SUBLIME

The structure of Kant's comparisons is obscured by the fact that the headings "Quality," "Quantity," "Relation," and "Modality," which in the "Analytic of the Beautiful" had already been wrenched loose from their original senses in the *Critique of Pure Reason*, are, in spite of the statement with which we began Section II of the chapter, even more roughly handled in the "Analytic of the Sublime." The first *Critique* introduced "Quantity," "Quality," "Relation," and "Modality," in that order, as headings for the logical "functions of judgment" (A 70 / B 95). The exact force of the term "function" is hardly self-evident, but it soon turned out that the first three of these headings subsume features of the logical forms of statements or propositions in virtue of which they might differ from one another even when employing the same nonlogical terms or predicates – that is, such structural features as being universal or particular, affirmative or negative, and categorical or hypothetical (a categorical proposition being a simple statement of the form "$x$ is F" and a hypothetical proposition a complex one of the form "If $p$ then $q$"). Only the last of the headings, "Modality," had anything to do with the epistemic status of judgments rather than with the internal structure of the propositions asserted in judgments (cf. A 74 / B 100). In the "Analytic of the Beautiful," however, these headings are not used to differentiate logically distinct forms of aesthetic judgment, for in fact all genuine aesthetic judgments have the same logical form: Every aesthetic judgment expresses a particular affirmative categorical proposition (*CJ*, §8, 5:215) because it simply asserts that a particular object is beautiful or sublime. Instead, the heading "Quantity," in addition to "Modality," is used to characterize the epistemic status of an aesthetic judgment as universally and necessarily valid, with the epistemic status of intersubjective validity being explicitly distinguished from the logical quantity of universality (*CJ*, §8, 5:215), whereas the headings of "Quality" and "Relation" are used to discuss neither the logical form nor epistemic status of the aesthetic judgment itself but rather epistemological aspects of the state of mind that grounds aesthetic response and of the relation between that state of mind and the objects which occasion it – the disinterestedness of the former and the merely formal finality or purposiveness of the latter.[14]

But Kant then obscures the theoretical relation between his discussions of the beautiful and the sublime by structuring the latter in a way that departs even from the scheme just established in the former. On the one hand, he reverts to the scheme of the first *Critique* by returning the heading of "Quality" to the second place it originally occupied rather than placing it first as in the "Analytic of the Beautiful,"[15] and also by once again confining the discussion of the epistemic status of judgments of sublimity to the single heading "Modality." On the other hand, although Kant now suppresses the labels "Quantity" and "Relation," he clearly has those concepts in mind in describing first magnitude and then moral superiority as features of objects and of our relation to them in virtue of which we experience sublimity. Further, in spite of the prominence given to the concept of disinterestedness in his statement of principle in Section 24, Kant then omits any discussion of the disinterestedness of judgments on the sublime at all from the remainder of the "Analytic of the Sublime" (resuming this theme only in the "General Remark" which follows), and uses the heading "Quality" to discuss the phenomenology of the experience of the sublime. This discussion has no direct parallel in the "Analytic of the Beautiful," let alone in the first *Critique*.

Nevertheless, from all of this confusion a structure for our own comparison of the beautiful and the sublime can in fact be derived. We may follow the lead of the "Analytic of the Beautiful" by beginning with the subject of quality rather than quantity, noting however, that precisely because the heading "Quality," as a reference to disinterestedness, has already been used to make the nonphenomenological distinction between all aesthetic judgments and nonaesthetic forms of judgment, it is now available to subsume the discussion of the phenomenological differences *within* the class of aesthetic responses that is crucial to the distinction between the beautiful and the sublime. Then, turning to the psychological mechanisms that explain these differences as well as to the different relations to the objects of the aesthetic response which those mechanisms imply, we may consider the two explanations of the feeling of the sublime which Kant develops by exploiting the concepts of quantity and relation. Finally, by examining Kant's brief discussion of the modality of judgments on the sublime, we can see how he suggests that judgments on the beautiful and the sublime may satisfy the general epistemic requirements imposed by the abstract concept of aesthetic judgment in specifically different ways.

## IV. THE PHENOMENOLOGY OF THE SUBLIME

Under the heading "Quality," then, Kant provides an extended description of how sublimity actually feels and how it differs in feeling from beauty. Some of Kant's descriptions, as we have already seen in passing, are couched in the metaphor of motion:

> The mind feels itself *moved* in the representation of the sublime in nature: whereas in the aesthetic judgment on the beautiful in nature it is in *restful* contemplation. This movement can be compared (especially in its beginning) with a vibration, that is, with a rapidly alternating repulsion and attraction to the same object. (*CJ*, §27, 5:258)

Such a passage reminds one of the "physiological" explanation of aesthetic response as due to "movements which . . . clear the vessels" or to "the relaxing, slackening, and enervating of the fibres of the body" which Kant repudiated when offered by Edmund Burke (*CJ*, §29 General Remark, 5:277). However, Kant is not literally describing a vibration of a bodily part. He is trying to capture an emotional vibration, a tension between felt elements of pleasure but also displeasure in the experience of the sublime. What he wants to express is that whereas the pleasure in the beautiful can be thought of as a simple feeling, the pleasure in the sublime must be characterized as a complex feeling, which, although on balance pleasurable, includes elements of pain as well. Indeed, Kant suggests that for this reason the straightforward concept of pleasure used in the "Analytic of the Beautiful" might not be quite right for our response to the sublime, which "contains not so much positive pleasure as admiration or respect, i.e., it deserves to be named a negative pleasure" (*CJ*, §23, 5:245).

Kant's characterization of this complexity, however, is itself unstable. Sometimes he treats the response to the sublime as a single yet complex feeling, but sometimes as not so much a single feeling at all but rather a sequence of feelings which ends in pleasure but which includes moments of pain among its stages. Thus, one of Kant's first contrasts between the responses to the beautiful and the sublime emphasizes a sequential complexity in the latter which has no parallel in the former: Although "the beautiful is directly attended with a feeling of life, and is thus compatible with charms and a playful imagination," in the case of our delight in the sublime "the mind is not simply attracted but also alternately repelled by it" (*CJ*, §23, 5:244–5). In other passages, however, Kant emphasizes the complex quality of our response to the sublime without implying that the response must consist of a temporal sequence of distinct feelings:

> The feeling of the sublime is, therefore, at once a feeling of
> displeasure arising from the inadequacy of the imagination in

the aesthetic estimation of magnitude to attain to its estimation through reason and a simultaneously [*dabei zugleich*] aroused pleasure arising from the harmony of this very judgment of the inadequacy of the greatest sensible capacity [in comparison to] ideas of reason. (*CJ*, §27, 5:257)

Again, "The quality of the feeling of the sublime is: that it is a feeling of displeasure about the power of aesthetically estimating an object, which is yet at the same time [*zugleich*] represented as purposive" (*CJ*, §27, 5:259), which is to say that the feeling must also be pleasurable, since pleasure is the only expression of purposiveness in the sphere of the aesthetic (cf. *CJ*, §VII, 5:189; *FI*, §VIII, 20:225 and §XII, 20:248). But in either case, whether the response to the sublime is a sequence of feelings of displeasure and pleasure or a single feeling simultaneously both painful yet pleasurable, the response to the sublime can be readily distinguished from that to the beautiful, first by the mere fact that it is complex at all, and second, by the fact that in at least some way "an object is apprehended as sublime with a pleasure that is possible only by means of a displeasure" (*CJ*, §27, 5:260). Thus, even if the ways in which the responses to the beautiful and sublime are disinterested, formally purposive, and universally and necessarily valid were the same, the judgments on these two aesthetic phenomena could indeed be meaningfully differentiated by qualitative differences in the feelings which satisfy these further criteria.

## V. THE MATHEMATICAL AND DYNAMICAL SUBLIME

### The general theory

But Kant's distinction between the beautiful and the sublime does not stop with their phenomenological differentiation. He also elaborates differences in the psychological mechanisms which explain these responses; and as a matter of fact

Kant's ambivalence about the precise way in which the complexity of the feeling of sublimity is manifested is probably due to underlying tensions in this explanation rather than to any phenomenological observations.

As we have seen, Kant's general analysis of the concept of aesthetic judgment yields the broad epistemological constraints that such a judgment must both concern yet also be made by means of a feeling of pleasure, but that it must also satisfy a claim of subjective universal and necessary validity. His explanatory theory is, then, that such a conjunction of constraints can only be fulfilled by feelings, whether simple or complex, which are caused by a free rather than conceptually guided or determined relationship or "play" of the cognitive faculties of mind. Yet this abstract explanation may be satisfied by a variety of specific states, and the psychological processes that produce our responses to beauty and sublimity, although both instances of "free play," are nevertheless significantly different. The general theory requires that aesthetic response be produced by the free rather than rule-governed conformity of the imagination to the law of a "higher" cognitive faculty. That is, an object of a genuine aesthetic response produces the pleasure we take in it when the imagination apprehends it in a way that is felt to fulfill the general objective of a higher cognitive faculty, even though the kind of determinate concept which ordinarily ensures the fulfillment of such an aim is not being employed, and such an apprehension is unusually pleasurable just because the fulfillment of this objective, in itself always desirable, is felt to be contingent rather than necessary in these circumstances and is thus especially noteworthy.[16] But differences in *which* faculties beyond the imagination are involved and *how* they are related to it mean that there is a variety of psychological states which can be subsumed under this general conception of an epistemological accomplishment felt to be achieved without ordinary epistemic guarantees.

In the response to the beautiful, the imagination's grasp of the form of a particular object apart from the evaluation of it under any determinate empirical concept directly satisfies the

understanding's general requirement for unity in our apprehension of a given manifold (*CJ*, §VII, 5:190), so the abstract
concept of a free play of the cognitive faculties is in this case
instantiated by what is felt as a simple and pleasurable harmony between the freedom of the imagination and the fundamental aim of all employment of the understanding – an aim
so fundamental to our mental life that we are, indeed, rarely
conscious of it as such (*CJ*, §VI, 5:187–8). In the response to the
sublime, however, it is not the understanding but rather *reason* (that is, not simply our ability to apply concepts to particular objects but our even higher-order ability to seek and find
unity and completeness among concepts and principles themselves, whether of a theoretical or practical nature) which en-
gages with the imagination. What results from "free play" of
reason and the imagination is not a simple feeling of harmony
but a complex psychological state, including both frustration
at the imagination's inability to satisfy the bidding of reason
through any finite synthesis of sensibility – hence the element of displeasure in our response to the sublime – and the
sense that this very frustration itself is a representation of the
infinite capacity of reason, a sensible representation which
satisfies the bidding of reason in an unexpected way and is
thus the ground of our ultimate pleasure in the sublime. In the
case of the sublime, the state of the imagination is freely
purposive and thus pleasurable in that its very "incapacity
discovers the consciousness of an unlimited capacity of the
subject, and the mind can aesthetically estimate the latter only
by means of the former" (*CJ*, §27, 5:259). The sublime, like the
beautiful, produces a psychological state in which the imagination is felt to satisfy the objective of a higher faculty of
cognition freely, but because this higher faculty is reason
rather than understanding, the response to the sublime differs from that to beauty both in its actual feeling and, ultimately, in some specifics of its epistemological status.

A further variety in the psychological states which may
instantiate the general conception of free play derives from
the fact that whereas the understanding has only the single
epistemic objective of unifying its manifolds, the objectives

of reason can be either theoretical or practical (that is, can concern the structure of inquiry or the principles of conduct) and thus give rise to two kinds of sublimity. It is to explain this that Kant tacitly preempts the headings of "Quantity" and "Relation" to expound, not the intersubjective validity and subjective finality of the sublime, but rather the two distinct ways in which the imagination can satisfy reason and thereby give us the pleasure of sublimity. In the discussion of the *"aesthetic* estimation of magnitude" (*CJ*, §26, 5:255), also called the "mathematically sublime" (*CJ*, §25, 5:248), which obviously occupies the place of a discussion of quantity, imagination is shown to please by representing theoretical reason's requirement of the representation of an absolutely great whole, which no synthesis of the imagination guided by the understanding alone can provide. In the discussion of the "dynamically sublime in nature" (*CJ*, §28, 5:260), which first by elimination and finally by explicit wording (see the last paragraph of §28, 5:264) can be seen to occupy the place of a discussion of relation, the imagination is argued to please by representing in a sensibly palpable form the dominion of our rational personality over the threats of phenomenal nature as that is represented by the deterministic understanding.

The general outline of Kant's two explanations of the feeling of sublimity is clear enough. In its ordinary conjunction with the understanding, the imagination is frustrated in fulfilling an objective of reason, but the very feeling of frustration which is thus engendered reveals the presence of "a faculty of mind transcending every standard of sense" (*CJ*, §24, 5:250), and in so doing itself becomes the occasion of a considerable feeling of pleasure. But the details of Kant's account are infected by several ambivalences, and it will be worth our while to tarry over these, precisely because they expose some problems in several of the most basic concepts of Kant's aesthetic theory. In particular, first, Kant's characterization of the response to the mathematical sublime suggests a problem with his fundamental conception of pleasure and displeasure as simple and unanalyzable feelings; second,

Kant's explanation of the mathematical sublime, and even more his account of the dynamical sublime, manifest a tension between the primacy of feeling and the primacy of judgment in his underlying model of aesthetic estimation;[17] and finally, a certain contrast between Kant's initial explanations of both forms of the sublime and his reprise of these explanations in the "General Remark" following this initial analysis reveals an indeterminacy in Kant's very conception of the imagination itself.

## Tensions in Kant's account

Kant's explanation of the mathematical sublime turns on the distinction between the "logical" and "aesthetic" estimation of magnitudes, which in turn revolves on his distinction between "apprehension" and "comprehension," or between the several successive representations of the elements of a given manifold (apprehension) and their joint display in a single further representation of them (comprehension) (*CJ*, §26, 5:251–2). Briefly put, his theory is this. By logical estimation, or the enumeration of separately apprehended items under some unit of measurement or other, a magnitude of any size may in principle be measured. But there are two different senses in which such a measurement will be relative rather than absolute. First, the units of measurement will always be either entirely arbitrary or at best relative to a merely empirical comparison group, so measurement by such units can give us only a comparative and not an absolute idea of the magnitude of the whole which is measured by them (*CJ*, §25, 5:248; §26, 5:251). Second, since the understanding can always conceptually represent the continuation of the synthesis of any manifold of apprehended units *ad infinitum* but can never complete the synthesis of an infinite whole, it is prevented from producing concrete comprehension in intuition of an absolute whole where that is taken to mean an infinitely large whole (*CJ*, §26, 5:251–2). Now of course as long as we confine ourselves to concepts of the understanding, "there is nothing compelling us to tax the utmost powers of the imagination . . . so as to enlarge the size of the measure, and thus make the single intuition holding the many in one (the *comprehension*) as great as possible"; that is, the understanding itself does not require the measurement of an absolute whole by an absolute unit. Yet, Kant holds, the mind – in particular the imagination – "does listen to the voice of reason, which for all given magnitudes – even for those which can never be completely apprehended . . . – requires totality and consequently comprehension in *one* intuition, and which calls for a *presentation* answering to all the . . . members of a progressively increasing numerical series, and does not exempt even the infinite" from this demand (*CJ*, §26, 5:254). That is, the imagination does recognize a call for the representation of an absolutely great series by an absolutely great unit of measurement. But of course it cannot succeed in actually producing such a representation, so it causes a feeling of inadequacy; yet it is that very feeling of frustration which reveals to us the existence of reason and its call, which is in turn the ground for our eventual pleasure in the mathematically sublime. Thus

> the idea of the comprehension of any phenomenon whatever, that may be given us, in a whole of intuition, is an idea imposed upon us by a law of reason. . . . But our imagination, even when taxing itself to the utmost on the score of this required comprehension . . . betrays its limits and inadequacy, but still, at the same time, its proper vocation of making itself adequate to the same as a law. Therefore, the feeling of the sublime in nature is respect for our own vocation, . . . and this feeling as it were renders intuitable the supremacy of the rational determination of our cognitive faculties over the greatest power of the sensibility. (*CJ*, §27, 5:257)

The general drift of Kant's argument is obvious. The very feeling of the inadequacy of the imagination to represent an absolute whole is the same feeling which manifests to us the existence of reason, and so this frustration turns pleasurable.

But at this point Kant's account succumbs to the ambivalence earlier mentioned; that is, Kant now makes it unclear whether what all this produces is a single but complex feeling which is both displeasurable yet pleasurable, or a succession of simple feelings which begins with displeasure but must end in pleasure. For it is at precisely this point in his argument that (as I noted in Section IV) Kant first claims that our response to the mathematically sublime is "a feeling of displeasure from the inadequacy of the imagination . . . and a simultaneously aroused pleasure from the agreement of this very judgment of inadequacy of the greatest sensible faculty with the ideas of reason" but then goes on to describe what is apparently a succession of pain and pleasure, rather than a simultaneous combination of them, by saying that the "mind feels itself *set in motion* in the representation of the sublime in nature," that it feels "a rapidly alternating repulsion and attraction to one and the same object" in which the idea of an absolute whole first seems "like an abyss in which it fears to lose itself" but then like a "rational idea of the supersensible [which] is not excessive, but conformable to law . . . and so in turn as much a source of attraction as it was repellent to mere sensibility" (*CJ*, §27, 5:257–8). What can account for this sort of ambivalence in Kant's view about the simultaneity or alternation in the feeling of the sublime?

One answer to this question would be that although Kant's explanation of the mathematical sublime points toward a situation in which a single feeling simultaneously reveals two different facts about our faculties, facts toward which we adopt contrasting evaluative attitudes, Kant's initial temptation to infer from this a single but complex feeling of pleasure and displeasure gives way before his Humean assumption that feelings of pleasure and displeasure are qualitatively unique and simple atoms of sensation. This phenomenology of feeling would permit a response that must for theoretical reasons be inferred to be displeasurable yet also pleasurable to be modeled only by a succession of distinct sensations.

Another possibility, however, suggested by Kant's slide (in the passage from *CJ*, §27, that I quoted in §IV of this chapter) from "a feeling of displeasure from the inadequacy" to "this very judgment of inadequacy" is that Kant's ambivalence on this matter is a reflection of his underlying unclarity about to just what degree aesthetic judgment can be understood as a psychological process that first becomes manifest to consciousness only in feelings of pleasure or displeasure and to what degree it must be understood as a process in which such feelings could result only from a conscious reflection that a certain objective is satisfied. The picture which predominates in the "Analytic of the Beautiful" is that, since the harmony of the imagination and understanding becomes manifest only in the feeling of pleasure, whatever reflection leads to the feeling must be essentially subconscious, and only reflection on the origins and intersubjective status of the given pleasure could be anything like a conscious process of inference.[18] Applying this model to the case of the sublime, Kant might have been tempted to regard both the recognition of the inadequate effort of the imagination and the recognition that its very inadequacy implies the vocation of our reason, since these both lead to feelings, as manifesting themselves only *in* such feelings; and with all that reflection taking place subconsciously there would be no obvious reason why both sorts of feeling should not become conscious simultaneously. However, Kant's inclination to move away from this suggestion to the picture of several successive feelings might well have been founded in an increasing suspicion of the implausibility of this basic model of aesthetic reflection as it is stretched to take in the case of the sublime. In particular, he might have recognized that while it is at least plausible to think of the striving of the imagination toward the comprehension of an absolute whole as actually manifesting itself to awareness only in a feeling of failure, the *interpretation* of this frustration as revealing the demand of reason – what Kant suddenly describes as "this very judgment of inadequacy" – would seem to require a conscious reflection in conceptual terms. Recognizing this, Kant might have been tempted tacitly to interpose a judgment between the feeling of frustration and the feeling of pleasure at its insignificance in the face of reason and thus to introduce a temporal separation between the two feelings.

The increasing necessity for giving primacy to the conscious occurrence of judgment rather than mere feeling may be even more evident in Kant's treatment of the dynamical sublime. In the discussion of the mathematical sublime, Kant's reference to the "judgment of inadequacy" is unique, and thus might be just a slip in an account otherwise intended to allow consciousness in the form of feeling only. In the case of the dynamical sublime, however, Kant's exposition appears throughout to describe a pattern in which a painful feeling must be accompanied by an explicit *judgment* of the superiority of reason, with a further feeling of pleasure succeeding only once that judgment is made. For what Kant describes is essentially the case in which mighty objects or vistas in nature are first *felt* to be *fearsome* but in which it is then *judged* that there is no (moral) reason to be *afraid* of nature (*CJ*, §28, 5:260) – and only on the "cessation" of this uneasiness due to this judgment does there arise a "feeling of joy" (*CJ*, §28, 5:261). At the very least, the language of beliefs or propositional attitudes is more in evidence in Kant's discussion of the dynamical sublime. The example that Kant uses to introduce this idea of the dynamical sublime is "the righteous man" who "fears God without being afraid of him." Although the righteous man feels the terrifying power of God, "he thinks of the case of his wishing to resist God and his commandments as one which need offer *him* no anxiety" (*CJ*, §28, 5:260–1) – because, of course, he has no desire to resist such righteous commandments. The example of the dynamical sublime that most interests Kant, however, is not that in which a human being humbles himself before the superior power of God but rather that in which the natural inclinations and fears of the human being are humbled before his own power of practical reason. In explaining how fear of the power of nature is overcome by the revelation of practical reason, although Kant does once use the ambiguous verb *beurteilen* (which can denote either an unconscious process of reflection leading to a feeling or the conscious judgment or assessment of a feeling),[19] the context suggests that what ultimately moves us from fear to "soul-stirring delight" is not the mere feeling that practical reason exists but a fairly explicit judgment that its dominion exceeds that of mere nature and nature's deterministic power of disposing over our "worldly goods, health, and life." Thus,

> The irresistibility of the might of nature gives us to recognize [*erkennen*] our physical helplessness, considered [*betrachtet*] as creatures of nature, but at the same time reveals [*entdeckt*] ourselves as independent of it and a superiority over nature on which is founded a self-preservation of quite another kind than that which may be attacked and brought into danger by the nature outside us, one where the humanity in our own person remains undefeated. (*CJ*, §28, 5:261–62)

It seems hard indeed to think of all of this, especially when described with such verbs, as a subconscious psychological mechanism. Instead, it seems that by this point Kant is being forced by the substance before him to characterize a state in which conscious reflection on highly articulated ideas of reason – although not, of course, "determinate concepts" in his technical sense – is necessary before any feeling of pleasure could plausibly be expected. This seems part of what he means when he says that sublimity resides "only in our own mind, insofar as we may become conscious of our superiority over nature within, and thus also over nature without us" (*CJ*, §28, 5:264).

None of this implies that Kant's explanation of the feeling of dynamic sublimity is intended to break with the idea of the harmony of the faculties apart from concepts. For Kant perserveres in the claim that it is the imagination rather than an explicitly conceptual faculty which is doing the work here – "Nature is here called sublime merely because it raises the imagination to a presentation of those cases in which the mind can make itself sensible of the sublimity of the sphere of its own being" – and he expressly abjures the objection that this explanation of the sublime makes it "too far-fetched and rationalized [*vernünftelt*]," so placing it "beyond the reach of an aesthetic judgment," claiming instead that "it may be the foundation of the commonest judgments" and indeed that "one is not always conscious of its presence" (*CJ*, §28, 5:262). The very fact that such a case can still be subsumed under the basic model of the harmony of the faculties, however, may well reveal the ambivalence of that conception between a strictly psychological and necessarily more propositional state of mind.[20]

The final point to be made concerning Kant's explanation of our response to the sublime is that although it clearly attempts to preserve the primacy of imagination's "free conformity to law" (*CJ*, §22 General Remark, 5:240) in aesthetic response in general, it also reveals the indeterminacy of Kant's conception of the imagination itself. In the detailed explanations of the mathematical and dynamical sublimes which we have just been considering, the imagination appears to function only within limits set for it by the understanding and to "represent" reason only indirectly, by producing a feeling of inadequacy which is the occasion for a further feeling of – or reflection on – our superior rationality; but in the summary "General Remark" which follows these particular explanations, Kant seems to envision the imagination entering into a direct harmony, rather than merely a significant contrast, with the faculty of reason. He writes:

> Thus, too, delight in the sublime in nature is only *negative* (whereas that in the beautiful is *positive*), that is to say it is a feeling of imagination by its own act depriving itself of its freedom by receiving a final determination in accordance with a law other than that of its empirical employment. In this way it gains an extension and a might greater than that which it sacrifices, though the ground of this is concealed from it, . . . and it [only] *feels* the cause to which it is subjected. (*CJ*, §29 General Remark, 5:269)

Precisely while attempting to restore the primacy of feeling rather than explicit judgment in the characterization of aesthetic response, that is, Kant seems to suggest that the imagination may enter into the direct service of reason rather than merely serve to point to its existence by contrast with its own limitations. And what this suggests is simply that Kant's conception of the imagination is not really subject to a strict set of either empirical constraints or theoretical ones independent of his aesthetic theory, but is sufficiently pliable – or, if one will be harsh, vacuous – to mold itself to the changing demands of his particular analyses of aesthetic phenomena. This is, of course, not a conclusion which would be a total surprise even to a reader of the "Analytic of the Beautiful" alone, but it is certainly strengthened by the evidence of the "Analytic of the Sublime."

This observation completes my remarks on the way in which the explanation of the sublime is specifically differentiated from that of the beautiful while remaining within a common generic framework – a conclusion which remains untouched by the various problems I have mentioned, as long as we consider that they may represent fundamental tensions within that generic model itself rather than essential differences between the beautiful and the sublime. I now turn to the final stage of my exposition, that is, the description of the ways in which the specific differences between the feelings and the explanations of the beautiful and the sublime lead to specific differences in their satisfaction of the generic constraints of disinterestedness, subjective or formal purposiveness, and universal and necessary validity.

## VI. THE DIFFERENCE BETWEEN THE BEAUTIFUL AND THE SUBLIME

### Subject and object

Perhaps the most obvious of these differences lies in the way that the beautiful and the sublime each satisfy the third moment's requirement that aesthetic responses be grounded in the special "relation" of subjective or formal finality in the perception of an object. This is the requirement that an aesthetic judgment express only the "*form* of finality in an object, so far as it is perceived in it *apart from the representation of an end"* (*CJ*, §17, 45:236): that is, the demand that an object of an aesthetic judgment please us only by satisfying our own subjective end or purpose in the pursuit of cognition and not because it is judged to satisfy any more particular objective concept or purpose, especially a practical purpose. Kant makes it clear from the outset that the case of the sublime is intended to satisfy this general constraint: "Judgment concerning the sublime in nature would not be excluded from the aesthetic of the reflective judgment, because it too expresses a subjective purposiveness that does not rest on a concept of the object" (*FI*, §XII, 20:250). What the "Analytic of the Sublime" now reveals is that this is a generic constraint which can be satisfied in different ways by different states of the imagination. This must be so, for although in the case of beauty the "bare form of finality" (*CJ*, §11, 5:221) is specifically exemplified by the imaginative apprehension of a "finality of form" in a particular object, that is, its perceivable form (e.g., *CJ*, §13, 5:223), an object which we experience as sublime, whether it impresses us through the idea of absolute magnitude or of absolute power, pleases us precisely because of its formlessness. Something which is sublime serves the subjective end of reason by allowing the imagination to reveal the power of the latter, but it does not manifest the finality of perceivable form characteristic of a beautiful individual object. Thus the "form of finality" must be a general constraint satisfied by both the beautiful and the sublime, but the "finality of form" characteristic of the beautiful is only a specific way in which this requirement may be satisfied, and one which may be contrasted to the formal finality of formlessness characteristic of the sublime.[21] In other words, in the case of the sublime it is the apprehension of an indeterminate rather than readily grasped form which advances our underlying intellectual objective.

At one point Kant goes so far as to claim that this difference between the ways in which they satisfy the requirements of subjective finality is the "most important and intrinsic distinction" between the beautiful and the sublime. He also uses it to argue for a distinction in the proper *grammar* of the verbal expressions of judgments about these two phenomena. Kant outlines his general claim that

> natural beauty . . . conveys a finality in its form, through which the object seems to be as it were antecedently determined for our faculty of judgment; whereas that which merely in its apprehension without any ratiocination arouses the feeling of the sublime in us may indeed appear, as regards its form, contra-final for our faculty of judgment, inappropriate for our faculty of representation, and as it were outrageous for the imagination, and yet just for this may be judged all the more sublime.

He then infers from this "that we express ourselves incorrectly when we call some *object of nature* sublime, though it is quite proper to call an object of nature beautiful" (*CJ*, §23, 5:245). Precisely because of the formlessness of that which causes us to feel sublimity, Kant insists, it is only "the disposition of the soul evoked by a particular representation engaging the reflective judgment, but not the object, which is to be called sublime" (*CJ*, §25, 5:250). Thus, Kant also differentiates the judgments on the beautiful and the sublime by holding that some particular object can always be treated as both cause and grammatical subject of the former, but as cause only and not grammatical subject in the case of the latter.

This inference seems peculiar. If we assume that it is the causal connection which the *theory* of aesthetic response postulates between a given object and our feeling of pleasure in its presence which is the ground for taking *that* object as *the* subject of our expressed aesthetic judgment, then Kant seems wrong to suppose that the "formlessness" of that which makes us aware of sublimity disqualifies it from being the grammatical subject of an aesthetic judgment. For something like the vastness of extent or force of a mountain range or stormhead, whether or not it could be grasped by the imagination without the aid of reason, is certainly as objective a property of as ordinary an object (or collection of objects) as the delicacy of a flower or the regularity of a (re-peated pattern in a) frieze; indeed, since it *could* be measured by a (relativistic) synthesis of the understanding, it may well be more objective than the latter. Thus its object should stand in as direct a causal relation to our feeling of sublimity as a flower or frieze does to our feeling of beauty. Kant's claim that we respond to the form of a specific object in the case of the beautiful alone thus appears to proceed only by a paralogistic confusion between some specific notion of *relatively confined* and/or *readily grasped* form and the more abstract notion of form *in general*.

Nevertheless, Kant's apparently unjustified claim about the grammar of judgments of sublimity may be based on at least a phenomenological point with genuine bearing on the practical possibility of individuating particular objects for our judgments of sublimity. For if we assume, as Kant often does, that in the aesthetic estimation of an object we must not merely refrain from evaluating an object according to whatever determinate empirical concepts we know to apply to it but actually abstract from these concepts altogether, then it may follow that we in fact discriminate a particular object, within the whole manifold of the experience which on a given occasion is accompanied by a feeling of pleasure, *as* the particular object of our judgment, only if something *other* than an empirical concept picks such an object out and secures the reference of our judgment to it; the merely theoretical knowledge that there *is* a connection between our feeling and some particular object(s) will not do this for us. But then, although the kind of specially coherent and readily graspable forms which Kant holds to be characteristic of the beautiful may well serve to delimit phenomenologically particular objects within the whole manifold of our experience as *the* proper objects of our judgments of beauty even without the use of determinate concepts, the very fact that it is an appearance of unlimitedness which is responsible for the feeling of sublimity may indeed mean that there is nothing so particular, nothing short of the *whole* of what we perceive on the occasion of feeling sublimity, which the feeling itself allows us to pick out as its proper object. This would remain true even in light of the theoretical concession that in an *explanation* of our feeling, only a finite (although perhaps very large) number of ordinary and particular empirical objects – mountains which *could* be measured, waves which *could* be counted – would ultimately be invoked.

It might seem harmless for Kant to express the view that it is the totality of the objects of our present experience which is responsible for its being an experience of the sublime by saying that it is our experience itself which is the proper object of our judgment of sublimity. But this presents a difference in phenomenology and, as it were, grammatical practicability as an ultimate difference in ontology, and to do this can mislead the reader into mistaking the *phenomenologically* indeterminate scope of the object of our experience of sublimity for an *epistemic* subjectivity that is greater than that which characterizes our experience of beauty. Kant's emphasis on his grammatical point thus tends to mask rather than clarify his underlying thesis that the beautiful and the sublime are phenomenological and psychological variants within the single logical and epistemological genus of aesthetic reflective judgment. But when we realize that his point is only phenomenological, this general thesis is confirmed: The formlessness of the sublime leads to a difference in the way in which the formal finality of the sublime is felt and expressed, but not to a fundamental departure from that generic constraint itself.

Consideration of the dynamical rather than mathematical sublime may suggest another reason for Kant's claim that sublimity, unlike beauty, is not properly predicated of external objects at all. In the case of beauty, the harmony of imagination and understanding is supposed to be induced solely by the form of an external object; thus, although the feeling of pleasure is of course internal and depends upon the propensity of our faculties to react to external objects in certain ways, it is not misleading to ascribe beauty to the object as well. But in the case of the dynamical sublime, our pleasure depends upon the way in which physically fearsome natural phenomena turn our thought to the indestructible moral personality which lies within us. The physical properties play a causal role in this reflection, but it is our own moral character which is ultimately the object of our pleasure. To this extent Kant is justified in denying that the property of sublimity can properly be attributed to the external objects which may stimulate our reflection.[22]

### Disinterestedness

Turning now from the "relation" of subjective finality to the "quality" of disinterestedness, we may find it more difficult to say whether Kant intends a specific difference in the ways the beautiful and the sublime satisfy this requirement. This is partly because, as we have already observed, there is little explicit discussion of disinterestedness in the "Analytic of the Sublime" proper, the rubric of "quality" having been preempted for other purposes; and it is partly because even in the "Analytic of the Beautiful" it is by no means clear that Kant employs a univocal concept of disinterestedness.[23] In fact, there are at least three different conceptions of disinterestedness at work in Kant's argument. But although there is no great difference in the way in which the beautiful and the sublime exemplify disinterestedness on the first two of these conceptions, when it comes to the last we do find the same pattern of significant phenomenological differentiation within a generally similar epistemological framework that we have found in the case of subjective finality.

Kant's official definition of an "interest," in the "Analytic of the Beautiful," is that it is a pleasure "which we connect with the representation of the existence of an object" (*CJ*, §2, 5:204). On this definition the independence of a feeling of pleasure from any connection to the existence of an object constitutes its disinterestedness. If the absence of such a connection is sufficient to determine disinterestedness, then pleasure in the sublime is disinterested in precisely the same way as our response to beauty is, for what Kant claims to be true in the case of the sublime is "that, although we have no interest at all in the object, that is, its existence is a matter of indifference to us, still its mere magnitude, even if it is regarded as formless, is able to convey a universally communicable delight" (*CJ*, §25, 5:249). The wording here is virtually identical to that of such paradigmatic passages as the original claim, in Section 2 of the *Critique of Judgment*, that when it comes to the question of beauty "one wants to know only whether the mere representation of an object is accompanied by delight in me, no matter how indifferent I may be in regard to the existence of the object of this representation" (*CJ*, §2, 5:205; see also §5, 5:209).

The notion of indifference to existence, however, stands in as much need of interpretation as the notion of disinterestedness itself. In view of the fact that Kant asserts, but offers no good argument to prove, that the beautiful is without any effect on desire or volition at all (*CJ*, §2, 5:205n.; §29 General Remark, 5:271), one strategy is to use his treatment of interest in the second *Critique*. There he defines an interest as a determinate *conception* of an object as an object of choice showing its suitability for a specific purpose prior to its existence.[24] We may then interpret the disinterestedness of the aesthetic as freedom from this sort of interest. But on this interpretation, too, there seems to be no significant difference between the beautiful and the sublime, for in saying that "a pure judgment of the sublime must have no end of the object as its determining ground, if it is to be aesthetic and not mixed up with any judgment of understanding or reason" (*CJ*, §26, 5:253), Kant again uses words that could have been lifted directly from any number of places in the "Analytic of the Beautiful" (e.g., *CJ*, §4, 5:207; §11, 5:221). Just as the disinterestedness of the pleasure in the beautiful consists not in its independence of objectives of cognition itself but only in its independence from any determinate concept of any particular end to be served by a given object, so too the disinterestedness of the sublime requires that in the experience of the sublime the imagination be felt to "subjectively harmonize with the ideas" of reason, "though quite without being set in connection with any determinate purpose" (*CJ*, §26, 5:256). There is a difference here in regard to *which* higher faculty of the mind is indeterminately satisfied, but not in regard to the indeterminacy, and hence disinterestedness, of its satisfaction.

However, when we consider Kant's final contrasts between the beautiful and the sublime in the "General Remark," a significant difference in the way in which they satisfy the requirement of disinterestedness does seem to emerge. For Kant emphasizes that "the beautiful is that which pleases in the mere estimate of it," thus suggesting that it is at least without any obvious connection to interest at all, but he claims that "the sublime is that which pleases immediately by reason of its very *opposition* to the interest of sense." As he also puts it, "The beautiful prepares us to love something, even nature, apart from any interest, [but] the sublime, to esteem something even *against* our (sensible) interest" (*CJ*, §29, General Remark, 5:267; emphases added). The disinterestedness of the sublime, it seems, consists not in freedom from any interest at all but only in freedom from the particular, presumably self-referential, interests *of sense;* the sublime appears to please *not* because it involves freedom from interest *simpliciter,* but rather precisely because its freedom from particular interests of sense is regarded as an aesthetic – imaginative rather than conceptual – satisfaction of the higher demand of "inner freedom." In Kant's words, the delight in the sublime "is from the aesthetic side (in relation to sensibility) negative, that is, against [sensibility's] interest, but considered from the intellectual side it is positive and connected with an interest" (*CJ*, §29 General Remark, 5:271). The disinterestedness of our response to the sublime seems more like a form of moral disinterestedness in which private interests are overridden by some *higher* interest than like the purely aesthetic disinterestedness of the beautiful, in which personal interests are supposed to be simply disengaged without being overridden by any other interest, higher or not.

Once again, however, these remarks describe a phenomenological difference in the satisfaction of an epistemological constraint – our pleasure in the sublime is *felt* as emerging out of a conflict of higher and lower interests, whereas our pleasure in the beautiful is not – but do not imply any fundamental departure from the basic epistemology of aesthetic judgment. For in both the case of the imaginative grasp of a relatively confined form that is typical of the beautiful and the case of imaginative apprehension of a relatively limitless force or magnitude that is typical of the sublime, what we have is a psychological state that is felt to satisfy the objective of a higher faculty of the mind in the absence of the employment of the sort of determinate concepts – whether theoretical or practical – in virtue of which such objectives are ordinarily satisfied; and *both* such objectives may be construed as interests of the relevant faculties of mind in light of Kant's statement, in his famous discussion of the "primacy of practical reason," that "to every faculty of the mind an interest can be ascribed," the "knowledge of objects up to the highest *a priori* principles" being just as much an interest as "the determination of the will with respect to the final and perfect end."[25] To be sure, the purpose which is felt to be satisfied in the case of imagination's harmony with the understanding – namely, that our manifolds of intuition be unified – is one which, with the exception of such unusual cases as directed scientific research, rarely presents itself to us as a conscious objective of action, and it is a purpose which rarely does or is felt to conflict with other purposes, as moral objectives certainly may do or be felt to do. On the contrary, the objective which is indeterminately satisfied in our response to the sublime – namely, that reason be shown to have a "dominion" (cf. *CJ*, §28, 5:260) superior to the limitations of mere sense – is one which is intimately involved in consciously undertaken actions having distinct objectives which frequently conflict with our purposes – namely, the acts of duty demanded by practical reason. Thus, as the objective of reason may well be *felt* as an interest in its own light, indeed as an interest in conflict with others, whereas the objective of understanding may never actually be *felt* as such, the disinterestedness of beauty may be *felt* as complete independence from interests, while that of the sublime is *felt* as a conflict between different interests, although as a conflict which is pleasurable because of its outcome. This is precisely to say, however, that there is in the case of disinterestedness once again a phenomenological difference in the way in which a more general constraint on the aesthetic is exemplified, so that the different phenomenologies of disinterestedness in the beautiful and the sublime are grounds for their specific differentiation within the same genus of aesthetic reflective judgment.

## Universal and necessary validity

We may now consider the requirement that the pleasure in the sublime, like that in the beautiful, be judged to be universally and necessarily valid. As we earlier noted, having already employed the heading "Quantity" for his discussion of the magnitude of the *objects* which occasion feelings of sublimity rather than for any discussion of the intersubjective validity of judgments about such feelings, Kant is now forced to consolidate the supposedly separate "quantity" and "modality" of aesthetic judgment into the single requirement of the "modality" on the judgment of the sublime, namely, "the necessity of the agreement of the judgments of others on the sublime with our own, which we include within our own judgment" (*CJ*, §29, 5:265). This textual feature represents only a superficial difference between Kant's expositions of the beautiful and the sublime, for the discussion should have been so consolidated in the "Analytic of the Beautiful" as well; the constraints on the epistemological status of judgments of beauty with which Kant was concerned in the second and fourth moments of the "Analytic of the Beautiful" constituted all along only a single requirement of a rationally grounded expectation of intersubjective validity.[26] However, there is also a more significant variation in Kant's treatment of the expectation of the satisfaction of the requirement of intersubjective agreement in the case of the judgment on the sublime. This lies in his claim that although the "universal voice" with which we speak in the case of the beautiful may find "easy entrance" among others in actual practice, the fact that reason and its ideas are involved in the explanation of our response to the sublime means that intersubjective agreement about such responses, although as well-founded in fundamental and indispensable features of human nature as the response to beauty, cannot reasonably be expected to emerge at the same point in actual practice or at the same stage in the actual development of different individuals and cultures.

In the case of beauty, Kant supposes, since the faculties of imagination and understanding and the possibility of co-operation between them that are necessary for its experience are necessary for any cognition at all, and since at most nothing more than a simple act of abstraction from determinate concepts of purpose or classification is needed for this free cooperation to occur, "agreement with our judgment may be imputed to everyone straight off and indeed expected without noticeably erring" (*CJ*, §29, 5:264). However, since the response to the sublime involves the imaginative satisfaction of ideas of theoretical or – what Kant now exclusively emphasizes – practical reason, the experience of sublimity in a particular situation may require not a mere act of abstraction but rather the considerable degree of culture and education which is necessary to develop the capacity of reason and moral feeling itself, even if we suppose a predisposition to this capacity in everyone. As Kant puts it, although we may indeed expect immediate agreement about "countless things in beautiful nature" without noticeable error, "We cannot so readily promise ourselves the accord of others with judgments on the sublime," for "without the development of moral ideas, that which we, prepared by culture, call sublime may strike the untutored person merely as terrifying" (*CJ*, §29, 5:264–5).

Although he emphasizes this point, however, Kant makes it even clearer than in his remarks on the subjective finality and disinterestedness of the sublime that he is describing an empirical difference in the specific phenomenologies and psychologies of the beautiful and the sublime, not a fundamental difference in their logical or epistemological status. For he insists that in both cases the sources of response are equally necessary to human nature. Because an *a priori* principle of human similarity underlies the judgment on the sublime as well as that on the beautiful (*CJ*, §29, 5:266), the expectation of agreement given the ideal conditions of response which are presupposed even in the case of beauty (*CJ*, §8, 5:216; §38, 5:290–1) is equally reasonable in both cases, although what counts as the ideal conditions of response may vary. As Kant argues,

> Just because the judgment on the sublime in nature requires culture (more than that on the beautiful), it does not follow that it is first generated by culture and introduced into society merely by convention; rather it has its foundation in human nature and indeed in that which we impute to everyone along with the healthy understanding and which we can require of everyone, namely the disposition for the feeling of (practical) ideas, that is, moral [feeling]. (*CJ*, §29, 5:265)

From an epistemological point of view, judgments on the beautiful and the sublime are equally capable of satisfying aesthetic judgment's generic criterion of universal and necessary agreement, even though differences in the psychological processes which underlie these judgments can only be expected to produce differences in the empirical circumstances in which this requirement is satisfied. Once again, the beautiful and the sublime both satisfy the generic requirements of aesthetic judgment but do so in specifically different ways.

We may conclude, then, that Kant's four moments are not used in an incoherent attempt to define formally distinct types of aesthetic judgment by identical attributes. Instead, these four moments loosely define a general conception of aesthetic judgments and concepts, which can then be seen as being satisfied by a variety of responses differing from each other in significant details of psychology and phenomenology even while they conform to a fundamentally similar linguistic analysis and epistemological justification. Kant is no more confused about the specific task of defining distinct forms of aesthetic judgment than he is about the general objective of linking both logical and epistemological considerations and psychological and phenomenological ones into a single but complex aesthetic theory: which is to say that although he is sometimes confused about the details, the basic distinctions of his theory of taste exhibit a subtle exploitation, rather than conflation, of these different levels of analysis and argument.

# Chapter 7

## Nature, art, and autonomy

Kant holds that pleasure in the beauty and the sublimity of nature has a moral value lacking in a taste for fine art. To the modern sensibility, irremediably transformed by the modern conception of the uniqueness of artistic creation, this must appear antiquated, as irrelevant to our own conception of the self and its expression in art as powdered wigs to our dress. For us, indeed, when artists reshape nature into earthworks or drape whole islands in cloth, nature itself may seem like nothing more than another medium for art. But a careful comparison of Kant's reasons for preferring nature over art with views about nature and art common among his contemporaries reveals a distinctly modern sensibility after all. Although his conclusions may seem typical of his time, Kant's grounds for them are radically divergent from those his peers accepted: Kant glorifies the aesthetic appreciation of nature and downplays that of art precisely because he thinks that the former displays the fundamental autonomy of the human will far better than the latter. He would not reconceive of nature as itself a product of human artistry –

This essay was originally published under the title "Nature, Art and Autonomy: A Copernican Revolution in Kant's Aesthetics," in the *Festschrift* volume for Dieter Henrich, *Theorie der Subjektivität*, ed. Konrad Cramer, Hans-Friedrich Fulda, Rolf-Peter Horstmann, and Ulrich Pothast (Frankfurt am Main: Suhrkamp, 1987), pp. 299–343. The postscript to this chapter has been added for the present edition.

art creates at best a second nature – but his own view that natural beauty and sublimity are so important just because they offer us a far greater opportunity to admire the magnificence of our own autonomy than any form of art is also a profound departure from his time. This revolution in Kant's thought is radical enough to be called Copernican, although (ironically) it returns mankind to the center of the moral universe.

In what follows, I will demonstrate the underlying modernity of Kant's apparently old-fashioned preference for nature over art in two steps. First, I will illustrate the conceptions of the value of natural beauty, the naturally sublime, and artistic beauty which were characteristic of many eighteenth-century writers. Then I will turn to Kant: first to his denigration of the "empirical interest" in beauty, which denies an account of the moral value of art accepted by his contemporaries, and then to his two positive accounts of the moral value of aesthetic experience: his account of the sublime, from which human art is largely (although not entirely) excluded; and his theory of the "intellectual interest" in beauty, from which fine art is explicitly and completely excluded. In this comparison, we will see that Kant does not share his contemporaries' view that in the naturally beautiful and sublime we can admire a benevolent artistry far greater than our own but that human art is nevertheless also morally valuable for its lesser (but still real) contribution to the perfection of creation and the happiness of its human subjects. Instead, Kant's view is that the beautiful and sublime in nature are morally significant because they represent – the former through symbolization, and the latter not primarily through symbolization but even more directly through feeling – the autonomy of our own practical reason, whereas fine art must be viewed with caution, both because it all too easily works on our inclinations rather than our autonomous will, which must be governed by principles, and also because its characteristic structure of intentions seems to disqualify it from the representation of our autonomy.

# Nature, art, and autonomy

## I. THE STANDARD VIEW

The sole project of aesthetic theory in the eighteenth century may seem to be the discovery of a standard of taste. In societies rent into many parts by divisions of class and confession (as in both Britain and Germany), and also by further divisions of sovereignty (as in Germany), it must indeed have seemed attractive to demonstrate that at least the realm of taste offered the possibility of a genuine community overriding such divisions.[1] But at least as fundamental as this project was that of justifying the appreciation of artistic and even natural beauty themselves. From midcentury and beyond – as in Hume and Kant – the project was to give a secular justification for aesthetic values in place of what may have seemed to be a traditional religious justification. But in the Protestant countries, which had suffered through the more extreme forms of puritanism, even a valid religious role for natural and artistic beauty first had to be theoretically reestablished.[2] Thus, the justification of aesthetic experience in the eighteenth century was really a two-stage process, in which it was first shown that theology itself permitted a place for natural and artistic beauty, although this had been excluded by some of the more radical Protestant sensibilities in the preceding century or two, and then shown that aesthetic appreciation had a fundamental place in human life independent of any religious significance whatever.

In spite of differences in detail, certain assumptions remained common throughout much of the period. Virtually all of the theories offered by German writers right up to Kant, and by British theorists at least up to the psychologistic and associationist writers such as Kames and Burke, grounded the value of the beautiful and even the sublime in what Kant classified as "objective finality," that is, determinate conceptions of metaphysical perfection or pragmatic utility. The perception of "uniformity amidst variety," which was the key to the rationalist explanation of the pleasure of beauty from

Christian Wolff to Marcus Herz, was what Kant called an "internal" objective finality, and an account such as Hume's, on which beautiful objects pleased because of a direct or sympathetic enjoyment of their apparent utility, fit Kant's model of "external" objective finality (see *CJ*, §15, 5:226; compare Kant's classification of moral theories in *Practical Reason*, 5:40). These alternatives for the explanation of the value of the aesthetic obviously led to certain conceptions of the moral significance of the beautiful and the sublime in nature and in art. The internal objective finality especially of beautiful natural objects was their uniformity amidst variety, thus their perfection and God's reason for their creation; so appreciation of natural beauty led to admiration of the benevolence of the creator and was, as such, of direct moral value – assuming, of course, a religiously based conception of morality. *Mutatis mutandis*, appreciation of the sublime was equivalent to admiration of the power of God. In the case of external objective finality such as directly or sympathetically enjoyed utility, moral value did not come through a suitable attitude toward the creator but rather through a direct contribution to human happiness or to an increase in the perfection of the human condition itself, which was of course assumed to be the natural object of morality. Such grounds for a moral justification of the aesthetic could not be used by a theorist of autonomy like Kant, for whom the only way to show that anything other than virtuous action itself has moral worth would be to show that it contributes to the development, or at least the representation, of the good will.

In his famous series of essays in the *Spectator*,[3] Joseph Addison organized the discussion of the "pleasures of the imagination" under the three headings "Beauty," "Greatness," and "Novelty."[4] By Burke and then more subtly by Kant himself, the category of novelty was incorporated into the fundamental explanation of the beautiful and sublime, and so the general forms of aesthetic merit were reduced to two. But this distinction was accompanied by another – that between the natural and artistic – and so there were in principle four categories for the objects of taste: natural beauty, the naturally sublime, artistic beauty, and the sublime in art. However, although the last category was sometimes recognized (as, for instance, by Kames, for whom literary models such as Homer and Milton were central), it was largely rejected, or else held to be derivative from the naturally sublime which art might sometimes represent. Thus, aesthetic theory revolved around the three categories of *natural beauty*, the *naturally sublime*, and *artistic beauty*. I will accordingly present some standard views about these three categories, so that we may then see how radically the moral evaluation of these three forms of the aesthetic that was necessitated by Kant's conception of autonomy departed from what was accepted by his contemporaries.

## Natural beauty

Although some held that the "native signification" of the concept of beauty restricted it to the visual only and allowed its application to objects of the other senses or the imagination merely by metaphor or association,[5] beauty was regarded by many as a universal source of value for objects of nature, art, and even the intellect.[6] Even more typically, beauty was characterized as grounded in the perception of maximal uniformity amidst variety. Francis Hutcheson stated the view clearly in 1725:

> The figures which excite in us the ideas of beauty seem to be those in which there is *uniformity amidst variety*. There are many conceptions of objects which are agreeable upon other accounts, such as *grandeur, novelty, sanctity,* and some others. . . . But what we call beautiful in objects, to speak in the mathematical style, seems to be in compound ratio of uniformity and variety: so that where the uniformity of bodies is equal, the beauty is as the variety; and where the variety is equal, the beauty is as the uniformity. This may seem probable, and hold pretty generally.[7]

Half a century later, Marcus Herz summed up the Wolffian tradition, without the mathematical imagery, but also without the modest disclaimer of more than inductive probability which Hutcheson attached to this otherwise potentially pretentious language:

> *First* . . . since in consequence of the highest principles of the human soul pleasure and displeasure attach to the representation of perfection and imperfection, the beautiful object must provide a representation of perfection. *Second:* This perfection must not consist in the object's serving as a means for the attainment of a particular final purpose, in which case it would merely be *good*, rather it must immediately please in itself. *Third,* the pleasure that it affords must not arise from the satisfaction of a sensible sensation, rather it must arise solely from the representation of the connection and harmony of its manifoldness.[8]

The anticipation of Kant's own claim about the immediacy of aesthetic response is striking; but equally so is the clear assumption that the unity amidst variety which produces that response is an objective ontological perfection in things.

This conception of the basis of beauty typically gives rise to three further thoughts. Borrowing a Kantian distinction, we might say that beauty as uniformity amidst variety was held to please internally by facilitating the perception or cognition of an object possessing such a quality, but also held to please externally as an instance of the perfection with which the creator has endowed his creation. Then we may note that it was commonly added that nature presented far greater uniformity amidst far greater variety than could be provided by art, and so offered greater scope for the internal pleasure of beauty but, even more importantly, for the external pleasure of contemplating the perfection of creation.

Hutcheson is cautious about explaining *why* the perception of uniformity amidst variety should please, since such an explanation cannot avoid trafficking in final causes. Nevertheless, he is willing to speculate that for creatures of limited understanding, the "manner of knowledge by universal theorems, and of operation by universal causes, . . . must be most convenient," and that for such creatures "those objects of contemplation in which there is uniformity amidst variety are more distinctly and easily comprehended and retained than irregular objects." And although no logical necessity connects pleasure with such conveniences, clearly it is reasonable to suppose "the Deity so kind as to connect sensible pleasure with certain actions or contemplations beside the rational advantage perceivable in them."[9] Later writers, including Kant himself, were to connect pleasure and cognitive convenience more closely. But whatever the manner of connection, it seemed clear to all that in responding to uniformity amidst variety, we are responding to the benevolent handiwork of the creator, and that there is far more of such handiwork in his creation than in ours.

Thus Hutcheson continues that the same benevolence which may well have led the creator to attach the feeling of pleasure to what would otherwise be affectless cognitive convenience may also have led him to provide ample objects for this response:

> But this we may probably say, that since the divine goodness . . . has constituted our sense of beauty as it is at present, the same goodness might have determined the Great Architect to adorn this stupendous theatre in a manner agreeable to the spectators, and that part which is exposed to the observation of man so as to be pleasant to himself, especially if we suppose that he designed to discover himself to them as wise and good, as well as powerful; for thus he has given them greater evidences through the whole earth of his art, wisdom, design, and bounty, than they can possibly have for the reason, counsel, and good-will of their fellow creatures, with whom they converse, with full persuasion of these qualities in them, about their common affairs.[10]

The existence of beauty is the work of the creator, and what we ultimately respond to in responding to beauty is that benevolent design.

This kind of sentiment is even plainer in a German work of a few decades later, which obviously had the task of transforming the aesthetic sensibilities of an even more pious readership than Hutcheson's. I refer to Johann Georg Sulzer's *Unterredungen über die Schönheit der Natur*, which was originally published in 1750 but reprinted at least as late as 1770, and thus was popular throughout most of Kant's intellectually formative years. In words that initially sound much like Kant's own, Sulzer's dialogue asserts that there is a close connection between a taste for natural beauty and moral virtue; but his explanation of this connection is precisely that in admiring beauty we are admiring the workmanship of the creator and that it is by modeling ourselves on that workman that we can also find the way to virtue:

> But just as the spirit forms itself after a perfect model . . . , so also do the mind and the moral qualities of the soul form themselves through the contemplation of nature. The moral taste stands in a very exact connection with the insights and taste of the spirit. Whoever has insight into the beautiful in nature will also all the more easily recognize the morally beautiful or good, which has the very same origin: and it almost seems as if he who has an elevated conception of natural beauty will be incapable of any demeaning sensations of the heart. Everywhere in nature he will see the sublime manner of thought of the highest being. . . . Whoever understands the regime of nature even in the least must necessarily be touched most sensitively by the universal care and good-will of the source of all that is good. . . . Consider further, oh friend!, to what a disposition we must be brought by the perfect order which rules everywhere in nature.[11]

The response to beauty is intuitively understood to be a response to the divinely created order of nature. Of course, such a response must have a morally beneficent effect, because virtue itself consists in conforming one's own character to this independent model of goodness. The emphasis must be on disposition, to be sure, because the individual agent in a Leibnizian world cannot well augment the objective perfection of what is already the most perfect possible world; but he can at least reflect its perfection in his own disposition. Thus the aesthetic response to natural beauty and the morally good disposition toward the perfection of creation are virtually identical. In writers of even a few years later, such as Moses Mendelssohn and Herz, the piety is not quite so unabashed, but the general idea that the admiration of natural beauty has an immediate moral value as the proper disposition to the work of the ultimate moral agent remains.[12]

And this leads naturally enough to the idea that human artistry and its beauties are but a pale reflection of the infinitely greater and more admirable artistry of this creator. Again, the purple prose of Sulzer's characters expresses this common sentiment. Eukrates, his advocate of natural beauty, asserts that "nature has made a wondrous work of beauty, in that all its productions are so uncommonly harmonious and yet at the same time so infinitely varied." Charites, who has not yet been enlightened, lamely objects that "however beautifully a plant or animal is formed, you must yet concede that a single statue by a good master has more richness in invention and beauty in its proportions than all plants or animals." This inspires Eukrates to the following response:

> Whence does the artist derive the originals of his works? Are they not from nature? Is not the human form, this truly magnificent edifice, in nature? Man is indeed one of the animals which nature forms. . . . But now she has made infinitely many; of which each in its way is just as perfectly formed as man. If now merely in the forming of humankind such a wealth of rules must be taken account of, as you have learned from the painter or the sculptor, then what a vastly greater wealth of rules must nature not have taken account of to form all these shapes? Thus you see, Charites, that the entire human artistry in painting and in sculpture is but an infinitely small part of the artistry of nature, a droplet in that immeasurable sea.[13]

We find similar sentiments in the plainer prose of Britain. Thus Lord Kames:

> When we examine the internal structure of a plant or animal, a wonderful subtilty of mechanism is displayed. Man, in his mechanical operations, is confined to the surface of bodies; but the operations of nature are exerted through the whole substance, so as to reach even the most elementary parts. . . . This power of diffusing mechanism through the most intimate parts, is peculiar to nature, and distinguishes her operations most remarkably from every work of art.[14]

Like Hutcheson, Kames views it as a special gift of a benevolent creator that we are fit to *appreciate* such wonderful uniformity amidst variety:

> But the most wonderful connection of all, though not the most conspicuous, is that of our internal frame with the works of nature: man is obviously fitted for contemplating these works, because in this contemplation he has great delight. The works of nature are remarkable in their uniformity no less than in their variety; and the mind of man is fitted to receive pleasure equally from both.[15]

Yet of course this is just one more instance of the superior harmony of nature itself, for it is nature (or its creator) that provides this additional harmony between human capacities and its other instances of uniformity amidst variety.

In spite of the common recognition that the artistry of nature is infinitely greater than our own, it was also a commonplace that art was morally valuable for its direct contribution to human happiness. Before we consider that view, however, we will examine the other aesthetic category paradigmatically exemplified by works of nature, that is, the sublime. Here too the most common way of expounding the moral significance of the aesthetic was ultimately still theological, although the moral attitude toward our creator suggested by this experience was humility rather than admiration.

## The sublime

The standard account of our pleasure in the sublime often began with a psychological description of the pleasure that the imagination takes in its unconstricted exercise. Although in such an account as Addison's explanation of the pleasure of the imagination in grandeur we do not find the tripartite division of mental faculties into imagination, understanding, and reason that is exploited in Kant's account of the sublime, the theory does not seem entirely dissimilar to certain aspects of Kant's more elaborate model. The imagination may be pleased by symmetry and proportion, in the case of beauty, but it also finds pleasure "in the largeness of a whole view, considered as one piece"; the imagination likes to *be* free, and even to contemplate an *image* of its freedom:

> Our imagination loves to be filled with an object, or to grasp at anything that is too big for its capacity. . . . The mind of man naturally hates every thing that looks like a restraint upon it, and is apt to fancy itself under a sort of confinement, when the sight is pent up in a narrow compass, and shortened on every side by the neighbourhood of walls or mountains. On the contrary, a spacious horizon is an image of liberty, where the eye has room to range abroad, to expatiate at large on the immensity of its views, and to lose itself amidst the variety of objects that offer themselves to its observation. Such wide and undetermined prospects are as pleasing to the fancy, as the speculations of eternity or infinitude are to the understanding.[16]

This is a less conflicted account than Kant's, on which the imagination is rather torn between the understanding's love of confinement and reason's striving for infinitude, and on which it is thus the satisfaction of reason rather than mere imagination which is the ultimate ground of our pleasure. But the basic ideas that there is something in our makeup which enjoys freedom and that the naturally sublime in some sense functions as an image of our freedom are hardly alien to Kant; indeed, they are the key to his own account of the sublime.

Yet the explanation of the concept of grandeur or sublimity did not usually remain confined to psychology; a turn to theology characteristically followed. The very next essay in the *Spectator* holds that the immensity of nature which the imagination so enjoys is really to be understood as an image of the immensity of nature's creator, and thus that the "final cause" of our pleasure in the sublime is a worshipful appreciation of the magnificence of God rather than of our own freedom. Unhindered by the scruples of more professional philosophers, Addison says that although we may not be "able to trace out the several necessary and efficient causes from whence the pleasure . . . arises," "final causes lie more bare and open to our observation." He then indulges in the following pious speculation:

> One of the final causes of our delight in anything that is great, may be this. The Supreme Author of our being has so formed the soul of man, that nothing but himself can be its last, adequate, and proper happiness. Because, therefore, a great part of our happiness must arise from the contemplation of our being, that he might give our souls a just relish of such a contemplation, he has made them naturally delight in the apprehension of what is great or unlimited.[17]

Although a feeling of pleasure is immediately attached to the unconstrained exercise of freedom, the ultimate cause of this pleasure and perhaps even its ultimate object is the immensity of God rather than anything in ourselves.

No more explicit link between sublimity and morality is drawn by Addison; perhaps it hardly needs to be. But an explicit consequence for our moral attitudes is drawn from such a conception of sublimity by Sulzer, and this is precisely that our attitude toward ourselves and our own character, in the face of the divine immensity revealed by the sublimity of nature, ought to be nothing other than humility. In a meditation on the magnitude of the world, the characteristic immensity of the sublime is used to yield a contrast between the magnitude of the universe as a whole and the insignificance of the earth, our own little portion of the whole. This leads to the following moralization:

> Learn to judge from these concepts, you proud fools who make bold to demand of the Lord of the world that he arrange and rule the whole world according to your individual prejudice. Judge from the magnitude of the whole how little or nothing the majesty of the all-powerful would suffer if you together with your whole race should be annihilated. . . . And even if he does preserve and love us, this is only because he is infinite, and his goodness spreads itself over all his creatures, and cares for the worm as well as for the seraph.[18]

The appropriate moral stance for one who fully understands the sublime immensity of nature is to regard himself as virtually nothing before God, as one who is allowed to live through no merit in himself but only because the goodness of God is as infinite as his power. Humanity and its works (it is of course inconceivable and in no need of mention that sublimity so conceived could be found in any human art) are nothing to be proud of; the sublime calls for no pride in ourselves but only humility before God.

We shall soon see how profoundly different is Kant's own account of the sublime. Beginning with a psychological explanation of the feeling not dissimilar to Addison's, he finds its moral significance to lie in the grandeur of our own autonomy rather than in our humility before God. Before we can consider what is indeed Kant's Copernican revolution in linking aesthetics and morality, however, we must conclude the presentation of the conventions which he overturns with an account of the standard interpretation of the moral significance of fine art.

## Artistic beauty

As I mentioned at the end of the discussion of natural beauty, it was standardly held that although natural beauty necessarily outstripped the achievements of human artistry, there was nevertheless an important and even distinctive contribution to human happiness that could be made by art. A quite sophisticated statement of such an assumption may be found in the already mentioned essay on taste by Marcus Herz. Although Kant greeted the initial publication of this work in 1776 with approval,[19] he did not refer to it in his own *Critique of Judgment* fourteen years later. Yet Kant's terminology strongly suggests that it was nothing other than Herz's explanation of our interest in art which was the target of Kant's own unfavorable contrast of our "empirical" to our "intellectual" interest in beauty, and especially of his exclusion of artistic beauty as a fit object for the latter.

After giving an essentially Wolffian account of beauty as the clear but indistinct perception of the objective perfection which lies in the harmony of a manifold, supplemented with a more psychological – even Humean – account of the *Haltungsgefühl* (literally, "feeling of attitude") as sensitivity to proportionality between actual and expected emphases in the manifold parts of a beautiful object, Herz goes on to raise a question about the source of our *interest* in beautiful objects. Such a question, he acknowledges, may seem to contradict his initial position that it is "the primary essential characteristic of beauty in general . . . that it please not as *good* and *useful*, but immediately in itself." But there is no contradiction, because there is a difference between "*enjoyment* and *pleasure in the enjoyment*," or between "having an agreeable sensation" and "finding pleasure in the enjoyment" of such a sensation. Although there is undeniably an immediate feeling of pleasure in the sensory perception of harmony in a manifold as such, it is a separate question whether reason will approve or disapprove of any instance of this first type of pleasure and thus add its own pleasure to it.[20] In fact, Herz holds, no such additional question arises in the case of natural beauty, either because nature is so obviously a grand and purposive design or else because it is so obviously nonintentional that in either case reason has no question to ask about its purpose. But in the case of art, which is obviously a prod-

uct of human intentionality, reason cannot avoid asking the
question "What for?" and can add its own pleasure to the
more immediate sensible pleasures of art only if given a satisfactory account of the fundamental human interest which
such beautiful art may serve. Thus, although we suspend the
question of interest in the case of nature, "The artist must in
the unity [of artistic beauty] itself represent something to us
that has an interest for us through its closer influence on our
inner [life]."[21] And although Herz begins by considering
whether art may not satisfy this demand by the *representation*
of morally interesting objects, he ultimately explains the satisfaction of this interest in terms of the direct contribution of
art to morality.

Herz's account of the connection between art and morality
works at two levels. At the base of the whole edifice is the
assumption that the "most important final purpose of mankind" is the "greatest happiness."[22] Conditions for the attainment of the greatest possible happiness can be conceived
in two ways. First, we may consider the concept of the human agent and the perfection of it, as well as the larger world
of which it is a part; we might think of these as constituting
the metaphysical – or, to use Herz's term, "objective" –
conception of the conditions for the greatest happiness. Second, we can consider the psychological or subjective element
in the greatest possible human happiness. Briefly put, Herz's
theory is that the objective final purpose of mankind lies in
the maximal development of human capacities and in the
maximization of the reality or perfection of the world itself, to
which we can contribute through the maximal development
of our own capacities;[23] that the subjective condition for the
attainment of this objective lies in the harmonization of our
inclinations, to which the development of the inclination to
sociability makes the greatest possible contribution; and that
beautiful art can make a genuine contribution to the attainment of these objective and subjective goals of morality. Let
us consider these two aspects of art's contribution to morality
in turn.

Herz gives the clearest expression of his perfectionist mo-

rality, indeed of the perfectionist morality of the whole rationalist movement, in a poetic passage in which nature calls to
mankind:

> Many and manifold capacities have been given to you as your
> portion. Beyond these you also possess a free will, which
> gives you an unlimited dominion over these; seek to maintain
> them in continuous activity, exercise them, and extend the
> scope of your effectiveness as far as possible in all directions,
> and you will be happy. And in all directions seek to make
> yourself more perfect; leave no single power, no single inclina-
> tion idle: for know that I am never wasteful in the distribution
> of my gifts. I would have stinted with even the smallest vessel
> in your body if it did not contribute to its greater perfection;
> with the least capacity in your soul, if it were not indispens-
> able to your greatest happiness![24]

In plainer language, Herz asserts that the moral agent must
strive for the maximal – or, more accurately, maximally
harmonious – development of his capacities; indicates that
this contributes to the perfection or maximization of reality
itself; and then explicitly connects beauty to this form of
perfection. First, the characterization of the development of
human capacities:

> In order to satisfy the request of nature man must not indiffer-
> ently extend this or that power beyond measure, or this or
> that inclination, rather in the development of his capacities he
> must observe a certain relationship among them, so that the
> less considerable are subordinated to the more considerable,
> all together advance each other, and so that the resultant
> perfection is not only the greatest in sum but there is also the
> greatest harmony among the powers which brings it forth.[25]

Such a maximally harmonious development of the capacities
of the human agent in turn contributes to the objective perfection of the world, for through whatever manifestation of virtue is most appropriate to their time and place do men

attain the highest goal of happiness, but to be sure only under the condition, *that they bring all their other inclinations and capacities into harmony with this, and preserve among them exactly that proportional extension which is requisite in order to bring forth the greatest sum of realities.*[26]

This model of morality then makes plain the place of artistic beauty. For if virtue itself "consists in a proportional development and expansion of [our] capacities, inclinations, and powers," and the key to beauty is also proportionality – the beautiful must be not only unified yet manifold, but also proportional, to bring forth the indispensable *Haltungsgefühl* which is the hallmark of aesthetic response – then the artist seeking to make a beautiful work "seeks to make the relationship among the manifold in his work exactly the same as that which the vocation of man requires." The artist gives the "greatest effect in the whole, the strongest light, and the liveliest expression" to that in his work which represents the most vital contributions to the greatest happiness, and correspondingly less to other elements, and by this means "becomes master of a work that contains an objective inner worth." In fact, Herz's view seems to be that the human creator of beauty both *represents* the nature of moral perfection and thereby *contributes* to it. Of course, complete attainment of the highest goal remains only an ideal for us, but it is

> enough that we have before us the exemplar of the highest perfection, in order to model both ourselves and our works after it. Let us strive so far as it is possible to attain it: Whoever among us comes closest to it will be the *relatively* most virtuous, have the *relatively* most perfect taste.[27]

But limits on the attainment of virtue, although natural, are not what concern us here. What is revealing is simply that Herz does not merely compare moral perfection and the perfection of taste but conjoins them. The perfection of taste is a part of moral perfection itself.

So much for the objective side of moral and aesthetic perfection. We may now turn to what I called the subjective side, or Herz's more specific characterization of the effect of beauty on human feelings as a psychological condition of virtue. Although touched upon in Herz's initial exploration of the connection between taste and morality in the second part of his essay, this aspect is more deeply considered in the third part of the book, where Herz considers the causes for differences of taste among nations or peoples. Here Herz argues as follows.

First, he premises that "since man is on the whole more a sensing than a *merely* thinking being, so also he wants the objects which afford him pleasure, that is, which strengthen his feeling of life, to stand in a closer connection with the greatest part of his self, with his inclinations and sensations, than with his merely distinct cognitions."[28] One need hardly mention how profoundly distant from Kant's conception of morality is the assumption that inclinations and sensations constitute the "greatest part" of our selves. Obviously, the connection between art and morality to be erected on this premise will be unacceptable to Kant.

Herz's next step is to interpret the most satisfactory effect of an object on our inclinations and sensations as a state in which, by means of the harmony of the inclination which is first touched by an object with other inclinations, as many inclinations as possible are touched and set into activity; in this manner there "arises a mutual play among different strings in the soul, which uncommonly elevates its self-feeling, and lets it sense the reality of its existence in the most gentle manner."[29] Again, the conception of maximal unity amid maximal variety as itself intrinsically valuable is at work, although this time it is applied to the passive rather than active side of human nature, to our feelings and inclinations rather than our powers and activities.

Now this general conception of subjective value is applied to the special case of works of art:

And nothing other is understood by the concept of *interest* in objects of taste than this very connection between one inclination and several others. A work of art, which otherwise most perfectly satisfies the requirements of beauty, nevertheless lacks an essential ingredient for pleasure if it is not sufficiently *interesting*, that is, if the manifold or the unity of the whole has such inclinations for its object which stand in connection with few others; and as the chief inclinations that are aroused through the work encounter more or fewer congenial ones in the soul, which are harmoniously excited with it, thus is the *interest*, and consequently the value of the beauty, greater or smaller.[30]

The value of beautiful art, or the ground of our interest in it – which is here obviously intended to be quite distinct from the simple pleasure aroused by the immediate apprehension of its form alone – lies in its production of a harmonious disposition of our inclinations. And, finally, Herz names that inclination which among all others possesses this desirable property to the highest degree. It is none other than the disposition to sociability itself: "And it is precisely those inclinations, which are most directed toward sustaining society, which among the entire crowd of others have the most adherents."[31] Herz does not argue, as Hume might have, that sympathy with others adds their enjoyments to one's own more direct pleasures. Instead, he argues the obverse: Self-directed pleasures, whether explicitly selfish ones like the miser's or even merely implicitly selfish pleasures like those of purely physical gratification, do not touch any of the "more noble inclinations and feelings" and even divide the soul, both from itself and from others. But the net result is the same. Satisfaction of the inclination toward sociability maximizes the harmonious disposition of one's inclinations and feelings in general.

Thus the sociable inclinations are at the same time those which set our actions into motion in the greatest and most manifold ways, which let us sense the inner feeling of our existence in the gentlest way: they are those, therefore, which attract us most strongly, and which are the most interesting objects for poets and artists . . . on which they must concentrate.[32]

In sum, then, Herz's account looks like this. A beautiful work of art is immediately pleasing because of the harmonious and proportional unity of its manifold of parts or contents. But without satisfaction of a deeper interest, a work of art will quickly seem to us "an empty effort, an insipid game."[33] Art can attain such interest by leading toward the increased perfection of our own capacities for action and thereby to the perfection of reality itself, and by its beneficial impact on our inclination toward society, which of all our inclinations and feelings is most harmoniously efficacious. Thus art contributes to the perfection of human nature conceived in both ontological and psychological terms and thereby makes a clear and direct contribution to morality.

Kant obviously shares Herz's view that unless it satisfies a moral interest the pleasure of artistic beauty quickly fades: His own statement that "if the fine arts are not brought into close or distant connection with moral ideas, which alone carry with them a self-sufficient satisfaction," then we quickly become dissatisfied with them (*CJ*, §52, 5:214), could easily have been borrowed from his former student. But, characteristically, Kant immediately goes on to add that it is the "beauties of nature which are most conducive to this aim" and to leave the lingering suspicion that in the end the beauties of art really are an empty game. That the moral theory on which Kant must ground any interest in beauty is profoundly different from Herz's, although the latter is far more typical of its time, is obvious; what remains to be seen is just why Kant's moral theory, given its own emphasis upon human will, should lead to such a glorification of natural beauty at the cost of artistic creation, which might otherwise seem the most natural emblem of human autonomy.

## II. KANT'S ALTERNATIVE

Needless to say, Kant's reasons for rating natural beauty higher than works of human artistry are not always original. Throughout his initial analysis of the judgment of taste in the

"Analytic of the Beautiful," of course, it is natural rather than artistic beauty which provides Kant's paradigm for the pure judgment of taste. The purity of such a judgment, however, is epistemological rather than moral. The purity of a judgment on the beauty of a natural object hardly means that such an object is of greater moral significance than a work of art, but rather precisely that our pleasure in it is produced entirely independently of the concern for human goals, indeed moral ends, which would conventionally be taken to lend art greater moral value than the natural objects of such epistemologically pure judgments. Kant's first explicitly normative argument, however, (in the "General Remark" which concludes the "Analytic of the Beautiful") expresses a preference for the beauties of nature over works of human artistry (although not of fine art) on grounds which would have been completely familiar to a Sulzer or a Kames. Criticizing the British orientalist William Marsden for his preference for the regular beauty of a well-tended pepper garden over the wild beauties of the Sumatran wilderness, Kant says that a day spent in the garden would quickly have revealed to him the "oppressive constraint" which such regularity imposes on the imagination, "whereas nature, which is there lavish with its multiplicity to the point of luxuriance, [and] which is subject to no constraint from artificial [*künstlich*] rules, could give his taste continuous nourishment" (*CJ*, §22 General Remark, 5:243). Like so many of his contemporaries, Kant here simply admires the greater variety of nature as compared to any works of humankind, but of course variety which also contains the unity requisite for pleasure in beauty.

On the assumption that increments of pleasure, especially such refined pleasure as that in natural beauty, make a direct contribution to happiness, and that contributions to happiness are in turn morally valuable, the greater pleasurability of natural beauty might lead to some moral significance for it. But Kant adds no moral significance to natural beauty on this account, precisely because increments to happiness have no intrinsic moral value for him. For Kant, the only thing that is of true moral value is the rational exercise of human freedom

itself, and what makes his grounds for his aesthetic prefer-
ences so paradoxically distinct from those of his contemporaries is precisely that he finds our aesthetic responses to natural beauty and sublimity to be more intimately connected
with our freedom or autonomy than is our taste for works of
art.

This is not the place for a detailed discussion of Kant's
theory of moral value.[34] Suffice it to say that underlying the
apparent formalism, especially of the *Critique of Practical Reason*, in which Kant seems to be persuaded by his own association of all human ends with the merely natural rather than
moral objective of happiness that the content and even the
value of the good will must be grounded in a formal law of
willing independent of all ends whatever, is a deeper conception on which the form of the moral law is derived from a
conception of the fundamental good for human beings after
all, although one in which this good lies in no material end of
the kind subsumed under the generic concept of happiness
but rather in the exercise of freedom itself. Freedom must be
governed by law in order not to be perverted into radical evil
rather than good, and so much of Kant's published treatment
of autonomy emphasizes its self-imposed lawfulness that it
might seem as if Kant somehow supposes that the most fundamental form of intrinsic value attaches to lawfulness itself.
But this is not so; the lawfulness of the free will is merely the
necessary condition for the actualization of the potential
value which attaches more fundamentally to freedom than to
anything else. This view is perhaps most apparent in the
lectures on ethics which Kant gave at the inauguration of the
great critical decade of the 1780s:

> If the will of all beings were . . . bound to sensuous impulse,
> the world would possess no value. The inherent value of the
> world, the *summum bonum*, is freedom in accordance with a
> will which is not necessitated to action. Freedom is thus the
> inner value of the world. But, on the other hand, freedom
> unrestrained by rules of its conditional employment is the
> most terrible of all things. . . . It must therefore be restricted,

though not by other properties or faculties, but by itself. The supreme rule is that in all actions which affect himself a man should so conduct himself that every exercise of his powers is compatible with the fullest employment of them. . . . The conditions under which alone the fullest use of freedom is possible, and can be in conformity with itself, are the essential ends of humanity.[35]

The consequences of this foundation for Kant's ethics are manifold and profound. Kant's assumption of the fundamental value of freedom itself clarifies his real difference with Wolffian ethics: In spite of the verbal similarities in the formulation of the moral law in Kant and in the Wolffians, for the latter freedom has only an instrumental value as the human means for the achievement of perfection, whereas for Kant freedom is itself the ultimate end of all morally valuable human action. That freedom is our essential end can explain how Kant's applications of the categorical imperative (as in, for instance, the argument against suicide or for the development of one's talent) can contain a teleological assumption without collapsing into naturalistic hedonism. But for aesthetics, freedom as the foundation of the "inner value" of the world creates a paradox. On Kant's own account, only art is "production through freedom, that is through a will which grounds its actions in reason" (*CJ*, §43, 5:303). Then why should nature monopolize morally significant aesthetic response?

Kant's answer to this paradox must be that although only the artistic production of aesthetic objects is literally rational – no will at all being involved in the production of the naturally beautiful or sublime – our *response* to the beauty and sublimity of nature stands in more intimate connection, both as it were theoretical and practical, to our freedom than does our response to art. And even in the special case of the artist or genius, whose productive activity might seem a suitable symbol of freedom, Kant seems to assume that the pragmatic rather than moral interest which must motivate his work cognitively overrides the element of freedom in it. In any case, in his moralizing about art Kant seems more concerned with the comparison of aesthetic response to nature and to art in the rest of us, the consumers rather than producers of aesthetic objects; and here, he clearly thinks, the aesthetic response to nature advances the interest of freedom whereas the response to art fails to do so and can even act against it.

At the conclusion of the "Critique of Aesthetic Judgment," Kant claims that the beautiful is the symbol of the morally good because the experience of beauty is felt to be an experience of freedom. Beauty is here the symbol of the morally good because the freedom of the imagination that is characteristic of the response to the former may be taken as a symbolic representation of the freedom of the will that is essential for the latter. "In the estimation of the beautiful the *freedom* of the imagination . . . is represented as harmonious with the lawfulness of the understanding," and in "moral judgment the freedom of the will is thought of as the agreement of the will with itself according to universal laws of reason" (*CJ*, §59, 5:354). But whereas the freedom of the will is represented only by concepts, the freedom of the imagination in responding to beauty is felt, and thus furnishes a sensitive representation which can symbolize an otherwise unintuitable object of pure thought.

In summing up the "Analytic of the Sublime," however, Kant awards the symbolic plum of representing the morally good to the sublime, in explicit comparison with the beautiful. Here he says that "a feeling for the sublime in nature cannot well be thought without connecting with it a disposition of the mind which is similar to the moral disposition"; he then continues,

> and although the immediate pleasure in the beautiful in nature likewise presupposes and cultivates a certain *liberality* of the manner of thought, that is, independence of delight from mere enjoyments of the senses, freedom is yet thereby represented more in *play* than as in lawful *business:* which is the true characteristic of the morality of mankind, in which reason must apply force to sensibility; only in the aesthetic judgment on the sublime this force is represented as exercised by

the imagination itself, as through an instrument of reason. (*CJ*, §29 General Remark, 5:268–9)

This leads to an even stronger claim a few pages later. Since the ultimate object of a pure intellectual delight can only be "the moral law in the power which it exercises over every and all *antecedent* impulses of the mind," and since it is only through "sacrifices" that this power makes itself "aesthetically cognizable" (*ästhetisch-kenntlich*), it is only the experience of the sublime, with its frustration of the imagination while that attempts to accomplish the task of understanding rather than reason, which can really symbolize the nature of morality.

> From this it follows: that the intellectual, intrinsically purposive (morally) good, aesthetically estimated, must not be represented as beautiful but rather as sublime, so that it arouses more the feeling of respect (which scorns charm) than of love and intimate inclination; for human nature does not accord with that good of itself, but only through the force which reason applies to sensibility. (*CJ*, §29 General Remark, 5:271)

The first of these passages might be explained by saying that the beautiful and sublime symbolize different aspects of human autonomy. The freedom of the imagination in the experience of the beautiful represents the potential that we have to be free from the determinism of impulse, while the more painful experience of the sublime reminds us that we can only achieve our potential for such freedom by the rigorous submission of even our most humane inclinations to the principle of pure practical reason. The second passage, which virtually excludes the beautiful from any role in symbolizing the morally good, seems harder to explain. But perhaps it reflects Kant's scruple that any representation of moral motivation as itself producing a feeling of pleasure, while not necessarily false, runs the risk of confusing us about the proper motive for morality, duty rather than the pleasure which doing our duty may actually produce. Thus, Kant's statements about the aesthetic symbolization of morality reveal a tension. On the one hand, the purely rational nature of morality requires to be made palpable to our senses, and it turns to the aesthetic – above all, the beautiful – for that purpose; on the other hand, morality cannot be associated too closely with pleasure, but instead of simply turning back from the aesthetic altogether Kant finds an aesthetic experience which itself contains an element of pain to drive the necessary wedge.

In the end it seems fair enough to say that Kant treats both the beautiful and the sublime as indispensable symbols of fundamental yet different features of morality, even if he is not quite sure how these different symbols should be related. In any case, Kant's interpretation of both the beautiful and sublime differed from what was commonplace. But before we can see how drastically Kant's interpretation of each of these symbols does differ from what was conventional, we must also note that Kant considers the direct influence of aesthetic experience on our affects or inclinations, as well as its symbolic and thus cognitive moral significance, and that in this context he implies a particularly negative assessment of the moral value of art.

## The empirical interest in the beautiful

Of course Kant shares the conventional view that to be of enduring interest art must not only be representational but also have moral content (*CJ*, §52, 5:326),[36] although his expression of this assumption in his doctrine of aesthetic ideas makes clear that morality in art cannot be straightforwardly didactic – for both aesthetic and moral reasons, that is, to preserve the freedom of the imagination yet by doing so also preserving the freedom of the imagination to make palpable the freedom of the will in moral motivation itself.[37] Nevertheless, Kant's heart really seems to be set against the moral value of the fine arts, and under the rubric of the "empirical interest" in beauty he delivers a stinging attack on precisely the kind of conventional assumption that the arts can make a direct contribution to morality by their beneficial effect on our inclinations that we found in his former student Herz's theory that the feeling of sociability is the highest point of our moral psychology and the ultimate basis for our rational interest in the arts. In an occasional remark Kant may sound as if he is willing to concede to this convention: "Taste as it were makes possible without too violent a leap the transition from the charm of sense to habitual moral interest, for . . . it teaches us to find a free delight in objects of the senses even without the charm of sense" (*CJ* §59, 5:354). But his real conviction seems to be that sound moral principles are necessary for the development of taste, rather than vice versa: "The true propaedeutic for the grounding of taste is the development of moral ideas and the culture of moral feeling: for only when these are brought into accord with sensibility can genuine taste assume a determinate, constant form" (*CJ*, §60, 5:356). Thus a primary concern of Kant's discussion of the arts seems to be precisely to reject a justification of our interest in them by an easy appeal to their beneficial impact on allegedly moral inclinations.

In fact, Kant does not explicitly say that the object of his attack on the allegedly beneficial but actually suspect "empirical interest" is artistic rather than natural beauty. But his examples make it clear that he is concerned with the use of the fine arts to gratify human inclinations, which use may have its origin in an original human tendency to put naturally beautiful objects to work for human purposes of self-aggrandizement. Thus Kant begins by observing that on a desert island no one would "adorn himself or his hut" even with naturally available flowers, and then suggests that in society there would be a gradual progression from self-adornment with mere colors, to the more varied use of "flowers, seashells, beautifully colored feathers," and finally to "beautiful forms (as in canoes, apparel, etc.) which carry no enjoyment, that is, delight in gratification, in themselves, but which become important and connected with interest in society" (*CJ*, §41, 5:297). Here he seems to contemplate a gradual emergence of fine art from naturally available objects for self-adornment and suggests that as art becomes more distant from the direct gratification of the senses it maintains our interest by allowing for what Hume might have called "artificial" opportunities for gratification. Art too refined to gratify the simplest desire for charms will gratify by showing off our good taste, wealth, and so on. And then art may even go beyond the confines of such apparently egoistic sources of pleasure and become an object of inclination simply because it affords an opportunity for sympathetic enjoyment of our agreement with others and of our membership, indeed, in a community of taste:

> Finally civilization which has reached its highest point almost makes refined inclination its chief business, and sensations are held to be of value only insofar as they allow of being communicated; here then, even if the pleasure which every one has in such an object is in itself inconsiderable and without noticeable interest, yet the idea of its universal communicability almost infinitely augments its value. (*CJ*, §41, 5:297)[38]

What is wrong with such an interest? Why does Kant scorn the idea of augmenting the value of art by its appeal to our entirely natural inclination to society, which he himself describes in teleological terms as a "property pertaining to the requirements of man as a creature destined for society" (*CJ*, §41, 5:296–7)? His objection may seem merely theoretical – that is, no more than the problem that an empirically recognized source of pleasure cannot ground an *a priori* judgment. What he is looking for, he says, "is something which may be related to the judgment of taste *a priori*, even if only indirectly" (*CJ*, §41, 5:297). But since Kant begins the discussion of both the empirical and intellectual interests in the beautiful by arguing that an interest cannot be the "determining ground" of a judgment of taste but can only enter into combination with it after the judgment has been made – which means that an interest can only add some further pleasure to that which is requisite for the original judgment of taste itself – it is simply unclear why any additional interest that attaches to the judgment of taste should have to be *a priori* in order for the original judgment to be *a priori*. Or, Kant's problem might seem to be aesthetic: a concern that an excessive interest in social acceptability may allow trends of taste to lend intrinsically indifferent objects a fraudulent appearance of genuine aesthetic merit. But Kant hardly makes such an argument clear.

Instead, his real animus emerges only at the end of the section. Natural and beneficial as the inclination to society may be, art cannot obtain moral value by means of a connection to this inclination, for the simple reason that even the most benevolent inclination does not have any intrinsic value; even worse, attempting to ground moral value in any inclination runs the risk of subjecting morality to the unreliability of all inclination. Since "the empirical interest in objects of taste and in taste itself . . . panders to inclination," then, be this interest "ever so refined, and happily blended with all those inclinations and passions which reach their greatest development and highest plane in society, the interest in the beautiful, if it is grounded therein, will be able to yield only a very ambiguous transition from the agreeable to the good" (*CJ*, §41, 5:298). On the standard view, our attachment to artistic beauty is elevated from the merely agreeable – which, as Herz emphasized, is highly transitory – to something of enduring moral significance by being associated with our inclination to society. But Kant's objection is simply that the inclination to society itself is an unreliable and even dangerous support for morality. Thus, while putting art at the service of this inclination might seem to others to ennoble it, for Kant it clearly runs the risk of making the beautiful too an unreliable crutch or even dangerous threat to morality.

The gist of Kant's attack on benevolent and sympathetic inclination as the basis for morality is well known: even benevolent inclinations are fragile and thus may be misapplied, or even perverted, if not governed by principle;[39] any theory on which favorable inclination, no matter how altruistic in content, is essential to moral motivation is ultimately a theory of self-love, because it rests the efficacy of morality on the contingencies of one's own gratifications;[40] and these threats of contingency, inconsistency, and even perversion can be avoided only by the autonomous regulation of one's potential for freedom by means of a principle of pure practical reason.[41] In other words, Kant's curt dismissal of the sociable interest in beauty, which is so readily directed to artistic beauty, follows from his theory of autonomy. The only thing that is unconditionally good is the rational use of freedom, and to ground the moral value of the aesthetic in its service of even benevolent inclinations to society makes it a potential enemy rather than loyal servant of autonomy. As with so much else in Kant's discussion of taste, the ground of the problem with the empirical interest in beauty is not to be found in aesthetics itself but in Kant's moral theory. The apriority of the judgment of taste itself is not threatened by the addition of an empirical interest; rather the theory of sociability as our highest inclination reveals the presupposition that morality is empirical rather than *a priori*.

None of this implies that the fine arts could not have a beneficial effect through strengthening the natural human inclination to society, if this inclination is governed by a principled commitment to autonomy as the sole intrinsic good. Is there any way in which aesthetic response can advance the interest of autonomy, rather than depend upon it?

## The sublime

As we saw, Kant treats both the beautiful and the sublime as symbols of the different aspects of morality. But since he at least once asserts that it is the sublime that is the better symbol, and in any case discusses it first in his own exposition, we may as well follow suit. We will thus defer consideration of the "intellectual interest" in natural beauty, which Kant discusses immediately after his attack on the empirical interest in artistic beauty, until after we have examined his radical revision of standard treatments of the sublime.

We have already noted that eighteenth-century writers explained the sublime in two different ways. Addison began with a psychological account with no obvious moral implications, according to which we simply take pleasure in the freedom of the imagination afforded by boundless vistas and the like. Such a purely psychological account was taken up by later writers such as Edmund Burke, who provided Kant's paradigm for a psychological approach to aesthetic experience. But Addison, as well as such writers as Sulzer, also went on to offer a theological account of the moral significance of the sublime as an occasion for reflection on our own finitude and for humility before the infinitely greater power, as well as goodness, of our creator. What Kant did was to transmute the psychological account into an alternative moral account, in which humanity is elevated rather than humbled. In the experience of the sublime, we stand in awe of the power of our own reason rather than of God. Indeed, God's creation is humbled before our own free reason, and even the sublimity of God himself can be appreciated only through the image of our own autonomy. Yet Kant also seems to assume that only nature, and not art, can produce this experience of the magnificence of our own rational freedom.

The premise of Kant's account of the sublime is that although the attempt to apprehend something quantitatively boundless in spatial and/or temporal extent – the "mathematical sublime" – or something qualitatively boundless in force – the "dynamical sublime" – exceeds the ability of the imagination to serve the understanding, and thereby causes displeasure, the very effort of the imagination to represent such boundlessness also reveals that the imagination serves an infinitely greater power of reason; the recognition of such a power within us is the occasion of a mediated, but profound, pleasure. Kant's distinction between the mathematical and dynamical sublime might seem to reflect a fundamental distinction between theoretical and practical reason, each form of the sublime revealing one form of reason. In fact, the *Critique of Judgment* reflects a more unitary conception of reason as a single faculty which can produce only illusion if misused for speculative purposes but sound postulates in its practical application; thus it seems more accurate to interpret the two forms of the sublime as progressively revealing two *aspects* of the single, and ultimately practical, faculty of reason. The mathematical sublime reveals the *infinitude* of its scope or power of comprehension, and the dynamical sublime then adds a representation of the *independence* or autonomy of reason from the influence of the natural world.[42] This already suggests that it must be nature which calls forth our experience of the sublime, precisely because this feeling represents the independence of our moral being *from* nature.

For the most part, Kant ascribes a cognitive significance to the sublime. The effort of the imagination to surpass the limits of understanding reveals the existence of the faculty of reason, and the pleasure which complements the frustration of the understanding is pleasure in the existence of that faculty of reason. That is, Kant's basic idea is that the feeling aroused by the effort of the imagination is proof or evidence of the existence of reason and may therefore be taken as a *representation* of that faculty or of its role in human conduct. This is clear in the terms of Kant's explanation of the mathematical sublime:

> Just because there is a striving for infinite progress in our imagination, while reason lays claim to absolute totality as if a real idea, the very incommensurability between our faculty for the estimation of the magnitude of the things of the sensible world and this idea is the awakening of the feeling of a supersensible faculty in us. . . . Therefore . . . *the sublime is that, which even the mere capacity to think proves the existence of a faculty of mind which exceeds every standard of sense.* (CJ, §25, 5:250)

And for this reason, even though ideas of reason cannot literally be presented (*dargestellt*), the feelings of both effort and pleasure in the experience of the sublime can nevertheless more generously be counted as "a presentation [*Darstellung*] of the subjective finality of our mind in the use of imagination for its supersensible vocation" (*CJ*, §29 General Remark, 5:268). At one place, to be sure, Kant does seem to ascribe a direct affective, rather than cognitive, significance to the feeling of the sublime: In the estimation of an object as sublime, the power of aesthetic judgment relates the imagination "to *reason*, in order to accord subjectively with its ideas . . . that is, to bring forth a disposition of mind which is commensurable and compatible with that which the influence of determinate (practical) ideas would effect on feeling" (*CJ*, §26, 5:256). As we have already seen, however, Kant is generally loathe to grant moral value to aesthetic experience on the basis of any direct effect on our inclinations, just because of the general unreliability of inclinations, and it seems clear that his general approbation of the sublime is based precisely on the fact that it provides a cognitive representation of our freedom, which our autonomous will can use for its own rational determination, but does not substitute inclination for principle in the act of free choice.

Thus, the experience of the sublime is morally significant because it represents the power of our reason to override all natural determinism, a power which can be represented only by representing nature at its most powerful as nevertheless powerless against our own autonomy. It is precisely the contrast between autonomy and the realm of nature which is the real basis for Kant's startling departure from the standard view that its vast extent and power makes nature itself sublime (as well as the sublime product of its equally sublime creator). For Kant, "True sublimity must be sought only in the mind of the judge, not in the natural object the estimation of which occasions this attitude of the mind." There is nothing intrinsically significant at all in the "wild disorder" of "shapeless mountain masses," "but the mind feels itself raised in its own estimation if, in the contemplation of such things without regard for their form, it abandons itself to the imagination and to a broadening reason which is connected to the former entirely without a determinate purpose" (*CJ*, §26, 5:256). It is the power of reason to form an idea exceeding all bounds of the imagination which is sublime, not the otherwise meaningless natural objects which can occasion such an idea in us. Moreover, what we admire in ourselves is not the sheer intellectual strength of reason. Rather, the feeling which "as it were makes intuitable the superiority of the vocation of reason in our cognitive faculties over the greatest capacity of imagination" is precisely a feeling of "respect for our own vocation" (CJ, §27, 5:257). And what is our vocation? Surely nothing other than what Kant elsewhere defines as the "essential end" of mankind: the exercise of our freedom conditioned by a law of reason so that it realizes the absolute value potential in it rather than collapsing into "the most terrible of all things." Thus, that sublimity is properly ascribed to ourselves rather than to nature is not a merely ontological technicality, as the similar claim about the subjectivity of beauty may be (CJ, §1, 5:202–3); rather it expresses the fundamental assumption of Kant's moral theory, that nature is "might that has no dominion over us" (CJ, §28, 5:260), a force which, for all its power, cannot even touch what is essential to human personality.

By asserting that nature has no dominion over us, Kant may seem to imply the immortality of the human personality. It may sound as if he means this when he claims that the dangers of nature have no power to do anything to "the human in our own personality" but can only submit us to "external violence" as "mortal men." But the real import of his claim is that nature by itself can do nothing of *moral* disvalue to us. For all the dangers or threats it may throw in our face by its power, just as for all the inducements it may put before our inclinations by its pleasures, there is nothing nature can do to us which can force us to surrender our ability to act freely under the guidance of practical reason alone. In fact, although the immense destructive power of nature outside us can remind us of the triviality of what we usually incline to accept as objects of choice – "worldly goods, health, and life" – and by that means remind us of our power to choose the unconditionally good end of freedom itself, Kant is even more concerned to interpret the experience as revealing the superiority of reason over our own natural being: "Sublimity is therefore contained in no object of nature, but only in our own mind, so far as we can become conscious of being superior to nature within us and therefore of nature outside us (insofar as it influences us)" (*CJ*, §28, 5:264). The real threat from external nature would not be our physical destruction but rather nature's effect, whether by threat or gratification, on the inclinations within us, which could lead to the heteronomous rather than autonomous determination of the will. It is in freedom from this that the "sublimity of our vocation even over nature itself" lies – the sublime is nothing other than the experience of our own autonomy (*CJ*, §28, 5:261–2) – and for this reason sublimity must be contrasted to nature rather than ascribed to it.

Thus, the idea of freedom which Kant finds in the experience of the sublime is a far cry from the humility before our infinitely better and more powerful creator which ordinary thinkers such as Sulzer read into it. The respect for our own vocation which this experience reveals is not a form of self-aggrandizement, for it is not a reason for one human to think himself superior to any other; but it is a ground for "true, noble pride": "We have reason to have but a low opinion of ourselves as individuals, but as representatives of mankind we ought to hold ourselves in high esteem."[43] And Kant does not hesitate to make plain the unconventional theology which is required by his new foundation of the sublime in the ethics of autonomy. Fear of God is obviously not the attitude of the virtuous man, but neither does Kant argue that the recognition of our own capacity for moral rectitude is merely the condition which frees us from fear of divine punishment. Rather, he seems to argue, it is only through the sublimity of the recognition of our own freedom that we can even form an image of the sublimity of God: "Only when [a person] is conscious of his own upright, God-pleasing disposition do these effects of power serve to awake in him the idea of the sublimity of this being [God], insofar as he recognizes a sublimity of disposition in himself suitable to the will [of God]" (*CJ*, §28, 5:263). The experience of the sublime is not an experience of humility, but an experience of freedom suitable for an image of God himself.

Why does Kant so plainly believe that through the experience of the sublime, aesthetic response to nature can gain a moral significance from which fine art is barred? To be sure, Kant does not explicitly deny that a work of art can produce the feeling of sublimity; somewhat like associationists such as Kames or Burke, he seems to assume that a work of art can have some claim to sublimity, at least by representing the naturally sublime.[44] Nevertheless, works of art seem to have no part in Kant's image of the sublime. Yet it may seem paradoxical that such free creations of the human spirit as works of genius should be incapable of producing an experience which is supposed to symbolize autonomy itself. Why should this be so? Two thoughts come to mind. First, Kant stresses the formlessness of objects that induce the experience of sublimity (*CJ*, §30, 5:280), and it is clear that an artistic representation of sublime seas or mountains must have a form, and thus has boundaries that what it represents does not have. This might seem unimportant until we remember that the significance of the sublime lies in nothing less than its contrast between the greatest powers of nature and the even greater force of human practical reason. No work of art, even an artistic representation of the sublime in nature, can itself so stretch our natural faculties as to reveal the even greater faculty of reason that lies beyond them. Second, although Kant stresses that art is production through freedom rather than nature (*CJ*, §43, 5:303), it is also clear that he thinks there is little autonomy of will involved in the reception of art and even that the production of art is not disinterested. Thus, he seems to assume that neither the experience of art nor even the figure of the artistic genius offers a genuine symbol of autonomy. The effects of this assumption may be clearer in Kant's discussion of the intellectual interest in nature than in his account of the sublime, however, where the status of art is indicated only by omission; so we will now return to that topic.

## The intellectual interest in the beautiful

Kant holds that in addition to gratifying our unreliable and therefore at best morally indifferent inclination to society, beauty can also stand in a connection to the *a priori* basis of morality which does legitimate an "intellectual interest" in it. But all "who have cultivated their moral feeling," he reports, credit a "beautiful soul" to the admirer of natural beauty and not to the "connoisseur and lover of art" (*CJ*, §42, 5:299–300), and he emphatically seconds this refined opinion. Yet again it is not clear why he should restrict this intellectual interest to natural beauty when his own theory of genius seems to break down the traditional boundary between nature and art and to ally the greatest products of human artistry more closely to the disinterestedly admirable glories of nature than to the obviously purposive products of more mundane human productivity.[45]

The answer can only be that although the existence of natural beauty can be given some moral significance (even if, unlike the experience of the sublime, it does not specifically make us feel respect for our own vocation), fine art, although obviously intentional, cannot well serve as an emblem of disinterested autonomy. On the one hand, a genius – that is, a producer of fine art – even though he has an artistic aim, has practical objectives as well, so his creative activity is not disinterested. Even more importantly, perhaps, the genius cannot achieve his artistic aim unless nature helps him get beyond concepts and techniques, so he is at the mercy of nature and can hardly symbolize its rule by human freedom. On the other hand, the consumers of art – who of course are far more numerous than creative geniuses – cannot appreciate art as art without recognizing the intentions of another, and Kant seems to interpret this as implying the domination of the consumer by that other. Thus the appreciation of artistic beauty is even less well suited to symbolize our autonomy than is its creation.

In fact, Kant's account of the intellectual interest in beauty does not make very clear why this interest should have moral significance. At the outset, at least, Kant seems to be employing the third *Critique's* standard definition of "interest" – as the pleasure that we attach to the actual existence of natural beauties (see *CJ*, §2, 5:204, and §41, 5:296) – and to be describing an additional mechanism by which we add pleasure to the initial – and already pleasurable – aesthetic response to a beautiful object. In this case, however, instead of the non-moral gratification of our inclination to sociability being the source of our additional pleasure, we take pleasure in the fact that beautiful objects exist in nature because of a general "interest" (here in the more ordinary sense) that nature conform to our will:

> But now since it also interests reason that . . . nature at least show a trace or give a hint that it contains in itself some ground to assume a lawlike harmony of its products with our own delight independent of all interest . . . therefore reason must take an interest in every expression in nature of a harmony similar to this; therefore the mind cannot reflect on the beauty of *nature* without thereby also finding itself interested. (*CJ*, §42, 5:300)

The idea seems to be that we have an interest arising from our need to have nature agree with our moral ideas, which can be extended to an interest in nature producing objects for any other disinterested pleasure.[46] The extension of this interest to beauty is not barred by the amorality of mere inclination, as in the case of the empirical interest in beauty. Further, it is clear why this interest should attach only to natural and not artistic beauty – it is an attitude toward nature from the outset. But it is not at all obvious what the direct moral significance of this interest is. Perhaps an interest in nature according with our ideas that is morally important when those ideas are themselves moral can extend itself to other disinterested responses without incoherence, but it is not clear that there is any intrinsic moral value in such an application. It might seem as if such an interest in the existence of natural beauty is merely morally *permissible,* because it does not involve morally pernicious mechanisms of inclination.

As Kant continues, however, it appears that he means to introduce the analogy between delight in beauty and delight in the morally good to which he returns in Section 59 and to imply that a moral interest attaches directly to the experience of the beautiful – and thus indirectly to the existence of objects which produce this experience – because of a specific cognitive contribution to morality which this experience can make. Kant does not in fact make a general claim that there is a moral value in the symbolic representation of the morally good; rather he implies that the case of beauty makes clear what may otherwise be obscure in morality itself: that a determination of the will can produce pleasure, and thus interest, without presupposing any pleasure and therefore without making that pleasure itself its object. Thus, the analogy which Kant actually states is that as the beautiful pleases independently of any antecedent desire and can thus create an interest in an object without presupposing one, so the moral law determines an object of the will without presupposing any antecedent desire for it it but also produces a pleasure, and thus interest, in virtuous action which is not presupposed by it. This is "the analogy between the pure judgment of taste, which, without depending on any interest, allows a delight to be felt and also to be represented *a priori* as proper to all mankind in general, and the moral judgment, which does the same from concepts" (*CJ,* §42, 5:301). That we can only take an interest in the existence of beautiful objects subsequent to finding them beautiful independently of antecedent interests is clear from the nature of aesthetic judgment. But that we can attach a feeling of pleasure to the determination of our will independently of antecedent desire, without thereby presupposing a desire to be gratified and without turning that pleasure into the object of our will, is one of the most difficult things to understand about our autonomy. Thus our disinterested interest in beauty does not merely stand in analogy to autonomy itself but offers a uniquely clear representation of one of the most obscure consequences of that autonomy. The intellectual interest in beauty is not merely not disqualified from the realm of morality by an unfortunate connection to inclination but also makes graphic a vital element of our freedom and thereby surely attains some moral worth of its own.

But now the question of art arises again. If the intellectual interest in beauty depends on nature's fortunate satisfaction of our own disinterested objectives, yet if in works of artistic genius nature itself supplements artistic intentions in ways that cannot antecedently be determined by any known rules or techniques of artistic skill (see *CJ*, §46, 5:307), why are works of fine art not just as useful as symbols of disinterested determination of the will as the delightful beauties of nature? Since Kant's theory of genius breaks down the ordinary ontological distinction between products of nature and of art, his answer to this question cannot lie in a simple denial that works of genius are also natural. Instead, he must suppose that there are additional elements involved in the production and reception of art which disqualify it from a symbolic role for which it would otherwise be suited. In fact, Kant makes it clear that the various intentions that may govern the production of a work of art disqualify either that production or the reception of the work from serving as a symbol of autonomy.

Kant does not say this explicitly but expresses it by the cases he considers in excluding an intellectual interest in artistic beauty. He supposes that a work of art may either be taken for a natural beauty, in which case it defrauds us and is thereby obviously disqualified from even symbolic moral significance by its own immorality, or else that it is explicitly recognized as the product of the intentional activity of another person, in which case it can hardly symbolize our own autonomy. This might seem enough, but Kant also intimates that the interests of the producer of a work of art are also incompatible with the use of his work as a symbol of disinterested determination of the will.

The first of these points is clear. Kant begins with a premise meant to cover all possible cases: A beautiful work of art may "be either such an imitation of [beautiful nature] which leads to an illusion, . . . or else it is visibly art which is intentionally directed toward our delight." If we are deceived into taking a work of art for a natural object, as the birds were fooled by Zeuxis's grapes, then the work of art "has its effect as a natural beauty (for which it is taken)" (*CJ*, §42, 5:301). Thus we fail to distinguish the object from an actual natural beauty and have no reason to take an interest in it other than that which we take in nature itself; but what is worse is that if we do so interpret the object, then we also have been the victim of a fraud (*Betrug*) (*CJ*, §42, 5:302), and a fraud can hardly be the basis of a moral interest. If anything, the perverse use of the skill necessary to accomplish such a deception, just like the use of gifts of nature unaccompanied by a good will, could only produce a strong sense of moral disapprobation.

One might object to Kant's characterization of the artist's motives in the first of his two cases, but it is at least clear what he thinks. It is somewhat less clear what the problem is in the case in which the status of the object as the product of intentional human artistry is clearly recognized and there is no question of fraud. What Kant says is that if a work of art is obviously directed to the production of our aesthetic pleasure, then although our pleasure in it "takes place immediately by means of taste" it can nevertheless "arouse none other than a mediate interest in the cause which lies at its ground, namely that of an art which can only interest through its end and never in itself" (*CJ*, §42, 5:301). What this seems to mean is that the artist's reasons for the production of his work prevent the work from serving as a symbol of autonomy. In fact, there are two different problems which Kant seems to have in mind here.

On the one hand, if a work of art is "visibly" and "intentionally" directed toward our pleasure, then our pleasure in it is the product of the intention of another and can hardly symbolize our own autonomy. To be sure, Kant emphasizes a few pages later that if we are to take pleasure in the beauty of a work of art at all we must not be overly conscious of the artist's intentions: "Art can only be called beautiful, if we are conscious that it is art and yet it appears to us to be nature" (*CJ*, §45, 5:306). But although we may be able to abstract from the intentionality of an art work enough to allow the imagination the freedom it requires for the bare experience of beauty, Kant seems to suppose that the concept of the artist's intention must dominate at the level of symbolic interpretation. Thus, to the extent that we recognize the success of the artist's intention, we also recognize the constraint rather than freedom of our own imagination.

On the other hand, by stating that we can only have a "mediate interest" in the end which art serves rather than in art itself, Kant may also mean to imply something about the reasons for which art is produced and thus about the motives with which even the genius must be supposed to undertake artistic production. Thus Kant appears to assume that even though the genius can have only an indefinite conception of the form of the object he intends to produce, he will have perfectly determinate reasons for attempting to produce this object. Kant implies that the pleasure produced by the work of art is only an instrument for some further end, so he appears to assume that the artist intends either simply to please his audience or else to accomplish some particular objective for himself, such as the achievement of fortune, fame, or honor. Aims of the latter sort are obviously of no moral value, and artistic production thus motivated could hardly serve as a symbol of the morally good. And even the former is not of intrinsic moral value but would be morally significant only if motivated by an application of the moral law, with its rather indirect requirement to advance the happiness of others (see especially *Practical Reason*, 5:34). In neither case would there be anything intrinsically moral about the artist's intentions, and thus his work would not be well suited to represent autonomy as the very basis of morality, let alone uniquely suited to represent any aspect of such autonomy. From this Kant seems to assume that works of art are disqualified from symbolizing autonomy, even though they often have ideas of reason as their *content* (in the form of aesthetic ideas) and can be produced only by means of that cooperation of nature which would otherwise be an object of intellectual admiration.

Thus we reach our conclusion. Like many of his contemporaries, Kant ascribes moral significance to the naturally beautiful and sublime; unlike most of them, he virtually rejects any moral significance for fine art at all. In both cases, his views depend upon his radical conception of autonomy as the basis of morality. The naturally beautiful can symbolize our moral autonomy, and in the experience of the sublime we can almost even feel it. But art gratifies our inclination to sociability, which is itself of no direct moral value, and can even represent fraud or at least the constraint rather than realization of autonomy – the constraint of the audience's autonomy by the will of the artist, and even the constraint of the artist's autonomy by his own ulterior motives. In this assessment, Kant certainly seems to go too far, reverting to a puritanical attitude toward art by focusing too narrowly on its capacity to symbolize autonomy. But precisely by so doing, he also reveals the centrality of the idea of autonomy throughout his thought.

### POSTSCRIPT

Subsequent to the original composition of this chapter, Salim Kemal published a book in which he argued that Kant's theory contains grounds implying that fine art rather than natural beauty must be considered the paradigmatic object of aesthetic experience from both a theoretical, and even more a practical, point of view.[47] Since I have examined Kant's reasons for finding natural beauty morally more significant than artistic products, it seems appropriate to examine Kemal's arguments for a diametrically opposed conclusion.

The gist of Kemal's argument is that the link to morality is external to natural beauty rather than internal to it, as he claims is the case in fine art.[48] More specifically, Kemal's argument can be reduced to four main headings. First, he argues that "fine art is better able to bear [the] symbolic relation to morality,"[49] by which he presumably means that the conceptual content which works of art may have can bear a more direct relationship to morality than is allowed by naturally beautiful objects, where the analogies are not between the objects and morality but between our *experience* of such objects and morality. He also puts this point by claiming that the analogy with morality is *constitutive* of the work of art, rather than merely added on to it afterward through reflection on the structure of the experience of it as is the case with natural beauty.[50] Second, he holds that Kant's concept of the highest good implies the primacy of artistic over natural beauty; his argument is that because in the case of the highest good the natural end of happiness must always be subordinated to the rational end of moral autonomy or freedom, the "freedom presupposed in fine art" therefore "circumscribes" "our experience of natural beauty."[51] Third, he maintains that Kant's theory of intellectual interest implies the superiority of art. "Nature is valued for its part in our attaining moral ends, but this evaluation is possible only because nature is like art."[52] Finally, he claims, the experience of natural beauty itself presupposes the more primary experience of art: "Natural objects are ascribed aesthetic qualities by analogy with fine art."[53]

I find these arguments extremely dubious. In general, it must be clear that within the Kantian framework there can be no immediate inference from what we might think of as ontological claims about objects to normative claims. That is, even if it were true that symbols of morality are somehow more immediately connected with works of art than natural beauties, it could never follow from that alone that the former are morally more significant than the latter. Thus, the fact that symbols of moral ideas may literally be parts of artworks, rather than connected to them only through reflection on the experience of them, does not imply that the creation or experience of artworks is morally more important than the experience of natural beauty. This is especially true if there may also be grounds weighing against the moral significance of art – which (as we have seen) is precisely what Kant holds, on the basis of grounds which Kemal never considers.

Kemal's more specific claims are also problematic. His appeal to Kant's conception of the highest good cannot prove his point, for Kant never allows that the kind of freedom manifested in works of art – especially in the audience's *response* to works of art, which is what he has in mind most of the time – is *identical* to moral autonomy. On the contrary, he explicitly claims that it is only analogous to it, since moral autonomy, unlike aesthetic freedom of the imagination, can only be achieved through the use of a concept or principle – the moral law itself – which is what is specifically excluded in the case of the aesthetic. And Kemal's appeal to the theory of intellectual interest is also misguided: Kant's claim there is specifically that natural rather than artistic beauty is paradigmatic because it is the satisfaction of our own objectives where we ourselves cannot guarantee their satisfaction that is so pleasing to us. What we have to do in order to bring fine art back under the aegis of our intellectual interest in the beautiful is to show by means of the theory of genius that works of art are really like products of nature after all, not vice versa.

Finally, Kemal's claim that natural objects are only assigned aesthetic properties by analogy with art is also deeply misleading. As we have seen in several essays in this volume, Kant's theory of aesthetic response is ultimately that what pleases us is the unexpected satisfaction of our own deepest objectives, in the first instance cognitive objectives, then more broadly moral objectives as well. Thus aesthetically satisfying objects are purposive in the specific sense of satisfying purposes in the responder, not the producer. Beyond that, there is certainly room for tension in Kant's account. On the one hand, his basic theory of pleasure requires that the satisfaction of our underlying purpose must be felt to be contingent, and thus cannot be ascribed to the intentional activity of any producer. On this ground, natural rather than artistic beauty must be the paradigmatic example of the aesthetic object. On the other hand, Kant also holds that reason has a natural tendency to posit a designer where something satisfies a design, which gives us an inclination to think of even natural beauties as the product of some kind of artistry, although obviously superhuman rather than human artistry. But here one can only say that there are analogies in both directions, which may be one of the very reasons why Kant insists upon characterizing aesthetic judgment as reflective rather than constitutive. There is room for thought here, but any dogmatic assertion that the creation of natural beauty was really similar, let alone subordinate, to human artistry would be entirely indefensible.

It therefore seems to me quite inappropriate to try to construct a theory of the primacy of artistic over natural beauty on Kantian grounds. Kant himself has a clear sense that there is a large and complicated set of analogies between our experiences of nature, art, and morality, and we do better to explore these many analogies as I have tried to do in this essay than to attempt to impose upon him a reductionist ontology giving uncontested primacy to art, from which he surely would have shied away.

# Chapter 8

## Genius and the canon of art:
## a second dialectic of aesthetic judgment

### I. AUTONOMY AND INTEGRITY IN TASTE

"That the *imagination* should be both *free* and yet *of itself conformable to law*, that is, that it should carry autonomy with it, is a contradiction" (*CJ*, §22 General Remark, 5:241). So Kant writes to express as a paradox the epistemological problem that the feeling on which an aesthetic judgment is based must be free of the constraint provided by determinate concepts, for otherwise there will be no reason why it should be pleasurable, yet must also be subject to some kind of rule, for otherwise the claim of universal validity which this judgment asserts will be irrational. And so understood, the remark is entirely rhetorical, for it is the express purpose of Kant's main argument in the "Critique of Aesthetic Judgment" to show that this conception of the judgment is coherent rather than contradictory. But taken out of its intended context, the remark need not be merely rhetorical, for it can be seen as an expression of competing demands for aesthetic integrity: demands for individual freedom on the one hand and social agreement on the other, demands which, unlike the two epistemological constraints on aesthetic judgment, cannot be si-

This chapter was originally published under the title "Autonomy and Integrity in Kant's Aesthetics," in volume 66 of *Monist* (1983, 167–88), a special issue on the general topic of "Integrity and Purity in Art and Morals," edited by Mary Mothersill. Copyright © 1983. *The Monist*, La Salle, IL 61301. Reprinted with permission. Minor revisions have been made for the present chapter.

multaneously satisfied but instead introduce a permanent source of instability into the history of art and taste. Indeed, it is even fitting that Kant's remark has to be taken out of context to be given this interpretation, for although Kant lays the theoretical basis for such a picture of art history, he also tries to suppress its consequence and to avert the destruction of the eighteenth-century ideal of aesthetic stability which is its inevitable outcome.

The tension which must arise on Kant's theory of taste may be seen as one between two competing demands for aesthetic integrity precisely because the concept of integrity has two distinct senses. On the one hand, it connotes a property of individual action or character. Individual agency possesses integrity when it is determined independently of anything other than principles freely chosen by the agent and is determined steadfastly by those principles. In a word, integrity in this sense is what Kant calls autonomy. On the other hand, the concept of integrity also has a sense in which it connotes not so much the autonomy of individual agency as the unity, coherence, or completeness of a whole such as an organism or an organization. It is in this sense of the term that a bridge, for instance, might be said to possess structural integrity.[1] Kant has included in his theory of taste demands for integrity in each of these senses. In his accounts of artistic creation and of individual aesthetic response, he has included requirements of individual autonomy or integrity in the first sense; and in his account of the reception of any work of art by its larger audience, a community or culture as a whole – a community, in fact, potentially including the whole of humankind – Kant has included a requirement of integrity in the second sense, a requirement of agreement in aesthetic response that will contribute to the coherence and stability of such a community. But Kant has also incorporated these two demands for aesthetic integrity into his theory in such a way that they inevitably conflict. This fact is only implied in Kant's discussion of the effects of art criticism on the individual appreciator of art, and when it becomes explicit in his theory of genius as the source of artistic creation Kant tries to confine the damage it can do. Nevertheless, Kant has described the theoretical basis for tensions which cannot readily be resolved at any single moment in the history of art and culture but which instead ensure that art and its reception will have an ongoing history typified by a repeating cycle of revolution, rejection, and assimilation that can appropriately be called dialectical.

The acknowledgment of such conflict is of course alien to the attachment to the ideals of unanimity in taste, stability in the status of classical (or canonical) works of art, and coherence in culture that Kant shared with so many other writers of the eighteenth century. Thus, when Kant claims that aesthetic judgment requires a person to criticize "his own judgment from a *universal standpoint* (which he can only determine insofar as he transposes himself to the standpoint of others")" (*CJ*, §40, 5:295), he appears to express his agreement with Hume's statement that the individual appreciator of art should strive to conform his own responses to the "true standard of taste and beauty" determined by the "joint verdict" of a small class of "true judges" who are rare characters "even during the most polished ages."[2] Kant also appears to share Hume's view that there must be that kind of canon of proper objects of good taste which could definitively be determined to include, for instance, Milton and Addison but not Bunyan and Ogilby;[3] indeed, Kant even seems to go beyond Hume in assuming not only that there must be such a canonical list of classics but also that this list is already closed. This is at least a natural reading of his statement that "art [must] somewhere come to a halt, insofar as there is a limit set for it, beyond which it cannot go, and which has also in all probability already been attained" (*CJ*, §47, 5:309).[4] So far from implying that art must have a history of perpetual change, such an assertion seems instead to accept the backward-looking view of someone like Winckelmann that "there is but one way for the moderns to become great . . . I mean, by imitating the ancients."[5] Kant also seems to anticipate Hegel's (admittedly more complex) celebration of classicism, and in so doing to limit significantly the autonomy of the artist in the choice of both subject and form for his work, when he claims that there are not only classical models in art but even a canonical content for art, the human form as the expression of human personality which constitutes the "ideal of beauty" (*CJ*, §17, 5:233). Finally, like authors as diverse as Hume and Schiller, Kant appears to wholeheartedly reject Plato's attack on the poets and to celebrate the arts as an agent for the development of community and social harmony. Just as Hume thinks that the arts must "diffuse their beneficial influence on the *public*, and render the government as great and flourishing as they make individuals happy and prosperous,"[6] so Kant suggests that the fine arts can serve to advance "the reciprocal communication of ideas between the most cultivated part of the populace and the ruder part and the reconciliation of the breadth and refinement of the former with the natural simplicity and originality of the latter" (*CJ*, §60, 5:356).[7]

In spite of the conformity of his opinions to such ideals of his age, however, Kant has included in his theory of taste the seeds of their destruction, or at least of the recognition that they constitute but one side of the competing demands that we place upon art and but one pole of the oscillations of innovation, rejection, and acceptance that our demands will generate in the history of art and its reception. Although Kant resists the conclusion, and indeed reserves the title of a "Dialectic of Aesthetic Judgment" for something entirely different,[8] what he in fact describes in his analysis of the judgment of taste and especially in his theory of artistic creation are sources for dialectical developments in art and taste that are in many ways more fundamental to the nature of aesthetic experience itself than those described by such an explicit dialectician as Hegel. In what follows, we will first consider how several demands for aesthetic integrity are generated by Kant's theory of taste and then examine the pattern of conflict these must generate in the creation and reception of art.

## II. INDIVIDUAL AND SOCIAL TASTE

There are two aspects of Kant's analysis and explanation of judgments of taste that give rise to a demand for individual autonomy in matters of taste, and a further aspect of his theory on account of which society as a whole can look on taste as an instrument of its own coherence or integrity, and indeed seek to exploit the phenomenon of taste with the aim of preserving and enhancing its integrity. I will briefly summarize these three points now and will later examine each of them in more detail.

I have mentioned two aspects of Kant's discussion that give rise to a demand for individual autonomy in matters of taste. First, for Kant the significance of an aesthetic judgment is not exhausted by the imputation of agreement about the pleasure produced by a given object to all members of an ideal community of observers that constitutes the propositional content of such a judgment; in addition, Kant's analysis requires that when individuals assert such propositions they do so on the basis of pleasures that they have *actually felt* for themselves. Second, Kant's explanation of the pleasure of aesthetic response does not merely require that the state of mind which produces such pleasure and thereby licenses a judgment of taste – the state of harmony or free play between imagination and understanding – be a state of which the epistemologically characterized property of manifesting unity without a determinate concept can be truly predicated; it also requires that this state of mind be one which is *actually felt to be free* of the kind of constraint on the imagination of which a determinate concept is the typical source. Finally, there is another aspect of Kant's treatment of judgments of taste which suggests that society as a whole can regard taste as something that promotes its own coherence or integrity. For Kant does not conceive of the intersubjective validity of aesthetic response solely as the epistemological status of such pleasure under ideal circumstances that is affirmed of it by the content of aesthetic judgment; he also sees inter-subjective agreement as something that is itself a further cause for pleasure in an object which occasions it.

This is all to say, however, that in addition to a purely logical and epistemological analysis of the content and status of aesthetic judgments, Kant's theory also includes theses about the individual and social psychology of the phenomenon of taste. And while Kant's theory cannot be made intelligible unless it is conceded that the theory properly includes such psychological as well as more purely epistemological elements,[9] it must also be recognized that it is these psychological elements which are chiefly responsible for the conflicting demands for individual autonomy and social integrity which the theory generates. For the demands that the individual appreciator of a work of art as well as the artist who has produced it must each feel free in his response to the object may not only conflict with each other, in that the freedom of the individual's response to the object seems like an affront to the artist's intentions for his work while the freedom of the artist's intentions seems like a constraint on the imagination of the audience responding to his work; it is even more likely that both of these forms of individual autonomy will conflict with society's demand for not just ideal communicability but actual communication, and that the autonomy of an individual's pleasure and the freedom of an artist's creative efforts will be both demanded by a society which values them yet will also be seen as obstacles to the attainment and maintenance of actual unanimity in taste. Before I can describe the particular ways in which these general possibilities of conflict emerge from Kant's text, however, we must consider in more detail the three sources of these tensions that I have enumerated.

Let us consider first Kant's requirement that those making judgments of taste do so on the basis of their own feeling of pleasure. It is easy to read Kant's analysis of the concept of aesthetic judgment as if it were exhausted by two constraints applying solely to the content of such judgments. The first of these constraints is the condition that insofar as it is aesthetic such a judgment must concern a necessarily subjective state, for which pleasure (or pain, in the case of a negative judgment) is the only candidate (see *CJ*, §1, 5:203; *FI*, §VII, 20:223–4). The second is the condition that such a judgment must impute agreement about the pleasure which it associates with its object to every potential (or at least ideal) observer of it, not because of any special element of the meaning of the particular predicate (such as "beautiful" or "sublime") that may be used in the judgment, but precisely because such predicates (unlike "agreeable") do *not* have the exceptional syntactic property of admitting of a personal index ("to me") that defeats the semantic assumption of intersubjective validity otherwise inherent in every use of judgmental form.[10] These two conditions are, of course, what is prominent in such a definitional statement as that "by the judgment of taste . . . the delight in an object is imputed to *everyone*" (*CJ*, §8, 5:213). However, although to his reader's detriment Kant does not himself introduce terminology that would make this fact clear, his analysis of the term "aesthetic" as meaning something which is necessarily subjective also introduces a third constraint, one on the *act* by which a particular judgment of taste is made or the state of mind in which it is made. That is, Kant also requires that the assertion that a given object ideally should produce a universally valid pleasure must itself be *made* aesthetically, by means of the evidence that is furnished by the pleasure *actually felt* by the person asserting such a judgment.

This condition is stated, if not emphasized, in the "First Introduction" to the *Critique of Judgment*, where Kant writes that an aesthetic judgment is one that determines something "by means of the sensation of pleasure or pain, though at the same time concerning the universality of the rule connecting the feeling with a given representation" (*FI*, §VIII, 20:229). It is, however, given more emphasis in the main body of the text of the *Critique of Judgment*. Thus, Kant's primary analysis of the "quality" of the judgment of taste in Section 8 holds that in making such a judgment one not only "speaks with a universal voice and lays claim to the concurrence of everyone" but also "wants to get a look at the object with his own eyes" (5:216); and Kant's peculiar discussion of the "ideal" of beauty, while searching for something that will satisfy the classicist – and thoroughly undefended – assumption that there must be one kind of object which most perfectly instantiates the concept of beauty, nevertheless also insists that each person must arrive at this ideal for himself, "for taste must be a faculty intrinsic to the self" (*ein selbst eigenes Vermögen*) (*CJ*, §17, 5:232).[11] This is precisely to say that a judgment of taste must not merely assert a certain content but also that it must do so on the basis of its asserter's direct evidence for this content.

Similarly, Kant emphasizes that what a "deduction of pure aesthetic judgment" must explain is the possibility of a judgment that asserts universal validity solely on the basis of the evidence supplied by one's own actually felt pleasure in an object:

> The problem can also be represented thus: How is a judgment possible, which merely from one's own feeling of pleasure in an object, independent of any concepts of it, judges *a priori* that this pleasure is connected with the representations of this same object in *every other subject*, without having to wait for confirmation from others? (*CJ*, §36, 5:288)

Finally, Kant makes it explicit that what he requires is that the act of aesthetic judgment be autonomous. In Section 31 of the *Critique of Judgment*, Kant argues that the problem of a deduction of taste arises precisely because even a correct assertion of universal validity cannot be made on the basis of indirect evidence, for instance by "gathering votes and asking around among others about their manner of sensation, rather it should rest as it were upon an autonomy of the subject passing judgment on the feeling of pleasure (in the given object), i.e., on his own taste" (5:281). In Section 32, Kant expressly asserts that "taste simply lays claim to autonomy. To make the judgment of others the determining ground of one's own would be heteronomy" (5:282). And in Section 33, Kant amplifies this by saying that "the approval of others can never yield a valid proof for the estimation of beauty," for although the observations of others may be an adequate basis for the acceptance of a "theoretical and therefore logical judgment," where presumably only the truth of the content is at issue, "that which has pleased others can never serve as the ground of an aesthetic judgment" (5:284). Throughout, the emphasis is that in order to make a genuine judgment of taste one must not merely have some reason to believe that an ideal observer would take pleasure in an object, but one must find that reason in the pleasure one feels in the object itself. One's own pleasure in an object may not be a sufficient reason to make a judgment of taste (as Kant's discussion of disinterestedness makes clear), but it is necessary.

Kant's argument for the requirement of autonomy is presented as if it were purely epistemological – he argues that since aesthetic response cannot depend upon the predication of any determinate concept of the object, the evidence for an aesthetic judgment, in turn, cannot lie in the applicability of any such concept to the object and can instead lie only in the actual occurrence of pleasure – but this argument results in a psychological requirement.[12] In fact, one might object that Kant's interpretation of the requirement of individual autonomy in the act of aesthetic judgment is too strong, for it would seem that an observer who for some reason believes himself to be in less than ideal conditions for the assessment of an object might base his assessment of it on pleasure actually felt, to be sure, but pleasure felt by someone other than himself, someone in a better position to evaluate the object. But Kant does not consider such an objection and holds firm to the view that the very concept of an aesthetic judgment requires that the individual "subject judge for himself, without having to grope about empirically among the judgments of others and antecedently instruct himself about their delight or displeasure in the given object" (*CJ*, §32, 5:282).

Next, I suggest that the significance of the demand for individual autonomy in matters of taste is broadened when we realize that Kant's explanation of the origination of the pleasure felt by an individual making an aesthetic judgment requires that this pleasure itself derive from a sense of *freedom* in the employment of the imagination in response to the object of the judgment. This may not be evident in some of Kant's initial characterizations of the basis of aesthetic response, which, cast in the abstract terms of his epistemology, appear to require merely that there be – or, more precisely, that there not be – a certain relation between concepts and the manifold of intuition presented by an object of taste. But as Kant's exposition continues, there is increasing emphasis on the need for an explicit feeling of freedom in the experience of something beautiful. In fact, the need for a feeling fitting such a description is entailed from the start by the theory of pleasure from which Kant's theory of aesthetic response is derived.

Kant's only direct discussion of the judgment of taste in the published introduction to the *Critique of Judgment* does not introduce the concept of freedom at all. Instead, Kant simply explains that the pleasure of an "aesthetic representation of finality" arises when a manifold of intuition presented to the imagination by a given object can be grasped by the understanding independently of the application of any concept to that manifold. Thus, "Pleasure is connected with the mere apprehension . . . of the form of an object of intuition without the relation of the form to a concept for a determinate cognition" (*CJ*, §VII, 5:189); and when it is also "judged that the form of an object . . . in the mere reflection upon it (without concern for a concept to be derived from it) is the ground of a pleasure in the representation of such an object," then the pleasure can be considered to be connected with the object "for everyone judging it at all" and "the object is then called beautiful" (*CJ*, §VII, 5:190). It appears to be required only that the unified perception of the form of an object of taste in fact be free – that is, independent – of the employment of a concept, although such employment is what ordinarily unifies a manifold, and that the fact of this independence be available to reflection in some form or other, so that the further inference to the universal validity of the response can be drawn.

Even when Kant first introduces an explicit reference to freedom in the characterization of this state, the relevant concept of freedom still seems to be only this formal notion of freedom as independence from concepts. Thus, the "key to the critique of taste" which Kant claims to offer in Section 9 (see 5:216) first refers to the "free play" of the cognitive faculties of imagination and understanding, but since it derives this notion from the purely formal notion of independence from concepts, it is not apparent that anything is being added to what has previously been said: "The cognitive powers which are set in play through this representation [of a beautiful object] are thus in a free play, since no determinate concept limits them to a particular rule of cognition" (5:217). Kant does add the claim that "therefore the mental state in this representation must be one of a feeling of the free play of the powers of representation in the case of a given representation," but this seems to mean only that since the state of mind is in fact one of free play, *any* feeling which represents it at all must in some sense represent a state of free play; nothing in the context appears to require that the state must be manifest *as* a feeling of freedom, that is, that it be phenomenologically and not just epistemologically free, or felt to be free rather than just inferred to be free.

However, consideration of the only explanation which Kant ever suggests for *why* a state of mind which seems like the unification of a manifold without a concept *should in fact be pleasurable* makes it clear that such a state must not just be one which happens to involve no determinate concept, but must also involve something like an actual feeling of freedom from the kind of constraint on the imagination that would be provided by a concept or any other form of antecedently determined rule. For Kant's explanation of why such a free play of the cognitive faculties should please, indeed his only real basis for the derivation of the requirement that aesthetic judgments be independent of concepts, lies in a theory of pleasure comprising two key claims. First, Kant holds that pleasure can be taken only in a state which may be interpreted as the satisfaction of an objective, and *a fortiori* that an intersubjectively valid pleasure can be taken only in the satisfaction of an intersubjectively valid objective – thus is the understanding's goal of unity as required for "cognition in general" ultimately introduced. Second, however, Kant also holds that such pleasure is actually felt – is, as he puts it, "very noticeable" (*sehr merklich*) – when the satisfaction of the objective involved is something "which we regard [*ansehen*] as merely contingent" (*CJ*, §VI, 5:187–8). As the verb here clearly describes an intentional attitude toward this contingency, it is evident that what is required is an actual feeling of contingency or freedom – not just that no concept be applicable to the manifold of intuition, but that no concept or rule be *felt* to determine its form.

That this requirement of an actual feeling of freedom can be defeated even in a case where the purely epistemological requirement of unity independent of concepts is satisfied, merely if there is a feeling of constraint due to something as simple as excessive familiarity with an object, appears to be the main point of the "General Remark" which Kant rather causally adds to the "Analytic of the Beautiful" after Section 22.[13] Kant begins this "Remark" with phrases that emphasize the word "free," but that could otherwise still be interpreted like the reference to "free play" in Section 9: A judgment of taste requires that its object be responsible for "the imagination's *free conformity to law*," or that the object be felt to have a form "containing just such a composition of the manifold as the imagination would project in harmony with the *lawfulness of the understanding* in general if it were left free by itself" (5:240). But these statements are now accompanied by examples which suggest that what is crucial is not the mere fact of independence from concepts but psychologically felt freedom from any form of constraint. Thus, Kant argues that what is necessary for beauty in ornamental gardens, interior decoration, and other such cases is that any "regularity which makes itself felt [*sich ankündigt*] as constraint be avoided as much as possible," even if this requires that "the freedom of the imagination be driven to the verge of the grotesque" (5:242) – a tendency which arises, it may well be, precisely because regularity can always come to feel like constraint, even if there is in fact no determinate concept of a purpose or classification in behalf of or as a result of which this regularity is present. And Kant's next example seems to make even clearer that what is required is a psychological sense of freedom, not just episte-mological independence from concepts. In this example, he holds that an explorer, surfeited with beautiful wilderness, who finds a cultivated garden charming will soon come to tire of it and want to return to "nature subject to no constraint of artificial rules," just because the garden will be felt to "impose a burdensome constraint upon the imagination" (5:243). But this can only be interpreted to mean that even though there is some way in which the form of the garden can be appre-hended as unified without a concept, for otherwise it would never have offered the explorer the pleasure of "regular beauty" at all, this formal independence from concepts is not enough to prevent the mere fact of familiarity from breeding a sense of constraint. Thus the imagination must be free of any such sense of constraint in order to ground an "unstudied and final play" that is "always new to us."

Further, Kant's discussion of fine art explicitly invokes this psychological requirement of a sense of freedom from con-straint. Emphasizing not just independence from concepts but freedom from whatever feels like a rule – anything in which "academic form is transparent" (*CJ*, §45, 5:307) – Kant argues that although one must be conscious that a work of fine art "is art and not nature, nevertheless the purposiveness of its form must appear as free from all constraint of arbitrary rules as if it were a product of mere nature," because the pleasure in a work of art, like that in a beautiful object of nature, must rest "upon this feeling of freedom in the play of our cognitive faculties" (5:306). The switch from a "feeling of free play" in Section 9 to "a feeling of freedom in the play" of the cognitive faculties in the present passage might have seemed insignificant at an earlier stage of the argument, but at this point it signals Kant's requirement that aesthetic re-sponse must actually be felt as free if it is to produce its charac-teristic pleasure. Yet insofar as this requirement is maintained in the case of art, it will generate serious tension with the ideal of a stable canon of classics for the formation of the taste of both connoisseurs and productive artists themselves.

Before we pursue this argument, however, we must consider the third and final source of tension in Kant's account of aesthetic integrity, the interest which society at large takes in actual and not just ideal agreement, on behalf of its own interest in coherence. As is already evident, the only kind of intersubjective agreement which is asserted by the actual content of a given judgment of taste is a merely possible agreement, an agreement to be expected only under ideal conditions which rarely obtain. Thus the "modality" of aesthetic judgment is that of a "merely ideal norm"; such a judgment "asserts not that everyone *will* be in accord with our judgment, but that they *should* agree with it" (*CJ*, §22, 5:239). That a judgment of taste asserts only this ideal possibility of unanimity in response rather than actual agreement is also implied by the language of Section 9, where Kant speaks of the "universal capacity for being communicated" (*Mitteilungsfähigkeit*) or "subjective universal communicability" (*Mitteilbarkeit*) of the state of mind occasioned by a given object (5:217). Nevertheless, as early as this same Section 9 Kant also suggests that we are not only concerned with the communicability *of* pleasure, but that in addition we have a "natural tendency" to attach pleasure *to* the opportunity for communicating our own state of mind (5:218), that is, to see the opportunity for agreement in feeling offered by a beautiful object as an additional source of value in it. Kant does not accept this natural tendency as the basic explanation of aesthetic response, because he does not consider it a necessary feature of the human constitution suitable for grounding an *a priori* judgment (it would also be circular for him to do so[14]); but he does not exclude it from his larger picture of the sources of pleasure in the experience of art. This becomes even clearer in his discussion of the "empirical interest in the beautiful" (*CJ*, §41, 5:296–8). Here Kant reiterates that there is a natural tendency toward society, and then argues that the ability to communicate with others is a condition of the satisfaction of this tendency and that objects of taste, especially works of art, are of interest to us precisely as occasions for the communication of our feelings:

> If one concedes that the drive to society is natural to mankind, and that suitability for society and the inclination to it, that is, *sociability*, are requisite for man as a creature destined for society, then it cannot but be the case that one will consider taste as a faculty for the estimation of everything by means of which one can communicate even his *feeling* to everyone else, thus as a means for the advancement of [society] which every inclination demands. (*CJ*, §41, 5:296–7)

By occasioning intersubjectively valid feelings of pleasure, objects of taste can strengthen the bonds of society where they would otherwise be weakest, in the subjective realm of feelings. This state of affairs, however, will not be brought about by the mere possibility of agreement (*Mitteilbarkeit*) but only by actual agreement or communication (*Mitteilung*). Thus Kant claims that a sociable person "is not satisfied with an object unless he can feel the delight in it in communion [*Gemeinschaft*] with others," a state which obviously requires actual and not just possible agreement. In fact, as if to make explicit the point that society attaches value to actual agreement and actual success in the communication of feeling, Kant points out that objects of fashion or tradition will provide this satisfaction even in the absence of genuine aesthetic merit, which is just to say that they will please because they allow the actual communication of feeling even without its ideal communicability:

> Finally civilization which has developed to its highest point makes [universal communication] the chief business of refined inclination, and attaches value to sensations insofar as they can be universally communicated, in which case the idea of its universal communicability can almost infinitely augment the value of the pleasure which everyone takes in an . . . object, even when it is itself inconsiderable and without any marked interest. (*CJ*, §41, 5:297)

Finally, Kant also implies that since society has an interest in its own coherence and sees objects of taste about which there can actually be agreement as a means for advancing the communication on which such coherence depends, society will actually demand that individuals develop their taste and, presumably, that artists produce objects of taste: "The concern for universal communication" (*not* communicability, as J. C. Meredith incorrectly translates *Mitteilung* at this point)[15] is "expected and demanded of everyone, just as if it were from an original contract dictated by humanity itself" (*CJ*, §41, 5:297). It is just this demand that individual aesthetic response and artistic production advance society's interest in successful communication that constitutes society's demand for aesthetic integrity.

As he did in Section 9, Kant again downgrades this account of a societal interest in actual agreement in matters of taste as an inadequate basis for any *a priori* connection. Here, however, he follows this account with an additional basis for a societal interest in art, although he does not himself recognize this implication. In Section 42, Kant describes an "intellectual" interest that we are alleged to take in beautiful objects of external nature only as instances of the kind of harmony between nature and reason that is assumed to be a necessary condition for the morally good (*CJ*, §42, 5:300–1). Now insofar as what is here called the morally good is equivalent to what Kant elsewhere calls the *summum bonum*, or the condition in which the actual distribution of happiness is in proportion to individual worthiness to be happy, this condition might indeed require some sort of harmony between human reason and external nature: but insofar as the worthiness to be happy itself requires the harmonization of human feeling with the dictates of human reason, it would seem that this condition should also require harmony between reason and nature *within* as well as outside of human beings. But since Kant shortly characterizes genius, as the source of fine art, precisely as the harmonious effect of nature working from within a human being, it would also seem that this intellectual interest

should attach to works of art as valid, if not indeed paradigmatic, products of the kind of harmony between reason and
nature necessary for morality itself.[16] Thus, it would seem,
society should take an interest in the production of art as
relevant to its *a priori* interest in morality, as well as taking
an interest in both the production and appreciation of art as
occasions for that unanimity of feeling which satisfies its
merely "empirical" interest in its own cohesion.

## III. THE DIALECTIC OF ART HISTORY

Demands for autonomy and a sense of freedom in the individual exercise of taste are thus consequences of Kant's basic
analysis of aesthetic judgment and explanation of aesthetic
response, and the demand that objects of taste function to
advance the goal of social integrity and perhaps even of morality itself is an aspect of Kant's psychology of taste more
broadly construed. However, although Kant ultimately resists this conclusion, there are good reasons, several of them
expounded by Kant himself, to believe that these demands
cannot be satisfied simultaneously by any single work of art
or stable canon of classics, but can only be satisfied partially
and successively in a history of artistic production and reception in which the autonomy of individual artists and appreciators requires them to break from the received traditions and
critical opinions of society, producing revolutionary works
and attitudes which society at large resists but then assimi-
lates in behalf of its interest in its own integrity, only to
encourage a new generation of individuals who will strive to
reject the constraints now imposed by these very models –
*ad infinitum*, as far as one can see. To see how the several
demands for autonomy and integrity described in the preceding section contribute to the generation of such a dialectic,
we will now consider in turn the three poles around which it
revolves: those of the individual appreciator of a work of art;
the artist or individual creator of a work of art; and a whole

society as the larger audience for a work of art and the pre-
server of artistic schools and traditions.

We can begin with the role of the individual appreciator.
Kant explicitly describes tensions that may arise between the
competing demands for the autonomy of an individual appreciator of a work of art and for the agreement in traditions of
taste that society expects as a condition of its own integrity,
although it is not evident that this particular locus of tension
is itself sufficient to generate a truly dialectical pattern in the
history of art and culture. In Section 32, Kant emphasizes
that the individual appreciator (his example is a "young
poet," in fact, but considered in the role of judge rather than
author of his own work) must make his judgment of a work
of art on the basis of his own feeling, even where that is at
odds with "the judgment of the public or of his friends"
(5:282), simply because the autonomy of aesthetic judgment
requires that it be made on the basis of a pleasure actually felt
in a given object rather than one merely reported by others.
In Section 33, Kant adds that such a procedure must also be
followed because the actual agreement of others about a
given object, even "a hundred voices all lauding it to the
skies," is no proof of the agreement of *ideal* observers which
is the true concern of aesthetic judgment; the "judgment of
others, where unfavorable to our own, can rightly make us
suspicious" of our own claim to have discerned a universally
valid response, but it is not itself direct evidence of error in
such an assessment (5:284). Yet the requirement that a judgment of taste be made autonomously, combined with the
possibility that the agreement of others about the object of
such a judgment may be erroneous, engenders the possibility that the individual judge of a work of art, in spite of his
ideal objective of attaining agreement with others, may be
forced to depart from the actual judgment of society as represented either by the opinions of his friends or immediate
public or else by such contemporary arbiters of taste as the
critics "Batteux or Lessing or still older and more famous
critics"; for when one's own response to an object remains at
odds with theirs, the autonomy of aesthetic judgment re-

quires one "to suppose that those rules of the critics were at fault, or at least have no application" (5:284). The autonomy of aesthetic judgment is thus a potential source of conflict between the individual appreciator of art and the opinion of society as a whole. Indeed, since each individual appreciator of art will share the natural inclination to society and the natural interest in its integrity, he will also feel within himself a tendency "to accommodate himself to the common error (even against his own judgment)" (*CJ*, §33, 5:282); thus the tension between the competing demands of individual autonomy and social integrity in matters of taste will express itself as a conflict within the individual as well as between the individual and society.

The tension generated in this way, however, is not itself adequate to introduce permanent instability into the history of art, for it might mean only that each individual must resist the judgment of society and its representative critics *until* he has experienced the socially requisite feeling himself, but that "later, when his judgment has been sharpened through practice" – much like one of Hume's "true judges" – he *will* experience the proper response, and thus "depart with a free will from his previous judgment" and accept the ultimately stable canon of classics already accepted by the rest of society (*CJ*, §32, 5:282). But at this point it must be recalled that Kant's interpretation of aesthetic autonomy requires not only that the individual make his aesthetic judgment on the basis of his own feeling, but also that this feeling itself be a feeling of freedom from constraint by anything that is manifestly a rule; and this might well mean that the mere fact that society as a whole has canonized certain works or schools of art will make them seem unacceptably constraining to the individual appreciator. Thus the mere ascription of classical status even to works of genius which might otherwise be expected to leave great scope for the imagination of the individual respondent to them can conflict with the sense of individual freedom from constraint, and the very status of a classic as an object of society's agreement will be self-defeating. Every individual would have a tendency to resist the recommendations not only of the critics of any particular period in the past, such as a Batteux or a Lessing, but also of the successors to these critics that intervening generations of resistant appreciators would have called forth, and this not merely because there is always the possibility that the judgments of such critics might in fact be erroneous but also because the very fact of their ratification of a particular work of art would be seen as a constraint on an individual's feeling of freedom in response to that work. Although Kant did not draw out this conclusion, then, it would seem that his requirement that aesthetic response itself be a feeling of freedom introduces a permanent source of instability into the history of art, for the only way for successive generations of individual appreciators of art to secure such freedom for themselves would seem to be by the constant creation of new works of art and new critical opinions for them, or at least constant change in critical opinions about which of the already extant works of art are true classics.

It might also seem that Kant's explicit account of the individual's response to a work of art should create a permanent source of instability in art history. For while Kant requires on the one hand that the individual's response to a work of art be free of any obvious constraint from any rule manifest in the work itself, he also requires that a work of art be recognized to be the product of a "determinate intention of producing something" on the part of the artist, and this intention itself, although it would be a product of the *artist*'s autonomy, might well seem like a constraint on the freedom of the imagination of the *appreciator*.[17] It would then appear that individual appreciators would constantly go to works of art for the satisfaction of their aesthetic sensibility, but equally constantly find them constraining and then attempt to resolve this paradox by the only available expedient, that of calling incessantly for new works of art.

Kant's theory of genius, however, can well appear to be designed to avert precisely this consequence. For the key claim of this theory is that the intention which the artist himself formulates for his work is not sufficient to determine the content or form of that work insofar as it is indeed a work of genius, nature instead filling the gap between the intention and the achieved object itself. And this would also mean that the content of the artist's intention would not be sufficient to determine – or constrain – the individual appreciator's response to the object. Thus, it would seem, any particular work of genius would leave scope for the freedom of the imagination of all respondents to it, and the nature of artistic intentionality itself would not appear to be a perpetual source of instability in the history of art.

This conclusion, however, would overlook the effect of the works of a genius on other geniuses, that is, on other individual producers of art, whose role we turn to now. More fully understood, the role of works of genius as models for the taste of society as a whole and also for other producers of works of art does indeed introduce such a permanent source of instability into the history of art and thus take us closer to an inescapable dialectic therein.

Kant's conception of genius requires it to be an optimal combination of freedom and taste, individuality and general acceptability. This is evident in his definition of it by two criteria. First, genius is "a *talent* for producing that for which no determinate rule can be given," so "consequently *originality* must be its primary property"; but second, as a test of their universal validity, "since there may also be original nonsense, its products must also be models, that is, *exemplary*," and "must be fit to serve as a rule for the judgment of others" even though they cannot themselves be derived from any such rule (*CJ*, §46, 5:307–8).[18] The requirement of originality is nothing but a requirement for freedom from constraint by any rule in the genius's autonomous production of a work of art and in his use of his critical faculties for the assessment of his own work at relevant points during the course of its production; this is made obvious when Kant says that in the production of an "aesthetic idea," which is the typical content of a work of genius, "the imagination is represented in its freedom from all instruction by rules but yet as final for the presentation of the given concept," and that there is an "unintentional subjective finality in the free harmony of the imagination with the lawfulness of the understanding" (*CJ*, §49, 5:317–18). The requirement that a work of genius be "exemplary" rather than "original nonsense," however, is nothing but the requirement that it produce this same free harmony of the cognitive faculties in all ideal observers of it. Yet, it turns out, this combination of demands cannot be satisfied by a stable canon of classics. Instead, it can only be expected to produce a history of artistic revolutions, efforts to break the grip on society exerted by the very works which are the models for those efforts.

This conflict is not implied by Kant's initial description of the relation between a work of genius and its audience, which presents the latter as if it constituted a stable but passive test of the permanent status, as a classic or a failure, of the former. Nor does it appear in Kant's descriptions of the effects of classics on a given genius regarded in isolation, for what Kant emphasizes in this context is the role of such models in the formation of the taste rather than the originality of a particular genius, and in this regard there seems to be no reason why any model should ever be removed from the list of classics, even if some may be added by subsequent geniuses. Such models are needed, Kant argues, because although taste is a native capacity, it also requires education. "Just because its judgment is not determinable by concepts or precepts, [taste is] among all faculties and talents the one most in need of examples of what in the course of culture has maintained itself longest in esteem" (*CJ*, §32, 5:283). However, when Kant considers geniuses in interaction, or the effects of the models created by one genius on other potential geniuses, the dialectical import of his theory of genius does at last become apparent. For in this context it becomes clear that works of genius are not merely models for the formation of the taste of a passive audience or even for the taste of other artists, but rather that they function primarily as stimuli for the *originality* of other geniuses. Works of genius are models not for the taste which may check the freedom of other geniuses, but for that freedom itself; the autonomy of one genius is a spur to nothing less than the autonomy of every successive genius. Geniuses stand in a line of succession, but this does not produce stability:

> Succession [*Nachfolge*]¹⁹ that relates itself to a precedent, not imitation, is the correct expression for the influence that the product of an exemplary originator can have on others; which means the same as this: to create from the same sources out of which the former has himself created, and to learn from one's predecessor only the way to proceed in such creation oneself. (*CJ*, §32, 5:283)

In other words, the work of one genius functions as a model for a successor only by providing a rule by which the latter "may put his own talent to the test" (*CJ*, §47, 5:309).

Yet the implication of this can only be that a work of genius, precisely because it is exemplary, must become the target of rejection by other creators, and even while it becomes a classic it must also become only a stage in the history of art:

> The product of a genius . . . is an example, not for imitation (for then that in which the genius lies and which constitutes the spirit of the work would be lost), but for succession by another genius, who is thereby aroused to the feeling of his own originality, to exercise freedom from the constraint of rules in art in such a way that for art itself a new rule is attained. (*CJ*, §49, 5:318)

The work of one genius must seem like a constraint to his successor and arouse the latter to reject the former and produce his own demonstration of the freedom of the imagination. But insofar as the latter truly has universal appeal and thus itself becomes a new rule for art, it too will be destined to arouse the originality of yet another successor and thus ensure its own rejection. Genius, then, is the only source for the production of works of fine art with a claim to universal validity and thus to a place in a permanent canon of classics, but as examples of artistic autonomy such works are also the cause of their own rejection and the stimulus to their own replacement, thus the source of a dialectical pattern in the history of art whereby every new candidate for classical status must itself be rejected and superseded by new aspirants to that same position. This is a process to which there is no obvious end, and Kant's theory of genius thus makes it clear that his classicist ideal of stability is undermined by his own demand for individual artistic autonomy.

Kant was clearly uncomfortable with this implication, however, and made several efforts to avoid acknowledging it. One such effort is the claim that art must come to a halt because there is some kind of limitation on genius (*CJ*, §47, 5:309), which was quoted in the opening section of this chapter. If intended to imply that there must be an end to artistic innovation, however, let alone that such a point has already been reached, this claim would be groundless. The premise that genius has a limit, for which in any case Kant provides no argument, would appear to mean only that there is some sort of quantitative limit on the degree to which humans can manifest genius, which, given the vast numbers of humans who have already lived, should in all probability already have been reached once if not numerous times; but this, of course, does not mean that the works produced by different artists of similar degree of genius will themselves be similar. Works of genius might take on perpetually changing forms even while manifesting a fixed degree of talent.

Another effort to preserve his ideal of stability is Kant's claim that "only those models can become classical of which the ancient, dead languages, preserved as learned, are the medium" (*CJ*, §47, 5:310). This appears intended to imply that the canon of classics must already be fixed simply because no artist, even a genius, who lives subsequent to ancient times can compose in the ancient languages and also manifest originality. But even if this claim could be made to bear on the cases of art in which media employed by the ancients are still very much in use – ceramics or marble sculpture, for instance – it would still be a *non sequitur*. Kant makes this claim as if it were a consequence of the prior claim that works of genius serve other artists as models only by setting them standards against which to test their own talents. But the sole explanation which he ever offers of it – that it is only by being in dead languages that these models can themselves remain stable and avoid "the changes that inevitably overtake living ones" (an explanation not in fact offered in §47 at all, but much earlier, at §17, 5:232n.) – would not imply the desired conclusion without the assumption of the further premise that in order to be available as a test for *any* aspiring genius the *same* object would have to remain available as a test for *all* geniuses. Yet Kant makes no attempt whatever to argue for such a premise, and it is obviously implausible. In fact, we can make most sense of what is going on in Kant's attempt to confine classical status to works of art in ancient media if we assume that, contrary to what he says, he is here thinking of the classics primarily as models for the taste rather than originality of geniuses, and that he is tacitly limiting such models to dead languages as media precisely to make sure that they do not excessively constrain the originality of budding geniuses.

Finally, Kant makes a frontal attack on the destabilizing influence of genius implied by his own theory. Because this attempt to stop the dialectic which he has set off involves a direct confrontation between the interest of individual autonomy in the creation of art and the interest of societal integrity in its reception, however, it will be best if further discussion of it is delayed until I have commented more directly than I have done so far on the implications of society's interest in art.

So let us now consider society's interest in art as a source of social union. As we saw in Section II of this chapter, Kant's psychology of taste postulates that as typical members of the human species individuals naturally tend to have an interest in the coherence of their society as a whole, and that this interest leads them to attach value to anything which can serve as an occasion for the kind of mutuality and communication of feelings which is the cement of social coherence. This interest thus attaches to works of art insofar as they actually are occasions for communication, producing a pleasure in them that is theoretically distinct from the purely aesthetic pleasure in them which is what is actually communicated and is thus the object of this social pleasure; indeed, since this as it were second-order pleasure attaches to objects of actual rather than ideal agreement, it is to this extent even independent of intrinsic aesthetic merit. Further, we saw that although Kant himself does not recognize the fact, his theory that the "intellectual" interest which we take in any free harmony between nature and reason is symbolic of the kind of harmony which is necessary for morality certainly ought to attach to genius as the paradigmatic case of a harmony between *human* nature and human intentionality. Thus, insofar as it is interested in the moral as well as merely psychological conditions of its own integrity, society should take an interest in works of art as products of the morally emblematic state of genius as well as occasions for social communication.

But the interest which society takes in art as an instrument of social coherence and the interest which even society as a whole will take in such individual aesthetic autonomy can only be expected to conflict. For since society's pleasure in communication requires actual rather than merely ideal agreement, it will attach most readily to works of art executed within well-entrenched traditions or schools of artistic style; at the very least, given Kant's emphasis on the fact that taste, although natural, must be cultured or educated, actual communication about such works of art will certainly be easiest when they are created within such traditions. But in behalf of his own interest in autonomy, which will also be encouraged by society, the individual artist and, for that matter, the individual connoisseur as well will strive to break from precisely such already-accepted traditions of appreciation and creation. Society will thus encourage originality, which defines itself by breaking from tradition, by taking from previous models of genius only their impulse to originality and not any of the outward forms which facilitate the communication on which the integrity of society is based. On behalf of its interests in both its own integrity and individual autonomy, society will then encourage the production of works of art which are themselves designed to break the bonds of tradition which ground actual, if not ideal, agreement. Society then will surely try to reject such art, feeling, perhaps, that originality has after all been pushed to the point of the grotesque. But we must also assume that given its interest in actual communication, society will eventually accommodate itself to even the necessarily revolutionary art of genius – at which point, of course, society's acceptance of the new work as well as the fact that such work represents the originality of a predecessor will come to feel like a constraint on the originality of a new claimant to genius, and the whole process will resume.

After exposing the basis for this inevitable clash between the individual's need to define his aesthetic autonomy by originality and society's interest in preserving its integrity by readily communicable traditions, Kant clearly recoiled, and attempted in Section 50 to return to the bottle the genie of individual autonomy in a way that the more purely literary theorists of genius of the preceding (*Sturm und Drang*) and succeeding (Romantic) generations did not. Suddenly Kant follows his exposition of genius as the joint exercise of taste and originality with the assertion that if the interests of these two capacities should come into conflict in the case of a given work, then "something should be sacrificed, [and] it must rather happen on the side of genius." He suddenly transforms taste from merely a "necessary condition" of genius into a "discipline" of genius, which "severely clips its wings" and "gives it manners" – or, if you like, "makes it sociable" (*macht es gesittet*). Only by this means, Kant suggests, can the very state of affairs which is otherwise precluded by the theory of genius be made possible, namely that artistic "ideas be made stable and capable of [receiving] enduring and also universal approval and [of grounding] an ever-progressing culture" (*CJ*, §50, 5:319–20). Kant's discovery of a theoretical basis for a dialectical picture of the history of art and culture is at odds with his own characteristically eighteenth-century inclination to a more stable or at best unidirectional picture of the flow of this history, and he attempts to satisfy this inclination by fiat, simply awarding the palm to the faculty of taste as the representative of integrity rather than to originality as the emblem of individual autonomy. But as with his other efforts to defuse the incendiary implications of his theory of aesthetic autonomy, Kant really provides no argument for this preference. The competing demands of individual autonomy and of social integrity in the shared reception of art are at best equally well-founded in Kant's theory of taste – in fact, as the discussion in Section II of this chapter might suggest, the demand for individual autonomy is if anything more basic to Kant's theory of taste than the interest in social integrity. There is thus no theoretical foundation for Kant's withdrawal from the edge of dialectical art history in Section 50 of the *Critique of Judgment*.

Although Kant himself was hesitant to admit it, he provided theoretical grounds for the expectation of a dialectical pattern in the history of art and culture that are directly linked to his conception of aesthetic experience and judgment themselves, virtual entailments of his idea of the aesthetic. Subsequent theorists of art have surely been more willing to recognize or even celebrate the existence of dialectical tensions in the history of artistic culture than Kant was, but the reasons for which they have done so – such theories as that art is only a stage in the self-realization of the Spirit; that art is but an aspect of the ideologies of dialectically competing economic classes; or that works of art, like all other manifestations of ego, must be subject to the strains of an Oedipal conflict with their authors' progenitors – are either extrinsic to any special conception of artistic activity and aesthetic appreciation themselves, as in the cases of the Marxist and neo-Freudian hypotheses just alluded to, or else have depended on a particularly restrictive view of art, such as Hegel's cognitivist account of art as significant only as a stage on the way to Absolute Knowing. Kant's grounds for recognizing the necessity of such a dialectic, however, although both expressed in terms of and constrained by the narrow tastes of his time and province, derive from his incorporation of ultimately competing demands for individual autonomy and social integrity into concepts of aesthetic response and assessment and artistic creation which are general enough to subsume a much more varied world of art than Kant himself ever imagined. The mere suggestion of such connections is a considerable theoretical accomplishment, even if one that he made *malgré lui*.

# Chapter 9

# Duties regarding nature

In the *Lectures on Ethics* which he gave at the outset of the period of his mature work in the 1780s, Kant reported to his students a traditional conception of the philosophical basis for our duties to nonhuman nature:

> Baumgarten speaks of duties towards inanimate objects. These duties are also indirectly duties towards mankind. Destructiveness is immoral; we ought not to destroy things which can still be put to some use. No man ought to mar the beauty of nature; for what he has no use for may still be of use to some one else. He need, of course, pay no heed to the thing itself, but he ought to consider his neighbor. Thus we see that all duties towards animals, towards immaterial beings and towards inanimate objects are aimed indirectly at our duties towards mankind.[1]

Aside from the passing reference to beauty, the assumptions expressed in this remark were characteristic of a widespread attitude toward nature. The foundation of any duty to conserve nonhuman nature which we might acknowledge is our

This chapter is a revised version of an address originally presented, under the title "Kant on Duties Regarding Nature," at the conference "Mensch – Welt – Kosmos" sponsored by the University of Lodz, Poland, in May 1988, and published in *Acta Universitatis Lodziensis*, Folia Philosophica 8 (1991), pp. 21–44. Reprinted with permission.

duty of consideration toward the needs of our fellow humans, and the indirect duty regarding nature to which this underlying duty can give rise is a duty to ensure that natural objects, whether animate or inanimate, are available for legitimate use by other persons as well as by ourselves.

A similar attitude, although founded upon explicitly theological reasoning absent from Kant's brief discussion, was also expressed in Locke's famous proviso restricting our appropriation and accumulation of the useful fruits and beasts "produced by the spontaneous hand of nature." Locke argued, first, that the earth and all its gifts have been given to men in common for use in the satisfaction of their needs: "God, who hath given the World to Men in common, hath also given them reason to make use of it to the best advantage of Life and convenience. The Earth, and all that is therein, is given to Men for the Support and Comfort of their being";[2] second, that individuals may appropriate particular properties out of the common gift of nature by annexing their labor to it;[3] and finally, that individual accumulation of natural goods must be restricted – as both reason and God dictate – by the need that others have to make similar use of these materials:

> *God has given us all things richly,* I Tim. vi. 17. is the Voice of Reason confirmed by Inspiration. But how far has He given it to us? *To enjoy.* As much as any one can make use of to any advantage of life before it spoils, so much may he by his labour fix a Property in. Whatever is beyond this, is more than his share, and belongs to others. Nothing was made by God for man to spoil or destroy.[4]

Whether based in reason alone or also in inspiration, this view holds, our duties regarding natural objects arise solely from their utility conjoined with our duty to others to respect their needs.

The passing reference to beauty might suggest Kant's (or Baumgarten's) recognition of an alternative to utility as a foundation of any duties regarding nature. But such a conclusion cannot be taken for granted, for the simple reason that eighteenth-century thinkers could interpret our favorable response to natural beauty as itself a veiled judgment of utility.[5] Hume expressed just such a view:

> 'Tis evident, that nothing renders a field more agreeable than its fertility, and that scarce any advantages of ornament or situation will be able to equal this beauty. 'Tis the same case with particular trees and plants, as with the field on which they grow. I know not but a plain, overgrown with furze and broom, may be, in itself, as beautiful as a hill cover'd with vines or olive trees; tho' it will never appear so to one, who is acquainted with the value of each. . . . Fertility and value have a plain reference to use; and that to riches, joy, and plenty.[6]

So natural beauty itself depends on utility, and any duty that it might have been thought to give rise to could also be reduced to a duty based on usefulness. Of course, Hume's own derivation of such a duty would have taken a very different path from Locke's. Hume was not really concerned to derive duties at all, but rather to explain moral attitudes of approbation, and indeed his discussion of natural beauty is offered as a case study of the operation of sympathy. It is sympathy with the needs and satisfactions of others which leads us to take pleasure in the utility-based beauty of a field or plain, even if we are not its owner. But the key point remains that it is the utility of nonhuman nature with respect to human needs that grounds our moral attitude to nature.

In the next phase of Kant's career, however – the period opening with the *Critique of Judgment* in 1790 and closing with the *Metaphysics of Morals* in 1797 – he suggests a very different foundation for duties regarding nonhuman nature. On this account, although the respect that we may owe to nonhuman nature is still grounded in our duties to mankind, two key differences emerge. First, the basis for such respect lies not in the utility of fruits, beasts, and fields but in nature's aesthetic properties, the beauty of individual natural forms; and Kant's critique of aesthetic judgment clearly distinguishes judgments of beauty from any judgments of utility, no matter how veiled or supplemented by sympathy. Second, in an even more striking reversal of the sort of view reported in the lectures cited earlier, Kant grounds the duty to which the beauty of nature may give rise not in our duties to *others* but in our duties to *ourselves*, and, indeed, not in duties we may have regarding the well-being of our animal nature, such as the cultivation of our bodily powers and talents, but in our duty to preserve and cultivate our moral character or disposition.

This reversal of attitudes is clearly summed up in the *Doctrine of Virtue*, the second part of the *Metaphysics of Morals*. First Kant observes that it is important not to confuse duty *regarding* other beings – he here provides us with an extensional definition of nature by listing the three realms of minerals, plants, and animals – with duty *toward* such beings (*Virtue*, §16),[7] so that he may then argue that although the fundamental principle of morality – to respect rational being as an end in itself – cannot give rise to duties directly *toward* nonrational nature, a duty that we have *toward* ourselves as rational beings may give rise to duties *regarding* nonrational nature. He then briefly characterizes such duties (indirectly, by describing their violation) and the ground on which they rest:

> A propensity to wanton destruction of what is *beautiful* in inanimate nature (*spiritus destructionis*) is opposed to man's duty to himself; for it weakens or uproots that feeling in man which, though not of itself moral, is still a disposition of sensibility that greatly promotes morality or at least prepares the way for it: the disposition, namely, to love something (e.g., beautiful crystal formations, the indescribable beauty of plants) even apart from any intention to use it.
>
> With regard to the animate but nonrational part of creation, violent and cruel treatment of animals is far more intimately opposed to man's duty to himself, and he has a duty to refrain from this; for it dulls his shared feeling of their pain and so

weakens and gradually uproots a natural predisposition that is very serviceable to morality in one's relations with other men. Man is authorized to kill animals quickly (without pain) and to put them to work that does not strain them beyond their capacities (such work as man himself must submit to). But agonizing physical experiments for the sake of mere speculation, when the end could also be achieved without these, are to be abhorred. Even gratitude for the long service of an old horse or dog (just as if they were members of the household) belongs *indirectly* to man's duty *with regard* to these animals; considered as a *direct* duty, however, it is always only a duty of man *to* himself. (*Virtue*, §17, 6:443)

The utility of nonhuman nature hardly loses all importance, and Kant continues to express the Judeo-Christian attitude[8] voiced by Locke that we are "authorized" to make use of the resources of nature. But, at least in the cases of the mineral and vegetable realms, it is clearly beauty rather than utility which is the salient ground of our indirect duty regarding nature; and in all cases it is clear that it is our duty concerning our own moral attitude and development, rather than any direct responsibility to the claims or needs of others, which generates this duty regarding nature.

Certain questions naturally arise in reflection upon Kant's introduction of duties regarding nature into the scheme of the *Metaphysics of Morals*. Perhaps the most obvious question concerns the reason for Kant's transformation of any sort of aesthetic response – which is, after all, supposed to be marked by disinterestedness, before all else – into something susceptible to moral evaluation and fit to ground a species of duty. In addition to this basic issue, however, one must also ask whether anything more can be said about the content of these duties beyond what Kant so briefly states. Finally, one may consider what might be inferred, from the position of these duties in Kant's general classification of duties, about the scope and strength of their claims regarding nature in relation to our other, more direct duties regarding ourselves and others. Most of what follows will concern the first of these questions, but some light will be shed on the other two as well.

## II. AESTHETICS AND MORALITY

As late as the *Critique of Practical Reason* of 1788, only two years prior to the publication of the *Critique of Judgment*, Kant characterized aesthetic response as a subjective state of pleasure which could not be seen as having any direct moral significance. In the former *Critique*, Kant considers an attraction to natural beauty to be a state of mind which, although commendable and perhaps even gradually productive of a morally good disposition, cannot be required as any sort of duty:

> Now there is no doubt that this exercise and the consciousness of cultivation of our reason which judges concerning the practical must gradually produce a certain interest even in its own law and thus in morally good actions. For we ultimately take a liking to that the observation of which makes us feel that our powers of knowledge are extended, and this extension is especially furthered by that wherein we find moral correctness, since reason, with its faculty of determining according to *a priori* principles what ought to occur, can find satisfaction only in such an order of things. Even an observer of nature finally likes objects which first offend his senses when he discovers in them the great design of their organization, so that his reason finds nourishment in observing them; Leibniz spared an insect which he had carefully examined under the microscope, and replaced it on its leaf, because he had been instructed by viewing it and, as it were, had received benefit from it.
>
> But this occupation of the faculty of judgment, which makes us feel our own powers of knowledge, is not yet interest in actions and their morality itself. It only enables one to entertain himself with such judging and gives virtue or a turn of mind based on moral laws a form of beauty which is admired but not yet sought. . . . It is the same with everything whose contemplation produces subjectively a consciousness of the harmony of our powers of representation by which we feel our entire cognitive faculty (understanding and imagination) strengthened; it produces a satisfaction that can be com-

municated to others, but the existence of its object remains
indifferent to us, as it is seen only as the occasion for our
becoming aware of the store of talents which are elevated
above the mere animal level.[9] (*Practical Reason*, 5:159–60)

Thus, Kant suggests, although a virtuous disposition may
grow out of aesthetic sensitivity to natural beauty, there is
no direct moral content to aesthetic contemplation; and apparently the causal connection that there may be between
aesthetic contemplation and what it reveals about our cognitive powers is not sufficient to license any direct claims of
duty. Instead, Kant continues, the "methodology of moral
cultivation and exercise" can only work by "calling to notice
the purity of will by a vivid example of the moral disposition in examples" (5:161, 160). Kant's view seems to be that
only our subjective responses to examples of moral behavior
itself – such as our admiration for the fortitude of a (fic-
tional) honest man's refusal to betray Anne Boleyn to the
accusations of Henry VIII (5:155–6) – can directly enter the
methodology of practical reason and thus, presumably, become connected to any actual duties.

As we have now seen, however, the *Critique of Judgment*,
although published only two years after the *Critique of Practical Reason*, contains several passages suggesting a closer link
between aesthetics and morality. In the first of these, Kant
introduces a notion of "intellectual interest" in the "beautiful
*forms* of nature" which, he says, is "always a mark of a good
soul" and, where habitual, "at least indicative of a temper of
mind favorable to the moral feeling" (*CJ*, §42, 5:298–9). The
use of the term "interest" might suggest that Kant now
means to bring our response to natural beauty more directly
into the sphere of practical reason than he seemed willing to
allow in the *Critique of Practical Reason*. But there are two
grounds for caution here.

First, the discussion of possible interests in beautiful objects is preceded by an explicit reference to duty which is far
from unequivocally recognizing any aesthetically grounded
interest as an actual duty of practical reason. If, Kant says,

we could "assume that the mere universal communicability of our feeling must of itself carry with it an interest for us, . . . we should then be in a position to *explain* how the feeling in the judgment of taste comes to be exacted from everyone as a *sort of* [*gleichsam*] duty" (*CJ*, §40, 5:296; my emphases). But this comment, while obviously reflecting a favorable attitude toward aesthetic response, does not say that an interest in beauty is an actual duty, nor does it say that exacting aesthetic response from others *as if* it were a duty can be *justified* by the possibility of connecting an interest with it. Instead, it seems as if Kant's point is precisely to suggest that he can *explain* why we may *respond* to the appreciation of natural beauty as if it were a genuine moral duty, even though it is not one.

Second, it should also be noted that even if Kant had meant to argue that intellectual interest in natural beauty could transform our attachment to it into a genuine duty of morality, rather than just something like one, the mechanism of this intellectual interest which he then goes on to describe might not suffice for this purpose. Kant argues as follows. A pure judgment of taste is neither founded upon an antecedent interest in an object – that is, a desire for the existence of its object which is grounded in a concept of it – nor does it produce such an interest. Moral judgment – "the power of intellectual judgment for the mere forms of practical maxims" – is analogous in being independent of an antecedent interest in the existence of its object, but it does produce a consequent interest. However, Kant adds, reason has a *general* interest in its ideas having objective reality – that is, presumably, being actually instantiated or at least approximated in external existence – and this general interest extends to the existence of naturally beautiful objects which satisfy the conditions of our aesthetic response, as well as to the existence of external circumstances complying with the direct interests of morality. As he puts it,

But, now, reason is further interested in ideas (for which in our moral feeling it brings about an immediate interest) having also objective reality. That is to say, it is of interest to reason that nature should at least show a trace or give a hint that it contains in itself some ground or other for assuming a uniform accordance of its products with our wholly disinterested delight. . . . That being so, reason must take an interest in every manifestation on the part of nature of some such accordance. Hence the mind cannot reflect on the beauty of *nature* without at the same time finding its interest engaged. But this interest is akin to the moral. (*CJ*, §42, 5:300)

Kant's idea seems to be that since (practical) reason is inevitably interested in nature complying with the demands of morality, it is interested in all signs that nature complies with any of our – at least not immoral – ideas and expectations at all. So although natural beauty has no directly moral content, and our disinterested contemplation of it no immediately obviously moral value, nevertheless the very existence of natural beauty, which, unlike artistic beauty, cannot be conceived of as having been intentionally created for our own gratification, shows that nature is not hostile to our own ideas and endeavors; and it should therefore give us encouragement in our effort to be moral as well – assuming that we have set ourselves to undertake the latter effort.

The problem with this argument, however, is that although it may give an explanation of our quasi-moral *interest* in natural beauty, it may not seem sufficient to transform such an interest into a *duty*. Such an objection may be suggested by Kant's concept of the *summum bonum*, at least as he interprets it in the *Critique of Practical Reason*.[10]

The *summum bonum* is the complete but bipartite object of rational willing for beings like ourselves who are both animal yet rational. One component of the highest good, that which Kant refers to as the *supreme* or *unconditioned*, but not *complete* or *consummate* good (*Practical Reason*, 5:110), is the maximal worthiness to be happy, or virtuousness, which of course consists in willing to do what duty requires for the reason that duty requires it. The other component of the highest good is happiness, indeed the maximal amount of happiness, which is not only naturally but also rationally willed by a rational being with desires (happiness being nothing but the satisfaction of desires), conditional only upon the being's worthiness to be happy.

> Happiness is also required, and indeed not merely in the partial eyes of a person who makes himself his end but even in the judgment of an impartial reason, which impartially regards persons in the world as ends in themselves. For to be in need of happiness and worthy of it and yet not to partake of it could not be in accordance with the complete volition of a . . . rational being. (*Practical Reason*, 5:110)

What is important for our present purposes is that Kant insists that the connection between happiness and virtue is "synthetic" rather than "analytic"; that is, that willing happiness is not identical with willing compliance with what duty requires but is an independent object, rationally willed as long as it is not in conflict with duty and is proportionate to one's worthiness.[11]

Kant makes this point clear in the *Critique of Practical Reason*, but stresses it even more forcefully in *Religion within the Limits of Reason Alone* of 1793:

> But that everyone ought to make the highest good *possible* in this world a *final end* is a synthetic practical proposition *a priori* (and indeed objectively practical) given by pure reason; for it is a proposition which goes beyond the concept of duties in this world and adds a consequence (an effect) thereof which is not contained in the moral laws and therefore cannot be evolved out of them analytically. . . . That is, the proposition: Make the highest good possible in the world your own final end! is a synthetic proposition *a priori*, which is introduced by the moral law itself; although practical reason does, indeed, extend itself therein beyond the law. This extension is possible because of the moral law's being taken in relation to the natural characteristic of man, that for all his actions he must conceive of an end over and above the law (a characteristic which makes man an object of experience).[12] (*Religion*, 6:7n)

The point is that we do not will the satisfaction of our objectives as part of willing to do our duty. We will the satisfaction of our objectives or happiness, as one form of practical willing, independently of willing our duty, and we will to do our duty, as another form of practical willing, independently of any promise of happiness; it is just that a fully rational will has an interest in the maximal satisfaction of its two distinct objectives, happiness and duty.[13]

The objection that is then to be drawn from this analysis of the highest good is that practical reason has *interests* in the satisfaction of its objectives which are not identical with its *duties*. Indeed, since dutiful action must be undertaken without regard to the bearing of its outcome on one's own happiness, it would seem as if practical reason's interest in happiness as a component of the highest good *must* be independent of practical reason's interest in the performance of duty. And this in turn suggests that reason's interest in nature's compliance with our objectives, which is supposed to be expressed in our interest in the natural existence of beautiful objects, is connected with practical reason's interest in happiness rather than duty. If this is so, then it would seem that the intellectual interest in natural beauty is something which must be *conditioned* by morality, as even happiness in the complete good must be conditioned by the supreme good of the worthiness to be happy, but is not something the interest in or pursuit of which can itself be considered a duty. Intellectual interest in the beautiful may reflect an interest of practical reason, but if it is analogous to practical reason's natural but only conditionally valid interest in happiness, then it is not the direct ground of any duty.

So how can our attachment to natural beauty, even if akin to an interest of practical reason, become transformed from something merely like a duty to a genuine duty toward oneself? To solve this puzzle, two pieces must be brought together. First, we must consider another line of thought in the *Critique of Judgment*, namely Kant's claim that the beauty of individual natural forms can be considered a *symbol* of the freedom which underlies morality; and we must then see how acknowledgment of symbols of morality can contribute to the development of a moral disposition. Second, we must consider Kant's position, clarified if not in fact introduced only in the *Metaphysics of Morals* at the end of his career, that the cultivation of a moral disposition is not irrelevant to, let alone in conflict with, the performance of duty and thus worthiness to be happy, but is itself a specific duty of virtue toward oneself. Only when we have seen that Kant thinks that attraction to natural beauty does not just *express* a morally good disposition but *contributes* to it and also that he recognizes the cultivation of such a disposition as a discrete duty will we be able to understand his claim that we have duties toward ourselves but regarding the objects of nature.

### III. SYMBOLS AND DUTIES

It is in its theory of beauty as the *symbol* of morality that the *Critique of Judgment* suggests a link between beauty and morality that is alternative to that expounded in the theory of intellectual interest.[14] The two chief claims in this theory are first, that beautiful objects can function as a symbol of morality not because of any directly moral *content* in them (as Kant puts it, they are not schemata of moral ideas) but because of parallels or analogies between the reflective *response* to beauty and moral judgment. Second, since moral ideas, as ideas of pure reason, cannot be presented to the senses at all, the analogical or symbolic presentation of the idea of morality through the experience of beauty is the only form available for the presentation – or "hypotyposis" – of moral ideas to sense. Thus, if it could be shown that the system of virtues requires any presentation of morality to the senses at all, it could then be argued that the response to beauty can give rise to a duty and not just an intellectual interest.

In fact, there are really two layers to Kant's theory of beauty as the symbol of morality. In his doctrine of aesthetic ideas, he argues that *specific* ideas of morality or virtue, such as the "kingdom of the blessed" (*CJ*, §49, 5:314), can only be presented through aesthetic symbols; in the exposition of the theory of beauty as the symbol of morality, however, the argument is rather that aesthetic experience in general is itself the symbol of morality in general. Since it is only in light of the latter connection that Kant suggests that taste for the beautiful may be demanded (although still "from others") as a duty (*CJ*, §59, 5:353), we may restrict our attention to the general connection. The basis of the analogy or symbolism is that in responding to beauty and making a judgment of taste the faculty of judgment "does not find itself subjected to a heteronomy of laws of experience as it does in the empirical estimate of things – in respect of the objects of such a pure delight it gives the law to itself, just as reason does in respect of the faculty of desire" (*CJ*, §59, 5:353). Kant then expands upon this analogy:

> (1) The beautiful pleases *immediately* (but only in reflective intuition, not, like morality, in its concept). (2) It pleases *apart from all interest* (pleasure in the morally good is no doubt necessarily bound up with an interest, but not with one of the kind that are antecedent to the judgment upon the delight, but with one that judgment itself for the first time calls into existence). (3) *The freedom* of the imagination . . . is, in estimating the beautiful, represented as in accord with the understanding's conformity to law (in moral judgments the freedom of the will is thought of the harmony of the latter with itself according to universal laws of reason). (4) The subjective principle of the estimate of the beautiful is represented as *universal*, i.e., valid for every man, but as incognizable by means of any universal concept (the objective principle of morality is set forth as also universal . . . and, besides, as cognizable by means of a universal concept). (*CJ*, §59 5:353–4)

Response to beauty is like the judgment of morality in being immediate, disinterested, free, and universal. It is unlike the latter in being represented to sense rather than through concepts. But since the pure idea of morality is not itself directly representable to sense, this disanalogy does not undermine the analogy between beauty and morality but is rather what requires that the former become the symbol of the latter.

That aesthetic response is the *only* form available for the sensuous representation of morality is not explicitly asserted by Kant. But several remarks in his discussion of "aesthetic ideas" suggest such a premise. There, for instance, he says that "it is easily seen, that an aesthetic idea is the counterpart (pendant) of a *rational idea,* which, conversely, is a concept, to which no *intuition* (representation of the imagination) can be adequate" (*CJ,* §49, 5:314). This may suggest that the aesthetic is indispensable to the sensible representation of morality, and if the latter is itself in some way a matter of duty, the argument for duty regarding natural beauty might be started here.

Such a claim might seem too strong to sustain and difficult to reconcile with Kant's doctrine of the "fact of reason," which seems to assume that the content of our moral obligation is always available to us without any sort of intervention by sensibility.[15] But perhaps there is no need for Kant to establish that beauty, or more accurately our response to it, is a *unique* symbol of morality; if he could establish that the experience of beauty is an instrument toward morality at all, and then introduce a general duty to cultivate *all* means toward the development of a morally good disposition, he would also have an argument generating duty regarding natural beauty.

There can be no doubt that Kant does regard beauty's symbolization of morality as one means toward the development of a morally good disposition:

> Taste makes, as it were, the transition from the charm of sense to habitual moral interest possible without too violent a leap, for it represents the imagination, even in its freedom, as amenable to a final determination for understanding, and teaches us to find, even in sensuous objects, a free delight apart from any charm of sense. (*CJ,* §59, 5:354)

Taste prepares us for disinterested attachments; that is, even if the *content* of objects of taste is independent of morality, the *experience* of taste is a cause of a disposition favorable to the performance of duty. The same causal language is used in an earlier remark as well: "The beautiful prepares us to love something, even nature, apart from any interest: the sublime, to esteem something highly even in opposition to our (sensible) interest" (*CJ*, §29 General Remark, 5:267). Thus, Kant clearly believes that experience of the beautiful can be an instrument or means for the development of a subjective disposition – he here calls it "love" – which is intimately connected to moral duty.

The question now becomes whether the cultivation of such a disposition is itself a moral duty. This question must be pressed, because, as we saw, the *Critique of Practical Reason* and many of Kant's other earlier presentations of his moral theory suggest the contrary. This question is finally addressed only in the *Metaphysics of Morals*. The key to its solution is Kant's recognition that cultivation of a sensible disposition favorable to the performance of duty, which in his earlier writing may have seemed irrelevant to the meritorious performance of duty or even, at least in the eyes of his critics, inimical to it, is in fact part of our general duty toward ourselves to advance the perfection of our whole character in respect to the end of morality. That is, although a sensible disposition favorable to duty is not itself either a necessary condition for the performance of the duty nor, in itself, a sufficient condition for willing our duty, Kant recognizes that our character as a whole includes a sensible side, and that our overall moral duty to perfect ourselves includes the perfection of this – although not, as in Wolffian perfectionist ethics, its perfection per se as part of our essence, but specifically its development in behalf of morality.[16] The cultivation of a respectful attitude regarding nature then becomes part of this duty. Although we have no duties directly toward nonrational being, since it is respect for rational being which is the source of all duties, the fact that the appreciation of natural beauty can contribute to the development of feelings favorable to morality in us, combined with the acknowledgment of a general duty to cultivate all such feelings, generates a duty toward ourselves but regarding nature.[17]

The development of Kant's ethical thought in this direction may first become evident in his eloquent reply, in *Religion within the Limits of Reason Alone*, to Friedrich Schiller's "Anmut und Würde" ("Grace and Dignity").[18] Schiller, Kant says, accused him of "representing obligation as carrying with it a monastic frame of mind." However, Kant denies that he and Schiller have any disagreement about the "most important principles." To be sure, he holds, the graces must keep a "respectful distance" when duty alone is the theme: "The attendants of Venus Urania [spiritual love] become wantons in the train of Venus Dione [corporeal love] as soon as they meddle in the business of determining duty and try to provide springs of action therefor." But he immediately adds that an irremediable conflict between duty and desire is not really possible but would, rather, represent a lingering denial of the law of duty itself:

> Now if one asks, What is the *aesthetic* character, the *temperament*, so to speak, of *virtue*, whether courageous and hence *joyous* or fear-ridden and dejected, an answer is hardly necessary. The latter slavish frame of mind can never occur without a hidden *hatred* of the law. And a heart which is happy in the *performance* of its duty (not merely complacent in the *recognition* thereof) is a mark of genuineness in the virtuous disposition. . . . This resolve, then, encouraged by good progress, must needs beget a joyous frame of mind, without which man is never certain of having really *attained a love* for the good, i.e., of having incorporated it into his maxim. (*Religion*, 6:23–4n.)

In other words, the kind of example which Kant imagines in the *Groundwork* in order to illustrate the true worth of motivation by the thought of duty – that is, the case of outright conflict between the demands of duty and the indifference of a deadened heart – is, in the end, neither permissible nor even possible. Kant will expand upon this theme in the *Metaphysics of Morals*. He will also take up the point suggested in the last sentence of this reply to Schiller: that although he has always argued that our real incentive in an action must ultimately remain inscrutable to ourselves, we nevertheless have a duty at least to strive for moral self-knowledge; and the sensible or, as he says here, aesthetic character of our moral disposition is in fact our best clue for such self-knowledge. Surprising as it may seem, it is in precisely this context that Kant's explicit discussion of our duty regarding nature occurs in the *Metaphysics of Morals*.

Kant introduces his discussion of duties to oneself by considering a contradiction which may, at first glance (as he says), appear to undermine the very idea of such a duty: "If the I *that imposes obligation* is taken in the same sense as the I *that is put under obligation*, a duty to oneself is a self-contradictory concept" (*Virtue*, §1, 6:417). Although one might be tempted to brush this aside as a pseudoproblem, like Kant's earlier opaque paradox about self-affection in the *Critique of Pure Reason*, Kant's solution to the paradox is actually very important. For what he claims is that the solution lies in man's twofold nature as both sensible and intellectual, as both *Sinnenwesen* and *Vernunftwesen*. The idea of a duty toward – and thus a constraint on – oneself makes sense, because as a being who is both sensible – or animal – and also rational, a human being has a reason that can place his sensible being under an obligation (*Virtue*, §3, 6:418). Contrary to what sometimes seems the view at least of the *Groundwork*, that the realm of the feelings must simply be ignored in ethics because it is not amenable to moral control, this suggests that the "pathological" domain of mankind's sensible being can be made to answer to reason and thus is an appropriate object of duty.[19] Thus, duties to oneself can be duties to have – or preserve and develop – certain kinds of feelings. Or, to put the point another way, although Kant may earlier have written as if one's sensible nature is a *given* and suggested that the determination of one's capacity of choice by the moral law must simply proceed *independently* of one's sensible nature – whether that puts feeling and duty into harmony or discord – this is not his final view; on the contrary, Kant recognizes that one's sensible being can, and also must, be made harmonious with one's duty. One cannot *rely* upon nature for the graceful state so

320

prized by Schiller, but out of the incentive of duty one can strive to *make* one's nature gracefully harmonious with duty. And, Kant now argues, one falls short of the demands of virtue if one does not try to do just this.[20]

Kant's next step is to introduce his customary distinction between what he variously calls "formal," "restrictive," or "negative" duties to oneself and "material," "ampliative," or "positive" duties. "Negative duties *forbid* man to act contrary to the *end* of his nature and so have to do merely with his moral *self-preservation;* positive duties, which *command* him to make a certain object of choice his end, concern his *perfecting* of himself." In other words, duties of the former sort require one to do what he can to preserve one's moral character or protect it from dimunition; the latter, to develop or improve it. In a striking metaphor, Kant glosses this point by saying that the former duties "belong to the moral *health* . . . of man, . . . to the *preservation* of his nature in its perfection (as *receptivity*). The second belong to his moral *prosperity* [*Wohlhabenheit*], . . . which consists in possessing a *capacity* sufficient for all his ends, insofar as this can be acquired; they belong to his *cultivation* (as active perfecting) of himself" (*Virtue,* §4, 6:419). Finally, in his organization of the subsequent discussion, Kant suggests that this distinction is congruent with the distinction between perfect and imperfect duties, that is, between those duties for which it is fully determinate what constitutes their fulfillment (usually omissions) and those duties the fulfillment of which (usually commissions) is indeterminate and therefore leaves open to judgment what actions and how much is required for fulfillment. We shall see that this last claim causes some trouble. Although Kant introduces the duty to oneself regarding nonhuman nature as a case of negative or restrictive – and therefore perfect – duty, it displays features of an imperfect duty as well.

Kant's division of duties toward oneself begins clearly enough with an enumeration of perfect duties toward oneself either as "an *animal* (natural) being and a moral being or *only as a moral* being" (*Virtue,* §4, 6:420). The perfect duties toward oneself as both animal and moral proscribe any con-

duct which would destroy or damage one's physical capacity for rational action; thus, suicide, self-abuse, and self-
stupefaction through the immoderate use of food and drink
are contrary to duty because they destroy or damage one's
capacity to act at all times as a rational agent (*Virtue*, §§6–
8).[21] Next, Kant enumerates perfect duties toward oneself
solely as a moral being; these proscribe any instance of certain actions alleged necessarily to demean oneself as a rational being without actually destroying or damaging the
physical basis of rational conduct. Here Kant proscribes any
instance of lying, avarice, or servility. Lying shows disre-
spect to the "natural purposiveness of [one's] capacity to
communicate his thoughts" (*Virtue*, §9, 6:429); avarice is simply irrational, because it restricts *"one's own* enjoyment of
the means to good living so narrowly as to leave one's own
true needs unsatisfied" (*Virtue*, §10, 6:432); and servility is
proscribed because to be servile is to fail to recognize the
dignity of rational being in oneself when comparing oneself
to others (*Virtue*, §11, 6:434–5).

Kant's next step, it would seem, should be to turn to the
imperfect duties toward oneself, which can only be described as broad duties to adopt certain ends or policies in
one's behavior toward oneself rather than duties to avoid (or
perform) any instance of specific forms of action. Using the
same distinction as before, Kant distinguishes two such duties. First, as both animal and moral, one has a duty to
"cultivate his natural powers (powers of spirit, mind, and
body), as means to all sorts of possible ends" (*Virtue*, §19,
6:444). This is a duty because it is clearly a policy enjoined
by respect for rationality, but it is broad or indeterminate
because it is not possible for any agent to cultivate all of his
potential talents; instead, "reflection and evaluation" on
one's circumstances and even desires are required to make
judgments about which talents to develop and to what degree (*Virtue*, §20, 6:445–6). Kant could also have added that
the development of talents may only be pursued as a general policy because there may be occasions on which the
implementation of the policy may have to give way before

the requirements of perfect duties to others or, for that matter, to oneself. Second, Kant adds an imperfect duty toward
oneself as a moral being alone. This is the general duty
always to strive to make the moral law itself one's incentive
in the performance of actions required by duty, or to "Be
holy!" (*Virtue*, §21, 6:446). One might wonder why Kant lists
this as a specific "duty of virtue" (*Tugendpflicht*) as opposed
to the general "obligation of virtue" (*Tugendverpflichtung*)
(*Virtue*, Introduction, §XVIII, 6:410) to perform all duties,
whether of virtue or of right, from "internal legislation"
(*Metaphysics of Morals*, Introduction, §III, 6:220–1); in fact, he
virtually concedes that his classification is misleading when
he says that this duty to oneself is imperfect not because it is
"in quality" anything less than "strict and perfect," but
rather only because the "fragility" of human nature means
that we can only hope for a "constant progression" to holiness and thus at best an imperfect *compliance* with what is in
fact a strict duty always to make the moral law our incentive
(*Virtue*, §22, 6:446–7).

## IV. DUTIES REGARDING NATURE

Falling between the cracks of this classification, however,
are two additional duties: a general duty to "moral self-
knowledge" (*Virtue*, §15, 6:441) and, finally, the specific
duty that we have to avoid the "wanton destruction of what
is *beautiful* in inanimate nature" and the "cruel treatment" of
animal but irrational beings (*Virtue*, §17, 6:443). These duties are included as a second part of the chapter on perfect
duties toward oneself as a moral being, but it is not clear
that they belong there rather than with the discussion of
imperfect duties. The first of these two additional duties, a
general duty to try to know one's real motivations as well as
to "test one's heart," which could mean to try out the
strength of one's commitment to morality, seems as if it
should belong with the general duty to make progress toward a holy will, perhaps as the epistemological presupposi-

tion of the latter, and as if it should be a strict although imperfect duty, for the same reason as that duty.

The case of the duty regarding nature, however, is more problematic. Kant discusses it in an "episodic section," a title which can hardly but reflect his uncertainty about the real status of this duty. The argument for the various forms of this duty do reflect the underlying rationale of perfect duties, yet converge upon his treatment of imperfect duties as well. Thus, as we saw at the outset of this chapter, what Kant finally argues is that a destructive spirit toward inanimate beautiful objects "weakens or uproots that feeling in man which, though not of itself moral, is still a disposition of sensibility that greatly promotes morality or at least prepares the way for it: the disposition, namely, to love something . . . even apart from any intention to use it" (*Virtue*, §17, 6:443). This reflects the proscriptive nature of the perfect duties toward oneself: Kant here proscribes an attitude of indifference toward natural beauties which "weakens or destroys" a feeling or disposition favorable to morality, rather than prescribing a general policy of aesthetic contemplation which might develop rather than just maintain this disposition. This is analogous to the requirement to preserve and respect one's rationality rather than cultivating oneself in behalf of rationality. At the same time, however, the nature of the disposition itself – that is, one which is not unconditionally necessary for the performance of other duties to oneself or others but rather one which "promotes" or "prepares for" a state of sensibility favorable to morals – suggests the idea of an open-ended improvement of moral character associated with the imperfect duty to moral self-knowledge and holiness rather than the determinacy characteristic of the perfect duties to oneself. On the one hand, then, Kant suggests a duty of conservation of an already-given element of our moral disposition, but on the other hand a duty to develop what must be one means to the improvement of this disposition among others. The latter form of duty can be only imperfect, both because of its open-endedness and because the cultivation of what is one causally significant but not obviously unique or indispensable means to the development of a disposition approximating a holy will may on occasion have to give way to the cultivation of other means to the same end or other, perfect duties.

The same complexity is even more evident in Kant's treatment of our duty regarding the third component of the natural rather than human realm, the animal as contrasted to the mineral and vegetable. Here Kant argues that savage and cruel treatment of irrational animals dulls one's compassion for their suffering, and thereby "a natural predisposition that is very serviceable to morality in one's relations with other men" is weakened and gradually obliterated. Compliance with this duty is compatible with mankind's "authorization" to slaughter animals painlessly or put them to work, but is incompatible with, for example, the experimental infliction of pain upon animals for purely speculative purposes which can be accomplished by other means (*Virtue*, §17, 6:443). Here Kant suggests, on the one hand, that humans have a "natural predisposition" which is useful for morality and which must be conserved, and that inhumane (as we say) treatment of animals tends to destroy this disposition and must therefore be avoided; this parallels the structure of his arguments for perfect duties toward oneself. On the other hand, Kant also makes it clear that the feeling of compassion toward animals and even other humans is neither a form of action nor an incentive which is required by morality itself, but rather a causal condition which is conducive or serviceable to morality; thus, it seems as if compassion, like attachment to natural beauty, is one means among many to the preservation and improvement of moral character, and that for that reason our duty either to conserve or improve it must be both open-ended and weighed against our other duties, and for that reason like an imperfect duty. The last point is also suggested by Kant's position that animals themselves have no rights and that our duty of compassion to them must coexist with our freedom to use them for our legitimate purposes. Although Kant does not explicitly argue this, our duty to avoid suicide or, for that matter, avarice, can clearly require the slaughter or other use of animals, under readily imagined circumstances. Even under those circumstances, obviously, compassion can usually be maintained and unnecessarily incompassionate behavior avoided; but clearly our duty to avoid destruction or injury to animals cannot be given the form of an absolute prohibition. Again, the conclusion seems unavoidable that our duty of compassion to irrational animals is most reasonably construed as an imperfect duty.

At this point, we can finally say something more about the content of the duties regarding nature which Kant has generated from the underlying principle of duty toward oneself. As far as our duty concerning mineral and vegetable nature is concerned, it is clear that our duty must be to conserve beautiful instances thereof in their natural state, so far as possible. This is implied by Kant's characterization of the way in which attachment to such beauty prepares us for moral conduct properly speaking: It does so by teaching us to find "pleasure in loving something without any intention of using it." Discovering the value of the beautiful object independent of any use of it is the key to its moral value. But the same point also emerges from Kant's underlying account of the experience of beauty itself. Kant characterizes a beautiful object as one by means of which "imagination (as the faculty of intuitions *a priori*) is undesignedly [*unabsichtlich*] brought into accord with understanding (as the faculty of concepts) by means of a given representation, and a feeling of pleasure is thereby aroused" (*CJ*, §VII, 5:190). His idea is that the unity of the manifold of intuition presented by a beautiful object, which must be detectable if our underlying purpose of cognition is to be served, must be detected independently of the subsumption of the manifold under any concept if it is to be unexpected and therefore pleasurable (*CJ*, §VI, 5:187). A *fortiori*, the form of a beautiful object must strike us as beautiful independently of any concept of its use – thus our pleasure in it must be disinterested; and this remains true even where we clearly *have* a concept of its use, such as in the case of a race horse or sanctuary – even in such cases, although our concept of the use of an object may *constrain* our sense of acceptable forms for it, it cannot fully or uniquely determine it.[22] And this applies not only to uses we might make of natural objects; it also applies to their own uses of their parts or capacities. For instance, even our judgment of the beauty of a flower must be independent of recognition of its use (to the plant) as a reproductive organ. As Kant puts it, "No perfection of any kind – no internal finality, as something to which the arrangement of the manifold is related – underlies this judgment"; natural beauties "are self-subsisting beauties which are not appurtenant to any object defined with respect to its end, but please freely and on their own account" (*CJ*, §16, 5:229 – 31). Now, this requirement gives Kant some difficulty when it comes to the case of *artistic beauty*, for "art has always got a definite intention of producing something," but Kant attempts to overcome this precisely by insisting that "fine art must be clothed *with the aspect of nature*, although we recognize it to be art" (*CJ*, §45, 5:306–7).[23] Thus, the point remains that for an object to please us as beautiful, it must please us not only independently of any inference from its usefulness but independently of any conception of it as having *been intended* to please us at all – thus, in its natural state.[24] Finally, we should note, the same point emerges from Kant's description of the analogy between the judgment on beauty and moral judgment, from which the value of aesthetic experience for the development of moral disposition arises. It is the "*freedom* of the imagination . . . in estimating the beautiful" that symbolizes the freedom of the will as the will in harmony "with itself according to universal laws of reason" (*CJ*, §59, 5:354).

That our duty to conserve our own predisposition to morality gives rise to a duty to conserve natural beauty, however, also makes it clear that in the end this duty must be conceived as an imperfect rather than perfect one. Just as Kant plainly believes that our duty to be compassionate to animals must be compatible with our freedom to use such animals and slaughter them for consumption, although not for experimentation that can be accomplished by other means, so he must also believe that our duty to conserve natural beauty must be balanced against our morally permitted or even required use of natural materials for our own preservation and for the advancement of the happiness of others. As with all imperfect duties, what we have is a *claim* which must always be respected, but not a specific form of action (for instance slaughter) which must always be avoided. Judgment must be used to decide when our material needs must outweigh the aesthetic and morally symbolic as well as instrumental value of natural beauty – and as Kant often emphasizes, although judgment must always be founded on principles it can never be furnished with precise rules, on pain of infinite regress (see *CJ*, Preface, 5:169). As with the cultivation of one's talents, the cultivation of one's moral disposition necessarily "allows a latitude for free choice" (*Virtue*, §20, 6:446).

That we have a duty to conserve natural beauty, although we are unable to say that in every case this duty must triumph, seems to me exactly right and to explain why we can never find a mechanical procedure for deciding between claims of the conservation and the development and exploitation of natural resources. But we must be careful to avoid one potentially misleading implication of the analogy with the imperfect duty to cultivate one's talents. In the latter case, Kant can argue that the choice of which of one's talents to develop can be fairly arbitrarily left to one's "own rational reflection about what sort of life he would like to lead and whether he has the powers necessary for it" (*Virtue*, §20, 6:445); because it is obviously, or at least normally, impossible for one individual to develop all of his potential talents, there may be no moral reason arguing for the development of any particular talents, and the individual is therefore free to rely on personal preference. But this is not in fact the kind of latitude that is normal for imperfect duties. The latitude that we must be allowed in fulfilling imperfect duties is not simply the latitude of personal preference or even whim, but the latitude requisite to balance the fulfillment of imperfect duties with the performance of other duties and with the uncertainties of moral judgment (see especially *Virtue*, Introduction, §VIII, 6:392). The claim of an imperfect duty is not one which can simply be dismissed with a promise to honor it on some other occasion; it is one which must always be honored, but which does not always dictate a specific action, both because of other claims of duty and because of indeterminacy and uncertainty in judgments as to how best to fulfill it.

Perhaps one rule of thumb might be added, however. In the *Metaphysics of Morals* Kant describes duties to oneself as duties to perfect oneself, and duties to others not as duties to perfect other people, since they can only do that for themselves, but rather as duties to advance their happiness (*Virtue*, Introduction, §VIII, 6:392–4). He does not give one of these forms of duty priority over the other. In his earlier *Lectures on Ethics*, however, Kant did suggest that our duties to ourselves have priority over our duties to others – that our first duty must be to maintain our own moral worth and that only if this is satisfied can we successfully perform our duties to others.

> Our duties to ourselves constitute the supreme condition and the principle of all morality. . . . Only if our worth as human beings is intact can we perform our other duties; for it is the foundation stone of all of our other duties. A man who has destroyed and cast away his personality has no intrinsic worth, and can no longer perform any manner of duty.[25]

The basis for Kant's assertion is not entirely clear, and perhaps all that he could persuasively argue is that fulfillment of our duties to ourselves is a necessary condition for acting out of the incentive of duty, but not that it is a necessary condition for all action in outward compliance with duty. But if the argument could be made out, then it might provide some support for a further inference that in a choice between action in behalf of one's moral perfection – for instance, conservation of natural beauty – and action in behalf of the happiness of others – the success of which is always so uncertain anyway, because of the difficulty both of knowing what would really please another and of knowing what the effect of any action is ever going to be anyway – then the duty

toward oneself, that is, action in behalf of the maintenance
and development of one's own moral character, must be
given a certain priority. Such an argument would give at least
some sense of the position of our duty regarding natural
beauty in the hierarchy of our duties.

## V. HUMANITY AS THE END OF NATURE

I think I have now gone as far as is reasonable in the effort
to elucidate a detailed doctrine of duty regarding nature
from Kant's powerful but brief statements on the subject.
Before concluding, however, one potential objection to the
very idea of Kantian duties regarding nature must be considered. Kant has argued that the beauty of individual forms in
the mineral or vegetable realms and the capacity for suffering of beasts in the realm of irrational animals give rise to
duties regarding them which are based in our duty toward
ourselves to cultivate our own moral dispositions. These
duties require that, at least *ceteris paribus,* we conserve these
beautiful objects in their natural form, for it is precisely in
light of the naturalness – that is, unintendedness – of their
beauty that they serve as symbols of morality and in turn as
means to the development of the disposition to morality. By
positioning these duties on the border between perfect and
imperfect duties to ourselves, Kant has also at least suggested some conclusions about the relations of these duties
to other forms of obligation. But now we must be struck by
another argument in which Kant apparently concludes that
nature as a whole exists solely to serve the purposes of
mankind, which might seem to undercut the very idea that
humans can have any obligation to the conservation of nature or humane use only of its other inhabitants. Does Kant
undermine the whole argument we have just considered?

The argument at issue is found in the "Critique of Teleological Judgment" in the *Critique of Judgment,* where Kant argues
that the system of nature as a whole can be seen as purposive
only if "teleologically subordinated" to mankind. Does this

mean that humans can put nature to use for whatever purposes they may have? Although much about Kant's purposes in the "Critique of Teleological Judgment" is opaque, it is clear that this is not at all the point he wants to make. For what Kant argues is that nature can be seen as "teleologically subordinated" to mankind only in the latter's purely *moral* capacity, and this seems naturally to suggest that mankind's uses of nature (as of anything else) must be subordinated to the conditions of mankind's *moral* use of nature – which certainly includes those duties to the self, but regarding nature, which have already been established. If anything, then, the argument of the "Critique of Teleological Judgment" provides a general foundation for the argument of the *Metaphysics of Morals* rather than undermining it.

The "Critique of Teleological Judgment" does not include a clear statement of its own purpose, but because it culminates in another statement of Kant's practical theology, it seems reasonable to conclude that Kant's deepest intention in this complex work was to give an account of the moral significance of our reflective judgments about nature.[26] As at least an intermediate step in this larger design, Kant argues that the system of nature can itself be seen as final or purposive only in relation to the moral end of mankind. Kant begins his discussion by distinguishing between the "intrinsic finality" of "physical ends" on the one hand and the "extrinsic finality" of "final ends" on the other. Intrinsic finality characterizes the relation of the parts or an organism to itself which constitutes it a physical end, that is, a thing which is *"both cause and effect of itself"* (*CJ*, §64, 5:371). Kant illustrates this opaque conception at the level of the species rather than the individual organism: A species of tree, for instance, both produces itself and is produced by itself (individual trees are produced by progenitors in the same species and produce further instances thereof). There is no suggestion of any moral relevance to the concept of a physical end, however, so we are spared from considering it further. We must instead consider what Kant means by *extrinsic* finality and the concept of a final end. Extrinsic, or relative, finality, is ascribed to "a means which other causes use in the pursuit of ends," and Kant illustrates the notion by the two cases of "utility, where it concerns human beings, and adaptability where it concerns any other creatures" (*CJ*, §63, 5:367). Such a notion is clearly a conditioned notion of reflective judgment – the end relative to which one means is extrinsically final can itself be a means that is extrinsically final to a further end. A final end, however, seems to be an "unconditional condition," or an end for which other things are means but which is not itself a means to any further end (*CJ*, §67, 5:378). Kant, then, seems to treat it as an inevitable task of reason – analogous to its pursuit of the unconditioned in such other forms as the cosmological ideas or the idea of the highest good – to seek for such a final end, or some conception which "necessarily leads us to the idea of aggregate nature as a system following the rule of ends, to which idea, again, the whole mechanism of nature has to be subordinated on principles of reason" (*CJ*, §67, 5:379).

Kant claims that such a conception self-evidently belongs to reflective rather than constitutive judgment – that is, is a regulative rather than constitutive idea – but he nevertheless seems to see the task of finding some conception in light of which nature as a whole can be seen as a final end as inevitable. So he eventually argues that there is only one candidate for an unconditional end in light of which nature can be seen as a final end: mankind's own unconditional end of freedom, the intrinsic value of which underlies the unconditional claim of morality. The only end which nature can serve as a whole is mankind, but mankind only insofar as it in turn serves an unconditionally valuable end, its own freedom, rather than any of the conditionally valuable ends which collectively constitute human happiness. Thus Kant argues,

> Now we have in the world beings of but one kind whose causality is teleological, or directed to ends, and which at the same time are beings of such a character that the law according to which they have to determine ends for themselves is represented by them as unconditioned and not dependent on

anything in nature, but as necessary in itself. The being of this kind is man, but man regarded as noumenon. He is the only natural creature whose peculiar objective characterization is nevertheless such as to enable us to recognize in him a supersensible faculty – his *freedom*. . . .

Now it is not open to us in the case of man, considered as a moral agent, . . . to ask the further question: For what end (*quem in finem*) does he exist? His existence inherently involves the highest end – the end to which, as far as in him lies, he may subject the whole of nature, or contrary to which at least he must not deem himself subjected to any influence on its part. – Now assuming that things in the world are beings that are dependent in point of their real existence, and, as such, stand in need of a supreme cause acting according to ends, then man is the final end of creation. For without man the chain of mutually subordinated ends would have no ultimate point of attachment. Only in man, and only in him as the individual being to whom the moral law applies, do we find unconditional legislation in respect of ends. This legislation, therefore, is what alone qualifies him to be a final end to which all of nature is teleologically subordinated. (*CJ*, §84, 5:435–6)

Whatever the exact nature of reason's underlying impulse to see nature as a whole as final, it is clear that it is only in service of mankind's moral end – freedom or autonomy – and not in service of mankind's ends in general that nature can be seen as ultimately final; for only the end of morality is unconditional or ultimate for humans themselves. Thus, it seems natural to conclude, just as the unconditional end of morality is an ineliminable constraint on humans' own pursuit of any of their other ends, so the moral finality of nature as a whole is an ineliminable constraint on other uses of nature which humans may propose. Kant makes this clear by his explicit exclusion of happiness (as always, his generic term for the satisfaction of whatever desires individuals may happen to have) as a source of the finality of nature:

But where in man are we to place this *ultimate end* of nature? To discover this we must seek out what nature can supply for the purpose of preparing him for what he himself must do in order to be a final end, and we must segregate it from all ends whose possibility rests upon conditions that man can only await at the hand of nature. Earthly happiness is an end of the latter kind. . . . Hence it is only culture that can be the ultimate end which we have cause to attribute to nature in respect of the human race. His individual happiness on earth, and, we may say, the mere fact that he is the chief instrument for instituting order and harmony in irrational external nature, are ruled out. (*CJ*, §83, 5:432)

Obviously nature is not to be made subordinate to any of our purposes whatever, although on Kant's theory of the primacy of practical reason it can only be subservient to the unconditional end of human morality.

*Chapter 10*

# Duty and inclination

In most of the preceding chapters I have approached the links between Kant's ethics and aesthetics from the side of the latter. I have argued that much of the novelty of Kant's approach arises from his exploitation of aesthetic phenomena for purposes of what I initially called "moral epistemology" rather than "moral psychology." That is, I have emphasized Kant's thought that the aesthetic experience of the freedom of the imagination in the response to beauty and of the power of reason in the feeling of the sublime can make our practical freedom palpable to us, thus supplementing the entirely nonexperiential inference of our freedom from our obligation under the moral law to which Kant had come to restrict us by the theory of the *Critique of Practical Reason*. But this is not to deny that Kant has left room for the more traditional use of aesthetics in moral psychology, that is, for the claim that "the beautiful prepares us to love something, even nature, apart from any interest" (*CJ*, §29 General Remark, 5:267). Yet this raises a fundamental issue: How can any possible effect of aesthetic experience on what we might ordinarily be tempted to call our "moral sentiments" be of the least interest to the Kant whose conception of duty and moral worth is usually supposed to have excluded any role for sentiment whatever? Indeed, is not Kant usually thought to have defined moral worth as consisting precisely in the performance of what duty requires only in the *absence* of any inclination to so act, or even in *opposition* to every natural inclination of the agent? To answer this question, a more systematic review of Kant's thought about the relation between reason and duty on the one hand and sentiment and inclination on the other than has thus far been provided will be necessary.

Virtually since its initial publication, Kant's *Groundwork of the Metaphysics of Morals* has been read to maintain that moral worth attaches only to actions performed out of the motive of duty in the absence of any inclinations to so act or even in the face of contrary inclinations, and that no moral worth attaches to the presence of any inclinations which would naturally incline the agent to perform the actions that are required by duty. This apparent moral rigorism has been scorned by many. Schiller's famous distich is an example of the ridicule heaped upon Kant's position:

> Gladly I serve my friends, but alas I do it with pleasure.
> Hence I am plagued with doubt that I am not a virtuous person.
>
> Surely, your only resource is to try to despise them entirely,
> And then with aversion do what your duty enjoins you.[1]

The idea that virtue lies not in benevolent sentiments or even in harmony between such sentiments and the requirements of principles of duty, but rather only in fulfilling the requirements of duty when one has no inclination to do so or even an aversion to doing so, it seems, must itself be a bad joke. Nevertheless, it has continued to be the target of attacks upon Kant up to the present day. Thus, Bernard Williams, among others, has criticized the notion that a true conception of virtue can even *permit* the thought of duty as a motive to intrude upon the operation of the sentiments in actions regarding those persons and projects to whom and to which one is most closely attached.[2]

There have been many able rebuttals of this line of criticism of Kant,[3] and my project here is not simply to add to their number. Rather, what I wish to do is to expose something of the complexity and also the evolution of Kant's own position on the relation between duty and moral sentiments:

first, to understand his argument not just that inclination cannot ground either the *principle* or the *motivation* of duty, but specifically that it cannot be used as the basis of attributions of *moral worth*; and second to show how Kant nevertheless comes to argue that it is both *metaphysically possible* and *morally requisite* for us to pay considerable attention to our inclinations *out of the motive of duty itself*, and, if not to create both general moral sentiments and particular attachments out of whole cloth, then to foster and cultivate our natural disposition to have them. In fact, I will argue, Kant's metaphysical account of freedom does not allow any *a priori* restriction of the effects of our adherence to principles of pure practical reason on our affective state. (In this regard Kant's position is actually much more radical than the position Schiller himself adopts in his great essay "Anmut und Würde," "On Grace and Dignity," which is not, I will suggest, a criticism of Kant, like Schiller's mean-spirited little joke, but rather his attempt to assimilate and defend the deepest truth of Kant's ethics.) Kant's doctrine of the necessary ends of virtue, I will argue, gives clear grounds for the *cultivation* of moral sentiments out of the motive of duty itself.

## I. INCLINATION AND MORAL WORTH

### *Kant's conception of moral worth*

The discussion must begin with Section I of Kant's *Groundwork of the Metaphysics of Morals* of 1785. Here Kant argues that moral worth attaches only to the performance of what duty requires *from* or *out of* (his word is *aus*), the motive of "respect" for the moral law itself, and not from any sentiments that might naturally incline one to do what the moral law requires; such inclinations are "in accord with duty" and "lovable" (*pflichtmäßig* and *liebenswürdig*) but "have no moral worth" (*sittlichen Wert*); "they deserve praise and encouragement but not esteem" (*Hochschätzung*) (*Groundwork*, 4:398). Kant then illustrates his claim with some now-notorious examples. Ordinarily we have a strong inclination to preserve our own lives, yet although it is always a duty to preserve our own lives, there is no "moral value" (*Gehalt*) in complying with this duty out of this usual inclination. It is only when one preserves one's own life in spite of experiencing such misery that one can *wish* only for death that one's maxim and action has moral value. Or Kant imagines someone who was formerly a "friend of mankind" moved by "sympathy with the fate of others," in whom that sympathy has now been extinguished by some misery of his own, yet who continues to perform actions benefiting others without any inclination to do so but solely out of duty, that is, moved solely by the thought that to do so is his duty. Kant says that it is only such an action by such an agent that "first possesses genuine moral worth" (*Wert*) (*Groundwork*, 4:398). What does Kant mean by this claim, and why does he make it?[4]

To understand the purport of these examples, we must pay close attention to their position in the text. By the time he delivers them, Kant has already (indeed in the preface to the work) asserted that nothing empirical (such as inclinations) can be the basis of the moral law and of our motivation to conform to it, but only an *a priori* principle of pure practical reason itself. In fact, as the text of the *Groundwork* suggests, and other works may make even clearer, Kant has two points in mind in making this claim: (1) first, no inclination can be a reliable *rule* for what duty requires, because any inclination may sometimes tell us to do what is lawful and at other times to do what is not lawful; (2) second, no inclination can be a reliable *motive* for us to do what is right, even if we know what is right, for inclinations will sometimes be there but sometimes will not (as Kant's subsequent examples make clear). Kant makes the first point by stating that the accord with the requirements of moral law on the part of any sentiment is "very contingent and spurious, for an immoral ground may sometimes bring forth actions in accord with the law but will often bring forth actions opposed to the law" (*Groundwork*, 4:390). Kant suggests the second point by stating that "the will of man . . . since it is affected by so many inclinations, is to be sure capable of the idea of a pure practical reason, but not so easily empowered to make it effective *in concreto* in its course of life" (*Groundwork*, 4:389). That is to say, no inclination can provide an effective *rule* for morality, because any inclination can sometimes incline one to do what is right but sometimes what is wrong. In an example given by Barbara Herman, an indiscriminate inclination to help anyone struggling to lift a heavy object might lead one to help someone in the midst of committing a theft just as readily as someone with a lawful claim to one's help.[5] And no mere inclination can provide an effective *motive* to morality, because it may be present on some occasion but absent on others, or prevail in the crowd of our inclinations on some occasion but be dominated on others.

Kant spells out these two shortcomings more explicitly in other texts. The conceptual distinction between a moral principle as a *criterion* of what duty requires and a moral principle as a *motive* for conformity to what is required by such a criterion was clearly made in his *Lectures on Ethics*, in the form in which these were delivered by 1780. Under the rubric of the "Supreme Principle of Morality," he says that

> in this connexion we must first notice that there are two points to consider: the principle of the discrimination of our obligation and the principle of its performance or execution. We must distinguish between measuring-rod and mainspring. The measuring-rod is the principle of discrimination; the mainspring is the principle of the performance of our obligation. Confusion between these has led to complete falsity in the sphere of ethics.[6]

In these lectures Kant was perhaps not yet clear that one thought, the idea of the universality of practical law itself, could serve as both the content of the moral law and motivation for adhering to it, that is, as both the *principium diiudicationis* and *principium executionis*, as he often called them;[7] but even when he did become clear about this, he retained the view that there are two different *roles* being fulfilled by the thought of duty. This is indeed one of the characteristic theses of his practical philosophy.

But even before he gave these lectures, Kant was quite clear that any mere sentiments or inclinations, no matter how good-hearted and admirable, would be inadequate to fulfill either of the functions which must be satisfied by a moral principle. The following brief note, apparently written in the second half of the 1770s, suggests by its very construction that Kant believes there to be two different problems about founding any moral decisions on the presence of sentiments:

> One must not only not cite the moral feeling as a *principium*, but one must also not leave any moral grounds as it were to the decision of feeling, e.g., suicide, also not leave the ground of decision to grounds [of] feeling, e.g., sympathy, aversion. For feeling has no rule, it is therefore changeable and fickle. (*R* 6902, 19:201)

Other texts spell out the two different problems separately.

Thus, some texts emphasize the first problem, that one cannot appeal to sentiments for a univocal rule of duty. So Kant writes in the much later *Metaphysics of Morals:*

> For since men's sensible inclinations tempt them to ends (the matter of choice) that can be contrary to duty, lawgiving reason can in turn check their influence only by a moral end set up against the ends of inclinations, an end that must therefore be given *a priori*, independently of inclinations.[8] (*Virtue,* Introduction §I, 6:380–1)

Here Kant supposes that inclination will inevitably set us a variety of ends, some of which may be in accord with the requirement of duty but others not, and that our pursuit of these ends must not only be constrained by a univocal law of duty but that this will in addition require the postulation of some necessary end. (This is a problematic inference, but it need not detain us here.)

Other passages emphasize the unreliability of sentiment or

inclination as a source of motivation to do what is right, even if what is right can in fact be univocally determined. Most important perhaps is this passage from the *Groundwork* itself:

> Whatever is derived from the particular natural disposition of mankind, from particular feelings and tendencies, indeed even where possible from a particular direction which would be unique to human reason and not necessarily valid for the will of every rational being, that can to be sure yield a maxim for us, but not a law, a subjective principle in accordance with which we might have a tendency and inclination to act but not an objective principle according to which we are *directed* to act even if all our tendency, inclination, and natural propensity were opposed to it. (*Groundwork*, 4:425)

Here the point is precisely that an adequate motivation for morality must be one which can ensure our obedience to the principle of duty, whether or not our sentiments or natural condition inclines us to such conformity. Sometimes we will be so inclined, but sometimes we will not, and therefore such inclination cannot serve as an adequate motive for conformity to the moral law.

Kant puts a similar point in much simpler language in the *Metaphysics of Morals*:

> But virtue is not to be defined and valued merely as an *aptitude* and . . . a long-standing *habit* of morally good actions acquired by practice. For unless this aptitude results from considered, firm, and continually purified principles, then, like any other mechanism of technically practical reason, it is neither armed for all situations nor adequately secured against the changes that new temptations could bring about. (*Virtue*, Introduction §II, 6:383–4)

One point here (if not the whole of Kant's argument) is precisely the same point he had made in a note written years before the publications of the *Groundwork*: No mere sentiment, no matter how favorable to duty, can be relied upon as the motivation to perform duty, for the simple reason that all of our sentiments and inclinations are liable to change in the course of nature (*R* 6902, 19:201).

But inclinations are not merely naturally unreliable sources of motivation to conform to the universal and unchanging requirements of moral law. In fact, Kant also suggests some ways in which inclinations could only be something like self-defeating or self-destroying motivations for morality. One point that Kant makes is that natural inclinations are never entirely satisfied, and thus create ever-changing sets of needs that cannot reasonably be expected to conform to a univocal moral law:

> No complete satisfaction for the senses can ever be discovered, it cannot even be determined with certainty and universality what would be in accord with their needs; their demands are always mounting, and they are unsatisfied without being able to say what then would be enough for them. Even less is the possession of this enjoyment secured on account of the change-ability of happiness and the contingency of favorable circumstances and the shortness of life.[9] (*R* 7202, 19:277)

Inclinations arising from our sensory nature, Kant suggests, are never satisfied; thus if at one time their object is in fact an action in conformity with duty, they may not remain satisfied with that but go on to create a desire for some other state which may not be in accord with duty.

Perhaps more persuasively, Kant suggests that any motivation to perform dutiful actions which is based in inclination is liable to frustration, and ultimately self-destruction, if the outcome of action falls short of expectation. Thus he writes in the *Lectures on Ethics:*

> But let us consider the man who is benevolent from love, who loves his neighbor from inclination. Such a man stands in need of people to whom he can show his kindness, and is not content until he finds human beings towards whom he can be charitable. A kindly heart gets more pleasure and satisfaction from doing good to others than from its own enjoyment of the

good things of life; the inclination to do good is a necessity to it, which must be satisfied. It is not this kindliness of heart and temper which the moralist should seek to cultivate, but good-will from principles. For the former is grounded in inclination and a natural necessity, giving rise to unregulated conduct. Such a man will be charitable, by inclination, to all and sundry; and then, if someone takes advantage of his kind heart, in sheer disgust he will decide from then onwards to give up doing good to others. He has no principle by which to calculate his behavior.[10]

Kant's remark that someone who is simply good-hearted by inclination will be benevolent to "all and sundry" suggests that such a person's benevolence will not be regulated by an appropriate moral rule, and that he may offer help where that is contrary to duty as well as where it is required by it. This repeats the general point that sentiment cannot supply a coherent and consistent rule for duty. But his further remark that such a man may become disgusted at the exploitation of his benevolence and thus lose his benevolent inclinations altogether is an example of the separate point that inclination cannot provide a reliable motivation for the performance of duty, even where it is clear what it is that duty requires to be done. The point is that a merely natural condition such as a benevolent inclination is liable to change in the face of such phenomena as frustration or anger. There is no reason why this should be the case, however, where the motivation to perform benevolent actions is not the satisfaction of a mere inclination but respect for the requirements of duty to begin with; here one knows that what one has done is right, and that one must continue to perform such actions, regardless of how others respond to them and what effect that response has on one's own further inclinations and emotions.[11]

Thus, Kant clearly believes both that (1) no agent's set of sentiments and inclinations at any one time can offer an adequate criterion for a universally valid moral law and also that (2) any agent's sentiments and inclinations offer an insufficiently reliable motivation to conform to a universally valid moral law, even if the content of that law is derived from elsewhere. No inclinations, whether in the form of a generally benevolent moral sentiment directed toward humanity at large or favorable inclinations toward particular persons or objects, can yield an unequivocal and generally valid determination of duty or be counted upon to motivate any agent to invariable compliance with such a law of duty; and thus a universally valid law that is not derived from the contents of our inclinations alone and can motivate us independently of them is a clearly *necessary* condition of any proper understanding of duty. But now the question arises, why shouldn't the requirement of such an *a priori* law of duty independent of inclination be *added* to the requirement of the presence of certain forms of inclination, perhaps both general sentiment and particular attachments, to constitute our complete ideal of the virtuous or morally admirable character? Why shouldn't we require that a virtuous agent acknowledge an *a priori* principle of pure practical reason but also have certain sentiments? In other words, why should one assume, as Kant clearly seems to do, that motivation by the universal principle of pure practical reason is a single *sufficient* condition of moral worth, and not merely one of several *necessary* conditions constituting a compound conception of genuine virtue?

This is a crucial question, for by themselves all of Kant's worries about the universal validity of a principle of duty based on sentiment and the reliability of motivation based in sentiment do not themselves provide reason for excluding the presence of moral sentiment from our conception of virtue; they could require merely the addition of an *a priori* principle to this conception. There must be an assumption at work in Kant's argument which has not yet been identified. And there certainly is. The underlying assumption of Kant's argument is nothing less than the assumption that moral worth can be ascribed only to products of agents' *activity*, and that what *principles agents adopt*, not what *inclinations agents have*, are an expression of their activity. Inclinations are products of nature, but our formulation of and adherence to principles can be products of freedom, and that is the proper locus for purely moral evaluation.

Kant does not make this fundamental point explicit very often in the *Groundwork,* but he clearly relies upon it at one of the most crucial steps in the argument of the first section of the work, his justification of the third and culminating proposition of this section that *"Duty is the necessity of an action out of respect for the law."* Kant's argument for this claim is precisely that respect for the law, although not any inclination, can be interpreted as an expression of the activity of the will of the agent rather than a mere effect of nature:

> I can certainly have an *inclination* for an object as the effect of my proposed action, but *never respect,* just because it is merely an effect and not the activity of a will. In just the same way I cannot have respect for inclination in general, whether it be mine or someone else's, I can at most in the first case approve of it, in the second sometimes even love it, i.e., see it as favorable to my own advantage. Only that which is connected to my will solely as ground but never as effect, what does not serve my inclination but overwhelms it, or at least excludes it from the calculation in making a choice, can be an object of respect and thus a command. Now an action from duty entirely abstracts from the influence of inclination and with this of every object of the will, and there remains nothing for the will which can determine it but objectively the *law* and subjectively *pure respect* for this practical law. (*Groundwork,* 4:400)

Here Kant excludes inclination from any role in determining the action of a dutiful agent, for the sole and simple reason that no inclination is an expression of the activity of the will of the agent. From this he draws the conclusion that the only thing worthy of "respect," or purely moral commendation, is an agent whose *principium diiudicationis* is nothing less than law itself and whose *principium executionis* is nothing other than pure respect for that law.

Kant's assumption that moral worth can attach only to what is an expression solely of the activity of the agent functions in the *Groundwork* as a first principle that cannot itself be argued for because it cannot be derived from anything more fundamental. Nevertheless one can identify several streams in Kant's thought over the years that flowed together into this unshakeable conviction. One of them is what might be considered the Stoic idea that the only true source of *happiness* is a source that is entirely within our own control and thus entirely a product of our own activity, which can be nothing other than the subjection of all of our desires to a law of reason rather than the satisfaction of any desires in particular. This line of thought comes to striking expression in one note from the mid-1770s:

> The *principium* of morals is autocracy of freedom in respect to all happiness or the epigenesis of happiness according to universal laws of happiness. Happiness has no self-sufficient [*selbständigen*] worth so far as it is a gift of nature or luck. The origination of it from freedom is what constitutes its self-sufficiency and harmony. Good behavior therefore, i.e., the use of freedom according to laws according to which happiness is the self-creation of the good or regular capacity for choice [*Willkühr*], has an absolute endurance [*Bestand*], and the worthiness to be happy is the agreement with the highest good through nothing other than the fulfillment of the faculty of free choice, so far as it agrees according to universal laws with happiness in the whole. The moral feeling here goes to the unity of the ground and the self-possession of the sources of happiness in rational creatures, to which all judgments of worth must be related. The good use of freedom is worth more than contingent happiness. It has a necessary inner worth. Thus the virtuous one possesses happiness in himself no matter how bad the circumstances may be. (R 6867, 19:186)

Here Kant's key image is autocracy, or absolute self-rule, and the argument is that the only source of happiness which is not susceptible to contingencies beyond our control is that which we can generate out of the use of our free will in accordance with reason itself. This argument, however, runs the risk of treating the governance of our will by reason as the proper object of judgments of moral worth because it is more *reliable* than any external source of happiness, not because it is the only form of action which can properly be attributed to ourselves rather than to nature or any agency external to us.

As Kant's thought evolved toward the *Groundwork*, however, the idea of the intrinsic value of autocracy began to supersede the idea of autocracy as valuable because it is the most secure source of happiness. Perhaps reflection on the conditions of moral merit took over, and, in particular, reflection on the difference between the purely juridical requirement of *mere compliance* with the moral law and the ethical ideal of *meritorious compliance* with the law. In the *Lectures on Ethics*, which represent the development of Kant's practical philosophy from the late 1770s to 1780 or 1781, thus between the period of the reflection just cited and the *Groundwork*, the idea of motivation by the thought of duty itself is originally introduced in a theological context, where Kant stresses that what God values in our behavior is not merely our compliance with (his) laws (*rectitudo juridica*) but our *willing* compliance.[12] This thought, of course, goes back to the Pietist, anti-Calvinist idea that divine grace must be earned and is not simply given, and thus was probably deeply rooted in Kant's psyche. As the lectures continue, however, the image of self-rule is separated from any theological context and linked instead to the idea of the intrinsic value of freedom, which is Kant's most fundamental axiological notion in these lectures and for the remainder of his career. Kant's ultimate idea seems to be that moral worth attaches to the active use of our free will, rather than to any inclinations that we have, precisely because it is this which distinguishes us from all other animals as mere products of nature.

Kant first introduces this general idea in explaining the very idea of duties to oneself. To understand the possibility of such duties, we have to distinguish our reason from our sensible inclinations, not simply so that we will have formal analogues for the roles of the two (or more) different persons involved in duties to others as ordinarily understood (as the later *Doctrine of Virtue* might be taken to suggest [§3, 6:418]), but more importantly so that we can conceive of duties to oneself as the most fundamental ethical duties of all, precisely because it is by the recognition and fulfillment of such duties that we elevate ourselves above the status of mere animals. Thus Kant writes, in a passage which I have already cited more than once in these essays,

> The inherent value of the world, the *summum bonum*, is freedom in accordance with a will which is not necessitated to action. Freedom is thus the inner value of the world. But on the other hand, freedom unrestrained by rules of its conditional employment is the most terrible of all things. The actions of animals are regular; they are performed in accordance with rules which necessitate them subjectively. Mankind apart, nature is not free. . . . Man alone is free; his actions are not regulated by any such subjectively necessitating principle; if they were, he would not be free. . . . What then is the condition under which freedom is restricted? It is the law. The universal law is therefore as follows: Let thy procedure be such that in all thine actions regularity prevails. What does this restriction imply when applied to the individual? That he should not follow his inclinations. The fundamental rule, in terms of which I ought to restrain my freedom, is the conformity of free behavior to the essential ends of humanity. I shall not then follow my inclinations, but bring them under a rule. He who subjects his person to his inclinations, acts contrary to the essential end of humanity; for as a free being he must be subjected to inclinations, but ought to determine them in the exercise of his freedom. . . . In the case of animals inclinations are already determined by subjectively compelling factors; in their case, therefore, disorderliness is impossible. But if man gives free rein to his inclinations, he sinks lower than an animal.[13]

At the deepest level, Kant believes that we realize the moral worth that is potential in us by elevating ourselves above the level of mere nature, where sentiments and inclinations rule. We should note that there is nothing inherently wrong with our inclinations, just as there is nothing inherently wrong with the inclinations of any animal, but we cannot achieve any special value through our inclinations alone. Indeed, even if there were any intrinsic value in inclinations themselves, it would not be open to us to realize such a value. For we possess free will, and cannot escape it. So if we are ruled by inclination – regardless of its content – then we in fact choose to let ourselves be so ruled, and risk using our freedom to sink lower than any animal which does not, because it cannot, make this choice. But if we choose to rule ourselves by reason, that is, to rule our nature and all the inclinations inherent in it – whatever their content – by reason, then we elevate ourselves above the animals. This is what our unique value lies in, and this can only be achieved by the activity of our own will.

Kant recurs to the image of autocracy when he subsequently describes "self-mastery" (*Oberherrschaft*), or the "discipline" and "rule" over the "rabble of acts of sensibility," as the "subjective condition of the performance" of all more particular duties to oneself.[14] What is crucial in his characterization of self-mastery is his emphasis on ourselves as active agents rather than passive effects of the ordinary forces of nature:

> The power of the soul over all our faculties and circumstances to make them submit to its free will, without being necessitated to do that, is an *autocracy*. If man does not cultivate this autocracy, then he is just a play of other forces and impressions against his will, and then he depends upon accidents and the arbitrary course of circumstances.[15]

Here the contrast between being a mere plaything of forces beyond our control, and realizing our potential for moral worth in the kind of control that is uniquely open to us, is particularly clear. Again Kant gives voice to his deepest conviction. There is nothing intrinsically wrong with inclinations, but inclinations are just a part of the ordinary ebb and flow of nature, and there is therefore nothing uniquely valuable about them either. Human beings achieve their unique moral value by elevating themselves above their inclinations, which is not to say by eradicating their inclinations but by ruling them through reason.

This is Kant's moral vision in its starkest form. It cannot be thought of as a merely rigoristic insistence on the value of law itself, as so many have conceived of it. Kant does not simply assume that we must be both governed and motivated by a pure moral law, without any explanation or justification. On the contrary, he sees our recognition of and motivation by a law of pure practical reason as the means by which we become entirely active agents of our own destiny, rather than passive playthings of nature, and thus realize our unique value. This is hardly to deny that there is anything attractive to us in sentiment or inclination, but only to insist that we do not achieve moral value through passive effects of nature but only through our own activity as manifested in self-governance by reason. Kant's underlying image is that what is unique to us is our capacity for self-activity, which can be realized only through self-governance, and that is where he places our sole moral worth.

It is because of his underlying assumption of the essential activity of the motivation of the will by a principle of pure practical reason and the equally essential passivity of all inclination that Kant insists upon considering the former alone as a sufficient condition of moral worth rather than merely a necessary condition which must be combined with the presence of certain sentiments in order to create a compound conception of virtue. If there is to be any relaxation of the *Groundwork*'s apparently rigorous exclusion of sentiment and inclination from the sphere of virtue, then it must be made within the terms of Kant's underlying distinction between the active and the passive elements in human nature. In particular, it must take the form of a recognition that reason cannot merely rule over inclinations which arise entirely independently of it, but that it can itself play a role in the origination, or at least the modification and cultivation, of our inclinations. The next step of my account will be to show that the argument in the *Critique of Practical Reason* makes room for precisely such a recognition, and indeed not just in fact but in principle. Before turning to this, however, I will make a brief comment on the most famous critic of Kant's position on reason and feeling.

## Schiller on grace and dignity

As I suggested earlier, Friedrich Schiller's considered response to Kant's practical philosophy is not contained in his famous joke but in his essay "On Grace and Dignity" of 1793. Schiller's conception of grace, which is ordinarily taken to be the vehicle of a radical criticism of Kant, seems to be a plea for precisely such a compound conception of virtue as requiring both a principle of pure reason and the presence of certain natural feelings as well of the sort which Kant rejects. However, it is by no means clear whether Schiller's conception of grace is even intended as a critique of Kant's rejection of moral sentiment from our requirements of moral worth. For one thing, Schiller's ideal of grace is not explicitly a combination of principle and *sentiment* or *inclination* at all. On the contrary, Schiller arrives at his conception of grace by distinguishing between the architectonic, physical beauty of a human being, or the beauty of a human body, which is an entirely natural phenomenon, and the beauty expressed in the voluntary movements of a human being, which can be seen as *"the sensible expression of a concept of reason"* effective in the agency of the person.[16] Because the grace expressed in an individual's voluntary movements is an expression of the individual's rational agency, Schiller argues, an individual's grace is an appropriate object of our approbation:

> Freedom therefore now reigns over beauty. Nature gave the beauty of the build, the soul gives the beauty of play. And now we know what we are to understand by grace and gracefulness [*Anmut und Grazie*]. Grace is the beauty of form [*Gestalt*] under the influence of freedom; the beauty of those

appearances which the person determines. Architectonic beauty brings honor to the originator of nature, grace and gracefulness to their possessor. The former is a *talent*, the latter a *personal merit* [*Verdienst*]. [17]

Second, Schiller himself also recognizes that although as a product of voluntary action grace might reasonably be required of moral agents, in a way in which purely physical beauty of body could not reasonably be required as an expression of personal merit, nevertheless the ground for the requirement of grace is not itself entirely moral. On the contrary, Schiller clearly recognizes that the requirement of grace is a compound requirement arising from both our demand for moral worth and our independent demand for beauty. Thus he writes, "As an appearance the human being is also an object of sense. Where the *moral* feeling finds satisfaction, there the *aesthetic* feeling will not be short-shrifted, and agreement with an idea cannot cost any sacrifice in appearance. As strongly as reason demands an expression of morality, equally firmly does the eye demand beauty." [18] So we find that Schiller does not reject Kant's view that purely moral worth rests in the rational principle of an agent's action alone; he simply argues that we demand more of agents than moral worth alone, that we have an aesthetic interest in beauty in general, and in particular an aesthetic interest in harmony, which includes the harmony between the agent's principles and outward appearance which is manifested in grace. And Kant never denied this. From the outset, he clearly stated that moral sentiments in harmony with moral principles are lovable and praiseworthy (*Groundwork*, 4:398). He merely denied that such matters of sentiment are part of our conception of and demand for purely *moral* worth, which in fact Schiller never actually denies.

It must also be noted that Schiller's conception of grace is not intended as his whole characterization of our standard for human behavior. On the contrary, Schiller makes it plain that his conception of grace can never be more than an incompletely realized ideal for human behavior:

Man is to be sure set the task of establishing an inner harmony between his two natures, always to be a harmonious
whole and to act with the full voice of his entire humanity
[*Menschheit*]. But this beauty of character, the ripest fruit of his
humanity [*Humanität*], is merely an idea, which he must
strive to live up to with ever-vigilant wakefulness but which
in spite of all his efforts he can never entirely attain.[19]

The reason why this ideal can never fully be attained is simply that the sphere of voluntary movements hardly exhausts
the natural side of human beings, for there are drives and
affects which are not subject to voluntary control at all. These
aspects of human nature must simply be brought under the
rule of reason, however forcibly or violently that may have to
be done, and it is in this that "dignity," as opposed to grace,
consists: "Grace therefore lies in the *freedom of voluntary movements; dignity* in the *domination of the involuntary.*"[20] Thus
Schiller writes,

The legislation of nature through drives can come into conflict
with the legislation of reason from principles, if the drive
demands for its satisfaction an action which runs contrary to
the moral principle. In this case it is the unalterable duty for
the will to subordinate the demand of nature to the pro-
nouncement of reason, since natural laws bind only conditionally but laws of reason absolutely and unconditionally.[21]

Schiller goes on to say that when man must subordinate his
drives to reason, "he cannot here act with his whole harmonious nature but exclusively with his rational nature."

In these cases man does not act *morally beautifully*, since in the
beauty of action inclination must also necessarily take part,
although that is here excluded. But he acts *morally greatly*,
since all of that and that alone is great which gives witness to
a superiority of the higher faculties over the sensible ones.[22]

Indeed, Schiller even imports the distinction between the
beautiful and the sublime from Kant's aesthetics to express

what I take to be his assimilation and defense of the fundamental point of Kant's ethics that there may be tension between reason and inclination which must always be resolved in favor of the former: in the case of the affects, "the beautiful soul" must transform itself into a "sublime" one.[23]

The principle, and ultimately even the language, of Schiller's argument is in fact the same as that of Kant's: "In dignity," Schiller writes, "the subject legitimates itself as a self-sufficient [*selbständige*] force."[24] Schiller clearly shares with Kant the belief that moral approbation is directed most of all precisely to the activity of reason by which we elevate ourselves above passive nature. In the end, surely, the point of Schiller's twofold ideal of grace and dignity is not primarily to criticize Kant's ethics but to use his artistic powers to defend Kant's view, perhaps from the more scornful tendency within himself and certainly from the many critics who had ridiculed Kant's separation between happiness and virtue from the moment the *Groundwork* was published.

Ironically, Schiller's account of dignity has even more conservative theoretical implications than the model of the relation between feeling and reason which Kant had already begun to suggest in the *Critique of Practical Reason*. For Schiller based his brief for dignity on the assumption that there are certain human drives and feelings which are necessarily beyond the control of the human will, and which can only be subordinated to the rule of reason but not themselves gracefully transformed by it. Such an assumption may be in accord with the apparent psychology of the *Groundwork*, where Kant does write as if natural inclinations are entirely beyond the influence of reason and must therefore simply be ignored by it. In the *Critique of Practical Reason* as well as in all his subsequent writings, however, Kant evinces both in practice and in principle the view that there is no aspect of human sentiment or inclination that is necessarily unamenable to accepting the rule of reason. On the contrary, he clearly expresses his conviction that although we can never turn to passive inclination to discover the principle and motivation that we need for the activity of reason, there is no reason why the activity of reason cannot exploit the passivity of feelings in its own behalf and transform them in its own image.

Kant commented on Schiller's essay himself in his *Religion within the Limits of Reason Alone* during the same year. His answer to Schiller is profoundly revealing. He begins by exploiting Schiller's own terminology to maintain that the concept of duty must always be portrayed with dignity rather than grace, in order to express its unconditional necessity. But he goes on to deny, as Schiller himself never did, that there can ultimately be any profound tension between the principle and the inclinations of a truly virtuous agent:

> Now if one asks: what is the *aesthetic* quality, as it were the *temperament of virtue*, courageous, thus joyful, or anxiously bowed down and repressed? then an answer is hardly necessary. The latter slavish determination of the mind can never take place without a hidden *hatred* of the law, and the joyful heart in the *prosecution* of its duty (not comfort in the *recognition* of it) is a sign of the genuineness of virtuous disposition. (*Religion*, 6:23–24n)

While Kant hardly denies that there can be particular inclinations or temptations the satisfaction of which would be contrary to duty, he clearly suggests that any general and lingering attitude of resentment toward duty would be a sign that one is not really committed to it, and that, on the contrary, a genuinely virtuous condition of the will (*Gesinnung*) cannot fail ultimately to make itself manifest in a joyful attitude. These claims make sense only if Kant is supposing that one's emotional condition, at least in some global sense, is in fact determined by one's deepest moral decisions and is therefore a reliable indicator of the latter. This does not suppose that any sentiment can be a motive for the performance of duty, but clearly does presuppose that one's purely rational motivation can itself be a cause of one's sentiment or overall psychological state.

But if our principles were to express the activity of our reason yet our inclinations were to express only our passivity in regard to the forces of nature, why should our psychological state reflect our underlying choice of moral maxim? To consider Kant's answer to this question must be our next step.

## II. FROM REASON TO SENSIBILITY

### *The feeling of respect*

We have now seen that Kant's restriction of the ground for moral worth to motivation out of duty alone depends on his assumption that only our principles, and not our inclinations, directly reflect our self-activity. If, however, our inclinations themselves can indirectly reflect our self-activity precisely by being affected by our choice of principles, then the contrast between duty and inclination may not be so simple, and there may be some role for inclinations in the achievement of moral worth after all. Kant's own reply to Schiller in *Religion within the Limits of Reason Alone* makes clear that he believed, at least in works published after the *Groundwork,* that our emotional condition does reflect our ultimate choice of maxims of practical reason. Two questions must now be asked. First, to put it in Kantian language, *How is it possible* for the allegedly entirely rational, and therefore purely active, decision to adopt the law of duty as one's fundamental maxim in all of one's actions to affect one's sentiments and inclinations, when those are supposed to be passively determined by mere laws of nature? Second, assuming that it is possible for an active, rational agent's choice of maxim to affect that agent's feelings, can morality have any ground for interest in these feelings other than as a mere sign of the agent's maxim? In other words, Is there any reason *why* morality should directly require the presence of any inclinations, whether a general moral sentiment or specific inclinations toward particular persons or states of affairs? I will address the first of these questions here and the second in Section III.

As we just saw, in replying to Schiller in the *Religion within the Limits of Reason Alone,* Kant evinced his belief that a complete commitment to the maxim of duty inevitably produces a joyful temperament, while an anxious and repressed performance of duty can only express an inward rejection of that maxim – with outward compliance presumably arising from some other motive, such as fear of public or juridical consequences of violation of duty's external requirements. But we did not have to wait until the *Religion* to find evidence of Kant's view that an agent's free choice of the maxim of duty does affect his psychological state, for such a view is already explicit in Kant's treatment of the feeling of "respect" in the *Critique of Practical Reason.* As Kant there says, "Respect for the moral law is a feeling which is effected by an intellectual ground" (5:73).

Kant initially characterizes respect in terms of the feeling of *pain* that is naturally consequent upon the restraint of one's natural inclinations often required by adherence to the principle of duty:

> All inclination and every sensible impulse is grounded on feeling, and the negative effect on feeling (through the check exercised on the feelings) is itself a feeling. Consequently we can see *a priori* that the moral law as the determining ground of the will, since it works to the prejudice of all of our inclinations, must effect a feeling which can be called pain, and here we have the first, perhaps also the only case where we can determine the relation of a cognition (here it is one of pure practical reason) to the feeling of pleasure or displeasure *a priori* from concepts. (*Practical Reason,* 5:73)

The mechanism of this pain might be readily understood as compatible with obvious laws of psychology. The decision not to satisfy one or more of one's inclinations, where such satisfaction would require actions excluded by duty, causes the frustration of those inclinations, which in turn naturally leads to pain. As long as we can understand the possibility of a decision of our will affecting our actions, we do not need to postulate any extraordinary mechanism to account for our pain. The pain can be understood as the natural effect of the frustration of the naturally present inclinations rather than as a direct effect of the decision of the will itself. Of course, in this case it may be hard to see why respect should be thought of as a *moral* sentiment, or why Kant should assume, as he does in the *Religion*, that discomfort in the performance of one's duty is a sign of inward *opposition* to the maxim of duty. On the contrary, such discomfort would seem to be the inevitable, natural result of the decision to adhere to this maxim.

But the pain of frustrated inclinations is by no means the whole of the feeling of respect. On the contrary, precisely by revealing our power to frustrate our own inclinations, indeed all forms of self-satisfaction or self-conceit, this very pain reveals the presence of the higher power of pure practical reason within us and thus generates a positive feeling in response to such an object:

> The moral law strikes down self-conceit. But since this law is yet something positive in itself, namely the form of an intellectual causality, i.e., freedom, it is, insofar as in opposition to subjective opposition, namely our inclinations, it weakens self-conceit, an object of *respect,* and insofar as it even *strikes them down,* i.e., humiliates them, it is an object of the greatest *respect,* thus the ground of a positive feeling that is not of empirical origin and is known *a priori.* (*Practical Reason,* 5:73)

Some commentators write as if Kant describes two different feelings here, the painful feeling of respect occasioned by the frustration of inclination and a separate, positive feeling, perhaps designated "moral feeling" to distinguish it from respect, which expresses our admiration for the superiority of the moral law.[25] Yet if anything Kant tends to reserve the term "respect" for the positive feeling of admiration toward the moral law. It would seem most accurate simply to treat "respect" and "moral feeling" as synonyms naming a single but complex effect of the decision to adhere to the maxim of duty on our emotional state. The painful frustration of our inclinations itself makes palpable to our senses the majesty of the moral law, which produces a positive feeling of admiration for the principle of our own will and activity:

> Insofar as the moral law excludes the inclinations and the tendency to make them into the highest practical condition, i.e., self-love, from all access to the highest legislation, it can exercise an effect on feeling, which is on the one hand merely *negative*, but on the other hand and indeed in relation to the limiting ground of pure practical reason *positive*. . . . Therefore this feeling can also be called a feeling of respect for the moral law, and from both grounds together a *moral feeling*. (*Practical Reason*, 5:74–5)

The structure of Kant's account is the same as that which he was to use two years later in his characterization of the feeling of the sublime. The palpable painfulness of the frustration of the imagination in attempting to grasp the infinite or of our fear of physical destruction itself reveals to us the higher power of reason to form the very idea of the infinite in the first place and to grant us a value that is immune from physical destruction. And presumably the underlying psychological law which accounts for pleasure in aesthetic cases is at work in this moral case as well: It is always pleasurable for us to realize the possibility of accomplishing our objectives (see *CJ*, §VI, 5:187), and there can certainly be no objective which is more profound, or the satisfaction of which is more pleasurable, than the objective of governing ourselves by reason rather than inclination and thus elevating ourselves above the sphere of mere nature.

Indeed, in spite of the absence of any explicit characterization of it in the *Groundwork*, the introduction of the feeling of respect in the *Critique of Practical Reason* is hardly a radical departure in Kant's thought, but is instead continuous with his long-held view of the natural response to the recognition of the role of reason in our actions. Thus Kant wrote in the mid-1770s

> The *ground of moral feeling*, on which the *delight* in [the] agreement [of our actions] according to principles rests, is the neces-

sity of delight in the form of actions, through which we are in harmony with ourselves in the use of our reason. The lack of *moral feeling* . . . comes from one not taking *so much interest in the form* as in the *matter* [of an action] and not considering an object from the viewpoint of *universality*. . . . This is no particular feeling, but rather a general manner of considering something from the universal point of view.

And, in a note on the "ground of moral feeling," he writes,

How can morality be felt, since it is an object of reason? It is related to all of our actions in accord with our pleasure or displeasure and contains the condition of the agreement of them in general; through that it is related to the feeling of pleasure according to form. (*R* 6864, 19:184–5)

It is a continuing principle of Kant's thought not only that we can take pleasure in action, but that we can take pleasure in the possibility of conducting our actions according to universally valid laws, at least as well as we can take pleasure in actions merely because of their promise to satisfy our inclinations.

The feeling of respect is thus a complex but ultimately pleasurable state of feeling produced by our decision to adhere to the moral law, grounded, like other feelings of pleasure, in the recognition of the possibility of the realization of our own objectives but reflecting in its very complexity the fact that not all of our objectives are conjointly satisfiable. Respect, or moral feeling, is a mixture of pleasure and pain precisely because we cannot always satisfy both our inclinations and the demands of duty. One must always keep in mind, however, Kant's insistence that this feeling is neither the source of the content or validity of the moral law nor our motive for adherence to it, but strictly the effect of our adherence to the moral law motivated by our recognition of the law itself: "This feeling (under the name of the moral [feeling]) is therefore merely effected through reason. It does not serve for the evaluation of actions, nor certainly for the grounding of the objective law of morality itself" (*Practical Reason*, 5:76). Thus when Kant wrote in the *Groundwork* that *"Duty is the necessity of an action out of respect for the law"* (4:400), he did not mean that moral feeling is the original motive for adherence to the law, but that moral worth requires that we act out of duty because of the intrinsic merit of so doing rather than out of any mere inclination to so do. But what he is now saying is that the decision to adhere to the law because of its intrinsic merit does indeed have an effect on one's feelings which can be called respect or moral feeling.

## The effect of reason on feeling

Once he has asserted that the purely "intellectual ground" of the decision to adhere to the moral law can have an effect on the feelings in the form of respect, can Kant simply infer that all of one's sentiments and inclinations can be influenced by one's moral maxims? Hardly, since he has said that the feeling of respect is, or at least is perhaps, the *only* feeling which is effected through a purely intellectual ground: "This feeling is the only one which we cognize fully *a priori* and whose necessity we can understand" (*Practical Reason*, 5:73).[26] This appears to preclude the possibility that the choice of the maxim of morality itself might produce or modify any sort of inclination in a direction favorable to morality. Kant's basis for this claim is not clear, however, unless he is simply construing the feeling of respect so broadly as to include all feelings whatsoever that might conduce to or accompany one's fulfillment of one's duties. But there is no ground for him to construe the feeling of respect so broadly, for, as we have seen, the feeling of respect in its positive aspect is defined specifically as a positive feeling directed at the moral law itself, and therefore does not include any positive sentiments or inclinations directed at the ordinary *objects* of duty, such as other persons. The feeling of respect is thus by no means identical with feelings of love or other benevolent sentiments toward other persons, whether in general or in particular (although presumably it may be directed toward the capacity for autonomous governance by the moral law *in* others, and perhaps must be so directed if Kant's most basic conception of treating others as ends and not mere means is to make sense). So if Kant's claim that the feeling of respect is the only feeling which can be produced by the intellectual commitment to morality is correct, then the existence of the phenomenon of respect by no means itself opens up the door to the possibility of any wider range of moral sentiments grounded in pure reason.

But this restriction of the effect of the "intellectual ground" of the decision to adopt the maxim of morality to the production of the feeling of respect by no means follows from Kant's basic account of action, although there may be a sense in which his claim that this is the only case in which we can *know a priori* that such a feeling must be produced is justified. In the account of respect thus far, we have been speaking loosely of this feeling as a result of an "intellectual ground." But of course we know that on the theory of choice which Kant was developing, especially in the works from the *Critique of Practical Reason* to the *Religion*, this "intellectual ground" is understood as a complex event consisting of a free but ultimately inscrutable *act of choice* (*Willkür*) to adhere to the maxim of universal law offered by pure practical reason or will (*Wille*) rather than to a maxim of self-love which would allow one to exempt oneself from the requirements of duty. Because this act of choice is free, it must be ascribed to a noumenal realm rather than to the causally determined realm of phenomena. But in contrast to the argument of the third section of the *Groundwork*, where Kant tries to characterize the noumenal realm as fully intelligible through our ordinary conception of reason, Kant's fully mature theory of action does not *identify* the free act of choice with reason as we may understand it through our phenomenal conception of reason, but considers it as a separate, although inexplicable act to cast our lot with reason rather than against it. But this means that there is no metaphysical ground why the effect of such an act of choice must be confined to anything like the phenomenal manifestation of reason itself – that is to say, why it must manifest itself only in the strength of reason, as contrasted to inclinations within the phenomenal sphere. On the contrary, and precisely because the noumenal act of free choice cannot be identified with any particular event in the phenomenal world, this act of choice can be considered to be the ground of the entire phenomenal world, and its effect can just as plausibly be manifested in the phenomenal sphere of sentiment and inclination as in anything that might be considered the phenomenal manifestation of rationality.[27]

And this is precisely the account which Kant gives in the discussion of freedom that follows the discussion of respect in the *Critique of Practical Reason*. There Kant specifically denies that freedom of choice can be associated with any specific feature of the phenomenal world, including "grounds of determination thought by reason," that is to say, reason as a phenomenon that would originally be contrasted to "instinct" or inclination, because even reason (in that sense) would be subject to deterministic laws of nature (5:96). Instead, freedom of choice can only be conceived of as the act of a "thing in itself," an underlying reality of which anything and everything in the sensible or phenomenal world can be the consequence. Thus Kant writes, in one of his most stirring if extraordinary passages:

The same subject, which is also conscious of itself as a thing in itself, also considers its existence, *so far as it does not stand under conditions of time*, but is rather itself determinable through laws which it gives itself through reason, and in this its existence there is nothing that precedes the determination of its will, but every action and in general every changing determination of its existence in inner sense, even the entire succession of its existence as a sensible being, is to be regarded in the consciousness of its intelligible existence as nothing but the consequence and never the determining ground of its causality as noumenon. In this consideration the rational being can say with right, of every action contrary to law which it commits, that although as an appearance it is sufficiently determined by the past and is insofar inexorably necessary, it could have left it undone; for

> that action, together with all that is past that determines it,
> belongs to a single phenomenon of its character, which it itself
> creates. (*Practical Reason*, 5:97–8)

Although it makes no difference whether reason as the
source of the principle of morality is identified with the phenomenal faculty of reason as contrasted with inclination,
since reason is not the source of action at all but only the
source of a principle of action which must be accepted or
rejected, the action which constitutes the decision or choice
to adopt this principle is not itself identical with any particular event within the phenomenal world, nor can its consequences be confined to any particular aspect of the phenomenal world. The noumenal act of choice can be thought of as
responsible for the entire phenomenon of the agent's character, if that is what is necessary to comprehend the possibility of his leaving undone an immoral action which would
otherwise seem to be necessitated by the laws of the sensible
world. There is therefore no reason why the effect of this
action of choice should be confined to reason as one aspect of
the agent's phenomenal character, that is, a phenomenal
quality typically contrasted to sentiment and inclination.
Rather, the effects of this choice can be manifested anywhere
and everywhere in the agent's empirical character.

As I suggested, there may be some basis for Kant's remark
that the feeling of respect is the only feeling which can be
known *a priori* to be a consequence of the "intellectual
ground," that is, the noumenal decision to adopt the pure
practical principle of duty. This basis would be Kant's conviction, voiced not in the *Critique of Practical Reason* but in the
*Critique of Judgment*, that pleasure is the inevitable consequence of our recognition of our capacity to fulfill our own
objectives, in this case our objective of acting as a rational
being. Given this premise, respect in the sense of a positive
feeling would be the natural accompaniment of the recognition of our power to overcome self-conceit by the adherence
to reason. But, as I have argued elsewhere,[28] Kant has no
ground for classifying this fundamental premise as strictly *a*

*priori*, although it may well be a fundamental law of human psychology. And if this is so, then it may be up to psychology, rather than metaphysics, to discover where the limits of the influence of the moral motive on the sentiments and inclinations of human beings lie.

## The psychology of moral sentiment

This next remark may seem a most un-Kantian thing to say, but I think in fact we can make the most sense of Kant's views about the development of moral sentiments and inclinations in his later works precisely if we think that it is psychology, rather than metaphysics, which tells us how reason can affect our feelings. We have already seen Kant's claim, in the *Religion*, that symptoms of anxiety and repression can be expected when an agent outwardly complies with the requirements of duty while inwardly hating it, whereas a joyful disposition can be expected to accompany an inward commitment to duty. There is no obvious metaphysical foundation for these claims, but they seem profoundly right as psychological observations. In the *Metaphysics of Morals*, Kant makes two key claims about the effects of our moral decisions on our psychological state. First, he asserts that moral feeling is not something which one has a duty to acquire but rather is a natural susceptibility, which no man is entirely lacking and which everyone is capable of cultivating (*Virtue*, Introduction §XII, 6:399–400). His thought here appears to be that one simply cannot create this feeling out of whole cloth if it is lacking (that would be "moral death"), but that one can take various measures to strengthen it, given any tendency toward it at all. Second, Kant also claims that although the feeling of love for other human beings cannot be directly commanded, precisely because "it is a matter of *feeling*, not of willing," nevertheless the development of this feeling will inevitably follow the duty of acting beneficently toward others, which can be commanded. Thus he writes,

> *Beneficence* is a duty. If someone practices it often and suc-
> ceeds in realizing his beneficent intention, he eventually
> comes actually to love the person he has helped. So the say-
> ing "you ought to *love* your neighbor as yourself" does not
> mean that you ought immediately (first) to love him and (after-
> wards) by means of this love do good to him. It means rather
> *do good* to your fellow man, and your beneficence will produce
> love of man in you (as an aptitude of the inclination to benefi-
> cence in general).[29] (*Virtue*, Introduction §XII, 6:402)

Again, there is no purely metaphysical basis for either of
Kant's claims. Just as no metaphysical consideration can demonstrate the incoherence of the *Groundwork*'s example of a
person who continues to act according to duty in spite of the
extinction of all sympathy for mankind in him, so no metaphysical fact can prove the necessity of the development of
love for others as the inevitable consequence of beneficence
toward them. If it is true that adherence to the principle of
beneficence eventually produces the feeling of love – the
truth of which would then suggest that the *Groundwork*'s
example is only a heuristic device – then this truth must be
discovered by psychology. It would not, indeed, be excluded
by the theory of the noumenal choice of all phenomenal character, but neither would it be necessitated by this theory.
And Kant does not claim otherwise. Although in the *Critique
of Practical Reason* he suggests that we can know *a priori* that
the motive of duty will produce the feeling of respect, neither
in the *Religion* nor the *Metaphysics of Morals* does he actually
assert that we can know *a priori* that our moral choices will
have these effects on our feelings. He simply describes these
effects. Their occurrence must then be thought of as metaphysical possibilities and psychological realities.

Kant's initial contrast between the activity of reason and
the passivity of all inclinations, the contrast which, as we
saw, is one of the deepest motives for his view that moral
worth lies solely in the agent's motivation out of duty and
not in the presence of any moral sentiments, must thus be
carefully restated. The *Critique of Practical Reason* implies, and

the Kant of the *Religion* and *Metaphysics of Morals* realizes, that there is no reason to suppose that our sentiments and inclinations are simply fixed by forces outside of our control and therefore need to be ignored in all moral contexts. On the contrary, our sentiments and inclinations are plastic, and can evolve in response to the actions of our will. To what extent they can evolve is a matter for psychology to discover, and that means, among other things, that we cannot tell in advance whether a moral revolution in our choice of maxims will require us to revise our conception of the laws governing our phenomenal behavior or will be compatible with those laws; psychology, not metaphysics, will have to tell us what sorts of changes and developments in moral sentiment are compatible with the laws of nature, so we cannot know *a priori* how our sensuous character would have to be changed in order to accommodate an unforeseen and inscrutable change in maxim from self-love to duty. But just because the extent to which changes in maxim can effect changes in inclination is ultimately a matter for empirical determination, it must remain true that we can never look to inclination rather than reason for the completely reliable motive for morality. On Kant's model, it remains true that only the free choice of the noumenal self can be ascribed unlimited power to adopt the maxim of pure practical reason *a priori*. Thus Kant can remain firm in his position that only the active agency of the rational self can be directly held to the standard of moral worth, while at the same time he appeals to experience to confirm that this activity of the rational self does have an effect on the sentiments and inclinations. The latter remain passive, but now in a metaphysical rather than merely empirical sense, and precisely because of that plasticity they can reasonably be expected to be at least modified by the agency of the active self itself.

If this account is correct, then we can now see how Kant thinks it is possible for the subjective state of one's feelings to reflect the moral choices of one's will. We can even understand why he claims that it is only the feeling of respect that we can know *a priori* to be the product of an "intellectual ground" and yet goes on to presuppose in practice that a wider range of sentiments, including love directed at other persons, will result from one's moral choices. What now remains to be asked is whether the development or cultivation of such moral sentiments should be considered merely as a natural concomitant of the fulfillment of duty and true moral worth, or rather whether within the framework of Kant's thought there is room for a conception of the production of sentiment through principle as itself a kind or part of duty and thus itself part of the ground for the attribution of moral worth.

## III. DUTIES OF FEELING

### The role of feeling in duty

To answer this question, we must seek guidance from Kant's most detailed account of the requirements imposed upon us by the general principle of duty, the *Metaphysics of Morals*, which was published in two parts, the *Doctrine of Right* and the *Doctrine of Virtue*, in January and August 1797. This was the work Kant had been intending to produce for most of his philosophical career and to which, he often suggested, the entire edifice of the three critiques was just a propaedeutic; but, in the end, what was produced was a slender and in many ways deeply confusing work. Nevertheless, the main lines of thought in this work are faithful to the underlying ideas of Kant's ethical thought and do provide us with materials for an answer to the question before us.

This is hardly the place for an extended commentary on the *Metaphysics of Morals*.[30] I will provide only a brief outline of its organization before considering its implications for the connection between duty and feeling. The most elementary distinction in the work, the basis of its division into the separate doctrines of right (*Recht*, often translated as "justice") and virtue, is the distinction between *juridical* duties, which can be enforced by external legislation, and *ethical* duties, which cannot (*Right,* Introduction §III, 6:218–19). Ethical duties are also characterized as duties to adopt a necessary end in one's actions, while juridical duties are those to comply with certain rules in one's external actions regardless of one's ends (*Virtue,* Introduction §I, 6:380). This might seem to suggest that the distinction between juridical and ethical duties is equivalent to that between perfect and imperfect duties: that is, the distinction between those duties requiring the commission or, more typically, omission of specific types of actions in specific types of circumstances, and those requiring the adoption of certain general aims or policies where what actions will be required in specific circumstances must always be left open for judgment in those circumstances (on this, see also Chapter 9). (This distinction was already used in the illustration of the categorical imperative in the *Groundwork,* 4:421.) This distinction is also correlated with the distinction between those duties the violation of which brings moral demerit but compliance with which does not merit any special praise (perfect duties), and those duties which can be left unfulfilled, at least on particular occasions, without demerit, but the satisfaction of which does entitle the agent to approbation and moral merit (*Right,* Introduction §IV, 6:227).

In fact, however, the division is not so simple, because not all perfect duties are classified as juridical duties, and because the class of ethical duties extends beyond the class of imperfect duties in two different ways. First, Kant holds that it is only an agent's injury of the freedom of others which can justifiably be threatened or punished with coercion, the sanction which is the necessary condition of external legislation, so in fact only perfect duties to others fall within the sphere of juridical duties (*Right,* §C, 6:231). Thus perfect duties to oneself, even though they require the avoidance of specific acts of destruction of oneself or one's capacity as a free agent, such as suicide or drunkenness, regardless of one's ends, are classified as ethical rather than juridical duties (*Virtue,* §5, 6:421), and the class of ethical duties therefore includes some duties which do not consist in the adoption and general advancement of a necessary end but are rather outright prohibitions. Second, Kant also includes among ethical duties not only specific duties of advancing specific morally necessary ends, or ethical duties (*Tugendpflichten*) properly so called, but also the general obligation to perform all of one's duties from the motive of duty itself, the general obligation of virtue (*Tugendverpflichtung*) (*Right*, Introduction §III, 6:219). This general requirement, satisfaction of which brings moral merit in any kind of situation, applies to perfect duties to others as well as all other duties, and so cuts across the initial distinction between juridical and ethical duties; of course, satisfaction of this general obligation, since it concerns strictly one's motive and not one's outward behavior, cannot be coerced by any external means, and cannot itself be a juridical duty, even though it applies to juridical duties (*Right*, Introduction §III, 6:220). It is an ethical requirement on the spirit in which juridical duties should be satisfied if their satisfaction is to be an occasion for praise rather than merely for the avoidance of punishment.

All of this would have been much more perspicuous if Kant had been as clear about the underlying structure of his ethical thought in his published books as he had been in his earlier lectures. In the *Doctrine of Virtue*, Kant introduces the idea of necessary ends, or ends that are also duties, by means of the argument that we could not comply with universally valid laws if we had only particular material objectives for our actions (*Virtue*, Introduction §§II, III, 6:382, 385). If we simply assume that rational agents must be bound by universally valid laws of practical reason from the outset, as the ultimate given of moral theory, this argument must seem invalid, for it is not obvious why every agent should not be able to apply this universal law to his own contingent ends and act only on those individual ends which do not require any violation of universal law. If we do not take the validity of universal law as the ultimate foundational assumption of Kantian ethics, however, but rather follow the guidance of Kant's lectures in assigning the inherent value of freedom that role, then the rationale for Kant's division of duties in the *Metaphysics of Morals* becomes clear. Freedom is the ultimate value or end to be considered in all action; thus, in one sense, all duties have freedom rather than any mere empirical desire as their end. Thus, any duty can be performed out of regard for freedom rather than out of interest in any more specific end which may also be served by compliance, and to so perform any duty can be considered to be the general obligation of virtue (*Tugendverpflichtung*). Specific laws of duty express the specific conditions by means of which the general end can be duly regarded. These specific conditions can take two forms. On the one hand, there are duties not to destroy or injure freedom by destroying free agents or unnecessarily restricting their freedom. On the other hand, there are specific ways in which the ability of both oneself and others to use and enjoy their freedom may be advanced or enhanced. The former give rise to the perfect duties, which generally require avoiding the destruction or limitation of freedom in ourselves and others; it is also both possible and justifiable to attach coercive sanctions to violations of the requirement not to destroy or injure the freedom of others, so perfect duties to others can be made the subject of external legislation and become juridical duties. Violations of the requirement not to injure one's own freedom and the general requirement to improve the conditions for the enjoyment of the freedom of both oneself and others cannot be made the subject of external legislation, for they cannot be made the subject of coercion, so perfect duties to oneself and imperfect duties to oneself and others remain in the class of specific duties of virtue (*Tugendpflichten*). On this account, then, all duties derive from the underlying value of freedom or freedom as an end, and all duties can be performed out of the motive which is simply respect for the value of this end; more specifically, some duties prohibit the impairment of freedom, and others enjoin improvement of the conditions for its exercise. The latter are duties which are also necessary ends in the narrower sense which Kant has in mind in the *Doctrine of Virtue*.

In his own exposition of that doctrine, Kant characterizes the necessary ends of the duties of virtue as one's own perfection and the happiness of others (*Virtue*, Introduction §IV, 6:385–6). The relation between this characterization and the general account I have just given is complicated. The underlying assumption is that the ultimate use of freedom is in fact the production of happiness. Since one naturally pursues one's own happiness, however, this pursuit cannot be imposed on oneself and cannot be any sort of duty; so the only candidate for duty to oneself is self-perfection, which is in fact preservation and advancement of the conditions necessary for the successful rational exercise of one's own freedom: avoidance of its destruction through acts like suicide, on the one hand, and its development through policies such as the cultivation of one's talents on the other. In the case of duties toward others, one cannot perform their own free actions for them, thus one cannot directly advance their freedom (although of course one can directly injure it), so Kant infers that what one can do for others is instead advance their happiness. In fact, however, Kant always emphasizes that one must advance their happiness *on their own conception of their happiness* (*Virtue*, Introduction §V, 6:388), thus respecting their freedom in advancing their happiness. Further, one's duty to respect the happiness of others is divided under the two headings of love and respect (*Virtue*, §§23–4, 6:448–9). The former is the requirement to be actively beneficent toward others rather than emotionally benevolent to them: that is, the requirement to act toward them in a beneficent way rather than feel toward them in a benevolent way (although such a feeling, as we saw, Kant supposes will naturally follow acting in that way toward them). The duty of respect is the requirement always to treat others as free agents worthy of respect, which can be violated by such attitudes as arrogance, defamation, and ridicule (*Virtue*, §41, 6:464). Avoiding such attitudes does not seem to require any direct advancement of the happiness of others, but rather the avoidance of injury to their dignity as free agents by means of one's attitudes toward them rather than by more direct actions; here again the boundary between imperfect and perfect duties seems to be violated in the classification of duties of virtue. That leaves the beneficent duty of love toward others as the main category of imperfect duty under which their happiness can be directly advanced. Here one must conjecture not only that their happiness must be advanced after their own conception and in this sense their freedom is consulted, but perhaps also that the primary form of beneficence is to assist others in obtaining the means to their own realization of their ends rather than in simply gratifying their needs. If this is so, one would aid their own pursuit of their happiness by improving the conditions under which they can exercise their freedom. It is indeed hard to see how free agents whose primary form of satisfaction lies in the exercise of their own free agency, as Kant describes human beings, could really have their happiness substantially advanced in any way that did not involve the free use of their own capacities.

This account then leaves us with the question of what roles feelings could play in the perfection of oneself and in the advancement of the happiness of others.

## Feeling and self-perfection

Kant's account of "Duties to Oneself in General" in Part I of the *Doctrine of Virtue* is more complicated than his account of "Duties of Virtue to Others" in Part II because it includes the perfect duties to oneself that have been excluded from juridical duty, as well as the imperfect duties to oneself, and describes ethical duties to others primarily as imperfect duties (although in fact, as we just saw, this distinction is not rigidly observed). The account of duties to oneself is also complicated by its use of what are really two not entirely congruent principles of division. On the one hand, it uses what we might call a paradigmatically Kantian distinction between duties to oneself as an animal, or duties concerning the physical basis of one's existence and activity as a free agent, and duties to oneself as a purely moral being, involving "what is *formal* in the consistency of the maxims of [one's] will with the *dignity* of humanity in [one's] person" (*Virtue*, §4, 6:420). On the other hand, Kant also employs what one might think of as a Wolffian distinction among the capacities of oneself that are eligible for self-perfection, distinguishing intellect, will, physical capacity, and finally feeling all as capacities of oneself that must be perfected not only for prudential but also for moral reasons.[31] Finally, Kant includes further discussion of the general obligation to act out of the motive of duty (*Tugendverpflichtung*) in his discussion of more specific duties to oneself. The rather "episodic" organization of the treatment of duties to oneself (to borrow a term Kant himself uses at *Virtue*, §16, 6:442) reflects this complexity of underlying distinctions. In the discussion of duties to others, Kant uses a distinction between duties of love (beneficence) and respect inspired more by Christian Thomasius than by Christian Wolff, and this also leads to some complexity in his classification of duties. But here, at least the general obligation to perform all of one's duties out of respect for duty is not placed on the same plane as specific duties, and to this extent Kant's treatment of duties to others enjoys a more straightforward exposition than his treatment of duties to oneself.

Forewarned of this complexity, let us summarize Kant's doctrine of duties to oneself, in order to see where duties of feeling might fit in. Under the rubric of "Perfect Duties to Oneself," Kant enumerates first the necessity to avoid the destruction or impairment of the physical basis for one's free agency, that is, one's bodily existence and health (*Virtue*, §§6–8, 6:422–8), and then the necessity of avoiding the debasement of the humanity of one's own person through lying, avarice, and servility (*Virtue*, §§9–12, 6:428–37). In a further discussion of perfect duties to oneself as a moral being, Kant discusses a separate duty to "judge" (§13, 6:437–40) and "know" (§§14–15, 6:441–2) oneself as a moral being, that is, to scrutinize and evaluate the purity of one's heart and motives. Although Kant does not say so, it is obvious that this discussion is separated from the preceding discussion of the avoidance of lying, avarice, and servility because he is here talking about conditions necessary for compliance with the general obligation to act out of the motive of duty, which is a requirement in one's performance of all specific duties rather than any additional specific duty to oneself: One cannot truly act out of the motive of duty unless one is willing to inquire into what one's inmost motive really is. Finally, Kant concludes with an "Episodic Section," in which he treats our duties regarding the treatment of nature other than human beings as a species of duty to ourselves, specifically the duty not to destroy a naturally occurring predisposition to "love something" such as natural beauty or a companionable animal, "even apart from any intention to use it"; this disposition is a "feeling in man which, though not of itself moral, is still a predisposition of sensibility that greatly promotes morality or at least prepares the way for it," a "natural predisposition that is very serviceable to morality in one's relation to other men" (§17, 6:443).[32]

The place of this duty in Kant's scheme is complicated. As a duty not to destroy, it does belong with the perfect duties, yet the predisposition which Kant describes is not exactly part either of one's physical being or of one's purely moral being, but a natural psychological tendency which is asserted to be conducive to morality. Thus our naturally favorable feeling toward nonhuman nature is a feeling of the sort which cannot simply be willed into existence but which is present in all who are not morally dead and which can be intentionally cultivated. The possible occasions for and extent of such cultivation are open-ended, and for this reason it would seem as if we should also have an imperfect duty not merely not to destroy but to cultivate this feeling. Before we can consider this feeling further, therefore, it is necessary to consider Kant's account of imperfect duties to oneself.

Kant's account of these duties is quite brief. "Man's Duty to Himself to Increase His Moral Perfection" is the duty to perfect "the *purity* (*puritas moralis*) of one's disposition to duty," that is, the duty to strive unceasingly to make the law "by itself alone the incentive" of all of one's actions, "even without the admixture of aims derived from sensibility." Thus, this duty is

375

nothing but the requirement to act "not only in conformity with duty but also *from duty*" (*Virtue*, §21, 6:446). But this is to say that it is not a specific imperfect duty to oneself at all, but again the general obligation of virtuous motivation (*Tugendver-pflichtung*) to perform all of one's specific duties out of the motive of duty; it is included here under imperfect duties only because our compliance with it can never be complete but can "consist only in continual progress." This leaves as the content of the specific imperfect duty to ourselves then only "Man's Duty to Himself to Develop and Increase His Natural Perfection." This is the requirement "to cultivate (*cultura*) [our] natural powers (powers of spirit, mind, and body), as means to all sorts of possible ends" (*Virtue*, §19, 6:444). Here the idea is that for the sake of our success in the exercise of free rational agency in general, not just in the pursuit of specific goals of happiness or prudence, we need to cultivate "the natural predispositions and capacities that . . . reason can someday use," although of course we have no way of telling in advance which talents any one person may most particularly need or most successfully develop. That must be left to judgment, which is why this duty must remain an imperfect duty (*Virtue*, §20, 6:445–6).

Here Kant is thinking in Wolffian terms of the perfection of our intellectual capacities such as mathematical reasoning (powers of spirit) as well as memory and imagination (powers of mind), and of the various powers of the body, all of which can be conceived of as furnishing "instruments for a variety of purposes" (*Virtue*, §19, 6:445). Thus he is thinking primarily of those of our natural capacities which can serve as means for the successful execution of whatever specific actions duty might someday call upon us to perform. However, it is not obvious why this idea of the necessity of developing natural capacities or predispositions as instruments for the performance of duty need be confined to those which can serve as instruments in the execution of specific actions; we might also think of natural predispositions such as sentiments of sympathy and benevolence as means to assist us in the formation of the intention to perform the actions required of us by duty, whatever those might turn out to be, in as yet unforeseeable circumstances. In this case, then, the naturally occurring predisposition to have feelings which may prepare the way for morality would not merely be something which we should avoid destroying, but something which we should seek to cultivate along with our other "natural powers" as a possible instrument for successful fulfillment of the tasks which duty may set for us. The cultivation of a wide range of benevolent sentiments toward nonhuman nature, but also toward other human beings both in general and in particular, would thus become part of our imperfect duty to ourselves to develop our natural powers in ways instrumental not merely for our pursuit of happiness but for our fulfillment of duty itself.

On this account, naturally occurring sentiments would not be relied upon to determine the content of our duty or to motivate us to fulfill it by themselves but would rather be cultivated out of the principle of duty, under the specific requirement to develop all of our natural capacities which may be useful in the fulfillment of our duty. It might nevertheless be objected, however, that there is a serious disanalogy between the instrumental role of natural powers in the execution of duty and the proposed role for naturally occurring sentiments in the performance of duty. The objection would be that while the natural powers of mind and body that Kant enumerates are useful solely in the execution of actions required by duty that we intend to perform solely because they are required by duty, sentiments and inclinations could be useful only by assisting in the formation and adoption of the intention to act in certain ways and would thus mar the purity of the moral motive. If so, they would not be instruments for the successful execution of duty which duty can require us to cultivate, but rather obstacles to action which is not merely in compliance with duty but genuinely from duty.

There are several levels at which this objection might be answered. At one level, we might construct a parallel with an argument that Kant offers concerning the moral status of the pursuit of one's own happiness. This is found in Kant's initial discussion of the duty to advance the happiness of others. Kant's position on the pursuit of happiness is complex. Kant advances two general claims which might seem to conflict. On the one hand, he argues that no one can have a duty to pursue his own happiness, because everyone has a natural tendency to do that anyway and thus the element of self-compulsion that is part of the concept of duty is missing (*Virtue*, Introduction §IV, 6:386); on the other hand, however, he also argues that one has no duty always to pursue the happiness of others at the cost of one's own, because that would give rise to an inconsistent maxim (*Virtue*, Introduction §VIII, 6:393). In the end, therefore, one has a duty to advance the happiness of others only in conjunction with a right to pursue one's own, and there can be no mechanical procedure for deciding which must be advanced on any particular occasion (see also *Virtue*, §27, 6:451). But in addition to this general consideration, Kant also suggests that one must take a certain amount of care about one's own happiness as an instrument for the successful pursuit of duty, because too much want of happiness might interfere with one's performance of duty:

> Adversity, pain, and want are great temptations to violate one's duty. It might therefore seem that prosperity, strength, health, and well-being, which check the influence of these, could also be considered ends that are duties, so that one has a duty to promote *one's own* happines and not just the happiness of others. But then the end is not the subject's happiness but his morality, and happiness is merely a means for removing obstacles to his morality – a *permitted* means, since no one else has a right to require of me that I sacrifice my ends if these are not immoral. To seek prosperity for its own sake is not directly a duty, but indirectly it can well be a duty, that of warding off poverty insofar as this is a great temptation to vice. (*Virtue*, Introduction §V, 6:388)

The pursuit of one's own happiness is not per se a duty, but it may be the instrument for the avoidance of a condition which would lead to the violation of duty and in that sense constitute an instrument for the fulfillment of duty that ought to be employed for the sake of duty. Similarly, one might propose, the cultivation of benevolent feelings toward others might not be a requirement of duty per se, but the presence of antipathetic or aggressive feelings toward others would certainly constitute a temptation to violate one's indisputable duty of beneficence or other duty toward them; and if the cultivation of one's natural predisposition to positive feelings toward others were the only or even just one of the means available for the eradication or limitation of hostile feelings toward them, then the cultivation of such a predisposition would after all be an instrument for the fulfillment of one's duty and would be required under that description. On this account, it would be a duty to cultivate positive feelings toward others as a means to blocking negative feelings which would themselves be an incentive for morally impermissible actions.

Kant does not explicitly draw this analogy. He does say that "Virtue Requires, in the First Place, Governing Oneself" (*Virtue*, Introduction §XV, 6:407), an assertion which he expands in this way:

> Since virtue is based on inner freedom, it contains a positive command to a man, namely to bring all his capacities and inclinations under his (reason's) control, and so to rule over himself, which goes beyond forbidding himself to be governed by his feelings and inclinations (the duty of *apathy*): for unless reason holds the reins of government in its own hands, man's feelings and inclinations play the master over him. (6:408)

This forbids allowing ourselves to be governed by inclination instead of reason. But it does not forbid reason from itself using one set of inclinations to govern another. That is the model that I am suggesting here, and I do not see why Kant need have excluded it.

But one might still feel the need for a more general answer to the objection, for it may seem as if the cultivation of sentiments and inclinations as an aid to morality runs the risk of conceding them a role in the formation of intentions in actions toward others which would preclude acting out of the motive of duty alone. To answer this objection, care in the interpretation of Kant's conception of action out of the motive of duty as the sole basis of moral merit is required. If it is supposed that the object or content of the morally worthy agent's intention must, in every action, be to do his duty solely for the sake of duty, then there will indeed be a problem if any other motive for the fulfillment of duty is also present, let alone cultivated. But if the requirement of moral merit is rather interpreted as the requirement that, out of his respect for duty, an agent must always intend to do what his duty requires, or, one might also say, to do what is necessary in order to fulfill his duty, then the situation is more complicated. On this account, where the motive of duty can be conceived of as a general or, so to speak, second-order intention governing one's conduct rather than as a specific or first-order intention in every action, then one will be considered morally worthy for having the general intention always to perform one's duty and to take whatever steps are necessary to do that, including the cultivation of moral sentiments and benevolent inclinations for use on specific occasions where the mere thought of duty might not be sufficiently strong to motivate one. In other words, out of a general motive of respect for duty one could form the general policy of cultivating moral sentiments for their use on particular occasions where they might help one comply with duty, that is, perform the actions required by duty.

Again, Kant does not explicitly expound this principle. In fact, he says things which might well be thought to preclude it. Thus, in his initial characterization of duties to oneself, when he describes the *"cultivation of morality* in us" as a duty of wide obligation, he is not implying that we should think of the requirement to do our "duty *from duty,"* that is, to make "the law . . . not only the rule but also the incentive of [our] actions," as a general policy rather than a thought which must be present as part of the intention in every action;

rather, he is emphasizing that we can only try to progress to this purity of motive without ever being sure that we have reached it. Thus it remains that what we need to strive for is precisely that the thought of duty alone be the incentive in every case of action: "The law does not prescribe this inner action in the human mind but only the maxim of the action, to strive with all one's might that the thought of duty for its own sake is the sufficient incentive of every action conforming to duty" (*Virtue*, Introduction §VIII, 6:393). However, one might argue that the very fact which is the premise of Kant's argument here for the classification of moral perfection as a duty of wide rather than narrow obligation – that complete moral purity is unobtainable for us, indeed that we not flatter ourselves with the fanatical idea that we can have an entirely holy will (cf. *Virtue*, §11, 6:436) – requires the approach I have suggested. For certainly the first requirement that would follow from a general commitment to the motive of duty would be that one use every means in one's power always to act in conformity with duty, even on those occasions where as a mere human rather than a holy will one cannot be guaranteed that one will be able to do so on the strength of the "thought of duty for its own sake." The cultivation of the natural predisposition to benevolence and sympathy would be one of the means in one's power for so acting, although of course only insofar as that predisposition was governed by rational reflection on what actions duty requires or permits in given circumstances. It would therefore seem to be a consequence of the general commitment to acting out of respect for duty that one cultivate such a predisposition at least as a fallback for those situations in which one knows that, as a human rather than a holy will, one might not be able to act out of the thought of duty alone.

Before concluding this discussion of duties to oneself, we might note that we can also reach a weaker conclusion than the principle under discussion by appealing back to Kant's original distinction between moral merit and demerit. Virtue, Kant had argued by means of one of his favorite conceptual devices, is opposed to "*negative lack of virtue*" as its "*logical opposite"* but to "vice" as its *"real opposite"* (*Virtue*, Introduction §II, 6:384). Thus the first thing that virtue requires is the avoidance of vice, or the avoidance of any actions the commission of which would bring moral condemnation even if their omission brings no special praise. If the cultivation of positive sentiments toward others was an instrument for the avoidance of vicious actions toward them, then virtue would require that cultivation as a condition for avoiding vice, even before any consideration of motivation by the thought of duty alone would be in order.

Virtue, in other words, is a complicated business. Its first requirement is that one comply with, rather than violate, the external demands of duty. Although one earns no special badges of merit for such compliance, failure to so comply is vicious. If one needs to cultivate certain natural predispositions of feeling in order to help ensure such compliance, then surely virtue in general requires this, even if the specific conditions of moral praise do not. But further, it might also be argued that complying with duty out of the motive of duty, which is what brings the additional element of moral praise, can be construed as a general intention which allows for or even encourages the policy of cultivating natural dispositions to feeling, just like other natural capacities, for their usefulness on particular occasions of action. If this is right, then one can adopt a praiseworthy policy of cultivating morally beneficial sentiments out of the general motive of always acting from duty.

## Feeling and the happiness of others

At this point I will turn to the question of whether our imperfect duty of advancing the happiness of others itself contains specific grounds for the cultivation of sentiments and inclinations.

As mentioned earlier, Kant divides our duties to others into the two classes of duties of love and duties of respect (*Virtue*, §23, 6:448). This division is complex. Like the basic distinction in the treatment of duties to oneself, it is grounded on the twofold nature of man as both a natural and a moral being. Duties of love are duties directed toward the "*natural welfare*" of others, the satisfaction of their needs, and duties of respect are directed at their "*moral well-being*" or "moral contentment" (*Virtue*, Introduction §VIII, 4:393–4). Kant also uses the fundamental distinction of his metaphysics of nature, and therefore likens love and respect to attraction and repulsion: "The principle of *mutual love* admonishes men constantly to *come closer* to one another; that of the *respect* they owe one another to keep themselves at a *distance* from one another" (*Virtue*, §24, 6:449), that is, always to treat one another with the dignity due to independent rational agents. But in fact this distinction is also a distinction between perfect and imperfect duties to others, and thus clouds the principle used for the distinction between ethical and juridical duties.³³ Duties of love are duties of wide – that is, indeterminate – obligation to advance the welfare or happiness of others through beneficence, gratitude, and sympathy (*Virtue*, §28, 6:452), and thus fit the model of ethical duties as duties to adopt an end that cannot be equated with the requirement to perform specific actions under specific circumstances. The duties of respect, however, are duties to avoid injury to the dignity of fellow human beings through self-conceit expressed in the specific forms of arrogance toward and defamation and ridicule of others (*Virtue*, §41, 6:465). These duties do not merely prescribe a general policy to be adopted, but rather proscribe specific forms of behavior to others under all circumstances, and for that reason are more like perfect than imperfect duties. Kant offers no explanation of why the duties to avoid these forms of conduct are classified as ethical rather than juridical duties; one can only conjecture that since such conduct would involve primarily the expression of certain attitudes toward others rather than outright actions against them, it would not be directly amenable to coercive sanctions and for that reason cannot reasonably be made the subject of any external legislation.³⁴

The duties of respect obviously touch upon the nature of our feelings toward others, for they prohibit us from expressing or conveying negative feelings about others to those who might be injured by them. If direct ethical significance for positive feelings toward others is to be found, however, it will have to be found under the duties of love. And here in fact Kant suggests three different models for the ethical role of feelings. Duties of love are characterized in general as duties of *benevolence*. This is not to be understood simply as a feeling of "pleasure in the perfection of other men" but as the policy or "maxim of *benevolence* (practical love), which results in beneficence" (*Virtue*, §25, 6:449). That is, the duty of love requires that we adopt a general policy of doing what we can to advance the welfare or happiness of others, which general policy will result in specific beneficent acts under appropriate circumstances, circumstances which will include not only compatibility with my other duties and consistency with my own pursuit of happiness but also the specific requirement that the ends of the others which I would help them advance not be immoral themselves (*Virtue*, §25, 6:450). As we noted earlier, Kant believes that the adoption of this maxim cannot be grounded upon the antecedent presence of a feeling of love, because feeling by itself may be erratic and cannot be counted on to determine whether the ends of others are moral or not; but he also believes that the adoption of this maxim can be expected to produce such a feeling "as an aptitude of the inclination to beneficence in general" (*Virtue*, Introduction §XII, 6:402). But there are also more specific links between the duties of love and the feelings.

*Beneficence.* The first duty of love is the duty of beneficence. It is not in fact clear what is the difference between this and the general duty of benevolence, except that here Kant defines benevolence as a general attitude toward others but beneficence as the actual maxim of helping them, the role that was previously assigned to benevolence: "Benevolence is satisfaction in the happiness (well-being) of others; but beneficence is the maxim of making others' happiness one's end." Aside from this difference in terms, the only other difference in the two accounts is the explicit suggestion here of an additional reason for treating beneficence as an imperfect duty, namely the restriction that the obligation to beneficence depends upon one's means: "Everyone who has the means to do so should be *beneficent* to those in need" (*Virtue*, §29, 6:452).

Given the virtual identity of the general duty of benevolence and the specific duty of beneficence, we can assume that adherence to the specific duty, like the general one, will tend to bring a positive feeling of love toward others in its train even if it is not grounded upon it. But there is another role for feelings in the practice of beneficence, which Kant describes in his general characterization of benevolence but which must also apply to the supposedly more specific duty of beneficence. Because benevolence or beneficence is a general policy, the specific actions performed to realize it must be appropriate to the circumstances. As we have now seen, the means of the one who would help and the morality of the ends of the one who would be helped are determinants of the appropriateness of actions under this general policy. But Kant makes clear that the degree of closeness among persons is also a relevant factor. While one "can be *equally* benevolent to everyone" in merely wishing for their well-being, no one agent can in fact help everyone else equally or effectively. So some additional consideration is necessary to allow one to target one's benevolence, and here Kant suggests that antecedent feelings of love toward particular persons are perfectly appropriate criteria: "In acting I can, without violating the universality of the maxim, vary the degree greatly in accordance with the different objects of my love (one of whom concerns me more closely than another)" (*Virtue*, §28, 6:452). Although feelings of love by themselves cannot be allowed to dictate one's beneficence toward others, because one's other duties and the morality of the ends of the objects of one's help must be considered, neither can the principle of beneficence itself determine its appropriate objects. Particular attachments are called upon to play this role.

One might expect some argument for this conclusion, perhaps an argument that beneficence directed toward those to whom one already has ties of affections will be more energetically, and therefore effectively, applied. Kant offers no such argument. Perhaps he takes the point to be too obvious to need it: Since one cannot help everyone, what could possibly be wrong in helping those nearest and dearest to one first? Of course this principle itself could not be applied mechanically. The depth and urgency of the needs of all of those whom one might be able to help would have to be considered, as well as the closeness of one's attachment to them. But it is in the nature of an imperfect duty that there be no mechanical principle for making such practical decisions in the realization of the general end prescribed by the duty. Indeed, imperfect duty illustrates Kant's general insight into the problem of the application of principles: At some point in the application of principles, we must appeal to an act of judgment for which no rule can be given, for otherwise we would be doomed to an infinite regress of rules, never reaching any concrete application of our principles (see *CJ*, Preface, 5:169).

*Gratitude.* The next duty of love is the duty of gratitude. Kant comes close to explicitly describing this as a duty to have certain feelings toward particular persons standing in a particular relation to oneself (the relation, namely, of having previously been beneficent to oneself): "*Gratitude* consists in *honoring* a person because of a benefit he has rendered us. The feeling connected with this judgment is respect for the benefactor" (*Virtue*, §31, 6:454–5). It is not entirely clear that the respect or honor that Kant refers to must be conceived of as a state of feeling, for it might be interpreted as a maxim of readiness to return the favor to the benefactor on some appropriate future occasion. Yet Kant explicitly says that a grateful attitude must extend to some whom one cannot help at all, such as "one's predecessors," for instance, "the ancients, who can be regarded as our teachers" (*Virtue*, §33, 6:455). It is hard to interpret honor or respect as anything but a positive feeling, "the *cordiality* of a benevolent disposition" (*Virtue*, §33, 6:456), under these circumstances.

Thus Kant seems to recognize the possibility that specific relations to specific persons can generate an obligation to have certain kinds of feelings. He does not explain here how one can have a duty to feel, rather than to act, in a specific way. He certainly says nothing to suggest that he believes here more than anywhere else that such a feeling can simply be willed into existence. Presumably he must believe here as elsewhere that we have a natural predisposition to such a feeling, and that we can make the choice to cultivate this disposition even though we could not simply choose to have the feeling. The duty of gratitude would thus be an example of the way in which specific relations in which we find ourselves or into which we voluntarily enter can create obligations for us to do whatever we can to maintain and encourage appropriate feelings, although we cannot simply will to have such feelings if they are entirely lacking.

And how are we to understand the requirement that benevolence be repaid with gratitude? Kant's laconic exposition does not justify this requirement. We might consider a purely instrumental justification: that is, that the repayment of benevolence with gratitude will serve as a positive reinforcement for benevolence, and thus assist in the continued fulfillment of that duty. But we might also suspect a more general, if more complicated, point here. By his benevolent concern for someone else's happiness, the benefactor also makes himself worthy of his own happiness; and if he places at least a part of his happiness in the reward of gratitude for his benevolence, as is only natural, then he is worthy of that and has some right to it. This in turn places some obligation on the person who has enjoyed the benefit to have certain feelings toward his benefactor, for the sake of the latter's happiness. This would thus be a case in which a person has a duty to have certain feelings as part of his duty to advance the happiness of others, which is after all the most general characterization of imperfect duties to others.

In other words, we might think of the case of gratitude as an example of a more general requirement to advance the happiness of others by having, or at least cultivating, certain positive feelings toward them. Of course, no one has an unrestricted right to gratitude or any other form of love from any or all persons. But people may enter into specific relations with each other that raise special expectations that their happiness will be advanced, and such expectations may in turn create obligations to have certain kinds of feelings toward one another. To the extent that feelings can be affected by will, the maintenance and cultivation of such feelings on the part of those involved can then be seen as part of the imperfect duty to advance the happiness of others.

*Sympathy.* The last of the duties of love is sympathy, which Kant introduces by stating that *"Sympathetic Feeling Is Generally a Duty." "Sympathetic joy* and *sadness (sympathia moralis)"* are defined as "sensible feelings of pleasure or pain (which are therefore to be called 'aesthetic')[35] at another's state of joy or sorrow." Here Kant explicitly invokes the model of naturally occurring feelings being employed as instruments for the accomplishment of goals set by principles of duty:

> Nature has already implanted in man susceptibility to these feelings. But to use this as a means to promoting active and rational benevolence is still a particular, though only a conditional, duty. (*Virtue,* §34, 6:456)

> But while it is not itself a duty to share the sufferings (as well as the joys) of others, it is a duty to sympathize actively in their fate; and to this end it is therefore an indirect duty to cultivate the compassionate natural (aesthetic) feelings in us, and to make use of them as so many means to sympathy based on moral principles and the feeling appropriate to them. (*Virtue,* §35, 6:457)

Here Kant plainly argues that while our direct duty, falling within the sphere of pure activity, is to adopt the principle of benevolence and take actions in accordance with it, the cultivation of naturally available feelings of sympathy will be a means for successful compliance with this requirement and is therefore also to be willed.

How exactly does the occurrence of sympathetic feelings serve as a means for the fulfillment of the duty of benevolence? Kant's answer to this question must be gleaned from his illustration:

> It is therefore a duty not to avoid the places where the poor who lack the most basic necessities are to be found but rather to seek them out, and not to shun sick-rooms or debtors' prisons and so forth in order to avoid sharing painful feelings one may not be able to resist. For this is still one of the impulses that nature has implanted in us to do what the representation of duty alone would not accomplish. (*Virtue*, §35, 6:457)

One might be inclined to read this as just another suggestion of the way in which feelings can be called upon to strengthen the resolve of duty. However, I think it is more natural to read Kant as here suggesting that our natural inclination to sympathy can be used as an instrument for the discovery of what actions need to be taken in order to realize our general policy of benevolence. We are to visit places of suffering, bringing along our predisposition to sympathy as a pair of moral eyes, the painful sensations in which will alert us to the need for action. In other words, Kant appears to be suggesting that the principle of duty can furnish us with an abstract rule for action, but that in the application of general rules we must rely upon the examples provided by our feelings. Just as concepts without empirical intuitions are empty (A 51/B 75), so are moral principles without sympathetic feelings. Of course, just as intuitions without concepts are also blind, so are feelings without principles. Feelings always need the guidance of principles, but principles without feelings cannot readily lead us to any particular actions.

*Love of humankind.* Kant concludes the discussion of the three duties of love with a Schillerian paean to love of humankind:

> Would it not be better for the well-being of the world generally if human morality were limited to duties of right, fulfilled

with the utmost conscientiousness, and benevolence were considered morally indifferent? It is not so easy to see what effect this would have on man's happiness. But at least a great moral adornment, love of man, would be missing from the world. Love of man is, accordingly, required by itself, in order to present the world as a beautiful moral whole in its full perfection, even if no account is taken of advantages (of happiness). (*Virtue*, §35, 6:458)

This might be interpreted, like Schiller's conception of grace, as placing an aesthetic requirement on morality that is to some extent independent of the strict requirements of duty, something that adds beauty as well as rectitude to our lives. But the three duties of love that we have just analyzed have suggested that the connection between duty and feeling is more intimate than that. Feelings of closeness to others can appropriately be used to delimit the sphere of otherwise un-limited, and therefore impracticable, imperfect duties; posi-tive feelings of one person toward another may be a part of the happiness of the latter which the former may have a duty to advance under appropriate circumstances; and our feel-ings of moral sympathy may be an essential instrument for the application of general principles of duty to the circum-stances we encounter in the particular circumstances of our lives. In all of these cases, the mere presence of feeling is never the sole ground of our moral principles or motive to their fulfillment. The natural predispositions to feeling must always be employed under the guidance and motivation of the principle of duty. But the cultivation of such feeling is not simply an aesthetically gratifying natural consequence of the fulfillment of duty; it is an essential part of the fulfillment of duty itself.

*Friendship.* At this point we have seen that Kant's metaphys-ics of agency certainly leaves room for the possibility that our noumenal choice to act out of duty rather than self-love can affect our feelings as well as the phenomenal manifestation of our reason, although psychology may suggest that this influence is more typically manifested in the cultivation of natural predispositions to feeling rather than the creation of feelings *ab novo;* and we have seen how the nature of our duties to both ourselves and others can mandate the cultivation of various sorts of feelings as both a means to the fulfillment of duty and even as a part of happiness, particularly the happiness of others, which is an explicit object of duty. At this point the argument of this chapter is completed. I will conclude, however, with a brief comment on Kant's theory of friendship, the subject of a brief but rich discussion, in the *Doctrine of Virtue,* in which many of Kant's views about duty and feeling come together.

Kant concludes the "Elements" of the *Doctrine of Virtue* with a consideration of the *"Most Intimate Union of Love with Respect in Friendship"* (*Virtue*, §46, 6:469), the placement of which does not make it clear whether the discussion of friendship is the conclusion of the discussion of duties toward others only or the conclusion of the treatment of duties toward both oneself and others. This ambiguity is entirely appropriate, since friendship involves elements of both. On the one hand, Kant posits a duty to friendship which is part of the duty toward the well-being of others: One of the ways in which people can realize the indeterminate ideal of advancing the happiness of others is by entering into relations of mutual love and respect with other persons whose well-being then becomes of special interest to them (and vice versa, of course):

> *Friendship* (considered in its perfection) is the union of two persons through equal mutual love and respect. It is easy to see that this is an ideal of each participating and sharing sympathetically in the other's well-being through the morally good will that unites them, and even though it does not produce the complete happiness of life, the adoption of this idea in their disposition toward each other makes them deserving of happiness: hence men have a duty of friendship. (*Virtue*, §46, 6:469)

On the other hand, Kant also suggests that the need for friendship arises from each person's need to share his deepest thoughts with at least one another person trustworthy enough to be entrusted with them. This need is not just a casual inclination but intimately connected with one's very status as a rational being, so satisfaction of it has something of the nature of a duty to oneself and is not a mere object of one's own happiness (*Virtue*, §47, 6:471–2). For both of these reasons, then, one has something like a duty to cultivate friendships. But friendship, even in the case of the latter, which Kant explicitly calls "moral friendship," cannot be grounded on principle alone; there must be natural feelings of mutual inclination to ground friendship. At the same time, Kant stresses that friendship cannot be left to depend on feeling alone:

> Although it is sweet to feel in such possession of each other as approaches fusion into one person, friendship is something so delicate (*teneritas amicitiae*) that it is never for a moment safe from interruptions if it is allowed to rest on feelings, and if this mutual sympathy and self-surrender are not subjected to principles or rules preventing excessive familiarity and limiting mutual love by requirements of respect, . . . the love in friendship cannot be an affect; for emotion is blind in its choice, and after a while it goes up in smoke. (*Virtue*, §46, 6:471)

As always, Kant's position is that principles are not complete without feelings, but that feelings must be both cultivated and governed under the guidance of principle. Principles by themselves cannot constitute the perfection of ourselves or the happiness of our friends without tender feelings, but feelings themselves cannot be relied upon to keep and preserve even our deepest attachments without the firm hand of principles behind them.

This position, finally, can provide a valuable corrective to one of the most notorious objections that has recently been lodged against Kant's view of duty and feeling. I have in mind Bernard Williams's well-known appropriation of Charles Fried's example of the man who finds himself forced with a choice between saving his wife and another person in equal peril and who is accused of having "one thought too many" if he first reflects on what his duty requires and permits before he lets his love lead him to save his wife.[36] Others have rightly argued that Kant does not require the man in this position to take the time to reflect upon general principles of duty before acting to save his wife; the Kantian motive of duty functions as a "limiting condition" on the moral agent's actions, not necessarily as part of his conscious thought process in every case of action.[37] But this is not Kant's only point; his discussion of friendship makes it clear that the principle of duty must not only serve as a limiting condition on all attachments of feeling but may have to support even the most intimate such attachments. The Fried–Williams case makes things too easy for itself by providing no description of the other person. This allows us to imagine that the rescuer is faced with the choice between saving his wife and someone to whom he is otherwise quite indifferent, say an unattractive middle-aged male. But what if the other person facing drowning is a younger and prettier woman than his wife, whom he had been eyeing admiringly throughout the cruise leading up to the present shipwreck? If the man were simply to act on his immediate feelings here, he might not rescue his wife at all. As she went under for the last time in this case, his wife could certainly accuse him of having one thought too few, and in the long run the husband himself might come to believe that not only duty but even his own happiness required him to save his wife. Not only in friendship but in marriage and every other personal relationship, our feelings are fragile and liable to interruption, and must always be governed as well as cultivated in accordance with principle. This is certainly one final lesson of Kant's complicated, but by no means unfeeling, examination of the relations between duty and feeling.

# Notes

## INTRODUCTION

1. The patron saint of deconstructionism, Jacques Derrida, has addressed himself to the *Critique of Judgment* several times, especially in his essays "Parergon," in *The Truth in Painting*, translated by Geoff Bennington and Ian McLeod (Chicago: University of Chicago Press, 1987), pp. 15–147, and "Economimesis," *Diacritics* 11 (1981): 3–25. Derrida's arguments are often wretched. In "Parergon," for instance, he argues that because Kant cannot succeed in mechanically distinguishing between the essential and inessential in art, even including the picture frame, in the case of painting (*parerga*, as Kant calls the frame at *CJ*, §14, 5:226), he can make no meaningful distinction between art and what is outside of art at all. This is just the crudest form of positivism, assuming that if there is no mechanical way to make the distinction between essential and inessential for all cases, then there is no way to make it in any particular case. Nevertheless, Derrida's essays have been very influential.

2. An interesting recent essay by Donald W. Crawford has also suggested that Kant's aesthetic theory should be viewed as a two-tiered structure, with a narrower "critique of taste," focusing more strictly on the question of the universal validity of judgements of taste, being embedded in a broader "critique of judgment," focusing on broader questions about the purposiveness of aesthetic experience itself; Crawford also suggests that this two-stage structure describes the historical development of the *Critique of Judgment*, with the critique of taste having been central to Kant's initial conception of the book, in

late 1787, and the broader issues of purposiveness having entered into the composition of the work only subsequently. See his essay "Kant's Principles of Judgment and Taste" in *Proceedings of the Sixth International Kant Congress*, vol. 2, pt. 2, ed. Gerhard Funke and Thomas M. Seebohm (Washington, D.C.: Center for Advanced Research in Phenomenology and University Press of America, 1989), pp. 281–92. I will not commit myself here to Crawford's historical thesis, although it does seem to me that much of Kant's broadening of the narrower theory of taste, as defended in the "Analytic of the Beautiful" (especially §§1–22), is meant to make up for the shortcomings of the moral epistemology and psychology of Kant's second *Critique*, the *Critique of Practical Reason* (see this volume, Chapter 1). And it is certainly plausible to suppose that Kant did not think of those problems immediately upon turning to the *Critique of Judgment* after completing the second *Critique* in 1787 but needed some further period of reflection for that purpose. I will stress the link to morality in the second stage of the theory more than Crawford does and indeed, as just suggested, see the chronological thesis as most plausible in light of the developments in Kant's moral views represented by that aspect of the *Critique of Judgment*.

3.  See Kant's letters to Reinhold of December 28 and 31, 1787, at 10:513–16. (For abbreviations of works frequently cited in the notes and text of the present volume, see the "Note on Citations.")

4.  This text is contained in the *Akademie* edition at 8:184–251; see also the note at 8:492–5. An English translation and commentary is available in Henry E. Allison, *The Kant–Eberhard Controversy* (Baltimore: Johns Hopkins University Press, 1973).

5.  For further discussion of these problems, see my *Kant and the Claims of Taste* (Cambridge, Mass.: Harvard University Press, 1979), chaps. 2 and 4.

6.  Kant made it available to his early commentator and publicist Jakob Sigismund Beck, who used extracts from it in his 1793–4 *vade mecum* to Kant, *Erläuternder Auszug aus den critischen Schriften des Herrn Prof. Kant*, 2 vols. (Riga: Hartknoch, 1793–4).

7.  For a fuller chronology of Kant's intellectual career and works, the reader may see my introduction to the *Cambridge Companion to Kant* (Cambridge: Cambridge University Press, 1992), pp. 1–25. A survey of Kant's intellectual development up to

1781 is provided in the chapter in that book by Frederick C. Beiser (pp. 26–61), and an overview of Kant's aesthetics is offered there by Eva Schaper (pp. 367–93).

8.  R. K. Elliott, "The Unity of Kant's 'Critique of Aesthetic Judgment,'" *British Journal of Aesthetics* 8 (1968): 244–59; Donald W. Crawford, *Kant's Aesthetic Theory* (Madison: University of Wisconsin Press, 1974).

9.  See also my reviews of Eva Schaper's *Studies in Kant's Aesthetics* (Edinburgh: Edinburgh University Press, 1979), in *Philosophical Review* 90 (1981): 429–36, and Jens Kulenkampff's *Kants Logik des ästhetischen Urteils* (Frankfurt am Main: Klostermann, 1978), in *Journal of Aesthetics and Art Criticism* 40 (1982): 212–17.

10. By a "judgment of taste," Kant means the proposition or the assertion of the proposition that a particular object is, for example, beautiful. Such a judgment is made or at least justified on the basis of reflection on the origin of the pleasure one feels in the object, when such reflection suggests that this feeling of pleasure is not merely a physiological response to the stimulus provided by sensation of the object but is the product of the harmonious reaction of the higher cognitive faculties of imagination and understanding to the perception of the object. Kant confuses the reader by suggesting that the process which leads from this feeling of pleasure, as well as that which leads from the feeling of pleasure to the assertion of the judgment of taste, are both acts of "reflective judgment." There are good reasons for thinking of both of these as expressing a reflective use of judgment, but it should be clear that the enjoyment of an object, on the one hand, and the judgment that other persons should also enjoy it, on the other, are, at least in principle, psychologically and epistemologically distinct acts of mind.

11. See also the similar structure employed by Anthony Savile, *Aesthetic Reconstructions: The Seminal Writings of Lessing, Kant, and Schiller*, Aristotelian Society Series, no. 8 (Oxford: Blackwell, 1987), pp. 109–27.

12. More properly, an aesthetic judgment of reflection, as contrasted with an aesthetic judgment of sense. The latter, for instance what Kant subsequently calls a "judgment on the agreeable," is a mere report of the physiological fact that one has been agreeably stimulated by contact with or consump-

tion of a certain object; the former does not merely report a physiological fact but also the origination of one's pleasure in a reflective involvement of faculties of cognition, and therefore can give rise to rationally justifiable claims about the appropriate responses of others besides oneself. See *FI*, §VIII, 20:223–4, and *CJ*, §3, 5:206.

13. Kant did cause a great deal of confusion for subsequent commentators by often putting this point as if concepts could be no part of the proper object of judgments of taste or no part of the response to them, thus suggesting that only purely perceptual form could be the object of a pure judgment of taste (e.g., *CJ*, §4, 5:207). This creates no end of difficulty for the interpretation and indeed for Kant's own exposition of his conception of the response to works of art, which paradigmatically involve the illustration of some leading concept called an "idea of reason" (*CJ*, §49, 5:317–18). All that Kant's basic analysis of the concept of an aesthetic judgment requires, however, is that our evaluative response to a beautiful object not be entailed by the subsumption of the object under any determinate concept, which does not exclude the possibility that harmony between perceptual form and conceptual content in the object is itself part of what we respond to in the way next to be characterized. See my article "Formalism and the Theory of Expression in Kant's Aesthetics," *Kant-Studien* 68 (1977): 46–70, and *Kant and the Claims of Taste*, chap. 6, especially pp. 237–48.

14. As was stressed by Karl Ameriks in "Kant and the Objectivity of Taste," *British Journal of Aesthetics* 23 (1983): 3–17. This does not, however, mean, as Ameriks suggested there, that there is no special problem about the *justification* of aesthetic judgments. Quite the contrary: The problem about judgments of taste is precisely that they raise the same claims to intersubjective acceptability as other empirical judgments do, without the apparent justification offered to the latter by well-established and widely accepted mathematical or empirical methods of confirmation.

15. For my argument that the two "modalities" of quantity and necessity explicate the same requirement of rationally expected intersubjective agreement under appropriate circumstances, see *Kant and the Claims of Taste*, pp. 160–7.

16. Even where that manifold might include concepts as part of its content, as in the case of aesthetic ideas in a work of artistic

genius. I have discussed this point in a variety of places, beginning with "Formalism and the Theory of Expression in Kant's Aesthetics."

17. Donald Crawford has objected to this kind of account of Kant's explanation of the pleasure of aesthetic response, on the ground that since it postulates the satisfaction of only necessary rather than sufficient conditions for the production of knowledge it "does not thereby guarantee knowledge," so "its attainment by itself need not result in pleasure"; "Kant's Principles of Judgment and Taste," in *Proceedings of the Sixth International Kant Congress*, vol. 2, pt. 2, ed. Gerhard Funke and Thomas M. Seebohm (Washington, D.C.: Center for Advanced Research and University Press of America, 1989), pp. 281–92 at p. 286. There must therefore be the satisfaction of some further, not merely cognitive purposes in the case of both natural and artistic beauty, he infers (p. 289). But this appears to miss Kant's point that it is precisely because the harmony of imagination and understanding is not felt to derive from any guaranteed source of knowledge that it is particularly pleasurable; if the unification of the manifold presented by a beautiful object were thought to contain sufficient conditions for knowledge, there would not be any ground for a specially noticeable pleasure in it. And as we will see in our discussion of the further purposes Kant finds to be satisfied in asesthetic experience, they presuppose this basic account of the origin of aesthetic pleasure (see especially Chapter 7).

18. Although judgments on the sublime make the same claim on the agreement of others as do judgments on the beautiful (*CJ*, §29, 5:265–6), Kant also claims that they do not need a transcendental deduction, because they do not ascribe a property to external objects but rather to the mind of the subject (*CJ*, §30, 5:279–80). This is a confusion on his part, for in judgments claiming universal validity on both the beautiful and the sublime there is a claim to know the minds of others on the basis of one's own response to an object that needs a theoretical justification, which is clearly the task Kant undertakes in his transcendental "deduction of judgments of taste" (*CJ*, §38, 5:289–90). See also *Kant and the Claims of Taste*, chap. 7, especially pp. 260–8.

19. See *Kant and the Claims of Taste*, chap. 8, pp. 288–97, and chap. 9, pp. 319–24.

20. *Kant and Fine Art: An Essay on Kant and the Philosophy of Fine Art and Culture* (Oxford: Clarendon Press, 1986).

21. *Kant's Aesthetics: The Roles of Form and Expression* (Lanham: University Press of America, 1986).

22. *Kant's Aesthetic Theory*, p. 149.

23. See *Kant and the Claims of Taste*, chap. 11, pp. 353–4. Rogerson adduces linguistic evidence to demonstrate that there is a normative demand, and not mere epistemological prediction, in Kant's analysis of the judgment of taste's claim to intersubjective agreement (*Kant's Aesthetics*, pp. 84–7). I never denied that there is, but only denied that this normative aspect can provide additional grounds for expecting agreement as opposed to presupposing a prior proof of the rationality of expecting agreement.

24. For example, see *Kant and the Claims of Taste*, chap. 11, pp. 365, 371–2, 386–7. Moreover, I would now add, since it is not Kant but only his commentators who have found the epistemological deduction of agreement in judgments of taste wanting, there is no reason to suppose that Kant himself had any intention of appealing to the connection with morality to complete the task of justifying the rational expectation of agreement in judgments of taste, which he clearly supposed had been completed prior to his major discussions of this issue. The official "deduction of judgments of taste" is offered in *CJ*, §38, which is explicitly focused on the question of the basis for a rational expectation of intersubjective agreement in aesthetic judgments; the idea of demanding agreement in such judgments as a "sort of duty" is not made explicit until §40, and the major grounds for thinking of taste as anything like a moral duty are not adduced until §42 and §59. So it seems fair to conclude that Kant may have intended the connection to morality to bear on the rational basis for demanding agreement in taste but not on the rational basis for expecting such agreement and that he thought the former issue could seriously be raised only after the latter had been resolved.

25. See *Kant and the Claims of Taste*, chap. 11, pp. 383–6.

26. *Kant and Fine Art*, pp. 159–60, where the *sensus communis* is treated as a normative, and presumably moral, idea.

27. See *Kant and Fine Art* (for instance, pp. 172–5).

28. The same criticism also applies to the interpretation of Kant's theory of taste offered by Howard Caygill, *Art of Judgment*

(Oxford: Blackwell, 1989), who similarly looks to actual social agreements for the completion of the deduction of aesthetic judgment, in an interpretation that, throughout, makes Kant far more preoccupied with historical traditions of taste than he really was (see, for example, pp. 348, 353, 363, 381).

29. See *Kant's Aesthetics*, chap. 2, e.g., p. 34.
30. *Kant's Aesthetics*, chap. 4, pp. 66–7.
31. *Kant's Aesthetics*, chap. 4, pp. 79–91.
32. *Kant's Aesthetics*, chap. 6, p. 154.
33. *Aesthetic Reconstructions*, pp. 169–72.
34. *Aesthetic Reconstructions*, pp. 185–6.
35. *Aesthetic Reconstructions*, p. 175.
36. *The Ideology of the Aesthetic* (Oxford: Blackwell, 1989), pp. 83–4.
37. *Ideology of the Aesthetic*, pp. 97–8.
38. Perhaps Eagleton's simplistic interpretation of Kantian ethics ought to be excused, for even within the literature of professional philosophy, this charge, originating with Hegel, has continued to be advocated by many writers. See, for instance, Lawrence Blum, *Friendship, Altruism, and Morality* (London: Routledge & Kegan Paul, 1980), and Victor J. Seidler, *Kant, Respect and Injustice: The Limits of Liberal Moral Theory* (London: Routledge & Kegan Paul, 1986). However, this view of Kant has also been ably refuted by many writers, including Mary J. Gregor, *The Laws of Freedom: A Study of Kant's Method of Applying the Categorical Imperative in the "Metaphysik der Sitten"* (Oxford: Blackwell, 1963); Onora O'Neill in *Faces of Hunger: An Essay on Poverty, Development, and Justice* (London: Allen & Unwin, 1986), and *Constructions of Reason: Explorations of Kant's Practical Philosophy* (Cambridge: Cambridge University Press, 1989), especially chaps. 8 and 11; and Barbara Herman, "Mutual Aid and Respect for Persons," *Ethics* 94 (1984): 577–602.
39. See especially *Groundwork*, 4:429–30.
40. See *Right*, §D, 6:231.

CHAPTER 1

1. I focus on this work, the metaphysics of morals in Kant's own sense, in Chapters 9 and 10.
2. This formula has an obvious affinity with Christian Wolff's rule "Do what makes yourself and the condition of yourself and

others more perfect." Wolff's perfectionism is readmitted into the framework of Kantian ethics in the form of imperfect duty.

3. The connection between feeling and virtue is explored in detail in Chapter 10.

4. Prior to this remark, Kant makes the distinct argument that because the feeling of the superiority of the moral agent to hindrances of sensibility is akin to the response to the beautiful or, even more, the sublime, it can itself be pressed into service for the aesthetic representation of the "lawfulness of action out of duty" without reducing such lawfulness to a matter of feeling (*CJ*, §29 General Remark, 5:267). This may suggest that morality stands in need of some sensible representation, but it does not imply, as ideas we will consider shortly do, that the aesthetic realm offers such a representation; it suggests rather that moral feeling is itself the sensible representation of the moral determination of the will, in part because of its analogy with the feelings involved in purely aesthetic response.

5. In his translation, J. C. Meredith writes of the art of "how to bridge the difference between the more cultured and ruder sections of the community" (*The Critique of Aesthetic Judgment* [Oxford: Clarendon Press, 1911], p. 227), thus suggesting an explicit reference back to Kant's original idea of bridging the gulf between nature and freedom, now seen as being accomplished through the development of culture. However, Kant does not use the word *brücken* or any derivative of it here, so this lovely echo is not to be found in his text.

6. "Capacity": Kant has *Vermögen*. I usually translate this term as "faculty," to capture its active rather than passive sense, but here the quantitative context requires something else.

7. Kant's conception of the sublime is anatomized more fully later in this volume, especially in Chapters 6 and 7.

8. Issues about the nature of artistic intentionality are explored in more detail in Chapters 7 and 8.

9. These two distinct aspects of morality that can be symbolized by beauty, namely the fact of freedom and its metaphysical or supersensible basis, have also been recognized in the treatment by A. C. Genova, "Aesthetic Justification and Systematic Unity in Kant's Third Critique," in *Proceedings of the Sixth International Kant Congress*, ed. Gerhard Funke and Thomas M. Seebohm (Washington, D.C.: Center for Advanced Re-

search in Phenomenology and University Press of America, 1989), vol. 2, pt. 2, pp. 292–309.

10. Through the formal parallels between aesthetic and moral judgment, Kant seems to suppose, the object of aesthetic judgment – i.e., beauty – is invested with the symbolic significance of representing the basis of morality. Kant does not linger over this point but instead quickly turns to symbolic relations between more specific aesthetic qualities and more specific moral conceptions or traits of character in general: "We call buildings or trees majestic and magnificent, or fields laughing and gay" (§59, 5:354). But Kant has little interest in any detailed analysis of such forms of expression.

11. In fact, Kant's solution to the antinomy of teleological judgment treats the mechanical as well as the purposive view of nature as merely regulative (*CJ*, §70, 5:387). This must imply that the completely deterministic conception of nature characterized in the *Critique of Pure Reason* is not something that we can literally impose on our experience of nature but rather, even if it is a necessary condition of the unity of our experience, it is still only a regulative ideal in our investigation of nature (although this may mean that the unity of experience itself must then also be treated as a regulative ideal rather than a constitutive principle). In this regard, the solution to the antinomy of teleological judgment is of a piece with Kant's treatment of the ideal of systematicity in the introduction to the *Critique of Judgment* and, together with that discussion, represents a fundamental revision in Kant's conception of the metaphysical status of the transcendental affinity of all appearances in the *Critique of Pure Reason*. See my "Reason and Reflective Judgment: Kant on the Significance of Systematicity," *Nous* 24 (1990): 17–43, and "Kant's Conception of Empirical Law," *Proceedings of the Aristotelian Society*, supplementary vol. 64 (Oxford: Blackwell, 1990), pp. 221–42.

12. This question has also been raised by Savile, *Aesthetic Reconstructions*, p. 175.

CHAPTER 2

1. See especially Jerome Stolnitz, "On the Significance of Lord Shaftesbury in Modern Aesthetic Theory," *Philosophical Quar-*

*terly* 11 (1961): 97–113, and "On the Origins of 'Aesthetic Disinterestedness,' " *Journal of Aesthetics and Art Criticism* 20 (1961): 131–43.

2. *Critique of Judgment* (1790), §§1–5.
3. The classical expression of this view is found in Edward Bullough, " 'Psychical Distance' as a Factor in Art and an Aesthetic Principle," in *Aesthetics: Lectures and Essays*, ed. Elizabeth M. Wilkinson (1912; Stanford: Stanford University Press, 1957), pp. 91–130.
4. *The Moralists*, pt. III, §II, in Anthony [Ashley Cooper, third] earl of Shaftesbury, *Characteristics of Men, Manners, Opinions, Times*, 2 vols., ed. John M. Robertson (Indianapolis: Bobbs-Merrill, 1964), vol. 2, pp. 3–151; quotation at pp. 136–7. See also *An Inquiry Concerning Virtue or Merit*, bk. I, pt. II, §III, in *Characteristics*, vol. 1, pp. 237–338, at p. 251: "The case is the same in the mental or moral subjects as in the ordinary bodies or common objects of sense. The shapes, motion, colours, and proportions of these latter being presented to the eye, there necessarily results a beauty or deformity, according to the different measure, arrangement, and disposition of their several parts. So in behavior and actions . . ."
5. *Moralists*, pt. III, §II, in *Characteristics*, pp. 126–7, hereafter cited as *Moralists*.
6. *Moralists*, pt. III, §II, p. 132.
7. *Moralists*, pt. III, §II, pp. 142–3.
8. Shaftesbury, "Miscellaneous Reflections," in *Miscellany III*, chap. 2, in *Characteristics*, vol. 2, p. 267.
9. "Miscellaneous Reflections," pp. 268–9.
10. Francis Hutcheson, *An Inquiry Concerning Beauty, Order, Harmony, Design*, 4th ed., ed. Peter Kivy (1738; the Hague: Nijhoff, 1973). Preface, p. 27.
11. *Inquiry*, Preface, p. 25. The word "private" was added in the fourth edition (see note 31 in the present chapter).
12. *Inquiry*, Preface, p. 24.
13. *Inquiry*, Preface, p. 25.
14. *Inquiry*, Preface, p. 24.
15. Although he does not say so, this is presumably why Peter Kivy entitled his study of Hutcheson's aesthetic theory *The Seventh Sense* (New York: Franklin, 1976): The sense of beauty is numerically distinct from the sense of virtue, which is the sixth sense, after the customary five external senses.

16. *Inquiry,* §I, ¶I, p. 30.
17. *Inquiry,* §I, ¶VI, pp. 31–2.
18. *Inquiry,* §I, ¶VI, p. 32.
19. *Inquiry,* §I, ¶VIII, pp. 33–4.
20. *Inquiry,* §I, ¶XI, p. 35.
21. *Inquiry,* §I, ¶¶XII–XIII, p. 36.
22. Alexander Gerard and Lord Kames, to whom I return later in this chapter, both accept Hutcheson's distinction without revision; one could argue that Kant's distinction between "free" and "dependent" beauty (*CJ,* §16) is still influenced by it.
23. *Inquiry,* §I, ¶XVI, p. 39.
24. *Inquiry,* §II, ¶III, p. 40.
25. *Inquiry,* §II, ¶III, pp. 40–1. For a criticism of Hutcheson's supposition that uniformity and variety are logically distinct properties that can vary independently, see Kivy, *Seventh Sense,* pp. 95–6.
26. *Inquiry,* §V, ¶XIX, pp. 71–2.
27. *Inquiry,* §VIII, ¶II, pp. 91–2.
28. This is a very different account of the motivation of eighteenth-century aesthetic theory from the one recently offered by Terry Eagleton in *The Ideology of the Aesthetic* (Oxford: Blackwell, 1989). He views the emphasis on consensus or unanimity of feeling as arising from disinterestedness, in characteristic theories by British writers beginning with Shaftesbury, as an ideological effort to paper over the rifts in British society and, in particular, to mask the striving for hegemony over other classes on the part of the protocapitalist bourgeoisie. I see no reason to cast such doubts on the motives of these theorists. To be sure, most came from families of locally significant landowners (Shaftesbury being the only one from a truly powerful family) or clerics, although it would be difficult to find many eighteenth-century British writers who did not. I believe that writers such as Hume, and ultimately Kant, recognized that it was unrealistic to look to politics to re-create the (at least supposed) feelings of community associated with the lost religiosity of earlier centuries, and indeed dangerous to do so, and that they were thoughtfully confining attempts to create human community (rather than a mere rule of law) to noncoercive arenas such as the realm of taste.
29. *Alciphron or the Minute Philosopher,* ed. T. E. Jessop, in *The Works of George Berkeley Bishop of Cloyne,* 9 vols., ed. A. A. Luce

and T. E. Jessop (London: Nelson, 1950), Dialogue III, vol. 3, p. 124.

30. *Alciphron*, Dialogue III, p. 127.

31. *An Inquiry into the Original of our Ideas of Beauty and Virtue*, 4th, rev., ed. (London: D. Midwinter et. al., 1738), following p. 304. Unfortunately this appendix is not included by Kivy in the sole modern edition of the *Inquiry*.

32. David Hume, *Essays Moral, Political, and Literary* (Oxford: Oxford University Press, 1963), p. 238.

33. Hume's published works contain no reference to Berkeley's *Alciphron*, although they certainly contain references to Berkeley's views on abstract ideas and other themes of his earlier works. But it would hardly be surprising if Hume was familiar with the work, published when he was twenty-one and already deeply, indeed feverishly, involved with philosophy; indeed, it would be astonishing if he had not known it.

34. *A Treatise of Human Nature;* originally ed. L. A. Selby-Bigge; rev. P. H. Nidditch (Oxford: Clarendon Press, 1978), p. 299.

35. *Treatise*, p. 299.

36. *Treatise*, p. 617. The word *"species"* here is used in its medieval sense of "form" or "aspect," not in its modern sense of "taxonomic type." I will leave it in italics to make the distinction clear.

37. *Treatise*, p. 299.

38. *An Enquiry Concerning the Principles of Morals*, 3rd ed., originally ed. L. A. Selby-Bigge, rev. P. H. Nidditch (Oxford: Clarendon Press, 1975), pp. 244–5.

39. See *Treatise*, Introduction (e.g., pp. xvi, xviii).

40. *Treatise*, p. 590.

41. *Treatise*, p. 364.

42. *Treatise*, p. 364.

43. *Treatise*, pp. 576–7.

44. See, e.g., *Treatise*, pp. 209, 215.

45. *Treatise*, pp. 584–5.

46. *Treatise*, pp. 364–5.

47. "Of the Standard of Taste," p. 246.

48. See Hume's famous claims that reason "is and only ought to be the slave of the passions" (*Treatise*, pp. 415–16) and that it is "perfectly inert" and thus "can never be the source of [an] active principle" (pp. 457–8).

49. Norman Kemp Smith long ago stressed the importance of the

influence of Hutcheson on Hume; see his *Philosophy of David Hume* (London: Macmillan, 1941), pp. 23–51. But he does not mention that Hume's substitution of the imagination for the Hutchesonian conception of the senses is necessary in order to make plausible Hume's radical generalization of the sensory model to the most fundamental beliefs of metaphysics as well as morality.

50. *A Philosophical Enquiry into the Origin of our Ideas of the Sublime and the Beautiful,* ed. James T. Boulton (London: Routledge & Kegan Paul, 1958), pp. 26–7.

51. *Enquiry,* pt. III, §VI, p. 105.

52. Burke distinguishes between "delight," as the feeling produced by a remission of pain or the absence of expected pain, and "pleasure," as an entirely positive state requiring no antecedent pain; he categorizes the experience of the sublime as one of delight and that of beauty as one of pleasure because the former (but not the latter) is a response to objects which are potentially or apparently – but, in the circumstances, not actually – dangerous (*Enquiry,* pt. I, §§II–IV and VII). This refinement need not concern us here.

53. See any standard source on Pufendorf, such as Alfred Dufour, "Pufendorf," in *The Cambridge History of Political Thought: 1450–1700,* ed. J. H. Burns (Cambridge: Cambridge University Press, 1991), pp. 561–88, especially p. 569, or J. B. Schneewind, in *Moral Philosophy from Montaigne to Kant,* 2 vols. (Cambridge: Cambridge University Press, 1990), vol. 1, pp. 156–82.

54. *Enquiry,* pt. I, §VI, p. 38.

55. *Enquiry,* pt. I, §XVIII, p. 51.

56. *Enquiry,* pt. I, §VIII, p. 40.

57. *Enquiry,* pt. III, §I, p. 91.

58. *Enquiry,* pt. III, §XV, p. 115.

59. *Enquiry,* pt. I, §XII, p. 44.

60. *Enquiry,* pt. III, §§II–VI.

61. *Enquiry,* "Introduction on Taste," p. 22.

62. Alexander Gerard, *An Essay on Taste* (London and Edinburgh: Millar, Kincaid, & Bell, 1759; reprint, Yorkshire: Scolar Press, 1971), pt. I, pp. 3–74.

63. *Essay on Taste,* pt. III, §I, p. 161n.

64. *Essay on Taste,* pt. III, §I, p. 162n.

65. *Essay on Taste,* pt. III, §I, pp. 162–3.

66. *Essay on Taste,* pt. I, §III, p. 31.

67. *Essay on Taste,* pt. I, §III, p. 38.
68. *Essay on Taste,* pt. I, §III, p. 42.
69. *Essay on Taste,* pt. I, §III, p. 39.
70. *Essay on Taste,* pt. I, §III, p. 31.
71. *Essay on Taste,* pt. I, §III, p. 37.
72. *Essay on Taste,* pt. III, §I, p. 163n.
73. *Essay on Taste,* pt. III, §VI, p. 202.
74. Henry Home of Kames, *Elements of Criticism,* ed. James R. Boyd (New York: Barnes, 1856), p. 7.
75. *Elements of Criticism,* chap. 1, p. 35.
76. *Elements of Criticism,* chap. 2, pt. I, §I, pp. 38–9.
77. *Elements of Criticism,* chap. 2, pt. I, §I, p. 40.
78. *Elements of Criticism,* Introduction, p. 28.
79. *Elements of Criticism,* chap. 3, p. 116.
80. See, for instance, his 1684 essay *Meditations on Knowledge, Truth, and Ideas,* in Gottfried Wilhelm Leibniz, *Philosphical Papers and Letters,* ed. and trans. Leory E. Loemker, 2nd ed. (Dordrecht: Reidel, 1969), pp. 291–4, especially p. 291.
81. Leibniz, "Remarks on Shaftesbury" (1712), in Loemker, p. 634.
82. See the *Monadology,* §58, in Loemker, p. 648.
83. *Vernünfftige Gedancken von Gott, der Welt, und der Seele des Menschen,* "new edition" (Halle: Renger, 1751), §278.
84. *Vernünfftige Gedancken,* §404; see also §§414, 417.
85. See *Vernünfftige Gedancken,* §152–3.
86. *Vernünfftige Gedancken,* §404.
87. *Vernünfftige Gedancken,* §423.
88. *Vernünfftige Gedancken,* §432.
89. Johann Christoph Gottsched, *Versuch einer critischen Dichtkunst vor die Deutschen,* in Gottsched, *Schriften zur Literatur,* ed. Horst Steinmetz (Stuttgart: Reclam, 1972), p. 62.
90. *Critischen Dichtkunst,* pp. 64–5.
91. *Critischen Dichtkunst,* p. 63.
92. *Critischen Dichtkunst,* p. 70.
93. Baumgarten has recently been receiving more scholarly attention than in the past. In addition to the useful commentary and partial translation of the *Aesthetica* in Hans Rudolf Schweizer, *Ästhetik als Philosophie der sinnlichen Erkenntnis* (Basel: Schwabe, 1973), see the discussion of Baumgarten in Howard Caygill, *Art of Judgment* (Oxford: Blackwell, 1989), pp. 148–71. Caygill gives a rather inflated picture of Baumgarten's impor-

tance in the development of Kant's conception of autonomy, ultimately characterizing the *Aesthetica* as describing "nothing less than the process by which reason gives itself both objects and law" (p. 171), as opposed to merely attempting a vindication of the role of the senses within the rationalist framework. The latter point was surely important for Kant; not, however, for his conception of autonomy but rather for his insistence on the indispensability of sensibility as well as understanding in cognition. Caygill's account of Baumgarten is interesting, but for a more judicious treatment see Mary J. Gregor, "Baumgarten's *Aesthetica*," *Review of Metaphysics* 37 (1983): 357–85.

94. *Aesthetica*, §14; partial reprint of the text is available in Schweizer, "*Ästhetik*, pp. 103–315; quotation at p. 114.

95. *Meditationes philosophicae de nonnullis ad poema pertinentibus*, Latin–German text, ed. and trans. Heinz Paetzold (Hamburg: Meiner, 1983), §§VII and IX, p. 10. For an English translation, see Karl Aschenbrenner and W. B. Holther, *Reflections on Poetry* (Berkeley and Los Angeles: University of California Press, 1954.)

96. *Aesthetica*, §§18–20; Schweizer, p. 116.

97. *Aesthetica*, §22; Schweizer, p. 118.

98. These phrases come from a surviving transcription of Baumgarten's lectures, published in Bernhard Poppe, *Alexander Gottlieb Baumgarten: Seine Bedeutung und Stelle in der Leibniz–Wolffischen Philosophie und seine Beziehungen zu Kant, nebst Veröfftenlichung einer bisher unbekannten Handschrift der Ästhetik Baumgartens* (Borna: Noske, 1907), §§182–3.

99. *Aesthetica*, §189; not reprinted in Schweizer.

100. So writes Mendelssohn; of course, Hutcheson was actually Scots-Irish, born in Ulster and professor in Glasgow.

101. "Über die Hauptgrundsätze der schönen Künste und Wissenschaften" (1757), in Moses Mendelssohn, *Ästhetische Schriften im Auswahl*, ed. Otto F. Best (Darmstadt: Wissenschaftliche Buchgesellschaft, 1974), pp. 175–6, hereafter cited as "Hauptgrundsätze." Mendelssohn was very impressed with Burke's book and published a highly favorable review of it in 1758 (*Ästhetische Schriften*, pp. 247–65); but since this review was based on the first edition of Burke's *Enquiry*, Mendelssohn could not have been directly influenced by Burke's own fairly obvious rejection of Hutcheson, which was added in the "Introduction on Taste" in the second edition. The convergence

of their views is, rather, evidence of a widespread rejection of Hutcheson's conception of aesthetic disinterestedness.

102. "Über die Empfindungen" (1755), in *Ästhetische Schriften*, p. 34, hereafter cited as "Über die Empfindungen." He also says, *"Pleasant sensation is nothing in the soul but the clear, but indistinct intuition of perfection"*; "Rhapsodie oder Zusätze zu den Briefen über die Empfindungen," in *Ästhetische Schriften*, p. 147, hereafter cited as "Rhapsodie."
103. "Hauptgrundsätze," p. 176.
104. "Hauptgrundsätze," p. 177.
105. "Hauptgrundsätze," p. 177.
106. "Rhapsodie," pp. 149–50.
107. "Rhapsodie," p. 151.
108. "On Enjoyment" (c. 1761), in *Ästhetische Schriften*, p. 115.
109. "Hauptgrundsätze," p. 174.
110. "Über die Empfindungen," p. 49.
111. See "Rhapsodie," pp. 129–30.
112. "Rhapsodie," pp. 129–30.
113. "Rhapsodie," pp. 129–30.
114. "Hauptgrundsätze," pp. 178–9.
115. See Chapter 4 for further discussion of this point.
116. "Attempt at a Unification of all beautiful Arts and Sciences under the concept of *that which is perfected in itself*," originally published in *Berlinische Monatschrift* in 1785, reprinted in Moritz, *Beiträge zur Ästhetik*, ed. Hans Joachim Schrimpf and Hans Adler (Mainz: Dieterich'sche Verlagsbuchhandlung, 1989), pp. 7–17; the citations come from pp. 8–9. The article was dedicated to Mendelssohn, although it clearly attempted to subvert his views. Kant published in the *Berlinische Monatschrift* in this period and can be presumed to have seen Moritz's article (see Chapter 4, note 1).
117. Both Mendelssohn and Moritz receive more detailed discussion in Chapter 4.
118. This claim is defended in Chapter 4.

CHAPTER 3

1. For more discussion of this issue, see Chapter 7.
2. See Introduction, note 17, for an objection to this interpretation, by Donald W. Crawford, and my reply to that objection.

3. Among numerous similar passages, see also *CJ*, §9, pp. 217–19, and §35, p. 287.

4. This is of course the issue of the transcendental deduction of pure judgments of taste. I have discussed this at length in *Kant and the Claims of Taste* (Cambridge, Mass.: Harvard University Press, 1979), chaps. 7–9. See also the penetrating discussion in Anthony Savile, *Aesthetic Reconstructions: The Seminal Writings of Lessing, Kant and Schiller*, Aristotelian Society Series, no. 8 (Oxford: Blackwell, 1987), chaps. 4–5.

5. I say "natural existence of beautiful objects" rather than "existence of beautiful natural objects" to leave for the possibility that objects of human art rather than nonhuman nature may also, contrary to Kant's suggestion in §42, have this moral significance when explained in a certain way; namely, in the naturalistic way afforded by Kant's own theory of genius.

6. See the similar distinction in the article by A. C. Genova, "Aesthetic Justification and Systematic Unity in Kant's Third *Critique*," in *Proceedings of the Sixth International Kant Congress*, ed. Gerhard Funke and Thomas M. Seebohm (Washington, D.C.: Center for Advanced Research in Phenomenology and University Press of America), vol. 2, pt. 2, pp. 292–309.

7. There has been an extensive literature on the role of the beautiful as the symbol of the morally good in completing Kant's argument, started in the so-called "Deduction of Pure Aesthetic Judgment," for the claim of universal agreement in judgment of taste, beginning with Donald W. Crawford, *Kant's Aesthetic Theory* (Madison: University of Wisconsin Press, 1974), and including Kenneth F. Rogerson, *Kant's Aesthetics* (Lanham: University Press of America, 1986) and, most recently, Savile, *Aesthetic Reconstructions*, chap. 6. As I stated in the Introduction, I stand by my original response to Crawford (see *Kant and the Claims of Taste*, chap. 11), in which I argued that the link to morality does not supplement the "Deduction" with any additional grounds for the *expectation* of agreement, but throughout these essays I am obviously more hospitable than I originally was to Kant's idea that such agreement is of so much interest to us that we do not just adopt the epistemic stance of expecting it under certain conditions but also adopt the practical stance of requiring it, *a fortiori* efforts toward the realization of it.

8. This was the key premise that ultimately caused me to revise

my original criticism of Kant's symbolism argument in *Kant and the Claims of Taste*, pp. 383–5.

9. I have discussed this argument in somewhat more detail, and mentioned the intervening premises, in Chapter 1.

10. For further discussion of this point, see Chapter 1.

11. This question was stressed in an earlier article of mine, "Interest, Nature, and Art: A Problem in Kant's Aesthetics," *Review of Metaphysics* 36 (1978): 449–60. The explanation that follows came only later and is explored more fully in Chapter 7.

12. For further discussion of Kant's conception of genius, see Chapter 10, as well as my article "Interest, Nature, and Art," cited in the preceding note.

13. Thus the explorer's initial enchantment with the regularity of the garden discovered among the jungle wild soon pales (*CJ*, §22 General Remark, 5:243).

14. Again, see Chapter 10 for further exploration of this point.

15. I have used the German text provided in Elizabeth M. Wilkinson and L. A. Willoughby, eds. and trans., *Friedrich Schiller: On the Aesthetic Education of Mankind in a Series of Letters* (Oxford: Clarendon Press, 1967). I have largely followed their translation but have ignored their nonstandard capitalization, restored Schiller's punctuation, and occasionally departed from their wording. Citations are located by the number of the letter and then by the page number in the facing German and English texts, separated by a slash (e.g., "pp. 146/147").

16. Chapter 10 explores other aspects of the relation between Kant and Schiller.

17. Kant distinguished *determinant judgment* and *reflective judgment* as two species of what is clearly theoretical rather than practical judgment (*CJ*, §IV, 5:179). He then distinguished three kinds of reflective judgment: (1) judgment on the forms of objects, paradigmatically natural objects, taken individually, or aesthetic judgment; (2) judgment on particular systems of natural objects, or teleological judgment in its ordinary form; and (3) judgment on the system of natural objects as a whole, which is the judgment of systematicity if considered purely with respect to classification but which is the ultimate form of teleological judgment if considered with respect to a final purpose of the whole system. (The first two kinds of judgment

are explicitly defined and distinguished at *CJ*, §VIII, 5:192; the third class is never explicitly defined.) Schiller makes no use of the general concept of reflective judgment or of Kant's third category of reflective judgments, and so is left with aesthetic and reflective judgments, which he then analyzes as analogues of ordinary theoretical and moral judgments.

18. Letter of February 8, 1793, in *Schillers Werke*, vol. 4, *Schriften* (Frankfurt am Main: Insel, 1966), pp. 81–2.
19. Letter of February 18, 1793; *Schillers Werke*, pp. 83–4.
20. Letter of February 18, 1793; *Schillers Werke*, p. 84.
21. Letter of February 18, 1793; *Schillers Werke*, p. 86. The emphasis is Schiller's.
22. Letter of February 18, 1793; *Schillers Werke*, pp. 86–7.
23. These were also originally written to a particular correspondent (Schiller's patron, like the duke of Augustenburg), but then, unlike the *Kallias* letters, were offered to the public in Schiller's own journal, *Die Horen*. See Wilkinson and Willoughby, *Letters*, p. xix.
24. *Critique of Pure Reason*, A 51 / B 75.
25. "Of the Delicacy of Taste and Passion," in *Essays Moral, Political, and Literary by David Hume* (Oxford: Oxford University Press, 1963), pp. 5–6.
26. In Chapter 10, I show how Kant's treatment of the duty of sympathy, in the *Doctrine of Virtue* of the *Metaphysics of Morals*, makes a similar point. Here, perhaps, he has learned from Schiller's work, which appeared prior to this last great work of his own.

CHAPTER 4

1. Moritz's essay, under the title "Versuch einer Vereinigung aller schönen Künste und Wissenschaften unter dem Begriff des in sich selbst Vollendeten," was published in *Berlinische Monatschrift*, vol. 5, pt. 3 (March 1785), pp. 225–36. Kant's essay "Über die Vulkane im Monde" was published on pp. 199–213 of this issue. His essay "Von der Unrechtmäßigkeit des Büchernachdrucks" was published in pt. 5 (May), pp. 403–17, and "Bestimmung des Begriffs einer Menschenrace" in pt. 11 (November), pp. 390–417. In these circumstances, it is inconceivable that Kant did not see Moritz's essay.

2. For a brief assessment and list of his works, see Erich Adickes, *German Kantian Bibliography* (New York: Franklin, 1970) (originally published in *Philosophical Review*, 1893–6), pp. 111–15.

3. "Über die Empfindungen" was first published anonymously (Berlin: Christian Friedrich Voß, 1755) and was reprinted in Moses Mendelssohn, *Philosophische Schriften*, "first part, improved edition" (Berlin: Christian Friedrich Voß, 1771). Cited from Mendelssohn, *Ästhetische Schriften im Auswahl*, ed. Otto F. Best (Darmstadt: Wissenschaftliche Buchgesellschaft, 1974), p. 34.

4. "Über die Hauptgrundsätze der schönen Künste und Wissenschaften," anonymously published under the title "Betrachtungen über die Quellen und die Verbindungen der schönen Künste und Wissenschaften," in *Bibliothek der schönen Wissenschaften und der freyen Künste*, vol. 1, pt. 2 (Leipzig: Johann Gottfried Dyck, 1757); reprinted in Moses Mendelssohn, *Philosophische Schriften*, "second part, improved edition" (Berlin: Christian Friedrich Voß, 1771); Best, p. 176. The phrase *schöne Künste* or *schöne Künste und Wissenschaften* was widely used (e.g., by J. G. Sulzer and G. F. Meier) in contexts where British writers of the time would have used "fine arts" and could easily be translated with that term. I have kept it more literal in translating the title, however, because the German expression raised issues for its users that the English did not: raising, for instance, the question of whether the subject of aesthetics must itself be beautiful, if aesthetics is not just a science of the beautiful but a beautiful science. I will not pursue this issue here, but would not like to foreclose it by a choice of translation.

5. "Hauptgrundsätze," p. 177.

6. "Rhapsodie, oder Zusätze zu den Briefen über die Empfindungen," first published anonymously in *Philosophische Schriften*, "second part" (Berlin: Christian Friedrich Voß, 1761), reprinted in the *Philosophische Schriften*, "second part, improved edition" (1771). Cited from Best, p. 129.

7. "Rhapsodie," pp. 129–30.

8. "Rhapsodie," p. 130.

9. "Hauptgrundsätze," pp. 177–8.

10. See "Rhapsodie," pp. 132–3.

11. This is the polemical point of "Hauptgrundsätze"; see pp. 174–5.

12. He reminds us of this initial assumption in the conclusion of his argument; see "Hauptgrundsätze," p. 179.
13. "Hauptgrundsätze," p. 178.
14. "Hauptgrundsätze," 177.
15. "Hauptgrundsätze," p. 179. Jan von Huysum (1682–1748) was a Dutch painter of still lifes.
16. "Von dem Vergnügen" ("On Enjoyment"), c. 1761. First published in the *Jubiläumsausgabe*, vol. 1, ed. Fritz Bamberger (Berlin: Akademie, 1919). Cited from Best, p. 115.
17. "Rhapsodie," p. 147.
18. See "Hauptgrundsätze," pp. 180–97.
19. The irony of Moritz's dedication has been noted by Martha Woodmansee, "The Interest in Disinterestedness: Karl Philipp Moritz and the Emergence of the Theory of Aesthetic Autonomy in Eighteenth-Century Germany," *Modern Language Quarterly* 45 (1984): 22–47; see p. 30. I would like to thank Professor Woodmansee for sending me this article and to mention that my use of a similar title in Chapter 3 predated my receipt of it.
20. "Versuch einer Vereinigung aller schönen Künste und Wissenschaften unter dem Begriff des in sich selbt Vollendeten." Cited from Karl Philipp Moritz, *Beiträge zur Ästhetik*, ed. Hans Joachim Schrimpf and Hans Adler (Mainz: Dieterich'sche Verlagsbuchhandlung, 1989), pp. 7–8.
21. "Versuch," in Schrimpf and Adler, pp. 8–9.
22. Perhaps "rhetorical" is a bit intemperate: Woodmansee argues that although Moritz's concept of the self-perfection of the artwork is not supported by philosophical analysis or argument, it does have deep roots in the Pietist conception of divinity with which Moritz was raised ("Interest in Disinterestedness," pp. 31–3).
23. "Versuch," in Schrimpf and Adler, p. 10.
24. "Versuch," in Schrimpf and Adler, p. 12.
25. *Über die bildende Nachahmung des Schönen* (Braunschweig, 1788); in Schrimpf and Adler, p. 65.
26. Karl Heinrich Heydenreich, *System der Ästhetik*, vol. 1 (Leipzig: Georg Joachim Göschen, 1790; reprinted with afterward by Volken Deubel, Hildesheim: Gerstenberg, 1978). Heydenreich makes one reference to Kant's "just published *Critique of Judgment*" on the last page of his preface, which is dated July 12, 1790 (p. xxxvi); it is obvious that the text was completed before Kant's book was available.

27. Quotations from *System der Ästhetik*, pp. 97; 100; 100; 102–3.
28. *System der Ästhetik*, p. 130.
29. *System der Ästhetik*, pp. 131–5.
30. *System der Ästhetik*, p. 135.
31. *System der Ästhetik*, p. 136.
32. *System der Ästhetik*, p. 141.
33. *System der Ästhetik*, p. 142.
34. *System der Ästhetik*, p. 143. Here Heydenreich seems to forget his original stricture against reducing all forms of beauty to some single metaphysical account. Perhaps he is saved from contradiction by the fact that his expressivist account is specifically an account of artistic beauty, not beauty in general, and is intended to be supported in an empirical rather than metaphysical way.
35. I obviously do not accept Woodmansee's argument ("Interest in Disinterestedness," p. 24) that Kant agrees with Moritz in advocating the autonomy of the aesthetic as Moritz understood this idea. Although later generations have certainly read Kant this way, the burden of this and the preceding chapters is that in so doing they have drastically distorted the complexity of Kant's aesthetic theory as a whole.
36. See, for instance, Hegel's statement that "in the beautiful object there must be both (i) *necessity*, established by the Concept, in the coherence of its particular aspects, and (ii) the appearance of their *freedom*. . . . Necessity should not be missing in beautiful objects, but it must not emerge in the form of necessity itself; on the contrary, it must be hidden behind the appearance of undesigned contingency"; from *Aesthetics: Lectures on Fine Art*, 2 vols., ed. and trans. T. M. Knox (Oxford: Clarendon Press, 1975), vol. 1, p. 115. This passage is discussed in Chapter 5.
37. See also the Introduction to the present volume.
38. In §15 of the published text of the *Critique of Judgment*, Kant clarifies his account by distinguishing between "external" objective purposiveness (for instance, the utility of an object) and "internal" objective purposiveness (i.e., perfection considered apart from a goal). However, the latter concept is obscured by a confusing distinction between "qualitative perfection," which presupposes a concept of *"what sort of thing* [the object] *is to be,"* and "quantitative perfection," where that issue is regarded as already determined and only the "complete-

ness of the thing in its kind" is considered (*CJ*, §15, 5:227); and Kant neglects to repeat his criticism that it is not obvious why perfection in this sense should have anything to do with pleasure at all.

39. This fundamental explanation of the sense in which beautiful objects are subjectively purposive must be distinguished from that which Kant connects with it at §10 of the *Critique*. There Kant defines purposiveness as a feature of an object which can only be caused by an antecedent conception of it; he defines purposiveness without an end, or a purposiveness merely in form, as a property objects have when they are intelligible to us only if we suppose that they have been designed by an intelligent agent even when we have no objective basis for assuming that they were (*CJ*, §10, 5:220). He suggests that objects which are subjectively purposive, in the sense of satisfying the basic aim of cognition without being subsumed under a concept, must also have merely formal purposiveness in this second sense, but simply seems to assume without argument that we cannot understand the possibility of a thing's harmonizing with our cognitive faculties (subjective purposiveness) without assuming, though not asserting, that it does so because it was designed to do so (merely formal purposiveness). This just seems to obscure his fundamental idea and even to introduce the misleading suggestion that there is some characteristic appearance of designed objects.

40. For further discussion of this issue, see Chapter 7.

41. Again, for more on genius, see Chapter 8.

### CHAPTER 5

1. Edited by H. G. Hotho in 1835 and revised in 1842; cited from G. W. F. Hegel, *Werke in zwanzig Bänden* (*Werkausgabe*), ed. Eva Moldenhauer and Karl Markus Michel, vol. 13 (Frankfurt am Main: Suhrkamp, 1970) (cited as *WA*); my translations are based on but modify that by T. M. Knox, *Aesthetics: Lectures on Fine Art*, 2 vols. (Oxford: Clarendon Press, 1975); I cite volume and page numbers from Knox's edition, following the citation to *WA*. Citations from Kant's works in this chapter employ the same conventions as elsewhere in this volume.

2. These comments are not meant to undermine Kant's own claim that the judgment of taste has an "exemplary necessity" (§18). What Kant means by that is that *if* an object seems beautiful to me then it must also appear beautiful to others, but not that there is any set of conditions that can be stated such that any given object *must* seem beautiful to me. See also *CJ* §37, where Kant argues that it is not the *pleasure* but only the *universal validity* of the pleasure in a beautiful object which is "represented *a priori* as a universal rule." As usual, "necessary" could be substituted for "*a priori.*"

3. The topic of the ideal of beauty is discussed further in Chapters 1 and 3.

4. For more on the conception of genius, see Chapters 4 and 8.

5. For further discussion of this relationship of symbolism, see Chapters 1 and 3.

6. This issue is discussed in Chapter 1.

7. *Enzyklopädie der Philosophischen Wissenschaften im Grundrisse,* ed. F. Nicolin and O. Pöggeler (Hamburg: Meiner, 1969), §557, pp. 441–2; in the translation by William Wallace and A. V. Miller, *Hegel's Philosophy of Mind* (Oxford: Clarendon Press, 1971), the final occurrence of *Sitte* is translated as "manner of life" (p. 293).

8. These passages are discussed in Chapters 9 and 10.

9. These subtleties are explored in Chapter 6 and 7.

10. See Chapter 7 for further discussion of this issue.

11. See my "Kant's Conception of Empirical Law," *Aristotelian Society,* supplementary volume 64 (1990): 221–42.


### CHAPTER 6

1. *Kant and the Claims of Taste* (Cambridge, Mass.: Harvard University Press, 1979), p. 400, note 2.

2. "Phenomenality and Materiality in Kant," in *The Textual Sublime: Deconstruction and Its Differences,* ed. Hugh J. Silverman and Gary E. Aylesworth (Albany: State University of New York Press, 1990), pp. 87–109, at p. 107. The "two terms" referred to in the sentence that I quote are imagination and reason.

3. Thomas Weiskel, *The Romantic Sublime: Studies in the Structure and Psychology of Transcendence* (Baltimore: Johns Hopkins University Press, 1976), p. 21.

4. Howard Caygill, *Art of Judgment* (Oxford: Blackwell, 1989), pp. 345–6.

5. Stanley Cavell, *Conditions Handsome and Unhandsome: The Constitution of Emersonian Perfectionism* (Chicago: University of Chicago Press, 1990), p. 57. Cavell refers to Thomas Weiskel, Harold Bloom, and Neil Hertz.

6. *The Ideology of the Aesthetic* (Oxford: Blackwell, 1989), p. 90.

7. The deconstructionist suggestion that there can be no finite limits to perception – that instead, perception of the finite floats on a sea of infinitude – is interesting and is indeed implied by Kant's own conception of the infinite given magnitude of space and time in the "Transcendental Aesthetic" in the first *Critique*, where he argues that the representations of space and time are not presented as subsuming an indeterminate number of instances, like ordinary general concepts, but are given as singular representations containing an infinite number of parts. But Kant does not suggest, in the discussion of what he calls the "mathematical sublime" in the *Critique of Judgment*, that perception as such is accompanied with a sense of its own inadequacy, because imagination and understanding are perfectly able to give sense to the idea of the infinite background of any objective perception, through what he calls "relative measures." It is only with the desire to have an absolute measure of infinitude that the sense of the inadequacy of imagination arises, and this desire is both raised and answered by the faculty of reason. So it seems inappropriate to read a general revision of Kant's theory of perception into his special discussion of the mathematical sublime.

8. See Chapter 8 for further discussion of this point.

9. This objection was raised by J. O. Urmson in a paper given at the April 1980 meeting of the Pacific Division of the American Society for Aesthetics at Pacific Grove, California; my reply to that paper was the ancestor of the present essay.

10. See pp. 50, 60, 80, 85, 94, and 118 in Meredith's translation of *Critique of Judgment* (Oxford: Clarendon Press, 1952; originally published 1911). Meredith's predecessor as translator of Kant, J. H. Bernard, avoided this particular problem by using the term "explanation" in his 1895 translation (London, Macmillan), although that term too may be more specific than *Erklärung*.

11. Kant's justification for this claim is admittedly problematic

(see *Kant and the Claims of Taste*, pp. 131–3), but this fact does not bear on the nature of his intentions in his claim.

12. For a discussion of the respects in which Kant's theory of taste did change over these years, see *Kant and the Claims of Taste*, chap. 1, and my "Pleasure and Society in Kant's Aesthetic Theory," in *Essays in Kant's Aesthetics*, ed. Ted Cohen and Paul Guyer (Chicago: University of Chicago Press, 1982), pp. 21–54.

13. The best examples of these two kinds of approaches in the current literature are the revised version of Richard E. Aquila, "A New Look at Kant's Aesthetic Judgments," in Cohen and Guyer, *Essays in Kant's Aesthetics*, pp. 87–114, and Eva Schaper, "Aesthetic Appraisals," in her *Studies in Kant's Aesthetics* (Edinburgh: Edinburgh University Press, 1979), pp. 53–77.

14. For a general discussion of the disanalogies between the use of these headings in the first *Critique* and in the "Analytic of the Beautiful," see Donald W. Crawford, *Kant's Aesthetic Theory* (Madison: University of Wisconsin Press, 1974), pp. 15–17; Jens Kulenkampff, *Kants Logik des ästhetischen Urteils* (Frankfurt am Main: Klostermann, 1978), pp. 12–18; and *Kant and the Claims of Taste*, pp. 128–31.

15. Kant's reason for reversing this order in the "Analytic of the Beautiful" was confused, in any case; see *Kant and the Claims of Taste*, pp. 124–5.

16. The key evidence for this interpretation is in *Critique of Judgment*, §VI, 5:187; it is argued for at length in *Kant and the Claims of Taste*, chap. 3, and discussed more briefly in Chapters 1 and 3 of the present volume.

17. This tension first manifests itself in the initial five paragraphs of Section 9 of the *Critique of Judgment*; I have discussed it at length in *Kant and the Claims of Taste*, pp. 151–60, and in "Pleasure and Society in Kant's Aesthetic Theory."

18. Kant's reason for this position is that since feelings of pleasure and pain are the only subjective states which cannot be included in concepts of objects, they are the only states available for the conscious representation of such a nonconceptual process as aesthetic reflection (*FI*, §VIII, 20:224; *CJ*, §VII, 5:189). This arugment is discussed in *Kant and the Claims of Taste*, pp. 99–105.

19. See *Kant and the Claims of Taste*, pp. 110–11.

20. See *Kant and the Claims of Taste*, chap. 3, especially pp. 105, 119.

21. In §13 of the "Analytic of the Beautiful," Kant does in fact treat "form of finality" and "finality of form" as equivalent concepts, rather than as genus and species (see *Kant and the Claims of Taste,* pp. 219–20); the present argument shows that there are more than purely syntactical reasons for regarding this as a lapse.

22. This paragraph has been added for the present volume. For further elaboration of this point, see the discussion of the sublime in Section II of Chapter 7.

23. For a general discussion of the problem with Kant's treatment of disinterestedness, see my "Disinterestedness and Desire in Kant's Aesthetics," *Journal of Aesthetics and Art Criticism* 36 (1978): 449–60, and *Kant and the Claims of Taste,* chap. 5.

24. See *Critique of Practical Reason,* 5:21, and *Kant and the Claims of Taste,* pp. 183–91.

25. *Critique of Practical Reason,* 5:119–20.

26. See *Kant and the Claims of Taste,* pp. 160–66, and Kulenkampff, *Kants Logik des ästhetischen Urteils,* pp. 12–16. This view of the relation between universality and necessity has now been controverted by Kenneth F. Rogerson, *Kant's Aesthetics: The Roles of Form and Expression* (Lanham, Md.: University Press of America, 1986), on the ground that the moment of necessity introduces the imperatival idea that others *ought* to agree with one's judgment of taste, which is not yet apparent in the moment of necessity (pp. 61–2). There can be no doubt that Kant wished to introduce this additional aspect on the basis of the moral connections that are being explored throughout these essays, but I am not sure that this explicitly occurs or was intended to do so in the discussion of necessity in the fourth moment of the "Analytic of the Beautiful."

CHAPTER 7

1. As I argued in the Introduction, the fact that eighteenth-century aesthetic theory was pursued in an ideological climate does not mean that it was itself part of the ideology by means of which the bourgeoisie attempted to gain and/or justify its hegemony over other elements of society; it seems more likely that it was intended by its authors as a sincere attempt to escape from the limits of class-bound ideology.

2. This is not to say that restoration in the arts themselves had to await for the theoretical reconception of their value; in Britain, for instance, the restoration of the theater succeeded almost immediately the demise of the Puritan Commonwealth. As usual, the owl of Minerva spread her philosophical wings in the dusk, rather than the dawn, of the day of change.

3. Nos. 411 through 421, Saturday, June 21, through Thursday, July 3, 1721. Citations are from the edition by A. Chalmers (Boston: Little, Brown, 1869), vol. 6.

4. *Spectator*, no. 412, pp. 126–9.

5. See Lord Kames [Henry Home], *The Elements of Criticism*, chap. 3, "Of Beauty." Citations to this work (originally published in 1762) are to the edition by James R. Boyd (New York: Barnes, 1856).

6. Hutcheson, for instance, devotes a whole chapter of his fundamental treatise in aesthetics to the discussion of the beauty of "theorems"; *An Inquiry Concerning Beauty, Order, Harmony, Design*, §III. I will cite passages from this work by section and paragraph number only, using the text of the fourth edition as edited by Peter Kivy (The Hague: Nijhoff, 1973).

7. *Inquiry*, §II, "Of Original or Absolute Beauty," ¶III.

8. *Versuch über den Geschmack*, 2nd ed. (Berlin: 1790), pp. 27–8. Unfortunately I have not been able to see a copy of the first edition of this work from 1776, with which Kant was familiar. Herz suggests that he made considerable revisions for the second edition, but since it came out at the same time as his former mentor's *Critique of Judgment*, it seems reasonable to assume that whatever revisions Herz made could not have been influenced by the latter work.

9. *Inquiry*, §VIII, ¶II. For further discussion of this point, see Chapter 2 of this volume.

10. *Inquiry*, §VIII, ¶III.

11. *Unterredungen über die Schönheit der Natur*, "new edition" (Berlin, 1770), pp. 133–4.

12. For further discussion of this aspect of Mendelssohn's views, see Chapter 4.

13. *Unterredungen*, pp. 22, 24–5.

14. *Elements of Criticism*, app. to chap. 9, p. 181.

15. *Elements of Criticism*, p. 183.

16. *Spectator*, no. 412, p. 127.

17. *Spectator*, no. 413, p. 133.

18. "Moralische Betrachtungen über besondere Gegenstände der Naturlehre," appended to *Unterredungen über die Schönheit der Natur*, pp. 198–9.
19. "It was with pleasure that I observed the purity of expression, the pleasantness of the style, and the subtlety of the remarks in your book on the difference of taste"; Kant to Herz, November 24, 1776 (10:184).
20. *Versuch*, pp. 94–5.
21. *Versuch*, pp. 85–6, 87.
22. *Versuch*, p. 143, among many others.
23. This is of course standard Wolffian doctrine; see the characterization of Wolffian perfectionism in Josef Schmucker, *Die Ursprünge der Ethik Kants* (Meisenheim am Glan: Hain, 1961), pp. 38–9, or my article, "Wolff," in *The Encyclopedia of Ethics*, ed. Lawrence Becker (New York: Garland, 1992), pp. 1324–7. See also such a contemporary popularization of it as that in J. C. Gottsched, *Erste Gründe der gesamten Weltweisheit*, 2 vols., "latest edition" (Leipzig, 1762), vol. 2, §§25–9.
24. *Versuch*, p. 110.
25. *Versuch*, pp. 111–12.
26. *Versuch*, p. 116.
27. *Versuch*, pp. 139, 139–40, 141.
28. *Versuch*, pp. 161–2.
29. *Versuch*, p. 163.
30. *Versuch*, pp. 163–4.
31. *Versuch*, p. 164.
32. *Versuch*, pp. 166–7.
33. *Versuch*, p. 88.
34. This issue is addressed more directly in my article "Kant's Morality of Law and Morality of Freedom," in *Kant and Critique: New Essays in Honor of W. M. Werkmeister*, ed. Russell Dancy (Dordrecht: Kluwer, forthcoming).
35. Immanuel Kant, *Lectures on Ethics*, trans. Louis Infield (London: Methuen, 1930), from the edition by Paul Menzer (Berlin, 1924), pp. 122–4; cf. Kant's *Moral Mrongovius*, 27:1482–4.
36. The force of this conventional view is particularly clearly expressed in Alexander Baumgarten's examples for his category of "aesthetic magnitude"; they are always examples of moral heroes.
37. See Chapter 3.
38. This sounds very close to the explanation of aesthetic pleasure

which Kant himself accepted around 1770–1 (see *Kant and the Claims of Taste*, pp. 14–32). The view that Kant criticizes in Herz may once have been his own, published by the student only to be criticized by the teacher from whom he had learned it.

39. See, e.g., *Lectures on Ethics*, p. 193; cf. *Moral Mrongovius*, 27:1538.
40. See *Practical Reason*, 5:34.
41. See Chapter 10 for further discussion of these arguments.
42. This account would thus go beyond that given in the last chapter by seeing Kant's exposition as a progression.
43. *Lectures on Ethics*, p. 126; *Moral Mrongovius*, 27:1486.
44. By saying that the sublime in objects "of art is always restricted by the conditions of an agreement with nature" (*CJ*, §23, 5:245), he seems to presuppose that there is such a thing as a sublime in art, or at least an artistic representation of the sublime.
45. See my "Interest, Nature, and Art," *Review of Metaphysics* 31 (1978): 580–603.
46. For further discussion of this point, see Chapter 1 and 3.
47. *Kant and Fine Art: An Essay on Kant and the Philosophy of Fine Art and Culture* (Oxford: Clarendon Press, 1986).
48. *Kant and Fine Art*, p. 14.
49. *Kant and Fine Art*, pp. 14–15.
50. *Kant and Fine Art*, p. 15.
51. *Kant and Fine Art*, p. 18.
52. *Kant and Fine Art*, p. 19.
53. *Kant and Fine Art*, p. 20.

CHAPTER 8

1. The *Oxford English Dictionary* recognizes three senses of "integrity": the sense of "wholeness" or "completeness"; a sense of intactness or uncorruptedness, illustrated, for example, by the condition of virginity; and the sense of "soundness of moral principle." These latter two senses, however, might be thought of as just passive and active forms, respectively, of what I have identified as the sense of autonomy, or independent but principled agency: a physical (or moral) *change* such as the loss of virginity might be thought to constitute *damage*

or *corruption* only if it occurs against the will of the person who undergoes it.

2. "Of the Standard of Taste," in David Hume, *Essays Moral, Political, and Literary* (Oxford: Oxford University Press, 1963), pp. 231–55; this quotation from p. 247.

3. "Of the Standard of Taste," p. 235.

4. Ingrid Stadler draws attention to this passage and seems to read it in this way in her article "The Idea of Art and Its Criticism: A Rational Reconstruction of a Kantian Doctrine," in *Essays in Kant's Aesthetics*, ed. Ted Cohen and Paul Guyer (Chicago: University of Chicago Press, 1982), pp. 195–218.

5. "On the Imitation of the Painting and Sculpture of the Greeks" (1755), in Johann Joachim Winckelmann, *Winckelmann: Writings on Art*, ed. David Irwin (London: Phaidon, 1972), p. 61.

6. "Of Refinement in the Arts," in *Essays Moral, Political, and Literary*, pp. 274–88; this quotation from p. 279.

7. One should not suggest that Kant thinks the fine arts an "unequivocally valuable" agent for the development of community, as I did in the original version of this essay. On the contrary, Kant is concerned that the arts can be used to advance a merely empirical interest in sociability, rather than the genuinely moral interest in universality, and that they can degenerate into mere fashion; see his discussion of the "empirical interest in the beautiful" (*CJ*, §41, 5:296–8). See also the concluding section of Chapter 7 in this volume.

8. He in fact reserves it for yet one more formulation of the epistemological problem of aesthetic judgment (*CJ*, §§55–8), although this fact is buried by Kant's desire to conform the structure of the *Critique of Judgment* to the architectonic of the *Critique of Pure Reason*. The result is that he presents a metaphysical solution to this epistemological problem.

9. I have argued this thesis in a number of places, including chapter 3 of *Kant and the Claims of Taste*, "Kant's Distinction between the Beautiful and the Sublime," now revised as Chapter 6 of this volume, and in my reviews of books on Kant's aesthetics by Eva Schaper, *Philosophical Review* 90 (July, 1981): 429–36, and Jens Kulenkampff, *Journal of Aesthetics and Art Criticism* 40 (1982): 212–17.

10. See *Kant and the Claims of Taste*, pp. 136–9.

11. For some explanation of Kant's doctrine of the ideal of beauty, see Chapter 1 of this volume.

12. In fact, as we will see in the next paragraphs of the present section, the premise of this argument, that aesthetic judgments must be free of concepts, is also ultimately dependent on psychological theory.

13. It was from this remark, it will be recalled, that the opening quotation of this chapter was drawn.

14. See *Kant and the Claims of Taste*, pp. 151–60, and my article "Pleasure and Society in Kant's Theory of Taste," in Cohen and Guyer, *Essay in Kant's Aesthetics*, pp. 21–54.

15. See p. 155 of Meredith's translation (Oxford: Clarendon Press, 1952; originally published 1911). The older translation of the *Critique of Judgment* by J. H. Bernard (originally published in 1895) does not in fact make this mistake.

16. I have discussed this point at greater length in "Interest, Nature, and Art: A Problem in Kant's Aesthetics," *Review of Metaphysics* 31 (1978): 580–603.

17. This tension was explored in Chapter 7.

18. Kant's contrast between originality and original nonsense is the subject of an interesting discussion in Timothy Gould, "The Audience of Originality: Kant and Wordsworth on the Reception of Genius," in Cohen and Guyer, *Essays in Kant's Aesthetics*, pp. 179–94.

19. The choice by both Bernard and Meredith of the term "following" rather than the term "succession" to translate *Nachfolge* seems to me to blur rather than clarify Kant's contrast with "imitation" (*Nachahmung*).


CHAPTER 9

1. Immanuel Kant, *Lectures on Ethics*, trans. Louis Infield (London: Methuen, 1930), p. 241.

2. *Second Treatise of Government*, chap. 2, §26; in Peter Laslett, ed., *John Locke: Two Treatises of Government*, 2nd ed. (Cambridge: Cambridge University Press, 1967), p. 304.

3. *Second Treatise*, §27; Laslett, p. 306.

4. *Second Treatise*, §31; Laslett, p. 308.

5. See Chapter 2 for further discussion of this point.

6. David Hume, *A Treatise of Human Nature*, ed. L. A. Selby-Bigge (1888), 3rd ed. (rev.) by P. H. Nidditch (Oxford: Oxford University Press, 1975), p. 364.

7. Translations are from the edition by Mary J. Gregor, Immanuel Kant, *The Metaphysics of Morals* (Cambridge: Cambridge University Press, 1991). Because this edition reproduces the *Akademie* edition pagination, only citations to the latter will be given.

8. See John Passmore, *Man's Responsibility for Nature* (New York: Scribner, 1974), pp. 3–15.

9. My translation here follows that of Lewis White Beck (Indianapolis: Bobbs-Merrill, 1956). This edition contains the *Akademie* edition pagination and so is not separately cited in the parenthetical references.

10. In some texts, Kant suggests a closer connection between virtue and happiness in the concept of the highest good than the one I am about to expound; see my "Unity of Reason: Pure Reason as Practical Reason in Kant's Early Conception of the Transcendental Dialectic," *Monist* 72 (1989): 139–67, especially pp. 166–7.

11. This synthetic interpretation of the derivation of the concept of the highest good is in opposition to the analytic account suggested by John Silber in "The Importance of the Highest Good in Kant's Ethics," *Ethics* 28 (1963): 178–97, especially pp. 190–2.

12. Translation by Theodore M. Greene and Hoyt H. Hudson (New York: Harper & Row, 1960), pp. 6–7n.

13. In the *Critique of Practical Reason*, Kant similarly argues that the connection between worthiness to be happy (duty) and happiness must be synthetic, but then also assumes that the connection must be causal, as if a causal connection was the only candidate for the basis of a synthetic judgment (5:111). This is obviously meant to pave the way for his argument that the postulation of the existence of God is necessary to establish a causal connection between virtue and happiness, which is otherwise literally unnatural, but does not undercut the basic point made in the *Religion*.

14. The theory of beauty as the symbol of morality is also discussed in Chapters 1 and 3.

15. I certainly argued as much in *Kant and the Claims of Taste*, p. 385.

16. For an account of Wolffian perfectionism, see my article on Wolff in Lawrence C. Becker, ed., *The Encyclopedia of Ethics* (New York: Garland, 1992), pp. 1324–7.

17. The exact basis for the claim of this paragraph is clarified in the more systematic discussion in Chapter 10, §III.
18. This interchange is also discussed further in Chapter 10.
19. The basis for this supposition is examined in Section II of Chapter 10.
20. One might argue that the *Critique of Practical Reason*'s sublime contention that "every action and, in general, every changing determination of [one's] existence according to the inner sense, even the entire history of his existence as a sensuous being, is seen in the consciousness of his intelligible existence as only a consequence, not as a determining ground of his causality as a noumenon" (*Practical Reason*, 5:97–8) already implies that one's feelings may literally be remade to accord with duty. Perhaps it does, but it does not make this explicit; and it certainly does not imply, as Kant argues in the *Metaphysics of Morals*, that one's feelings *should* be so made, or remade, as the case may be. I will pursue this issue further in the next chapter.
21. Note again that the violation is not simply an injury to the conditions for the development of one's intellect and will as constituting one's metaphysical essence (as assumed by Wolffian perfectionism) but destruction of the conditions necessary for the exercise of one's rational agency – or freedom.
22. This is the case of "dependent" rather than "free" beauty, of course (*CJ*, §16). See Chapter 3 for further discussion of this distinction.
23. Complexities surrounding this remark have been discussed in Chapters 5 and 7.
24. This obviously creates a problem about *cultivated* natural objects, such as Hume's hills of olives instead of furze. Obviously Kant must treat these as cases of fine art rather than purely natural beauty – but then argue that they please us as beautiful precisely insofar as they strike us *as if* their unity of form were natural rather than intended.
25. *Lectures on Ethics*, trans. Infield., p. 121.
26. I have offered some characterization of the purpose and structure of the "Critique of Teleological Judgment" in "Natural Ends and the End of Nature," in *System and Teleology in Kant's Critique of Judgment*, *Southern Journal of Philosophy* 30, Supplement (1992): 157–65.

CHAPTER 10

1. From "The Philosophers" (1796). Quoted from Henry Allison, *Kant's Theory of Freedom* (Cambridge: Cambridge University Press, 1990), p. 110, who quotes it from H. J. Paton, *The Categorical Imperative* (London: Hutchinson, 1947), p. 48, who in turn quotes it from Hastings Rashdall, *The Theory of Good and Evil* (London, 1907), vol. 1, p. 120 but cites the wrong footnote from Rashdall, thus sending the reader to Schopenhauer!

2. See Bernard Williams, "Morality and the Emotions," in his *Problems of the Self: Philosophical Papers, 1956–1972* (Cambridge: Cambridge University Press, 1973), pp. 207–29, especially pp. 225–9, and "Persons, Character, and Morality," in his *Moral Luck: Philosophical Papers, 1973–1980* (Cambridge: Cambridge University Press, 1981), pp. 1–19, especially pp. 17–19.

3. The literature on this issue is extensive, but some of the key works are Hans Reiner, *Pflicht und Neigung: Die Grundlagen der Sittlichkeit*, rev. ed. (Meisenheim am Glan: Hain, 1974; originally published 1951), chaps. 1–2; Dieter Henrich, "Das Prinzip der kantischen Ethik," *Philosophische Rundschau* 2 (1954–5): 20–37; Barbara Herman, "On the Value of Acting from the Motive of Duty," *Philosophical Review* 90 (1981): 359–82, and "Integrity and Impartiality," *Monist* 66 (1983): 213–32; and Marcia Baron, "The Alleged Moral Repugnance of Acting from Duty," *Journal of Philosophy* 81 (1984): 197–220.

4. For particularly useful discussion of the examples of virtuous persons in the *Groundwork*, see Herman, "On the Value of Acting from the Motive of Duty," pp. 362–6, and Lewis White Beck, *A Commentary on Kant's "Critique of Practical Reason"* (Chicago: University of Chicago Press, 1960), pp. 228–9.

5. Herman, "On the Value of Acting from the Motive of Duty," pp. 364–5.

6. *Lectures on Ethics*, trans. Louis Infield (London: Methuen, 1930), p. 36; *Moral Mrongovius*, 27:1422.

7. See among other instances R 6628 (1769–70), 19:117, R 6864, 19:184, and R 6915, 19:205.

8. Translation by Mary J. Gregor (Cambridge: Cambridge University Press, 1991), p. 186.

9. Adickes, in the *Akademie* edition of Kant's works, simply as-

signs the lengthy note from which this paragraph comes, "Loses Blatt Duisburg 6," to the 1780s without further specification (19:276). Paul Schilpp, in *Kant's Pre-Critical Ethics*, 2nd ed. (Evanston: Northwestern University Press, 1960; originally published 1938), p. 127, assigns it to 1775 but gives no reason for this departure from Adickes's dating. Other papers from the *Duisburg Nachlaß* are dated to 1774 and 1775, but not all are. There are features of the note as a whole which suggest that it must have been written some years before the *Groundwork* but nothing I can see to link it specifically to 1775.

10. *Lectures on Ethics*, p. 193; *Moral Mrongovius*, 27:1538.

11. This passage is quite intersting in light of one of Hegel's well-known criticisms of Kant's ethics. Hegel claims that the Kantian conception of the universalization of maxims contradicts itself, because if everyone were to help the poor, for instance, then there would no longer be any poor people and thus no one could help the poor (*Natural Law: The Scientific Ways of Treating Natural Law, Its Place in Moral Philosophy, and Its Relation to the Positive Sciences of Law*, trans. T. M. Knox [Philadelphia: University of Pennsylvania Press, 1975; originally published 1802], p. 80). Ironically, this is precisely the kind of result Kant's distinction in the *Lectures* – which of course Hegel had no access to – was meant to avoid: If someone helps the poor simply for the *emotional satisfaction* that so doing brings him, he may indeed feel an emotional void if he is so successful that there is no one left to help; but if someone helps the poor out of his attachment to a principle (say, that everyone deserves equal economic opportunity), there will be no reason for him to feel any emotional letdown if the principle is realized.

12. *Lectures on Ethics*, p. 35; *Moral Mrongovius*, 27:1422.

13. *Lectures on Ethics*, pp. 122–3; *Moral Mrongovius*, 27:1482–3.

14. *Lectures on Ethics*, p. 138; *Moral Mrongovius*, 17:1495.

15. *Moral Mrongovius*, 27:1496; here I depart from Infield's translation (*Lectures on Ethics*, p. 140).

16. "Über Anmut und Würde," in *Schillers Werke*: vol. 4, *Schriften*, introduced by Hans Meyer and Golo Mann (Frankfurt am Main: Insel, 1966), p. 150.

17. "Anmut und Würde," p. 153.

18. "Anmut und Würde," p. 164.

19. "Anmut und Würde," p. 175.

20. "Anmut und Würde," p. 182.
21. "Anmut und Würde," p. 177.
22. "Anmut und Würde," p. 179.
23. "Anmut und Würde," p. 179.
24. "Anmut und Würde," p. 185.
25. Thus Karl Ameriks describes respect primarily in terms of the painful check on our inclinations; see "The Hegelian Critique of Kantian Morality," in *New Essays on Kant*, ed. Bernard den Ouden and Marcia Moen (New York: Lang, 1987), pp. 179–212; p. 187. See also Beck, *Commentary on Kant's Critique of Practical Reason*, pp. 223–4.
26. See also the other passage from *Practical Reason* 5:73, which was cited as the first block quotation in this section.
27. This point is suggested by Ameriks, "Hegelian Critique," p. 187, although the argument for it is not spelled out.
28. See *Kant and the Claims of Taste*, p. 81.
29. Gregor translation, p. 203.
30. The only work in English which does provide a commentary on the whole of the *Metaphysics of Morals* remains Mary J. Gregor, *The Laws of Freedom: A Study of Kant's Method of Applying the Categorical Imperative in the "Metaphysik der Sitten"* (Oxford: Blackwell, 1963).
31. For a brief outline of Christian Wolff's ethics that will enable one to see the Wolffian elements still at work in Kant's account of self-perfection, see my article on Wolff in Lawrence C. Becker, ed., *The Encyclopedia of Ethics* (New York: Garland, 1992), pp. 1324–7.
32. This discussion in section 17 of the *Doctrine of Virtue* has already been considered in Chapter 9.
33. It may be noted that the discussion of duties toward others is not divided into separate chapters on perfect and imperfect duties, as is the discussion of duties toward oneself. This would seem to reflect the fact that perfect duties to others are subject to external legislation, and thus juridical rather than ethical duties, but in fact the discussion of duties toward others tacitly comprises both imperfect and perfect duties to others.
34. Worries about excessive coercion or limitation of free speech aside, it would indeed be difficult to write statutes prohibiting the expression of these attitudes, because they could always be conveyed through manner rather than by the normal semantic content of any particular expressions; the man of the

world always knows how to express utter contempt while using only the most polite verbal expressions.

35. Recall that for Kant the root meaning of "aesthetic" implies a connection to feeling, not to art (as it has since Hegel). See *CJ*, §1, 5:203.
36. "Persons, Character, and Morality," in *Moral Luck*, p. 17.
37. See Herman, "Integrity and Impartiality," p. 240.

# Bibliography

I. PRIMARY SOURCES

Addison, Joseph, and Richard Steele. *The Spectator*. 1710–14. Edited by A. Chalmers. Boston: Little, Brown, 1869.

Baumgarten, Alexander Gottlieb. *Aesthetica*. 1750–8. Partial Latin text and German translation in Hans Rudolf Schweizer, *Ästhetik als Philosophie der sinnlichen Erkenntnis*. Basel: Schwabe, 1973. Pp. 103–315.

A transcription of Baumgarten's lectures on the *Aesthetica* is available in Bernhard Poppe, *Alexander Gottlieb Baumgarten: Seine Bedeutung und Stelle in der Leibniz-Wolffischen Philosophie und seine Beziehungen zu Kant, nebst Veröffentlichung einer bisher unbekannten Handschrift der "Ästhetik" Baumgartens*. Borna: Noske, 1907.

*Meditationes philosophicae de nonnullis ad poema pertinentibus*. 1735. Latin–German text, edited and translated by Heinz Paetzold. Hamburg: Meiner, 1983. Translated into English by Karl Aschenbrenner and W. B. Holther as *Reflections on Poetry*. Berkeley and Los Angeles: University of California Press, 1954.

Beck, Jakob Sigismund. *Erläuternden Auszug aus den critischen Schriften des Herrn Prof. Kant*. 2 vols. Riga: Hartknoch, 1793–4.

Berkeley, George. *Alciphron, or the Minute Philosopher*. 1732. Volume 3 of *The Works of George Berkeley Bishop of Cloyne*. Edited by A. A. Luce and T. E. Jessop. London: Nelson, 1950.

Burke, Edmund. *A Philosophical Enquiry into the Origin of our Ideas of the Sublime*. 1757, revised edition 1759. Edited by James T. Boulton. London: Routledge & Kegan Paul, 1958.

Gerard, Alexander. *An Essay on Taste*. London and Edinburgh: Millar, Kincaid, and Bell, 1759. Reprinted, Yorkshire: Scolar Press, 1971.

Gottsched, Johann Christoph. *Erste Gründe der gesamten Weltweisheit.* 2 volumes. "Latest edition." Leipzig, 1762. Originally published 1733–4.

*Schriften zur Literatur.* Edited by Horst Steinmetz. Stuttgart: Reclam, 1972.

Hegel, Georg Wilhelm Friedrich. *Aesthetics: Lectures on Fine Art.* 2 volumes. Edited and translated by T. M. Knox. Oxford: Clarendon Press, 1975.

*Enzyclopädie der Philosophischen Wissenschaften im Grundrisse.* Third edition, 1830. Edited by Friedhelm Nicolin and Otto Pöggeler. Hamburg: Meiner, 1969.

*Hegel's Philosophy of Mind.* Translated by William Wallace and A. V. Miller. Oxford: Clarendon Press, 1971.

*Natural Law: The Scientific Ways of Treating Natural Law, Its Place in Moral Philosophy, and Its Relation to the Positive Sciences of Law.* Translated by T. M. Knox. Philadelphia: University of Pennsylvania Press, 1975.

*Werke in zwanzig Bänden (Werkausgabe).* Volume 13, *Vorlesung über die Ästhetik I.* Edited by Eva Moldenhauer and Karl Markus Michel. Frankfurt am Main: Suhrkamp, 1970.

Herz, Marcus. *Versuch über den Geschmack.* Second edition. Berlin, 1790.

Heydenreich, Karl Heinrich. *System der Ästhetik.* Volume 1. Leipzig: Göschen, 1790. Reprinted Hildesheim: Gerstenberg, 1978.

Hume, David. *An Enquiry Concerning the Principles of Morals.* 1751. Edited by L. A. Selby-Bigge, second edition, revised, 1902; third edition, revised, edited by P. H. Nidditch. Oxford: Clarendon Press, 1975.

*Essays Moral, Political, and Literary.* 1741–2. Oxford: Oxford University Press, 1963.

*A Treatise of Human Nature.* 1739–40. Edited by L. A. Selby-Bigge, 1888; third, revised edition by P. H. Nidditch. Oxford: Clarendon Press, 1978.

Hutcheson, Francis. *An Inquiry into the Original of our Ideas of Beauty and Virtue.* 1725. "The Fourth edition, corrected." London: D. Midwinter et al., 1738. Facsimile of fourth edition, Westmead, U.K.: Gregg, 1969. Modern edition of the first of the two parts of the work (fourth edition): Francis Hutcheson, *An Inquiry Concerning Beauty, Order, Harmony, Design.* Edited by Peter Kivy. The Hague, Nijhoff, 1973.

Kames, Lord [Henry Home]. *The Elements of Criticism.* 1762. Edited by James R. Boyd. New York: Barnes, 1856.

Kant, Immanuel. *Critique of Judgement.* 1790. Edited and translated by J. H. Bernard. London: Macmillan, 1895.

*Critique of Judgement.* Edited and translated by J. C. Meredith. Oxford: Clarendon Press, 1952. Originally published in two volumes, with indexes and supplementary essays, 1911 and 1928.

*Critique of Practical Reason.* 1788. Translated by Lewis White Beck. Indianapolis: Bobbs-Merrill, 1956.

*Kant's gesammelte Schriften.* 27 volumes. Edited by the Königlichen Preussischen (later Deutschen) Akademie der Wissenschaften. Berlin: Reimer (later de Gruyter), 1900–.

*Kritik der reinen Vernunft.* 1781 and 1787. Edited by Raymund Schmidt. Second edition. Hamburg: Meiner, 1930.

*Lectures on Ethics.* Translated by Louis Infield. London: Methuen, 1930. From the edition edited by Paul Menzer, Berlin, 1924.

*The Metaphysics of Morals.* 1797. Translated by Mary J. Gregor. Cambridge: Cambridge University Press, 1991.

*Religion within the Limits of Reason Alone.* 1793. Translation by Theodore M. Greene and Hoyt H. Hudson, introduction by John Silber. New York: Harper & Row, 1960.

Leibniz, Gottfried Wilhelm. *Philosophical Papers and Letters.* Second edition. Translated and edited by Leroy E. Loemker. Dordrecht: Reidel, 1969. First edition: Chicago: University of Chicago Press, 1956.

Locke, John. *Two Treatises of Government.* 1690. Edited by Peter Laslett. Second edition. Cambridge: Cambridge University Press, 1967.

Meier, Georg Friedrich. *Anfangsgründe aller schönen Künste und Wissenschaften.* 3 volumes. Halle: Carl Hermann Hemmerde, 1748–50.

Mendelssohn, Moses. *Ästhetische Schriften im Auswahl.* Edited by Otto F. Best. Darmstadt: Wissenschaftliche Buchgesellschaft, 1974.

Moritz, Karl Philipp. *Beiträge zur Ästhetik.* Edited by Hans Joachim Schrimpf and Hans Adler. Mainz: Dieterich'sche Verlagsbuchhandlung, 1989.

Schiller, Friedrich. *Friedrich Schiller: On the Aesthetic Education of Mankind in a Series of Letters.* Edited and translated by Elizabeth

M. Wilkinson and L. A. Willoughby. Oxford: Clarendon Press, 1967.

*Schillers Werke.* Volume 4: *Schriften,* introduced by Hans Meyer and Golo Mann. Frankfurt am Main: Insel, 1966.

Shaftesbury, Earl of [Anthony Ashley Cooper]. *Characteristics of Men, Manners, Opinions, Times.* 1711; revised edition 1714. Edited by John M. Robertson. Indianapolis: Bobbs-Merrill, 1964.

Sulzer, Johann Georg. *Unterredungen über die Schönheit der Natur.* "New edition." Berlin, 1770.

Winckelmann, Johann Joachim. *Winckelmann: Writings on Art.* Edited by David Irwin. London: Phaidon, 1972.

Wolff, Christian. *Vernünfftige Gedancken von Gott, der Welt, und der Seele des Menschen.* 1720. "New edition." Halle: Renger, 1751.


II. SECONDARY SOURCES


Adickes, Erich. *German Kantian Bibliography.* New York: Franklin, 1970. Originally published in *Philosophical Review* 2 (1893), 3 (1894), and suppl. (1896).

Allison, Henry. *Kant's Theory of Freedom.* Cambridge: Cambridge University Press, 1990.

*The Kant–Eberhard Controversy.* Baltimore: Johns Hopkins University Press, 1973.

Ameriks, Karl. "The Hegelian Critique of Kantian Morality." In *New Essays on Kant,* edited by Bernard den Ouden and Marcia Moen. New York: Peter Lang, 1987. Pp. 179–212.

"Kant and the Objectivity of Taste." *British Journal of Aesthetics* 23 (1983): 3–17.

Aquila, Richard E. "A New Look at Kant's Aesthetic Judgments." In Cohen and Guyer, *Essays in Kant's Aesthetics,* pp. 87–114.

Baron, Marcia. "The Alleged Moral Repugnance of Acting from Duty." *Journal of Philosophy* 81 (1984): 197–220.

Beck, Lewis White. *A Commentary on Kant's "Critique of Practical Reason."* Chicago: University of Chicago Press, 1960.

Blum, Lawrence. *Friendship, Altruism, and Morality.* London: Routledge & Kegan Paul, 1980.

Bullough, Edward. " 'Psychical Distance' as a Factor in Art and an Aesthetic Principle." 1912. In *Aesthetics: Lectures and Essays,* edited by Elizabeth M. Wilkinson. Stanford: Stanford University Press, 1957. Pp. 91–130.

Cavell, Stanley. *Conditions Handsome and Unhandsome: The Constitution of Emersonian Perfectionism.* Chicago: University of Chicago Press, 1990.

Caygill, Howard. *Art of Judgment.* Oxford: Blackwell, 1989.

Cohen, Ted, and Paul Guyer, editors. *Essays in Kant's Aesthetics.* Chicago: University of Chicago Press, 1982.

Crawford, Donald W. *Kant's Aesthetic Theory.* Madison: University of Wisconsin Press, 1974.

"Kant's Principles of Judgment and Taste." In *Proceedings of the Sixth International Kant Congress,* edited by Gerhard Funke and Thomas M. Seebohm. Washington, D.C.: Center for Advanced Research in Phenomenology, and University Press of America, 1989. Volume 2, part 2, pp. 281–92.

De Man, Paul. "Phenomenality and Materiality in Kant." In *The Textual Sublime: Deconstruction and Its Differences,* edited by Hugh J. Silverman and Gary E. Aylesworth. Albany: State University of New York Press, 1990. Pp. 87–109.

Derrida, Jacques. "Economimesis." *Diacritics* 11 (1981): 3–25.

*The Truth in Painting.* Translated by Geoff Bennington and Ian McLeod. Chicago: University of Chicago Press, 1987.

Dufour, Alfred. "Pufendorf." In *The Cambridge History of Political Thought: 1450–1700,* edited by J. H. Burns. Cambridge: Cambridge University Press, 1991. Pp. 561–88.

Eagleton, Terry. *The Ideology of the Aesthetic.* Oxford: Blackwell, 1989.

Elliott, R. K. "The Unity of Kant's 'Critique of Aesthetic Judgment.' " *British Journal of Aesthetics* 8 (1968): 244–59.

Genova, A. C. "Aesthetic Justification and Systematic Unity in Kant's Third *Critique.*" In *Proceedings of the Sixth International Kant Congress,* edited by Gerhard Funke and Thomas M. Seebohm. Washington, D.C.: Center for Advanced Research in Phenomenology, and University Press of America, 1989. Volume 2, part 2, pp. 292–309.

Gould, Timothy. "The Audience of Originality: Kant and Wordsworth on the Reception of Genius." In Cohen and Guyer, *Essays in Kant's Aesthetics,* pp. 179–94.

Gregor, Mary J. "Baumgarten's *Aesthetica.*" *Review of Metaphysics* 37 (1983): 357–85.

*The Laws of Freedom: A Study of Kant's Method of Applying the Categorical Imperative in the "Metaphysik der Sitten."* Oxford: Blackwell, 1963.

Guyer, Paul, editor. *The Cambridge Companion to Kant*. Cambridge: Cambridge University Press, 1992.

"Disinterestedness and Desire in Kant's Aesthetics." *Journal of Aesthetics and Art Criticism* 36 (1978): 449–60.

"Formalism and the Theory of Expression in Kant's Aesthetics." *Kant-Studien* 68 (1977): 46–70.

"Interest, Nature, and Art: A Problem in Kant's Aesthetics." *Review of Metaphysics* 31 (1978): 580–603.

*Kant and the Claims of Taste*. Cambridge, Mass.: Harvard University Press, 1979.

"Kant's Conception of Empirical Law." In *Proceedings of the Aristotelian Society*. Supplementary volume 64. Oxford: Blackwell, 1990. Pp. 221–42.

"Kant's Morality of Law and Morality of Freedom." In *Kant and Critique: New Essays in Honor of W. H. Werkmeister*, edited by Russell Dancy. Dordrecht: Kluwer, forthcoming.

"Natural Ends and the End of Nature: Reply to Richard Aquila." *Southern Journal of Philosophy* 30, supplement (1992): 157–65.

"Pleasure and Society in Kant's Theory of Taste." In Cohen and Guyer, *Essays in Kant's Aesthetics*, pp. 21–54.

"Reason and Reflective Judgment: Kant on the Significance of Systematicity." *Nous* 24 (1990): 17–43.

Review of Eva Schaper, *Studies in Kant's Aesthetics*. *Philosophical Review* 90 (1981): 429–36.

Review of Jens Kulenkampff, *Kants Logik des ästhetischen Urteils*. *Journal of Aesthetics and Art Criticism* 40 (1982): 212–17.

"The Unity of Reason: Pure Reason as Practical Reason in Kant's Early Conception of the Transcendental Dialectic." *Monist* 72 (1989): 139–67.

"Wolff, Christian." In *Encyclopedia of Ethics*, edited by Lawrence C. Becker. New York: Garland, 1992. Pp. 1324–7.

Henrich, Dieter. "Das Prinzip der kantischen Ethik." *Philosophische Rundschau* 2 (1954–5): 20–37.

Herman, Barbara. "Integrity and Impartiality." *Monist* 66 (1983): 213–32.

"Mutual Aid and Respect for Persons." *Ethics* 94 (1984): 577–602.

"On the Value of Acting from the Motive of Duty." *Philosophical Review* 90 (1981): 359–82.

Kemal, Salim. *Kant and Fine Art: An Essay on Kant and the Philosophy of Fine Art and Culture*. Oxford: Clarendon Press, 1986.

Kivy, Peter. *The Seventh Sense*. New York: Burt Franklin, 1976.

Kulenkampff, Jens. *Kants Logik des ästhetischen Urteils.* Frankfurt am Main: Klostermann, 1978.

O'Neill, Onora. *Constructions of Reason: Explorations of Kant's Practical Philosophy.* Cambridge: Cambridge University Press, 1989.

*Faces of Hunger: An Essay on Poverty, Development, and Justice.* London: Allen & Unwin, 1986.

Passmore, John. *Man's Responsibility for Nature.* New York: Scribner, 1974.

Reiner, Hans. *Pflicht und Neigung: Die Grundlagen der Sittlichkeit.* 1951. Revised edition. Meisenheim am Glan: Hain, 1974.

Rogerson, Kenneth F. *Kant's Aesthetics: The Roles of Form and Expression.* Lanham, Md.: University Press of America, 1986.

Savile, Anthony. *Aesthetic Reconstructions: The Seminal Writings of Lessing, Kant, and Schiller.* Aristotelian Society Series, no. 8. Oxford: Blackwell, 1987.

Schaper, Eva. *Studies in Kant's Aesthetics.* Edinburgh: Edinburgh University Press, 1979.

Schilpp, Paul. *Kant's Pre-Critical Ethics.* 1938. Second edition. Evanston: Northwestern University Press, 1960.

Schmucker, Josef. *Die Ursprünge der Ethik Kants.* Meisenheim am Glan: Hain, 1961.

Schneewind, J. B. *Moral Philosophy from Montaigne to Kant.* 2 volumes. Cambridge: Cambridge University Press, 1990.

Seidler, Victor J. *Kant, Respect and Injustice: The Limits of Liberal Moral Theory.* London: Routledge & Kegan Paul, 1986.

Silber, John. "The Importance of the Highest Good in Kant's Ethics." *Ethics* 28 (1963): 178–97.

Smith, Norman Kemp. *The Philosophy of David Hume.* London: Macmillan, 1941.

Stadler, Ingrid. "The Idea of Art and Its Criticism: A Rational Reconstruction of a Kantian Doctrine." In Cohen and Guyer, *Essays in Kant's Aesthetics,* pp. 195–218.

Stolnitz, Jerome. "On the Origins of 'Aesthetic Disinterestedness.' " *Journal of Aesthetics and Art Criticism* 20 (1961): 131–43.

"On the Significance of Lord Shaftesbury in Modern Aesthetic Theory." *Philosophical Quarterly* 11 (1961): 97–113.

Weiskel, Thomas. *The Romantic Sublime: Studies in the Structure and Psychology of Transcendence.* Baltimore: Johns Hopkins University Press, 1976.

Williams, Bernard. *Moral Luck: Philosophical Papers, 1973–1980.* Cambridge: Cambridge University Press, 1981.

*Problems of the Self: Philosophical Papers, 1956–1972.* Cambridge: Cambridge University Press, 1973.

Woodmansee, Martha. "The Interest in Disinterestedness: Karl Philipp Moritz and the Emergence of the Theory of Aesthetic Autonomy in Eighteenth-Century Germany." *Modern Language Quarterly* 45 (1984): 22–47.

# Index

Addison, Joseph, 50, 232; on the sublime, 239–40, 259

Adickes, Erich, 429–30n9

Aesthetic education, Schiller on, 121–30

Aesthetic ideas: in art, 38–9, 158–60, 173, 174–6, 254, 295; and freedom of imagination, 158–60; and morality, 316–18; Rogerson's view of, 16–17

Aesthetic judgment: analysis of, 8–9, 103, 149–50, 152, 168–9; character of Kant's theory of, 196–201; Hegel's interpretation of Kant's analysis of, 162–6; logical form of, 201–2; of reflection and of sense, 198–9; the sublime and analysis of, 192–201, 227–8; and symbolization of the morally good, 40–1; tensions in Kant's account of, 208–16. *See also* Beauty; Taste, judgments of

Aesthetic response: and freedom, 251, 283–7; as sensory, 49, 81–2, 88–89; in sublime, 206–8; and types of aesthetic judgment, 196–201, 202. *See also* Aesthetic judgment; Beauty; Taste, judgment of

Aesthetics: and ideology, 19–23; and morality, 2–4, 6–7, 12–19, 27–47, 335; and morality in Schiller, 351–3; possibility of, 5; structure of Kant's, 8. *See also* Beauty; Taste; Taste, judgment of

Ameriks, Karl, 398n14, 431n25, 431n27

Aquila, Richard E., 420n13

Art: and aesthetic ideas, 158–60; autonomy of, 2, 48, 92, 131–3, 141–4, 160; Baumgarten on, 85; dialectical history of, 276–8, 291–303; differences from beauty, 10; empirical interest in, 254–8; and genius, 113–15; Gottsched on, 83–4; Hegel on, 178–9; Herz on, 242–8; Hume on, 69–70; intentions in, 114–15, 148–9, 155, 268–71, 280, 294–5, 327; Kant on, 148–60, 161–2, 173–9, 248–71; Kemal's view of, 15–16, 271–4; Mendelssohn on, 132–41; and moral epistemology, 38–9; versus natural beauty, 229–74; Schiller on, 129; in society, 299–301; and the sublime, 264; Wolff on, 82

Association of ideas, in Hume's theory of beauty, 67, 69

441